FINAL SOLUTIONS

FINAL SOLUTIONS

MASS KILLING AND GENOCIDE IN THE TWENTIETH CENTURY

BENJAMIN A. VALENTINO

CORNELL UNIVERSITY PRESS
ITHACA AND LONDON

A VOLUME IN THE SERIES
CORNELL STUDIES IN SECURITY AFFAIRS

Edited by
Robert J. Art, Robert Jervis, and **Stephen M. Walt**

First published 2004 by Cornell University Press
Printed in the United States of America
Book design: Teresa Bonner

Library of Congress Cataloging-in-Publication Data

Valentino, Benjamin A., 1971–
    Final solutions : mass killing and genocide in the twentieth century /
Benjamin A. Valentino.
        p. cm. — (Cornell studies in security affairs)
    Includes bibliographical references and index.
    ISBN 0-8014-3965-5 (alk. paper)
    1. Genocide—History—20th century.   2. Massacres—History—20th
century.   3. Political atrocities—History—20th century.   4. War
crimes—History—20th century.   5. Crimes against
humanity—History—20th century.   6. Genocide—Prevention.   7.
Intervention (International law)   I. Title.   II. Series.
HV6322.7 .V35 2004
364.15'1'0904—dc22   2003019941

CONTENTS

ACKNOWLEDGMENTS

This book would not have been possible without the generous help of many friends, colleagues, and institutions. I conducted much of the research for this book at the Massachusetts Institute of Technology. Stephen Van Evera, Barry Posen, and Tom Christensen deserve much of the credit for what is good about it. I suspect it would have been even better if I had always found ways to follow their advice. The responsibility for what is not so good, of course, belongs to me alone. Myron Wiener also provided me with many valuable insights and criticisms during my time at MIT. Although he passed away before my research was completed, his contributions helped to shape this book.

Many colleagues have offered thoughtful comments on earlier drafts. John Mueller's ideas have had a major influence on my own. His extensive comments on several drafts of this manuscript were invaluable. At Cornell University Press, Robert Art and Roger Haydon guided me through the arduous task of transforming my research into a book. For their input I also thank Omer Bartov, Dan Byman, Jim Fearon, Ben Frankel, Taylor Fravel, Andrea Gabbitas, Kelly Greenhill, Paul Huth, Alan Kuperman, Norman Naimark, Dan Nexon, Daryl Press, Anne Sa'adah, Jeremy Shapiro, Taylor Seybolt, Ronald Suny, and Bill Wohlforth.

I owe special debts to Scott Sagan and Lynn Eden of Stanford's Center for International Security and Cooperation (CISAC). I have benefited from their constant guidance and support since my years as an undergraduate. CISAC first sparked my interest in studying international security and later provided the resources and environment to complete this book. The Olin Institute, the MIT Security Studies Program, and the MacArthur Foundation also provided generous financial support.

Tom Murphy proved a true friend to me throughout. In addition to quietly suffering through innumerable unsolicited lectures and diatribes, he was invaluable as a proofreader and copy editor. My wife, Laura Hercod, also deserves my deepest thanks. Spending my days with the heartbreaking subject of my research would have been unbearable without her.

I dedicate this book to my mother and father, Catherine and Dominic Valentino. I am forever grateful for their encouragement and support. Words cannot convey how profoundly they influenced my thinking. Their love of learning provides the example I have tried my best to follow in this book and in my life.

FINAL SOLUTIONS

INTRODUCTION: MASS KILLING IN HISTORICAL AND THEORETICAL PERSPECTIVE

Why do some human conflicts result in the intentional killing of massive numbers of unarmed civilians? This remains one of the most important questions facing humanity today. As the threat of global nuclear conflict recedes in the wake of the cold war, mass killing seems poised to regain its place as the greatest unnatural threat to human life. Episodes of mass killing in the former Yugoslavia and Rwanda are but the latest entries on a long list of atrocities extending back to earliest recorded history, even into the archeological record.[1] Mass killings have been perpetrated by and against a wide range of nations, cultures, forms of government, and ethnic and religious groups. Between 60 million and 150 million people probably have perished in episodes of mass killings during the twentieth century alone.[2] By comparison, international and civil wars have accounted for approximately 34 million battle deaths during the same period.[3] In light of this grisly balance sheet, it is regrettable that mass killing and genocide have received comparatively little scholarly attention as a general class of events. With the bloodiest century in human history behind us, we still know little about what accounts for this era's violence or whether the next one hundred years will be as savage as the last.

Many of the most widely accepted explanations of genocide and mass killing see the causes of these events in the social structures, forms of government, or collective psychology of the societies in which they take place. In particular, many scholars have focused on the dangers of dehumanizing attitudes and deep cleavages between social groups, on the psychological and political consequences of major societal crises such as wars or revolutions, and on the concentration of unchecked power in undemocratic political systems.

Although these theories have generated many important insights, each of them also has significant problems or limitations. Structural factors such as severe ethnic, racial, national, or religious divisions between social groups fail to provide a reliable indicator of mass killing. Indeed, some of the bloodiest mass killings in history have occurred in relatively homogeneous societies, between groups of the same or closely related ethnicity, nationality, religion, or class. Conversely, many deeply divided societies have endured for extended periods without experiencing mass killing.

Nor can mass killing adequately be explained by the presence of highly undemocratic governments or the occurrence of major social crises. While there is substantial evidence that these factors increase the risk that mass killing will occur, the great majority of undemocratic governments and social crises are not associated with massive violence against civilians, suggesting that other important causes are at work.

I believe that an understanding of mass killing must begin with the specific goals and strategies of high political and military leaders, not with broad social or political factors. Previous theoretical studies of genocide have tended to diminish the role of leadership on the grounds that the interests and ideas of a few elites cannot account for the participation of the rest of society in the violence. My research, however, suggests that society at large plays a smaller role in mass killing than is commonly assumed. Mass killing is rarely a popular enterprise in which neighbor turns against neighbor. On the contrary, the impetus for mass killing usually originates from a relatively small group of powerful political or military leaders. Sometimes even individual leaders can play a decisive role in instigating and determining the course of the slaughter. Scholars have long struggled, for example, to imagine the Great Terror without Stalin, the Holocaust without Hitler, or the Cultural Revolution without Mao.

It is true that these tyrants could not have accomplished their crimes without help from others in their societies. Nevertheless, a broad examination of the phenomenon of mass killing in the twentieth century reveals that the minimum level of social support necessary to carry out mass killing has been uncomfortably easy to achieve. Leaders have powerful methods to recruit the individuals needed to carry out mass killing and to secure the compliance or at least the passivity of the rest of society. The broader public sometimes approves of mass killing, but often it does not.

Whatever the sympathies of the public, the active support of a large portion of society is usually not required to carry out mass killing. The violence itself is typically performed by a relatively small group of people, usually members of military or paramilitary organizations. They carry out their bloody work often with little more than the passive acceptance of the rest of society, including members of the perpetrators' own social groups.

In light of these unsettling findings, I argue that the causes of mass killing will be best understood when the phenomenon is studied from what I call a strategic perspective. The strategic perspective suggests that mass killing is most accurately viewed as an instrumental policy — a brutal strategy designed to accomplish leaders' most important ideological or political objectives and counter what they see as their most dangerous threats.

Like war, mass killing can be a powerful political and military tool. Unfortunately, leaders throughout history have proved all too ready to use this tool when it seemed to serve their purposes. Many scholars have sought to draw a clear line between warfare and mass killing, but I believe that the two phenomena are closely related. This is not merely because mass killing so often occurs during times of war. Rather, it is because both phenomena involve the use of organized violence to compel others to do what they would not otherwise do. Contrary to common perceptions, perpetrators seldom view mass killing as an end in itself. Violence against victim groups is rarely intended to physically exterminate entire populations as such. More often, its purpose is to force victims to submit to radically new ways of life, to give up their homes and possessions, or to cease their support for political or military opposition groups. Some perpetrators, most notably the Nazis, have attempted to totally exterminate victim populations. Policies of extermination, however, usually emerge only after leaders have concluded that other options for achieving their ends, including less violent forms of repression or even limited concessions to victim groups, are ineffective or impractical.

The most meaningful distinction between war and mass killing, therefore, is not the purpose of its violence but the nature of its victims. War merges with mass killing when its intended targets become unarmed civilians rather than soldiers.

Thus, perpetrators see mass killing as a "final solution" in two respects. Mass killing is a final solution because it is permanent. It obviates the need for future efforts to resolve the perceived problems posed by its victims. Mass killing is also final, however, because it is usually the last in a series of efforts to "solve" these problems using other means. It usually emerges out of leaders' frustration with conventional military and political strategies for dealing with their victims. Perhaps perpetrators hesitate to resort immediately to this level of violence because some shred of humanity or compassion compels them to consider alternatives. More likely, perpetrators first seek less violent solutions because strategies of mass killing can carry substantial risks — inciting violent resistance from victim groups, alienating domestic populations and foreign powers, or provoking intervention by third parties. When perpetrators perceive the stakes to be high enough, and when less violent alternatives appear to be blocked or unworkable, however, the incentives to consider mass killing multiply.

As with war, even the most despotic leaders do not see mass killing as the most appropriate solution to every problem. Many scholars have noted that perpetrators may view genocide or mass killing as a "rational" response to a perceived threat, but few have attempted to explain why perpetrators see this kind of violence as an appropriate response to some threats but not others. I contend that leaders are likely to perceive mass killing as an attractive means to achieve their ends only in very specific circumstances. My research identifies several real-world scenarios that seem to generate powerful incentives for leaders to consider mass killing. Three of these scenarios, which account for the greatest number of episodes of mass killing in the twentieth century as well as the greatest number of victims, serve as the major focus of this book.

First, mass killing can be an attractive strategy for regimes seeking to achieve the radical communization of their societies. Indeed, communist regimes probably have been responsible for the most violent mass killings in human history. Radical communist regimes have been so closely associated with mass killing because the changes they have sought to bring about in their societies have resulted in the nearly complete material dispossession of vast populations. Communist policies such as agricultural collectivization have stripped tens of millions of people of their homes and property and have obliterated traditional ways of life. In practice, few people have been willing to submit to such severe changes in the absence of violence and coercion. Communist leaders did not set out with the desire to exterminate millions of people, but they did not shy away from mass murder when they believed it was necessary to achieve their goals. Nevertheless, if communist leaders had limited the scope of their repression to only those individuals implicated in active resistance, their lists of victims never would have been so long. I contend that the adherence of communist leaders to a pseudo-Marxist notion — that resistance to communist policies was motivated by the immutable "class consciousness" of certain groups — greatly magnified the scale of communist mass killings. This perception led communist leaders to seek the prophylactic suppression of entire social groups or classes, even in the absence of evidence of individual involvement in counterrevolutionary activities. It also led to bloody political purges that consumed countless victims within the communist party itself.

Second, regimes seeking to implement policies of large-scale ethnic cleansing also face significant incentives to consider mass killing. The mass killing of ethnic, national, or religious groups has often been portrayed as the result of deep-seated hatred of victims by perpetrators, or sometimes simply as killing for killing's sake. I argue, however, that ethnic mass killing occurs when leaders believe that their victims pose a threat that can be countered only by removing them from society or by permanently destroying their ability to organize politically or militarily. This perception may be based on perpetrators' racist or nationalistic ideological beliefs, or it may be a reaction to real, although almost always exaggerated, threatening actions of victim groups. Ethnic cleansing and mass killing are not one and the same, but they have often gone hand in hand. Forcing people to abandon their homes, belongings, and history for an unknown life in distant lands often requires considerable coercion. Even after victims have been coerced into flight, the process and aftermath of large population movements can be deadly. The bloodiest episodes of ethnic mass killing, however, occur when perpetrators conclude that physically expelling victims from society is impossible or impractical. Perpetrators may reach this conclusion when there simply are no territories available to receive large numbers of victims, or because they fear that victims will continue to pose a threat from across the border. Whatever the reasons, once perpetrators reject the possibility of expulsion as an effective of dealing with victim groups, the impulse for ethnic cleansing can escalate to systematic extermination.

Third, regimes seeking to defeat major guerrilla insurgencies may be drawn to strategies of mass killing. My research suggests that the intentional slaughter of civilians in the effort to defeat guerrilla insurgencies was the most common impetus for mass killing in the twentieth century. Guerrilla warfare has so often led to mass killing because the use of guerrilla tactics by insurgent groups generates powerful incentives for counterinsurgency forces to target civilians. Much more than conventional armies, guerrilla forces must rely directly on the civilian population for food, shelter, and information. Although the support of the civilian population is one of the primary strengths of guerrilla warfare, it can also be a weakness. Unlike guerrilla forces themselves, the civilian populations upon which insurgents rely are largely defenseless, immobile, and impossible to conceal. Military organizations seeking to defeat guerrillas therefore often find it easier to target their base of support in the people than to engage the guerrillas themselves. This effort to isolate the guerrillas from their civilian support has often resulted in mass killing.

I begin in chapter 1 with a discussion of the contentious debate surrounding the definition of the term "genocide." I argue that many previous formulations of the term genocide are problematic, at least for the purposes of this book. A new term is needed to address the full range of events I wish to explore. I introduce and define the term "mass killing," which includes most commonly accepted cases of genocide but also encompasses a broader range of events distinguished by the large-scale, intentional killing of noncombatants. In addition, this chapter provides a brief review of several of the most influential ideas and theories about genocide and mass killing. These theories, I suggest, tend to overemphasize the role of social and structural variables and neglect or underestimate the importance and power of small groups in causing and carrying out such violence.

In chapter 2, I assess the available historical evidence on the role of public support for mass killing and the psychology and motives of the individuals who actually carry it out. I argue that mass killing does not require widespread, active public support, only passivity or indifference to the fate of victims and compliance with authority. Unfortunately, these characteristics exist in many or even most societies. Where they have been absent, perpetrators intent on mass killing often have been able to create them through propaganda and indoctrination. Two processes — the preferential selection of sadistic or ideologically fanatic individuals and the influence of situational pressures and elite manipulation — provide the best explanations for the behavior of most rank-and-file perpetrators of mass killing. These two processes are dissimilar in many ways, but each helps explain how leaders can recruit the necessary support for mass killing even in societies that are largely indifferent or actively opposed to it.

I present the primary theoretical framework of this book in chapter 3. Here I provide a typology of mass killing that identifies the specific circumstances that encourage leaders to consider mass killing. I also present an inventory of cases of mass killing in the twentieth century and estimates of the numbers of people who perished in each episode.

The next three chapters apply the strategic perspective developed in chapter 3 to eight historical cases of mass killing: in chapter 4, communist mass killings in the Soviet Union, China, and Cambodia; in chapter 5, ethnic mass killings in Turkish Armenia, Nazi Germany, and Rwanda; in chapter 6, counterguerrilla mass killings in Guatemala from 1978 to 1996 and in Afghanistan from 1979 to 1988 during the occupation by the Soviet Union.

These cases were selected primarily because of the well-developed secondary literature associated with them, but they also provide wide variations in culture, geography, time period, and regime type. These variations serve as a means to isolate the potential influences of geographic, temporal, governmental, and cultural influences on the causes of mass killing. They thereby bolster confidence that the strategic theories described in this book are generalizable.

The examination of each of these historical cases relies primarily on "process tracing" — identifying the causal processes which link the factors and conditions implicated by the strategic perspective to the outcome of mass killing.[4] These case studies are not intended to provide comprehensive historical accounts of the events they examine. Nor do they forward radically new historical interpretations based on novel documentary evidence. Rather, in each case I highlight how leaders' strategic goals and beliefs interacted with situational pressures and exogenous events to produce strong incentives for mass killing. I attempt to show how leaders conceived of mass killing as a means to an end, to examine what other means they considered to achieve those ends, and to explain why leaders ultimately rejected these less violent alternatives.

In chapters 4–6 I also briefly investigate a variety of historical cases in which mass killing did not occur: in chapter 4, communist regimes that did not engage in mass killing; in chapter 5, racist regimes and episodes of ethnic cleansing that were not associated with mass killing; and in chapter 6, guerrilla insurgencies that did not precipitate mass killing. I explore these episodes in considerably less detail than the eight primary case studies of mass killing, but these limited case studies are sufficient to serve two related purposes. First, they help diminish the risk of overemphasizing factors and conditions that, though relevant to the occurrence of mass killing in the cases examined, are also common in numerous cases in which mass killing never materialized. Indeed, one reason that much of the theoretical literature on genocide has tended to exaggerate the role of factors such as negative social relations or national crises is because it has focused narrowly on a few cases in which mass killing occurred and neglected the many other cases in which deep social divisions, dehumanized intergroup relationships, or major crises did not lead to mass killing. Second, only by comparing cases in which mass killing does not occur with those in which it does can we isolate the specific conditions and intervening factors that increase or decrease the incentives for perpetrators to consider mass killing, or extend or limit their ability to carry it out.

In the final chapter I summarize the conclusions of this book and discuss some implications of the strategic perspective for preventing or limiting mass killing in the future. I suggest that efforts to prevent mass killing by addressing "root causes" such as discrimination or nondemocratic forms of government are likely to prove impractical at best and ineffective at worst. These social ills are so common that it is simply impossible to intervene preemptively to address them everywhere they exist. The strategic perspective, on the other hand, identifies a number of easily identifiable conditions that create strong incentives for mass killing and therefore serve as more reliable indicators of the likelihood of mass killing.

Because leaders resort to mass killing in defense of their most important goals, often in desperation when other strategies have failed, preventing mass killing will often require the use of force. On the other hand, because the perpetrators of mass killing often constitute a relatively small group without broad-based social support, intervention to prevent mass killing need not result in open-ended "nation building" missions designed to foster democracy or end discrimination between groups. Rather, intervention should seek to defeat perpetrators and protect victim groups from harm.

1. MASS KILLING
AND GENOCIDE

No generally accepted terminology exists to describe the intentional killing of large numbers of noncombatants. The most likely contender, of course, is the term "genocide." This term, however, fails to capture the broad range of events I wish to examine. The most important limitation of "genocide" is its relatively narrow meaning, both in its etymology and in the formal United Nations definition of groups that qualify as its victims.

Raphael Lemkin, a Polish jurist of Jewish descent, first coined the word "genocide" in 1944. To create the term, Lemkin combined the Greek word *genos*, meaning "race or tribe," with the Latin derivative *cide*, which means "to kill." Lemkin defined genocide as "a coordinated plan of different actions aiming at the destruction of essential foundations of the life of national groups, with the aim of annihilating the groups themselves."[1] The United Nations Genocide Convention of 1948, which Lemkin played a major role in drafting, limits the victims of genocide to "national, ethnical, racial or religious" groups.[2] Similarly, the *Oxford English Dictionary* defines genocide as "the deliberate and systematic extermination of an ethnic or national group."[3]

Many of the most infamous and important "genocidal" events of this century, however, including the deliberate killing of between 10 million and 23 million people in the Soviet Union, between 10 million and 46 million in China, and between 1 million and 2 million in Cambodia, have not primarily involved clashes between different ethnic or national groups. In many other episodes of large-scale, systematic killing, ethnic, national or religious groups have been targeted, but not because of their group identity per se. Because "genocide" is a term of general interest to society, however, and because it carries with it the weight of powerful moral sanction, many authors have been reluctant to give it up. Indeed, so politically powerful is the term that activists have applied it to policies such as abortion, interracial adoption, and lack of government funding for AIDS treatment and research.[4] As a result, the precise definition of the term has become the subject of intense debate among genocide scholars, policy makers, and human rights advocates.[5] Ever since the Genocide Convention was drafted, many authors have dissented from the UN definition, taking issue with, among other things, its apparent exclusion of political and other non-ethnic groups from the definition of genocide.

I strongly believe that understanding the causes of the systematic murder of noncombatants is important, regardless of the group identity of the victims. In academic works, however, it is useful if central terms coincide with their common English usage and etymology so that they can be readily understood, even by readers from outside the field. From a political perspective, it may be more effective to include non-ethnic groups in the definition of genocide and in the international agreements designed to prevent this kind of violence. From a scholarly perspective, however, clarity is paramount.

WHAT IS MASS KILLING?

In order to avoid this and other difficulties with the term "genocide," I utilize the term "mass killing" — defined here simply as *the intentional killing of a massive number of noncombatants.*[6] Victims of mass killing may be members of any kind of group (ethnic, political, religious, etc.) as long as they are noncombatants and as long as their deaths were caused intentionally. Three aspects of the definition of mass killing warrant further elaboration.

First, the mass killing must be intentional, which distinguishes it from deaths caused by natural disasters, outbreaks of disease, or the unintentional killing of civilians during war.[7] This definition is not limited to "direct" methods of killing such as execution, gassing, and bombing. It includes deaths caused by starvation, exposure, or disease resulting from the intentional confiscation, destruction, or blockade of the necessities of life. It also includes deaths caused by starvation, exhaustion, exposure, or disease during forced relocation or forced labor.

Determining the intentionality of deaths due to these causes can be extremely difficult, since it requires knowledge of the specific aims of the perpetrators. For the purposes of this definition, deaths need not be the result of policies designed specifically to kill in order to be considered mass killing. I also consider deaths to be intentional if they result from policies designed to compel or coerce civilian populations to change their behavior — and if the perpetrators could have reasonably expected that these policies would result in widespread death. Thus, civilians killed by aerial bombardment would be considered victims of mass killing only if their attackers intentionally aimed to kill or terrorize civilians as part of an effort to coerce survivors to surrender. If the civilians were killed as the attackers attempted to destroy nearby military forces or infrastructure, however, these deaths would be considered unintentional even though the attacker might have expected a certain level of civilian casualties. Deaths resulting from forced marches, forced labor, or forced deportation are considered intentional if perpetrators could have reasonably expected that implementing these policies would lead to large numbers of civilian deaths — even if perpetrators did not set out to kill these victims, per se. Unlike the civilian deaths caused by the bombing of factories or nearby military installations, civilian populations are the direct objects of forced marches, forced labor and deportation, not the coincidental victims of policies targeted against soldiers or physical structures.

Deaths resulting from these kinds of policies, whether perpetrators devise them to kill civilians or simply to coerce them, should not be underestimated. Starvation, malnutrition, exposure, exhaustion, and disease were responsible for a large proportion of mass killing deaths in the twentieth century. Fatalities resulting from these factors sometimes rival direct methods of killing, even in cases notorious for their violence and brutality. Starvation inside and outside labor camps was a primary means of mass killing in the Soviet Union, China, and Cambodia. During the Holocaust, starvation and harsh conditions killed vast numbers of Jews. Raul Hilberg estimates that over eight hundred thousand Jews, more than 15 percent of all those who perished, died of privation inside and outside ghettos in Eastern Europe.[8] Other authors have suggested that a third or more of Jewish victims died of starvation, disease, and malnutrition rather than gassing or shooting.[9]

The second aspect of the definition of mass killing that requires further specification is the meaning of "a massive number." Unlike most scholarly definitions of genocide, mass killing does not specify that perpetrators must possess the intent to destroy an entire group or even a specific percentage of it.[10] Rather, for the purposes of this definition, a massive number is defined simply as at least fifty thousand intentional deaths over the course of five or fewer years.[11] These specific numerical criteria are to some extent arbitrary, but selecting these relatively high thresholds helps establish with a greater degree of confidence that massive violence did, in fact, occur and that the killing was intentional. Utilizing relatively high thresholds is especially important given the generally poor quality of the data available on civilian fatalities. Nevertheless, although I will not examine such cases in this book, it seems plausible to assume that theories that can explain events in which fifty thousand or more people were killed can also explain events in which twenty or thirty thousand died.

Limiting mass killing to the total annihilation of a group, on the other hand, would create a highly restrictive definition. In fact, by this standard genocide actually may never have been committed. For this reason, the UN Genocide Convention, and most genocide scholars, have chosen to focus instead on the perpetrators' intent (or attempt) to destroy the group. Yet even the attempt to destroy an entire group has been exceedingly rare. By this definition, the Holocaust itself would qualify as attempted genocide only if the victim group were defined narrowly as European Jews, since there is little evidence that the Nazis attempted to kill, for example, Jews living in the United States.[12] Employing this kind of flexible definition of the victim group, however, opens the door to an infinite regress through which the attempted murder of a single individual, if he or she is the sole member of a narrowly defined group, could constitute genocide.

The Genocide Convention introduces additional ambiguity by defining genocide as "the intent to destroy, in whole or in part" the group "as such," and by including not only killing but acts ranging from "causing serious bodily or mental harm to the members of the group," to "imposing measures intended to prevent births within the group," to "forcibly transferring children of the group to another group."[13] Even if we accept the notion that the intent to destroy a group, rather than the actual destruction of the group, is the defining characteristic of genocide, and even if we accept that actions other than killing should be included in its definition, it is not at all clear what part or how much of a given group the perpetrator must intend to destroy in order to qualify as genocide.

Specifying that perpetrators must intend to kill a specific percentage of a victim group might seem to be the most objective way to resolve this problem. Utilizing a specific percentage, however, would also depend on an arbitrary quantitative criterion. Perhaps more importantly, it would also introduce an additional set of conceptual problems.[14] In the case of very small groups, a definition based on specific percentages might include events in which perhaps a few hundred lives were lost—still a great tragedy, but hardly comparable to the more infamous atrocities of the bloody twentieth century.[15] Such a definition would also depend heavily on what kinds of groups qualify as victims. Yet one of the principal difficulties with previous attempts to define terms such as genocide has been that the definition of ethnic, national, or religious groups has proven nearly as contentious as the definition of genocide itself. As the Nazis' evolving and sometimes contradictory policies toward so-called *Mischlinge* (persons of mixed Jewish ancestry) reveals, even the perpetrators of mass killing can have difficulty precisely defining their victims.[16]

Including political groups or economic classes as potential victims of genocide in a definition based on the perpetrators' intent to destroy the victim group introduces even more difficulties. Membership in such groups can be extremely volatile and is even more vulnerable to subjective classification than ethnic groups. In some cases, political victims belong to groups that seem to exist only in the imaginations or ideologies of their killers. How could it be determined, for example, what percentage of "kulaks," "counterrevolutionaries," or "wreckers" were murdered by Stalin, Mao, or Pol Pot? Even if the potential pool of victims could be identified accurately, would the killing of, say, the entire Romanov family by the Bolsheviks constitute genocide if we define the political group as "the Romanovs"? On the basis of what criteria are such groups to be excluded?

A numerical criterion avoids each of these difficulties. It should be emphasized, however, that any definition that relies on an absolute numerical criterion cannot avoid a bias toward victim groups with relatively large populations. As a result, such a definition does not adequately capture the threat to human diversity posed by attacks against smaller groups. Nevertheless, such a bias seems justified in light of the greater absolute cost in human lives incurred by attacks against large groups and by the greater objectivity with which such a standard can be applied. Nothing in this discussion, on the other hand, implies that threats posed to small groups are not worth studying or that these groups do not deserve protection from violence.

The third aspect of the definition of mass killing that warrants clarification is the term "noncombatant." This definition focuses on the killing of noncombatants because it is violence directed against noncombatants that distinguishes mass killing from other forms of warfare and that most offends our moral sensibilities. A noncombatant is defined as any unarmed person who is not a member of an organized military group and who does not actively participate in hostilities by intending to cause physical harm to enemy personnel or property.[17] It should be noted that simply associating with combatants, providing food or other nonlethal military supplies to them, or participating in nonviolent political activities in support of armed forces does not convert a noncombatant to a combatant. Because these activities pose no immediate threat of physical harm to combatants, individuals who engage in them deserve protection from killing — although they may be subject to judicial punishments. As I will show in subsequent chapters, this distinction is of vital importance. When it has been disregarded, entire populations easily come to be treated as enemies.

Mass killing as defined above encompasses a wide range of phenomena. It should be recognized as distinct from the phenomenon of genocide as that term has been commonly defined. Unlike most definitions of genocide, mass killing applies to the intentional killing of noncombatants caused by practices ranging from aerial bombardment and starvation blockades during wars to mass executions and gassing. It applies to the intentional killing of victims drawn from any group of noncombatants and is not limited to attempts to destroy these groups as such. What all of these disparate events share is the perpetrators' calculated decision to take the lives of vast numbers of unarmed human beings. It is this decision that separates mass killing from other forms of violence and that makes it so disturbing. Understanding the motives for this decision is the primary object of this book.

This broad formulation of mass killing might seem to expand the universe of cases to virtually unlimited proportions. In fact, this definition includes relatively few events that are not encompassed by those definitions of genocide that include the killing of non-ethnic groups.[18] Nevertheless, many scholars have objected to the incorporation of these events under the same terminology, claiming that their root causes and motivations are different.[19] Frank Chalk and Kurt Jonassohn, for example, write that killing by aerial bombardment should not be considered genocide because "in this age of total war belligerent states make all enemy-occupied territory part of the theater of operations regardless of the presence of civilians. Civilians are regarded as combatants so long as their governments control the cities in which they reside."[20] Similarly, Helen Fein argues that "to equate Auschwitz and Hiroshima belies the distinctive ends and root of each plan, focusing instead on the number of victims."[21] Lucy Dawidowicz claims that deaths caused by strategic bombing are not genocide because "America's decision to use the atomic bomb against Japan was not motivated by a wish to wipe out the Japanese people. The purpose of the bombing was to demonstrate America's superior military power and thus convince the Japanese that they had to capitulate, thereby ending the war and further killing."[22]

While the causes of events such as the Holocaust and the strategic bombings of the Second World War are surely distinct, this fact alone does not mandate that a separate term be used to describe each of them. Scholars regularly use the same term to describe phenomena with multiple causes. "War," for example, is often defined very broadly by scholars and applied to a wide range of phenomena in its common English usage. Few scholars suggest that all wars have the same cause, however. Even scholars who adopt the narrow definition of genocide usually accept that different episodes of genocide may have significantly different causes.

The broad definition of mass killing utilized in this book is justified because it can yield important insights into the causes of an important class of events. Indeed, a major premise of this book is that previous research into the causes of genocide often has been biased by a narrow focus on a limited set of historical cases. This focus has tended to overemphasize explanations that stress social-structural variables or the nature of relations between groups. Examples such as the strategic bombing of Germany and Japan during the Second World War are particularly illuminating because they emphasize the instrumental and strategic motives for mass killing. In the following pages, I will argue that strategic motives played a central role in many more commonly accepted cases of genocide as well.

Because the term "mass killing" encompasses such a wide range of events, some readers undoubtedly will wish to draw moral distinctions among these cases. Most Americans, for example, continue to justify the nuclear bombardment of Japan with the belief that the victims of the bombing were in some way guilty of supporting the Japanese war effort, or that the bombing served a greater good by ending the war without the need for an American invasion of the Japanese home islands.[23] It is not the purpose of this book to judge the appropriateness of such distinctions. The intentional killing of vast numbers of unarmed civilians, no matter what its cause, should raise profound moral questions. This is one of the most important reasons for studying mass killing. It should be emphasized, however, that referring to two distinct events as mass killing does not imply any moral equivalency between them. Just as the same words may apply to events with different causes, so may they apply to actions of differing moral rectitude. Scholars who study wars or revolutions, for example, need not imply that all wars or revolutions occupy the same moral domain. Readers should consult their own convictions about the subject of this book and draw moral distinctions on a case-by-case basis.

THE LITERATURE ON GENOCIDE AND MASS KILLING

Although the term "genocide" has existed for over fifty years, there are few formal theories of genocide or mass killing. Much has been written about specific episodes of mass killing and genocide, especially the Holocaust, but little scholarship has been produced on mass killing as a general class of events. A relatively small body of theoretical work has begun to accumulate, however, particularly during the last two decades.[24]

Three broad families of writing on genocide and mass killing will be examined below. Each family identifies a different set of factors as central causes or important preconditions of genocide and mass killing.[25] Because authors commonly suggest several different explanations for genocide and mass killing—often without identifying when different explanations are likely to operate, or without addressing the contradictions between them—a discussion of the literature is most productively organized around specific theoretical concepts and explanations rather than the writings of particular authors. Although these three families do not exhaust all scholarship on the subject, the explanations they suggest and the small set of causal factors and conditions they emphasize appear repeatedly throughout the literature.

The first family focuses on the importance of deep social cleavages between groups as a primary cause or precondition of genocide and mass killing. A second family suggests that factors such as wars, revolutions, and other national crises provide the spark for mass killing. The third family emphasizes the concentration of political power in certain forms of government as the most important cause of this kind of violence. Although each of these perspectives offers important insights and observations about mass killing, I argue that none provides a wholly satisfying explanation.

Social Cleavages and Dehumanization

One of the factors most commonly cited as a central cause or precondition of genocide is the presence of deep divisions between different groups living in the same society. I will refer collectively to explanations of genocide or mass killing that focus on the impact of social cleavages as the plural society theory. The plural society theory is most closely associated with Leo Kuper, a pioneer of comparative genocide studies, although several other scholars have proposed similar explanations.[26] Scholars have defined social cleavages variously with reference to deep ethnic, cultural, religious, or class divisions, high levels of overt or de facto discrimination, political or economic exclusion, and distrust or hatred between groups. A distinct, but related group of theories focuses specifically on the dehumanizing character of relations between groups.[27] According to different authors, social cleavages can lead to genocide by polarizing society, by increasing the likelihood of intergroup conflict, by sparking rebellions among oppressed groups, by facilitating the identification of enemies, or by eroding norms of moral responsibility.

There is little question that the perpetrators of mass killing often consider their victims different, inferior, or even less human than themselves. It is hard to imagine how anyone could participate in the wholesale slaughter of a group of defenseless people he believed to be exactly like himself. Nor is it surprising that the victims of mass killing and genocide are often subjected to economic and political discrimination before they are killed. These observations, however, do not imply that preexisting social cleavages or negative attitudes toward victim groups are prime, independent causes or crucial preconditions of mass killing. A closer look at this kind of violence indicates that unusually deep, preexisting social cleavages are neither sufficient nor universally necessary conditions for mass killing. Even the most severe social cleavages do not provide a reliable indicator of mass killing. This is not to deny that cleavages between social groups often play a central role in the causal process of mass killing. But substantial evidence suggests that genocide or mass killing may take place even when these attitudes are not unusually severe.

Although some level of discrimination, hatred, or dehumanization exists between groups in nearly all cases of mass killing, these divisive attitudes plague relations between at least some groups in virtually all societies. In order to distinguish peaceful societies from those at high risk of genocide and mass killing, therefore, most variants of the plural society theory focus on unusually severe or pervasive social cleavages. As Kuper writes, plural societies are not simply those that "contain a diversity of racial, ethnic and/or religious groups." Rather, plural societies are "characterized by a superimposition of inequalities. The same sections are dominant or subordinate, favored or discriminated against, in the political structure, in the economy, in opportunities for education, in human rights, in access to amenity."[28]

Proponents of the plural society theory, however, offer surprisingly little evidence that social cleavages are more intense in societies that have experienced genocide or mass killing than in those that have not. To date, quantitative research on ethnic conflict and genocide has found little correlation between indicators of ethnic, social, economic, and cultural differences and the likelihood of large-scale violence between groups.[29] Nor do ethnic wars appear to be more likely to result in mass killing than political or ideological conflicts.[30]

While reference to some level of preexisting social cleavages may be necessary to explain most cases of mass killing, even low levels of hatred or discrimination do not appear to be a universal precondition for this kind of violence. Indeed, history provides several striking examples of mass killing between members of similar social and economic groups with little record of unusually intense discrimination or dehumanization.

Mass killings carried out by communist governments in the Soviet Union, China, and Cambodia—three of the bloodiest episodes of mass killing in history—are especially illustrative.

Although specific ethnic and national groups were singled out for violence in each of these states, vast numbers of victims were also drawn from dominant social groups. Ethnic and national minorities appear to have been targeted primarily because of suspected resistance to communist rule, not because of their ethnic or national affiliations per se.[31] Nor can deep cleavages between economic classes explain the violence in these countries. Victims in all three states often were drawn from the same social and economic groups as their executioners. In the infamous Khmer Rouge prison known as S-21, for example, the prisoners were, David Chandler finds, "socially and ethnically indistinguishable from the people who held them captive."[32] Violent political repression in all three states eventually consumed large numbers of the communist party's highest-ranking members. Nowhere was this more evident than during the Great Terror in Soviet Union.[33] Many of the regime's most prominent political and military elites were executed or deported to the Gulag to die. Not even the Soviet secret police, the primary instrument of the Terror, managed to escape the violent purges.[34]

Even in the countryside—where Soviet, Chinese and Cambodian leaders attributed the massive violence during land reform and the collectivization of agriculture to "class warfare," there is surprisingly little evidence that class cleavages were stronger than in other societies that never experienced mass killing.[35] Tensions between peasant classes undoubtedly existed, but they do not seem to have produced unusually intense hatred or dehumanizing attitudes. On the contrary, communist leaders in all three countries greatly overestimated the degree of antagonism between peasant classes. In fact, they openly lamented their inability to draw on preexisting class hatreds to encourage more widespread participation in attacks on perceived enemies of communist rule.[36] Ties of family, clan, and village frequently proved stronger than those of class. In many locales, spontaneous support for violence against communist enemies often failed to materialize, and leaders were forced to acknowledge that even the poorest segments of the peasantry lacked the necessary "class consciousness."

This pattern is well illustrated by Jean-Louis Margolin's description of the conditions prevailing in rural China before the implementation of Mao's bloody land reform. According to Margolin:

> In comparison with the extreme social contrasts found in Europe before 1945 and still visible in much of South America even today, rural Chinese

society was in fact relatively egalitarian. Conflict between rich and poor was far from being the principal cause of the [land reform violence]. . . . Communists, including Mao himself, began to play at social engineering by trying to artificially polarize carefully defined rural groups and then decreeing that this polarization was the major cause of peasant discontent.[37]

In some cases, communist elites seem to have created new social categories for their victims out of whole cloth. In the Soviet Union, for example, violence during the forced collectivization campaign of 1929–32 was directed against the so-called kulaks. It is now widely recognized, however, that the peasant population of the Soviet Union had little concept of the kulak as an economic class until communist propagandists seized upon it in an effort to spark class warfare.[38] As one Russian peasant recalled, before the revolution "we were just neighbors in this village. We quarreled, we fooled, sometimes we cheated one another. But we were neighbors. Now we are bedniaki, seredniaki, kulaks . . . and we are supposed to have a class war. . . . One against the other, you understand? What the devil!"[39] This device was even more transparent in Cambodia, where Khmer Rouge propaganda railed against the subhuman "new people," a completely manufactured social group consisting of businessmen, city dwellers, foreigners, and virtually anyone with an education.[40]

Proponents of the plural society theory have generally refrained from applying their theories to cases such as the Soviet Union, China, and Cambodia, on the grounds that communist mass killings have different causes from ethnically motivated genocides like the Holocaust. The fundamental causes of events such as the Holocaust and the Great Terror are assuredly different. What the history of communist mass killing so strongly suggests, however, is that even the most extreme levels of violence can be supported in the absence of deep, preexisting social cleavages between groups. This conclusion suggests, in turn, that we should be careful not simply to assume a central causal role for social cleavages, even in cases of ethnic mass killing.

Indeed, upon closer examination the severity of preexisting cleavages between ethnic groups involved in genocidal violence often appears exaggerated. It is easy to overemphasize the significance of cleavages between groups after violent conflict has broken out. Widespread violence tends to exacerbate the negative aspects of group relations, coloring the interpretation of the past and making it harder to appreciate long periods of relative harmony and cooperation between groups. In fact, deep cleavages between ethnic groups often seem more like effects of mass violence than independent causes or preconditions. Even in relatively tolerant societies, powerful groups have proved capable of dehumanizing their enemies, intensifying existing social divisions, and even inventing new ones. Severe discrimination, moral exclusion, and dehumanizing attitudes are often the result of conscious strategies designed to facilitate violence against victim groups, not preexisting attributes of society.[41]

In the former Yugoslavia, for example, overt discrimination between Serbs, Croats, and Muslims does not appear to have been especially severe or pervasive before the outbreak of large-scale violence in 1991. By most objective indications, ethnic relations, while not entirely harmonious, did not seem significantly worse than relations between ethnic groups in many other countries. Public opinion polls taken as late as 1989–90 showed high levels of ethnic tolerance between groups. Even in November 1991, majorities of 70–90 percent opposed separation from Yugoslavia or an ethnically divided republic.[42] Much of the fighting, especially in Bosnia, took on religious overtones, but before the war less than 25 percent of Bosnians considered themselves religious believers (which compares to over 70 of percent Americans who identify themselves as such).[43] In the decade before the war, 29 percent of Serbs living in Croatia married Croatian spouses (compared to only 12.1 percent of blacks who married white spouses in the United States in 1993).[44] Most observers of the conflict seem to agree that although some animosity and prejudice did exist between ethnic groups before the war, for the great majority of people these feelings were not intense enough to provoke widespread violence until political leaders launched inflammatory rhetorical campaigns deliberately designed to exacerbate distrust among ethnic groups and mobilize their people for war.[45]

Even some of the violence perpetrated by Nazi Germany poses problems for the plural society theory. The Nazi "euthanasia" campaign, for example, killed at least ninety-three thousand physically disabled, mentally ill, or simply destitute Germans, including thousands of children.[46] Yet there is little reason to suspect that, before the Nazi seizure of power, most Germans felt differently about their sick and poor than did the people of other nations. In fact, German propagandists were compelled to try to overcome public opposition to forced euthanasia with a propaganda campaign designed to dehumanize the chronically and mentally ill and to remind Germans of the burdens that such "life unworthy of life" imposed on society.[47]

Conversely, as proponents of the plural society theory usually acknowledge, even societies torn by exceptionally deep social cleavages can exist for long periods without erupting in mass killing.[48] Such societies actually appear to be quite common. Many historians, for example, agree that during the late 1800s and early 1900s anti-Semitic attitudes and discrimination directed against Jewish minorities ran even deeper in Russia, Poland, France, and other European nations than in Germany itself. Jews in Germany were unquestionably the objects of significant discrimination and hatred, but, as Michael Marrus concludes, "it is highly unlikely, by any scale of judgment, that Germany would be deemed the most anti-Semitic country in Europe" prior to the Nazi seizure of power.[49] As Sarah Gordon points out, "had the German population been uniquely rabid in its hatred of Jews, it is inconceivable that Jews could have fared so well, especially compared to Jews in other nations."[50] Jews outside of Germany, however, avoided genocide until after the Nazis occupied their countries in the Second World War.

African Americans living in the Southern United States during the Jim Crow era also escaped genocide, despite being subjected to overt discrimination, intense economic and political exclusion, and dehumanizing hatred and violence by significant segments of society.[51] Likewise, Palestinians living in Israel and Israeli-occupied territories, and black Africans in apartheid-era South Africa, each suffered extremely high levels of hatred and discrimination for decades without becoming victims of genocide. René Lemarchand, in his comparative study of the relatively peaceful democratic transition of South Africa and the genocidal paths of Rwanda and Burundi, finds that "if all three states are (or were) hierarchically structured societies, only in South Africa was the once politically dominant minority judicially, culturally, and racially distinct from the African majority. History, language, and institutionalized discrimination conspired to mark them off from each other in ways unknown in Rwanda and Burundi."[52]

The evidence cited above strongly suggests that unusually severe preexisting social cleavages are neither universally necessary nor sufficient conditions for mass killing or even for more narrowly construed definitions of genocide. That said, this conclusion does not exclude a role for these factors in the causal process of mass killing and genocide. It is simply impossible, for example, to understand why the Nazis sought to murder the Jews without reference to the long history of German anti-Semitism. My claim is not that such factors did not matter, but only that they cannot reliably distinguish countries like Germany from many other societies that did not launch campaigns of systematic extermination against minority groups. The search for general factors that may help to distinguish societies at high risk for such violence from those that are not is one of the fundamental distinctions between the mission of the social scientist and that of the historian. Although this book will focus on factors of primary interest to social scientists, both modes of inquiry are necessary to develop a fully satisfying explanation of individual cases of mass killing, such as the Holocaust, as well as the phenomenon in general.

National Crises and Mass Killing

A second prominent family of explanations of mass killing and genocide suggests that wars, revolutions, severe economic depressions, and other catastrophes — hereafter referred to as "national crises" — provide the critical spark for mass killing. As many studies have documented, nearly all cases of mass killing follow or occur during some kind of national crisis. Explanations for the correlation between national crises and mass killing can be divided into two primary groups.[53] The first group, referred to here as the scapegoat theory, focuses on the social-psychological effects of national crises as the trigger for genocide. The second group of explanations, referred to as the political opportunity theory, focuses on the opportunities and incentives for mass killing generated by national crises.

The Scapegoat Theory

The scapegoat theory is one of the most common and carefully articulated social-psychological theories of mass killing.[54] This approach combines features of sociological research, often including some of the same factors and explanations highlighted by the plural society theory, with insights from individual and social psychology.[55] Proponents of the scapegoat theory claim that mass killing results when societies wracked by severe crises seek to place the blame for these hardships on minority groups or powerless majorities. According to these theories, individuals suffering from exceptionally difficult life conditions have a powerful psychological need to understand and identify the sources of their problems and frustrations. Proponents of the scapegoat theory hold that choosing a scapegoat allows individuals to comprehend the source of their problems, to believe that these problems can be predicted and controlled, to project their fears or insecurities onto others, and to escape feelings of guilt and personal responsibility for life's difficulties.

National crises do not inevitably or even usually lead to mass killing. While national crises are relatively common, mass killing is rare. Thus, most proponents of the scapegoat theory suggest that certain aspects of the perpetrators' society and culture predispose some states or societies to scapegoating and ultimately to genocide or mass killing. A wide variety of different risk factors have been proposed, including a tradition of obedience to authority, aggressive cultural dispositions, and certain types of social and governmental institutions. Nearly all proponents of the scapegoat theory, however, accept the premise that unusually strong preexisting social cleavages make the resort to mass killing more likely in the wake of national crises.

Although the historical record largely confirms the scapegoat theory's prediction that mass killings occur after national crises, other evidence casts doubt on the theory's explanation of the causal relationship between these events. First of all, as discussed above in reference to the plural society theory, unusually deep cleavages between social groups are not necessary for mass killing to take place. Genocide and mass killing commonly occur between members of similar social groups with little history of discrimination or violent conflict. This finding is damaging to the scapegoat theory because the theory suggests that preexisting social cleavages are crucial factors that help distinguish the relatively few societies that respond to national crises with mass killing from the great majority which do not.

More important, historical evidence casts doubt on the relevance of the basic psychological mechanisms described by many proponents of the scapegoat theory. The scapegoat theory suggests that mass killing serves to alleviate the psychological frustration and fear generated by national crises in society at large. If this claim is correct, we should find that mass killing is usually a popular undertaking among members of dominant social groups. Members of these groups should demonstrate spontaneous support for the killings.

My research finds surprisingly little confirming evidence for these propositions. Mass killing is often carried out with little public support, even from members of dominant social groups. It is difficult to imagine, for example, how the Great Terror in the Soviet Union could be characterized as a reaction to the desires of Soviet society. Scholars of the Terror often portray this episode as the impetus of a single man.[56] Those in the general population who supported the arrests, show trials, and purges did so largely on the basis of propaganda, forced confessions, and other fabricated evidence supplied to them by the Soviet government. Fear, coercion, and blackmail played a significant role in securing the participation of many of Stalin's accomplices, many of whom seem to have understood that they too could become victims at any moment.

Even the Holocaust offers considerable confounding evidence for the scapegoat theory. This evidence is particularly relevant because proponents of the scapegoat theory often cite the Holocaust as the paradigmatic example of the theory. Although a small group of authors, most notably Daniel Goldhagen, assert that most Germans wished to see the Jews exterminated, the weight of scholarly opinion firmly opposes this interpretation.[57] Research on German public opinion before and during the Nazi era refutes Goldhagen's conclusions as well as the scapegoat theory's implication that genocide should be broadly popular among members of the perpetrators' social group. Although no serious scholar disputes that anti-Semitism was prevalent in German society before the Holocaust, most agree that the majority of the German population stopped well short of calling for the extermination of the Jews.[58] Hitler, the Nazi regime, and many of the less violent anti-Jewish measures the Nazis promoted before the war were broadly popular, but forced deportation and systematic ex-termination received much less support. Michael Marrus's review of Holocaust scholarship concludes that "historians have been unable to identify a murderous impulse outside the Nazi leadership. . . . Popular strains of antisemitism were never strong enough on their own to sup-port violent persecution in the modern period."[59]

The contention that most Germans supported the mass killing of the Jews is also contradicted by the behavior of the German people and the Nazi government itself. Spontaneous violence against Jews remained rare even after the Nazis gained power. Far from reacting to the impulses of the German population, as proponents of scapegoat theory suggest, Nazi leaders felt they had to intensify and disseminate anti-Semitic feelings through a sustained propaganda campaign beginning from the moment they seized power. Even this steady stream of anti-Semitic slogans and images, however, appears to have been unable to convince the majority of Germans that the Jews should be killed—although it probably did re-duce their willingness to defend the Jews. According to Ian Kershaw, the propaganda campaign was unsuccessful in generating widespread sup-port for extermination precisely because, contrary to the predictions of the scapegoat theory, most Germans did not see the Jews as responsible for their own hardships. Rather, the "constant barrage of propaganda failed to make Jews the prime target of hatred for most Germans, simply because the issue seemed largely abstract, academic, and unrelated to their own problems."[60]

Indeed, fearing a negative reaction, the Nazi government ultimately felt compelled to try to keep the final solution secret from the German people.[61] Some scholars have suggested that German leaders believed that this secrecy was necessary, not because they suspected that the Ger-man people would not support the killing, but because revealing it would have provoked adverse foreign reactions or increased resistance among the intended victims. These concerns were undoubtedly taken seriously, but high-ranking Nazi leaders often framed the requirement for secrecy in terms of the expected negative reaction of the German people.[62] Himmler himself described the final solution to his senior officers as "an unwritten and never to be written page of glory in our history."[63] "Per-haps," he told them, "at some later, some very much later period we might consider whether to tell the German people a little more about this. But

I think we had better not! It's us here who have shouldered the responsibility, for action as well as for an idea, and I think we had better take this secret with us into our graves."[64]

Interestingly, recent research suggests that scapegoating may not have been the primary motivation for violence against Jews even among those most directly involved in the killing itself. Michael Mann's examination of the biographies of 1,581 Holocaust perpetrators tried for war crimes found that these men appear to have suffered substantially *less* from factors such as unemployment or the loss of a parent before the war than did the broader German population. While acknowledging the potential for biases in his sample, Mann concludes that "few perpetrators seem to have had very disrupted lives of the kind that might produce severe frustrations, aggression, or scapegoating for personal unhappiness."[65]

In the final analysis, the scapegoat theory may do a better job of explaining the psychology and actions of the individual leaders who conceive of and organize mass killing than it does of the broader societies over which these individuals rule, or even the individuals they recruit to help them carry out the killing. The chief architects of genocide and mass killing obviously do believe that their victims are responsible for causing great suffering. Yet mass killing can occur even if this suffering is not experienced by the rest of society and even if the belief that victim groups are responsible is not widely shared. Hitler, for example, clearly blamed the Jews for Germany's humiliating defeat in World War I and for the severe economic crises that ensued. Many authors have speculated that Hitler's unique personal misfortunes, rather than those suffered by most Germans, may have encouraged him to seek a scapegoat in the Jews.[66] Although national crises may provoke some members of society to seek violent revenge on scapegoats, this psychological reaction appears to be far from universal. This path to mass killing becomes operative only when such individuals achieve positions of high political or military authority. This outcome, however, is so rare relative to the occurrence of national crises as to provide little basis by which to identify societies at high risk for mass killing.

Political Opportunity

Another family of explanations that focuses on the effects of national crises suggests that crises encourage genocide not because they prompt societies to seek scapegoats per se but because these events provide the incentives, opportunity and cover for revolutionary elites seeking to consolidate political power or implement genocidal ideologies.[67] Indeed, wars, revolutions, and severe economic depressions can create the opportunity for relatively small radical groups to assume control of the powerful political and military machinery of the state. From this perspective,

Germany's military defeat and economic collapse are relevant to the Holocaust, not primarily because they induced the German people to blame the Jews for their problems, but because they seriously undermined the fledgling German democratic political system. These crises contributed to the creation of political factions, destabilized the democratic process, raised the specter of communism, and encouraged a minority of voters to consider radical solutions to Germany's economic problems, including both communism and fascism, thereby easing the way for extremely radical groups such as the Nazis to assume control of the German state.

This process was not unique to Germany. The political, military, and economic chaos caused by the First World War, for example, undoubtedly helped the Bolsheviks gain power in Russia. The turmoil wrought by twenty-five years of conflict in Southeast Asia, culminating in the American invasion and bombardment of Cambodia, helped create conditions in which the Khmer Rouge was able to seize power.[68] National crises, especially major wars, can also create situations that force even moderate leaders to consider the most brutal options available to them. The intentional bombardment of German and Japanese civilians during the Second World War and France's bloody tactics during the Algerian war of independence were, after all, not the work of radical dictators but of democratically elected leaders.

Unfortunately, although the political opportunity theory offers a convincing explanation of the correlation between national crises and mass killing, it ultimately provides relatively little leverage for understanding or predicting genocide and mass killing. National crises may raise substantially the probability of mass killing relative to more stable societies, but the absolute likelihood that a national crisis will spark such violence is extremely small.[69] As noted above, the vast majority of national crises, be they wars, revolutions, or severe economic depressions, do not lead to mass killing. Most proponents of the political opportunity theory acknowledge this limitation. Few, however, have devoted much effort to identifying and elaborating the specific conditions and factors that may determine when political elites will take advantage of the genocidal opportunities presented by national crises or, on the contrary, when these crises are likely to be resolved more peacefully.[70] Without this information, we can neither fully understand the causes of mass killing nor anticipate with confidence when it is likely to occur.

Democracy and Mass Killing

The third and final group of authors examined here search for the causes of genocide and mass killing in the form of government of the societies in which it takes place. Rudolph Rummel is the most forceful advocate of this explanation of mass killing. According to what Rummel terms the "power principle," "The more power a government has, the more it can act arbitrarily according to the whims and desires of the elite, and the more it will make war on others and murder its foreign and domestic subjects. The more constrained the power of governments, the less it will aggress on others."[71]

Rummel and others have marshaled strong evidence to demonstrate that democratic forms of government are associated with lower levels of mass killing and human rights abuses than other governmental systems, especially totalitarian and communist regimes.[72] The fact that democracies engage in less mass killing of their own citizens than other forms of government is one of the most carefully documented findings of the theoretical literature on mass killing. Nevertheless, two problems limit the utility of this insight.

First, as Rummel acknowledges, although democracies almost never kill their own citizens, they do engage in mass killing during foreign wars and in their own colonies abroad. The United States killed as many as 200,000 civilians, many of them intentionally, during its occupation of the Philippines from 1899 to 1902.[73] The United States also intentionally killed between 268,000 and 900,000 Japanese civilians during the Second World War and, in collaboration with Great Britain, between 300,000 and 600,000 Germans.[74] Democratic France, in concert with its native Algerian allies, killed hundreds of thousands of civilians during its war in Algeria and perhaps 250,000 in Vietnam.[75] In both cases, much of the killing was intentional.

Democracies have also perpetrated mass killings against domestic groups not defined as citizens. Most notably, the United States waged a relentless series of wars on the indigenous people of North America, a process that eventually resulted in their near-total extermination.[76]

In addition, democratic states have provided economic and military assistance to foreign regimes known to be perpetrators of mass killing. The Guatemalan Historical Clarification Commission, for example, found that U.S. training of the Guatemalan military in counterinsurgency techniques in the early 1980s "had a significant bearing on human rights violations" and that "the United States Government . . . lent direct and indirect support to illegal state operations" that ultimately killed well over 100,000 people.[77] In 1965, American officials also appear to have provided Indonesia with lists of thousands of names that the Indonesian army used to identify victims in its massacre of between 250,000 and 1,000,000 suspected supporters of the Indonesian Communist Party.[78]

Rummel writes that "all this killing of foreigners by democracies may seem to violate the power principle, but really it underlines it. For, in each case, the killing was carried out in a highly undemocratic fashion: in secret, behind a conscious cover of lies and deceit, and by agencies and power holders that had the wartime authority to operate autonomously."[79] This argument is misleading. American actions such as the bombings of Japan and Germany and the wars against the Native Americans were not kept secret from the general population. Not only were most citizens fully aware of these events, they strongly supported them.[80] The majority of Americans continue to express support for the atomic bombing of Japan in 1945, even now that the civilian death toll is widely known.[81] Rummel is surely correct in his assessment that democracies engage in less mass killing because, unlike other forms of government, democracies guarantee the basic rights of their citizens and require a much higher degree of public support for their policies. This does not mean that democratic publics will never support mass killing, or that they will do so only on the basis of misinformation.

A second and perhaps more important limitation of Rummel's power principle is that it provides relatively little ability to predict when mass killing will occur. As Rummel concedes, power is a necessary but not a sufficient condition for mass killing.[82] Thus, while it is important to understand that democracies engage in less killing than other forms of government, it is equally important to recognize that even the most undemocratic regimes do not engage in mass killing most of the time.[83] In light of this observation and the fact that democracies do resort to mass killing under certain circumstances, we know that other important factors and processes must also be at work. A more comprehensive theory of mass killing should specify the conditions under which some groups, democratic or otherwise, decide to exterminate their opponents rather than deal with them peacefully.

The notion that underlies each of the theories described above — that factors that impact or permeate society at large should provide the most significant clues to understanding which societies are likely to experience genocide and mass killing — has strong intuitive appeal. Indeed, these factors often, but not always, operate as background causes or preconditions for systematic violence. Because factors such as hatred, discrimination, national crises, or undemocratic systems of government need not be unusually severe to play their part in the causal process leading to mass killing, however, they are simply too common to serve as accurate indicators of this relatively rare kind of violence. Like the availability of weapons to carry out the killing, they are also present in many societies that never experience genocide or mass killing.

In the next chapter, I argue that the main reason that broad social structures do not provide reliable indicators of mass killing is because such
killing does not require as much support from society at large as is commonly assumed. Rather, small but powerful groups often play a determining role not only in instigating but also in physically carrying out this
kind of violence. Only by understanding the specific goals of these
groups, as well as the constraints on the achievement of those goals, can
we understand why these groups choose to tap into the latent capacities
for mass killing available in so many societies.

2. THE PERPETRATORS AND THE PUBLIC

In the early morning hours of July 13, 1942, approximately five hundred men from German Reserve Police Battalion 101 surrounded the small Polish town of Józefów with orders to shoot anyone attempting to escape.[1] The policemen entered the town, rounded up every Jewish man, woman, and child, and escorted them to the village marketplace. Those victims too sick or too old to walk were shot, as was anyone who showed the least signs of resistance. Male Jews of working age were separated from their families and prepared for deportation to slave labor camps. The rest of the villagers were loaded in small groups onto trucks and transported to the forest a short distance away. They were ordered to lie face down on the ground. The policemen then methodically shot each person in the back of the neck. Women were murdered with their infant children. The killing lasted all day and into the evening. When it was over, the policemen were literally covered in the blood of their victims. Fifteen hundred bodies littered the forest floor.

Events such as this have been a disturbingly common feature of twentieth-century history. Massacres similar in scale, if not always in the details of implementation, have been visited upon villages in Turkish Armenia, China under Japanese occupation, Indonesia, Guatemala, Rwanda, and dozens of other countries throughout the world. Why do societies allow such atrocities to take place? Why do the individuals charged with carrying out these bloody operations agree to take part in the murder of defenseless civilians? These are the most troubling and difficult questions confronting scholars of genocide and mass killing.

Although a wholly satisfying explanation for human cruelty of this magnitude probably will remain beyond our reach, this should not deter us from seeking to advance our understanding of mass killing and those who carry it out. This chapter contributes to such an understanding. In the first of three sections, I analyze the nature of public support for mass killing. I show that the active support or participation of the majority of the public is not generally necessary for mass killing to take place. The actual violence in most episodes of mass killing is carried out by relatively small groups, usually members of military, paramilitary, or police organizations. The rest of society typically remains passive or indifferent to the fate of the victims. In the second section I explore the motives and psychology of the rank-and-file perpetrators of mass killing. Through a review of the historical evidence on the behavior of perpetrators of mass killing, especially in the Holocaust, and the findings of several relevant psychological experiments, I conclude that deep hatreds or fervent ideological convictions are not necessary to explain the behavior of most perpetrators. Two processes, the preferential selection of a relatively small number of violent or fanatical individuals and the psychological influence of situational factors, such as authority and peer pressure, seem to provide the best explanation for the behavior of most perpetrators. In the third section, I argue that the limited degree of public support necessary for mass killing and the relative ease with which individuals can be led to kill renders it possible for small groups or even individual leaders to wield a determining influence over the instigation and organization of mass killing. This conclusion, in turn, suggests that the effort to understand and anticipate mass killing should begin with an examination of the specific goals, beliefs, and motives of these groups, rather than the broad attributes of the societies from which they are drawn or the characteristics of the individuals whom they recruit to carry out their bloody work.

PUBLIC SUPPORT

Perhaps one reason why so many scholars have searched for the causes of genocide and mass killing in the structure or psychology of society at large is due to an implicit assumption that implementing mass killing requires the direct involvement, or at least the active support and sympathy, of a large portion of society. This belief has even led some authors to suggest that societies involved in mass killing should be considered collectively mentally ill.[2] Upon closer examination, however, this assumption appears unfounded. Although the public sometimes supports mass killing, often it does not.

Unfortunately, reliable evidence about public attitudes toward mass killing and about the exact extent of public participation in it remains scarce. Perpetrators of mass killing have seldom felt the need to engage in public opinion polling. Nevertheless, the anecdotal evidence presented below demonstrates that even in some of the most violent episodes of mass killing in human history, the active support or direct participation of the broader public is simply not necessary for this kind of violence to take place.

The British statesman and political thinker Edmund Burke famously counseled that "the only thing necessary for the triumph of evil is for good men to do nothing." Indeed, rather than positive support from society at large, mass killing often seems to require little more than what might be called "negative support" — the inability of victims to escape or defend themselves, the absence of organized domestic or international opposition to perpetrators, and the lack of public willingness to take personal risks on behalf of others. Hatred, discrimination, and negative stereotyping directed at powerless social groups may not be enough on their own to provoke support for extermination, but widespread attitudes of this kind may be sufficient to block effective opposition to it. Since active opposition to mass killing can mean prosecution or death, most citizens manage to look the other way, even when the victims are neighbors, friends, or relatives. Nadezhda Mandelstam, whose husband perished in Stalin's Gulag, described the attitude of many of her fellow citizens during Great Purges: "We all took the easy way out by keeping silent in the hope that not we but our neighbors would be killed."[3]

Only democratic governments require broad-based, active political support for their policies. The vast majority of mass killings, however, have not been carried out by democracies.[4] Leaders who possess the political or military support necessary to gain control of a state, therefore, usually also possess sufficient support to carry out mass killing. In nondemocratic states this minimum level of support can be remarkably thin.

The Bolshevik rise to power in Russia, for example, paved the way for some of the most deadly episodes of mass killing in history. Scholars continue to differ over the degree of support the Bolsheviks received in October 1917 and in the civil war that followed, with some arguing that the revolution was little more than a coup d'état and others pointing to a larger role for the masses.[5] Few scholars today, however, suggest that the Bolsheviks won the support of the majority of the Russian people, the great preponderance of whom were peasants. Trotsky estimated that at most twenty-five or thirty thousand people actively participated in the October insurrection.[6] The Bolsheviks owed their ultimate victory less to their own popular appeal than to the ravages of the First World War, the weakness of Russian social and governmental institutions, and the unpopularity and disorganization of their principal adversaries. Socialist parties and revolutionary organizations, after all, existed throughout Europe at the time. Russia, with its backward economy and tiny working class, was a highly unlikely birthplace for the world's first communist society. According to Martin Malia, "the Bolsheviks were able to achieve this extraordinary feat only because of the immaturity and fragility of pre-revolutionary Russian society. . . . There were simply no structures capable of opposing them effectively." Socialism triumphed in Russia and not elsewhere in Europe, he concludes, because "only in Russia was there a social void that permitted ideological politicians to get away with acting on it."[7] As Lenin himself famously described the October Revolution, the Bolsheviks all but "found power lying in the streets and simply picked it up."[8]

In Germany, the 13.5 million vote plurality (37.3 percent of the ballots cast) that the Nazi party received in the July 1932 elections indicated high absolute levels of support for the Nazis. Yet these returns also indicate that almost two-thirds of German voters cast their ballots *against* the Nazis in 1932. The two left wing "workers parties" the SPD (socialists) and KPD (communists) received a combined 35.9 percent of the vote in that election. Moreover, the July returns represented the highest percentage of the vote that the Nazi party ever garnered in a free election. Less than three months later, the Nazis' share of the vote dropped to 33.1 percent, while the combined SPD and KPD vote grew to over 37 percent.[9] More than half a million Germans had joined the Nazi Storm Troopers (SA) by January 1933; but the Reichsbanner, the Socialists' paramilitary, was even larger, with approximately a million active members. One hundred thousand Germans also joined uniformed communist paramilitary groups.[10]

The Croatian Ustasa regime, which presided over the murder of at least 125,000 Serbs and 60,000 Jews in Yugoslavia during the Second World War, also appears to have been supported by only a small fraction of Croatian society.[11] Branimir Anzulovic concludes that "the vast majority of Croatians were . . . hostile towards the actions of the Ustasa regime."[12] The commander of German forces in Croatia estimated that only 2 percent of the population supported the Ustasa, and he complained that the unpopularity of the regime was actually driving people to join Tito's communist insurgents.[13]

Even apparently high levels of political support for murderous regimes and leaders should not automatically be equated with support for mass killing itself. Individuals are capable of supporting violent regimes or leaders while remaining indifferent or even opposed to specific policies that these regimes have carried out. As Vladimir Brovkin argues, "a vote for the Bolsheviks in 1917 was not a vote for Red Terror or even a vote for a dictatorship of the proletariat."[14] Nor do most scholars attribute the Nazis' electoral success to the appeal of radical anti-Semitic ideas, let alone support for the extermination of the Jews.[15] It is true that the Nazi regime, especially Hitler personally, remained broadly popular even as increasingly radical anti-Semitic measures were enacted. Yet scholars of German popular opinion overwhelmingly reject the notion that most Germans favored violent measures against the Jews.[16] Rather, as Saul Friedländer concludes,

> among the traditional [non-Nazi] elites and within the wider reaches of the population, anti-Jewish attitudes were more in the realm of tacit acquiescence or varying degrees of compliance. . . . [T]he majority of Germans, although undoubtedly influenced by various forms of traditional anti-Semitism and easily accepting the segregation of the Jews, shied away from widespread violence against them, urging neither their expulsion from the Reich nor their physical annihilation.[17]

Nationalist appeals, especially when associated with wars of national defense or liberation, can also rally public support behind a violent regime despite widespread indifference or opposition to its specific policies or brutal methods. Chalmers Johnson, for example, argues that it was Chinese nationalism and opposition to the Japanese occupation, not the appeal of radical communist economic ideas, that accounted for early mass support for the communists in China.[18] Yet these ideas would later provide the rationale for policies that resulted in the deaths of millions of Chinese men, women, and children.

Likewise, the Khmer Rouge exploited the outrage caused by the American invasion and bombardment to help turn many Cambodians against the Lon Nol regime and recruit the support necessary to implement their radical plan to transform Cambodian society.[19] They ultimately succeeded, not because their policies attracted the active support of the masses, but because, as Karl Jackson has suggested, by 1975 "they were the only organized coercive force in Cambodia."[20]

Finally, it also should be emphasized that even those who do lend their support to policies of mass killing—or those who choose not to oppose it—may do so not out of preexisting convictions but as the result of government propaganda and misinformation designed to win their support or at least compliance. In societies without freedom of speech and the press, or lacking access to trusted centers of alternative information, propaganda can have a powerful effect on public attitudes. During the civil wars in Russia and China, for example, many peasants joined communist armies under the slogan of "land to the tillers." Yet few understood that the leaders of these revolutions were planning not simply for the redistribution of farm land but for the eventual elimination of private farming altogether.

Propaganda issued by perpetrators often attempts to conceal from the public the full extent or true motives for mass killing. Throughout the conflict in the former Yugoslavia, Belgrade sought to cover up its atrocities or characterize them as legitimate military actions. Many Serbs appear to have accepted these arguments.[21] Propaganda has frequently been used to link victims to intervention by foreign powers or subversive internal plots, a technique vigorously exploited by Stalin during the show trials of the 1930s. Perpetrators often utilize their control over the media to promote the perception that their victims represent a mortal threat to the survival of dominant groups. In Rwanda, for example, Human Rights Watch has documented how prior to the 1994 genocide, Hutu extremists launched a coordinated propaganda campaign designed to portray the Tutsi as bloodthirsty foreigners intent on exterminating the Hutu.[22]

Paradoxically, propaganda can also lead the public to support individual leaders, even while opposing the broader regime or its policies. Both Stalin and Mao appear to have been the objects of genuine affection by large numbers of their countrymen. Their deaths were greeted with a surprising outpouring of public grief. Even many of those who had been imprisoned, lost family members, or suffered starvation as a result of Stalin and Mao's directives apparently refused to accept that these "devoted" leaders were responsible for the brutality that characterized communism in Russia and China.[23]

If widespread public approval of mass killing is often absent, even in the bloodiest episodes of this kind of violence, how is mass killing carried out? The central reason that broad public support of mass killing is seldom required is that, regardless of the degree to which society supports the violence, large numbers of civilians almost never play a major role in the killing itself. In nearly all instances of mass killing, the majority of the actual violence is carried out by a relatively small segment of society. These killers are almost always young men, typically members of an organized military group, militia, or police organization. A tiny minority of such men, well armed and well organized, can generate an appalling amount of bloodshed when unleashed upon unarmed and unorganized victims. When perpetrators are unopposed, the scale of the slaughter becomes a matter of mathematics. A group of twenty-five thousand determined killers, for example, each murdering an average of one victim a week, could kill a hundred thousand victims in a month, or 1.2 million in a year. This may be a conservative estimate of the carnage determined killers can accomplish.

In the case of the Holocaust, Daniel Goldhagen estimates that over a hundred thousand Germans "knowingly contributed in some intimate way to the mass slaughter of the Jews."[24] This number may be shockingly large in absolute terms, but it constitutes less than 1 percent of the adult male population of Germany in 1938, or roughly one German perpetrator for every fifty or sixty Jewish victims.[25] Even if wider participation might have been forthcoming, it simply was not necessary. As Raul Hilberg documents, in the mobile killing operations that followed the German invasion of the Soviet Union, "victims outnumbered their captors 10 to 1, 20 to 1, or even 50 to 1; but the Jews could never turn their numbers to their advantage. The killers were well armed, they knew what to do, and they worked swiftly."[26] Since the same killers participated in numerous killing operations of this kind, the overall ratio of victims to perpetrators must have been considerably higher. The notorious death camps were even more efficient. At any given time, an average of three thousand SS guards administered the Auschwitz concentration camp complex, where more than 1.1 million people likely perished.[27] Nearly all the actual killing during the Holocaust was performed by members of German military, police, or allied organizations, including military units from Axis countries and paramilitary groups recruited from foreign populations.[28]

Other episodes of mass killing also have been perpetrated by similarly small numbers of men. At one German psychiatric institution tasked with carrying out Hitler's euthanasia campaign, for example, approximately seventy-five to a hundred personnel, including less than twenty-five individuals involved directly in the killing, managed to murder over ten thousand patients in less than eight months in 1941.[29] In the Soviet Union, a prison guard force of approximately 135,000 men presided over a Gulag of at least 1.5 million in 1941.[30] Between 12 and 19 million people probably passed through the camps from 1934 to 1947.[31] Millions were killed or died from exposure, malnutrition, and exhaustion. In Cambodia, the Khmer Rouge army of approximately seventy thousand soldiers and a thousand political cadres gained control of the lives of nearly eight million of their countrymen in 1975.[32] Less than four years later, as many as two million Cambodians were dead.[33] At the most important political prison of the Khmer Rouge, a staff of less than three hundred people, including many workers not directly involved in violence, presided over the torture and execution of almost fourteen thousand victims.[34]

The 1994 genocide in Rwanda usually is depicted in direct contrast to these cases, as an example of how virtually an entire society can turn to murder. Many observers have attributed the widespread participation in the genocide to a cultural predisposition for obedience to authority, or to the administrative legacy of Rwanda's unique system of peacetime civil-ian-mobilization campaigns for public works projects.[35] After the geno-cide, some Tutsi spoke of the Hutu as "a criminal population."[36] As one Tutsi official described it, "In Germany, the Jews were taken out of their residences, moved to distant far away locations, and killed there, almost anonymously. In Rwanda, the government did not kill. It prepared the population, enraged it and enticed it. Your neighbors killed you."[37]

Participation in the Rwandan genocide was extensive in comparison to most other cases of mass killing, but it was far from universal. Civil-ians played a significant role in the violence, but military and paramilitary groups were probably responsible for organizing and carrying out most of the actual killing.[38] Scholars have estimated the total number of hard-core Hutu perpetrators at fifty thousand to a hundred thousand—many of them members of extremist militia groups, the Presidential Guard, or the army.[39] Larger numbers of civilians may have contributed to the genocide in some fashion, perhaps increasing the total number of partic-ipants to two hundred thousand or more.[40] Many of these civilians did not kill anyone but were present in Hutu mobs that did, or participated by manning roadblocks, or identifying Tutsi victims to the *génocidaires*. Even this larger group, however, amounts to less than 9 percent of the male Hutu population over the age of thirteen.[41] These perpetrators were responsible for massacring between 500,000 and 800,000 people in less than four months, perhaps two-thirds of them within the first thirty days.[42] The fact that the perpetrators succeeded in killing so many so quickly, although most were equipped with nothing more than small arms and edged weapons, suggests the astonishing efficiency with which such groups can function.

It should be noted that more significant segments of the public fre-quently lend their assistance to mass killing in ways that do not involve direct participation in violence. Indirect cooperation may involve activi-ties such as producing weapons, providing logistical and administrative support to organizations directly involved in the killing, or informing on fellow citizens. Indeed, many episodes of mass killing would not have been possible without widespread participation of this kind. Yet collabo-ration of this nature does not always indicate unhesitating approval of mass killing. Individuals may participate in these activities for a variety of other reasons: patriotic duty, material or careerist ambition, fear or coer-cion. Just as individuals are capable of supporting a murderous regime while at the same time disapproving of or ignoring its violent policies, they are capable of psychologically separating their own indirect collaboration in the violence from any sense of approval or responsibility for the killing itself.[43]

Even these indirect forms of cooperation with mass killing, however, seldom involve the majority of the public. All that is usually required of most citizens is their powerlessness, passivity, or disregard for others' torments. Thus, James J. Sheehan's review of research on public opinion in Nazi Germany concludes:

> While it is always frightening to imagine a nation swept away and dominated by the Nazis, it is surely no less frightening to consider that the Nazis were able to accomplish most of what they set out to do without acquiring unquestioning allegiance or imposing complete control. Apparently they did not need to: it was not necessary for Germans to believe, nor necessary for them to approve; compliance, not conviction was required. For the Nazi state to thrive, its citizens had to do no more than go along, maintaining a clear sense of their own interests and a profound indifference to the suffering of others.[44]

One of the central reasons that compliance or "bystanding" seems to be the norm in cases of mass killing is that active opposition to mass killing usually raises classic problems of collective action.[45] Organizing for collective action is always difficult, but it is hardest when the costs of participation are high and the benefits of action accrue even to those who do not participate. In such circumstances, each individual has a strong incentive to let others pay the costs of action, since all will share in the benefits.

These negative incentives can severely hamper the ability of bystanders to organize to prevent violence against victim groups. The costs of active opposition to mass killing can be very high, including prosecution or even death. Moreover, the most direct benefits of preventing mass killing accrue to the potential victims rather than their protectors. Since victims are commonly drawn from small, insulated minority groups, those who oppose mass killing often find themselves in the position of risking their own lives to save the lives of strangers. Germany's Jewish population, for example, was concentrated in large cities and accounted for less than 1 percent of the country's inhabitants. Many Germans had little or no contact with Jews.[46]

From this perspective the truly unusual society is not one in which most people stand passively by as mass killing takes place, but one in which people manage to organize and take risks in the defense of victims. After all, mass killing often has succeeded in large part because the victims themselves have failed to organize for their own defense. For example, scholars have long puzzled over the lack of more determined Jewish resistance to the Nazis.[47] In Cambodia, the barriers to resistance were so high that an effective national opposition to the Khmer Rouge failed to emerge despite the fact that as many one in four of the country's citizens fell victim to the regime. If victims of mass killing cannot overcome these barriers, it is little wonder that bystanders often fail to do the same.

THE PERPETRATORS

Although mass killing typically requires the participation of only a relatively small group of people in acts of violence, it remains important to understand how these individuals are recruited and motivated to engage in such brutal behavior. Unfortunately, direct evidence of the personal beliefs and motives of such persons is exceedingly rare. Perpetrators seldom record their inner thoughts and feelings about their deeds. Outside observers are rarely in a position to provide personal information of this kind. Moreover, the few existing accounts from perpetrators are of questionable reliability, since perpetrators usually have strong incentives to diminish their personal responsibility for any atrocities and portray their actions in the best possible light. This problem is particularly acute if, as is often the case, such testimony is recorded long after the fact when memories may be cloudy, or in the course of a criminal investigation when the threat of prosecution makes admissions of guilt unlikely.

No doubt largely because of these difficulties, historians have devoted surprising little systematic effort (with the notable exception of the Holocaust) to explaining the behavior of the rank-and-file perpetrators of mass killing. In addition to this admittedly limited historical evidence, however, important insights into the behavior of perpetrators can be found in a substantial body of psychological research on the sources of violent behavior. Together, the evidence available from both historical and experimental sources indicates that the task of recruiting individuals to participate in extreme acts of violence may be significantly easier than we might expect.

At some level, there are probably as many motives for taking part in mass killing as there are individual perpetrators of such acts. Nevertheless, I believe that two distinct social and psychological processes go a long way toward explaining the recruitment and motivation of most perpetrators of mass killing. The first process involves the concerted recruitment or self-selection of sadistic or fanatic individuals into the organizations responsible for mass killing. The second process relies on situational pressures, including authority and peer pressure, to induce otherwise ordinary human beings to participate in acts of extreme violence. Most episodes of mass killing seem to include substantial numbers of perpetrators motivated by each of these mechanisms. Although these two processes point to very different motivations for the individual perpetrators of mass killing, both help to explain how it may be possible to recruit a sufficient number of people to carry out mass killing even in the absence of broad public support for violence against victim groups.

Selection Effects

The most obvious explanation for participation in mass killing may also be the most disturbing. Some people seem to like it. All societies contain a certain number of individuals who, for whatever reasons, appear to derive satisfaction from violence and killing.[48] Some actively seek out violence. Others participate on a more opportunistic level. Psychological studies of perpetrators of violent crimes have consistently found that approximately 5 percent of these criminals enjoy participating in acts of violence and inflicting suffering on others.[49] Some violent perpetrators actually appear to develop something akin to an addictive need for violence.[50] Psychological studies of combat veterans have also found that a small percentage of soldiers, probably between 2 and 15 percent, seem to lack any reluctance to kill and are able to do so without remorse or regret.[51] Like some violent criminals, a small percentage of these soldiers may even take pleasure in the act of killing.[52]

In most societies, the police, penal intuitions, and the mental-health care system keep truly sadistic individuals in check. Their individual violent tendencies are uncoordinated and not channeled against a common group of victims. When a mass killing is being organized and implemented, however, such people naturally are drawn to the opportunity for violence without risk of punishment. Sometimes, leaders actively recruit them to serve as killers. In a surprising number of cases, perpetrators have been enlisted directly from prison populations to fill out the ranks of killing organizations.[53] These kinds of individuals represent a very small percentage of any society. But since mass killing seldom requires the direct participation of large numbers of perpetrators — often a fraction of 1 percent of the adult males in the societies in which they take place — these men may account for a significant percentage of the actual killers.[54] Among the formations involved in killing operations, these individuals also may be responsible for a disproportionate share of the actual killing, allowing more reluctant perpetrators to serve as sentries or fulfill other, less violent duties. An extreme example demonstrating the potential for this kind of division of labor comes from a massacre outside Riga, Latvia, in 1941, in which German troops and the Latvian forces under their direction murdered an estimated thirteen thousand Jews in a single day. Descriptions of the killing suggest that as few as a dozen men may have been responsible for the shooting, while 1,700 soldiers and policemen supported the operation, herding victims to the executioners and guarding the site.[55]

According to John Mueller, self-selection and intentional recruitment for brutality strongly influenced the composition of killing units during the wars in the former Yugoslavia.[56] Much of the violence against civilians appears to have been carried out by a relatively small number of gang members, thugs, and even prisoners specifically recruited to perform the bloody work of ethnic cleansing. "Arkan's Tigers," perhaps the most infamous of the Bosnian-Serb paramilitaries, numbered no more than five hundred to a thousand men and was composed largely of criminals and gang members.[57] As Tim Judah writes, it is difficult to avoid the conclusion that some "real psychopaths were rampaging across the countryside indulging in cruel and sadistic killings."[58] The main force of the Yugoslav national army, whose membership reflected a more representative slice of Serbian society, on the other hand, often avoided the task of executing civilians directly, preferring instead to secure the perimeter of targeted towns and leave the "dirty work" to the paramilitaries.[59]

The identity of the victims matters little to truly sadistic individuals. Before becoming perpetrators of genocide, many of these sadists appear to have occupied themselves with violence directed against other members of their own ethnic or social groups. These men seem driven more by an undifferentiated urge to hurt others than by a well-developed hatred of their specific victims. As Mueller concludes, "rather than reflecting deep, historic passions and hatreds, the violence [in the former Yugoslavia] seems to have been the result of a situation in which common, opportunistic, sadistic, and often distinctly nonideological marauders were recruited and permitted free reign by political authorities."[60]

It would be a mistake, on the other hand, to conclude that all self-selected perpetrators are merely psychopaths or criminals seeking to participate in mass killing for the sheer thrill of violence. Another group of perpetrators could be described more accurately as "true believers." These perpetrators are drawn to mass killing because they are deeply convinced that it is both necessary and just. True believers may derive no sense of pleasure from the violence itself. On the contrary, it may disgust them. Even Heinrich Himmler was reportedly shaken by the sight of a mass execution and proclaimed that he was "revolted by this bloody job."[61] Men such as these are motivated by a commitment to the ideological principles that justify the killing or by a profound hatred of their victims.

This kind of ideological selection may be a particularly powerful process in recruiting leaders and higher-level organizers of mass killing.

Michael Mann's systematic analysis of the biographies of more than fifteen hundred Germans involved in the Nazi genocide, for example, concludes that "those farther up the hierarchy were almost always more fervent Nazis than those lower down."[62] Mann finds that early supporters of the Nazi party—drawn from specific German subpopulations and geographic regions where the Nazi regime was especially popular—and individuals involved in prewar Nazi violence or fanaticism were overrepresented among high-ranking perpetrators. Given the inherently violent character of the ideologies that justify mass killing, however, in many cases, it is impossible to differentiate those individuals simply willing to kill for the cause from those attracted to the cause by the opportunity to kill. In research based on extensive interviews with three hundred former members of the Nazi SS, for example, John Steiner found that a self-selection process favoring both individuals attracted to military life in general and those who identified with Nazi ideology strongly influenced the membership of the SS.[63]

In practice, political and military leaders interested in mass killing undoubtedly prefer the true believer to the pure sadist. Sadists, thugs, and criminals are, almost by definition, difficult to control. They are seldom capable of the discipline necessary to function in professional military formations. Thus, during the early stages of the war with Croatia, an internal Yugoslav army memo reported that the army was concerned that the paramilitary units composed of such men were bad for "military morale" because their "primary motive was not fighting against the enemy but robbery of private property and inhuman treatment of Croatian civilians."[64] Likewise, in the effort to enforce discipline among the ranks, the Nazi SS legal office decreed that the unauthorized killing of Jews was to be treated as murder or manslaughter if "the motive is selfish, sadistic or sexual."[65]

True believers, however, are not always easy to find. As one disillusioned revolutionary described recruitment for the Cheka, Lenin's political police: "The party endeavored to head it with incorruptible men . . . sincere idealist[s], ruthless but chivalrous. . . . But the Party had few men of this stamp and many Chekas: these gradually came to select their personnel by virtue of their psychological inclinations. The only temperaments that devoted themselves willingly and tenaciously to this task of 'internal defense' were those characterized by suspicion, embitterment, harshness and sadism."[66]

This is undoubtedly one reason why the political and military organizations tasked with carrying out mass killing seem to expend so much effort attempting to produce their own true believers in the ranks. As Charles Sydnor documents, members of the notorious SS Death's Head

Division received daily political training that sought to instill hatred of Nazi racial enemies and "shape them into political soldiers of the Führer."[67] Each member of the division was required to spend one week each month on guard duty at Nazi concentration camps, a duty the division's commanding officer felt "would strengthen [each soldier's] belief that the prisoners were inferior but implacable enemies of the German nation against whom the SS had to wage an unending struggle."[68] So powerful was the indoctrination and peer pressure to which these soldiers were subjected that a substantial majority of them agreed to officially renounce their church affiliations in order to comply with the SS doctrine that portrayed the church as an enemy of National Socialism. Sydnor notes that many recruits agreed to take this step despite the fact that it "periodically resulted in serious and permanent breaches" with their own families.[69]

Situational Pressures

Although the selection effects described above appear to account for the behavior of many perpetrators of mass killing, they are inadequate to explain the behavior of many others. Most societies probably contain enough sadists and true believers to carry out mass killing, but in practice, such individuals are seldom the sole source of perpetrators. This is particularly apparent among units recruited through a general military draft or other processes that limit the potential for selectivity. Christopher Browning's study of one German police battalion involved in mass killing operations in Poland, for example, discounts selection effects as the major explanation for the behavior of the men in the unit. Browning acknowledges that there was a relatively high percentage of Nazi party members among the battalion's rank and file (about 25 percent), but with respect to most other factors, he argues, the unit's composition "did not represent special selection or even random selection but for all practical purposes negative selection for the task at hand."[70]

How, then, can we account for the actions of what Browning calls these "ordinary men"? Some of the most powerful evidence for understanding the behavior of these and other perpetrators of mass killing can be found in the results of a now famous series of experiments performed by the psychologist Stanley Milgram in the early 1960s.[71] Under the pretext of studying learning and memory, Milgram asked his subjects to administer an ever more severe series of electrical shocks to a complete stranger whenever that person was unable to remember specific items from a list of words. What the subjects did not know is that the shocks were not real and the "victim" was actually an actor cooperating with the experiment. Milgram was astonished to find that nearly two-thirds of his subjects were willing to deliver shocks until the victim was screaming for his life. Many subjects went on shocking the victim even after he had lapsed into what could only be interpreted as unconscious silence. Milgram also conducted a number of variations on this "baseline" experiment. In one particularly disturbing test, Milgram found that 30 percent of his subjects administered the highest level of shock — past a row of buttons labeled "Danger: Severe Shock" and ominously marked "XXX" — even when the experiment required them to hold the victim's hand forcibly on the electrode.

Milgram's experiments were initially met with incredulity by psychologists, but his extraordinary findings have proven remarkably robust. Milgram tested more than a thousand subjects in the numerous variations of his experiment. His results have been repeatedly replicated with subjects from a variety of different countries and socioeconomic and educational backgrounds. Similar experiments have elicited equally disturbing behavior from ordinary people.[72] Although Milgram's experiments focused specifically on obedience to authority, many social psychologists suggest that their wider significance is to emphasize the extraordinary power of situational factors in influencing human behavior more generally.[73] Authority is only one of many situational pressures capable of promoting extreme and violent behavior from ordinary individuals.

This tendency was powerfully demonstrated by another extraordinary experiment conducted by a team of psychologists led by Philip Zimbardo at Stanford University in 1971.[74] In an effort to study the psychological effects of imprisonment, Zimbardo created a simulated prison and randomly selected individuals from a pool of college students to play the roles of guards or prisoners. All of the subjects had scored within the normal range on a battery of personality tests, including tests designed to screen out "authoritarian personalities." By the second day of the experiment, however, some of the guards began to subject their prisoners to brutal, sadistic, and humiliating treatment. Although physical violence was prohibited, guards blasted prisoners with freezing carbon dioxide from a fire extinguisher, stripped them naked, forced them to do repeated pushups, exiled some to solitary confinement, and inflicted a variety of other mental tortures on the inmates. The guards' cruelty increased in severity until, after only six days, Zimbardo was forced to terminate the experiment prematurely out of concern for the well-being of the prisoners. Zimbardo concluded that the simulation had demonstrated "the relative ease with which sadistic behavior could be elicited from normal non-sadistic people. . . . [T]he pathology observed in this study cannot be attributed to any pre-existing personality differences of the subjects. Rather, their abnormal social and personal relations were a product of their transaction with an environment whose norms and contingencies supported the production of behavior which would be pathological in other settings, but were 'appropriate' in this prison."[75]

Unsurprisingly, evidence regarding perpetrators of mass killing in the real world is considerably more ambiguous than the findings produced in these controlled experimental settings. Perpetrators of mass killing in the real world face a much more complex and often conflicting array of pressures, rewards, and aversions than Milgram's and Zimbardo's subjects did. Perhaps most notably, perpetrators of mass killing must often take part in extremely gruesome tasks, sometimes becoming soaked in the blood of their victims. The realities of face-to-face killing undoubtedly reduce the willingness of most individuals to comply with orders to kill. Nevertheless, other situational aspects of mass killing in the real world that could not be replicated in the laboratory appear to bolster rather than undermine the propensity for participation in killing operations.[76]

While the subjects of both Milgram and Zimbardo's experiments were ordinary civilians who had received no special training prior to their participation, most perpetrators of mass killing are members of military, paramilitary, or police organizations. These organizations have developed powerful tools for producing violent behavior and ensuring obedience to authority.[77] Furthermore, unlike most perpetrators of mass killing, the subjects of Milgram and Zimbardo's experiments were not exposed to propaganda or other indoctrination designed to justify doing harm to their victims. On the contrary, the subjects were given no reason to believe anything but that their victims were completely innocent people no different from themselves. The subjects of Milgram's experiments had no prior contact with the scientists who ordered them to administer the shocks and no reason to accept the legitimacy of these orders beyond the inherent presumption of the experimenter's scientific license. Orders for mass killing, on the other hand, are likely to come from authorities known personally to the perpetrators and vested with significantly more legitimacy. Most importantly, however, neither experiment could faithfully reproduce the effects of peer pressure and group conformity on their subjects.[78] Evidence from historical cases of mass killing indicates that these factors may play a significant role in motivating the participation of many of the men who carry it out.

Browning states that peer pressures were central to compliance with orders to kill in the units he studied. Although individual soldiers were offered the option of not participating in the killings, Browning writes that

80 to 90 percent of the men proceeded to kill, though almost all of them — at least initially — were horrified and disgusted by what they were doing. To break ranks and step out, to adopt overtly nonconformist be-

havior, was simply beyond most of the men. It was easier for them to shoot. Why? First of all, by breaking ranks, nonshooters were leaving the "dirty work" to their comrades. Since the battalion had to shoot even if individuals did not, refusing to shoot constituted refusing one's share of an unpleasant collective obligation. It was in effect an asocial act vis-à-vis one's comrades. Those who did not shoot risked isolation, rejection, and ostracism—a very uncomfortable prospect within the framework of a tight-knit unit stationed abroad among a hostile population, so that the individual had nowhere else to turn for support and social contact.[79]

Despite the limitations of Milgram and Zimbardo's experiments, many scholars have found them useful for understanding the behavior of perpetrators in the real world. Indeed, Arthur Miller's review of Holocaust scholarship finds "a remarkable degree of consensus regarding the generalizability of the obedience experiments. Clearly they are viewed by many commentators from a diversity of disciplines and orientations as convincing and meaningful to an understanding of the Holocaust, and of other instances of what is often referred to as 'social evil.'"[80]

Perpetrators of the Holocaust: Willing Executioners, Ordinary Men, or Some of Each?

Not all scholars are convinced that the two processes described above provide a satisfactory account of the behavior of most perpetrators of mass killing. Focusing specifically on the Holocaust, a small number of critics have argued that it is impossible to explain the actions of most perpetrators without acknowledging that they were driven above all by a profound hatred of their victims and a fanatical adherence to an ideology that justified the killing.[81] In the words of Daniel Goldhagen, who is the foremost proponent of this position, the perpetrators of the Holocaust were "assenting mass executioners, men and women who, true to their own eliminationist anti-Semitic beliefs, faithful to their cultural anti-Semitic credo, considered the slaughter to be just. . . . [T]he perpetrators' own convictions moved them to kill." Moreover, Goldhagen argues, these committed perpetrators did not simply represent a small minority of true believers selected from the broader German society—they were "neither martial spirits nor Nazi supermen." On the contrary, Goldhagen claims that the "overall character of the [perpetrators'] actions can, indeed must be, generalized to *the German people in general*."[82] This ideological explanation of perpetrator behavior stands in stark contrast to the explanations focusing on the selection effects or situational pressures described above.

Goldhagen points to two main strands of evidence to support this argument. First, unlike the subjects of Milgram's experiments, many Holocaust perpetrators appear to have been convinced that the orders they followed were just. Most of Milgram's subjects seem to have recognized that the commands issued by the experimenter were morally wrong. As Milgram himself reported, "Many of the people studied in the experiment were in some sense against what they did to the learner, and many protested even while they obeyed. . . . Some were totally convinced of the wrongness of what they were doing but could not bring themselves to make an open break with authority."[83] They complied with orders because they felt the situation left them no other choice and because they believed they were not responsible, or at least would not be held responsible, for any harm that might result from their actions.

This description clearly fails to capture the attitudes and behavior of many Holocaust perpetrators as conveyed in contemporary accounts of killing operations and sometimes as affirmed in the perpetrators' own words. Most perpetrators of the Holocaust appear to have found their orders troubling and unpleasant, especially at first.[84] Yet many, perhaps even most, also seem to have believed the killing to be ultimately necessary and just. In private correspondence and in other situations that were not directly monitored by their superiors, rank-and-file perpetrators regularly expressed their beliefs in the necessity of exterminating the Jews and other victims.[85] The comments of one member of the SS involved in the killing of Russian Jews might be considered typical. In a letter to his family he wrote:

> We have to eat and drink well because of the nature of our work. . . . Otherwise we would crack up. . . . It's not very pleasant stuff . . . it is a weakness not to be able to stand the sight of dead people; the best way to overcome it is to do it more often. Then it becomes a habit. . . . [T]he more one thinks about the whole business the more one comes to the conclusion that it's the only thing we can do to safeguard unconditionally the security of our people and our future. I do not therefore want to think and write about it any further. . . . [E]verywhere we go we are looked upon with some degree of suspicion. That should not divert us from the knowledge that what we are doing is necessary.[86]

The second kind of evidence cited by Goldhagen and other proponents of ideological explanations is the fact that Holocaust perpetrators frequently appear to have exceeded their orders in anti-Jewish operations, obeyed commands to kill in the absence of direct supervision, or acted with unnecessary brutality toward their victims. Contemporary observers recorded numerous examples of perpetrators actively searching out Jews, faithfully carrying out orders even in the absence of direct supervision, and inventing gratuitous and appallingly grotesque cruelties to inflict upon their victims.[87] Contrary to the claims of many perpetrators following the war, there is virtually no evidence to suggest that the refusal to obey orders to kill would have resulted in severe penalties.[88] Indeed, as Browning's research found, officers in some units involved in killing operations offered their men the option of not participating, yet the vast majority proceeded to kill. Thus, Goldhagen concludes that "the initiative that the perpetrators routinely showed in their cruel and lethal actions towards the Jews, the zeal that characterized the Germans carrying out the retributive and exterminatory policy against European Jewry, cannot be accounted for by the conventional explanations."[89] This behavior, he asserts, can only be explained with reference to the perpetrators' personal convictions — their deep hatred of Jews and their acceptance of the Nazi ideology that necessitated and justified the extermination of every Jewish man, woman, and child.

Goldhagen's research provides ample historical evidence that many perpetrators of the Holocaust considered their savagery to be essentially just and that at least some perpetrators carried out their actions even in the absence of direct supervision or with excessive cruelty. Although few scholars would dispute this evidence, Goldhagen is correct to point out that these behaviors too often have been overlooked or minimized in previous attempts to understand the behavior of Holocaust perpetrators. Upon closer examination, however, these facts are not sufficient to establish what Goldhagen seeks to prove — that deeply held personal convictions were the primary motivation for participation in the Holocaust and that such convictions were shared by the great majority of Germans.

There are two main reasons to question Goldhagen's conclusions. First, most rank-and-file perpetrators of the Holocaust — as opposed to the high military and political leaders who directed them — appear to have had a surprisingly shallow belief in the Nazi ideology that justified such brutality. Second, acts of gratuitous brutality and compliance with orders in the absence of direct supervision are not incompatible with the selection effects and situational pressures described above, as Goldhagen claims they are.

Shallow Beliefs

Three main lines of evidence cast doubt on the independent role that personal convictions played in inspiring the participation of most Holocaust perpetrators, suggesting instead that the beliefs that motivated many perpetrators of the Holocaust were relatively shallow. First, as Browning's research reveals, many rank-and-file perpetrators appear to have lacked a deep understanding of the Nazi racial ideology that motivated the killings.[90] One contemporary witness of another German police battalion recalled that political conversations or expressions of virulent anti-Semitism were surprisingly rare among the men.[91] Jürgen Matthäus's study of some of these same police units concludes that while pervasive anti-Semitism probably facilitated participation in mass killing operations, "there is little proof . . . [that these men] were driven solely or even to a significant extent by what Daniel Goldhagen calls 'Nazi common sense'. . . . [T]he impulse for murder seems to have come from a variety of factors more closely linked to specific surrounding circumstances than to an anti-Semitic grand design."[92]

For the most part, the rank-and-file German soldiers involved in the mass killings seemed to understand little more than that Jews were inferior beings somehow responsible for much of the world's problems and that they had to be exterminated for the good of Germany. A more thorough comprehension of the complex, "scientific" racial ideology of Nazi theoreticians was simply not necessary for the individual soldiers who helped carry out the final solution. Although many perpetrators of the Holocaust believed their actions to be just and necessary, most did not seem sufficiently enthusiastic about the killing that, were they given the opportunity, they would have ordered it themselves. They were willing, sometimes even eager, to go along with murder, but it probably would not have been their idea.

The second observation that points to the shallowness of Holocaust perpetrators' convictions is the powerful role that Nazi propaganda and indoctrination appears to have played in the shaping of these convictions. Although many Holocaust perpetrators believed their actions were justified, their convictions often seem to have stemmed not from deeply held prior beliefs but from recently inculcated notions provided to them through propaganda that portrayed their victims as a serious threat and was specifically intended to promote acts of violence against them. To the extent that perpetrators' convictions were influenced by indoctrination designed to promote violence, however, these convictions can hardly be seen as a primary cause of participation in the Holocaust. On the contrary, these attitudes were the intended *result* of campaigns conceived by leaders who had already decided for their own reasons that genocide was both necessary and just.

Unlike the perpetrators of the Holocaust, subjects in the Milgram experiment were not exposed to any form of indoctrination or propaganda designed to justify violence against their victims. The lack of any effort to provide subjects with a justification for why their victims deserved to be hurt may at least partially explain why Milgram's subjects appear to have struggled with the morality of their actions much more than many Holocaust perpetrators did. Milgram himself speculated that "in all likelihood, our subjects would have experienced greater ease in shocking the victim had he been convincingly portrayed as a brutal criminal or pervert."[93] In fact, Milgram's speculation would be tested directly several years later when a team of psychologists led by Albert Bandura extended Milgram's basic research design to investigate the effects of dehumanizing the experiment's "victim" in the eyes of the subject. Bandura found that even a brief dehumanizing characterization of the unseen learner/victims prompted his subjects to deliver substantially higher levels of shocks.[94]

How much more powerful, then, years of incessant Nazi propaganda must have been in facilitating violence against Jews.[95] I have already described the powerful impact indoctrination had on highly specialized and intensely politicized units such as the SS Death's Head Division. Evaluating the effects of propaganda outside such units is considerably more difficult. Few scholars claim that indoctrination alone could have turned German soldiers into fanatic Nazis, but few suggest that it had no effect at all. For example, Omer Bartov's study of German Wehrmacht units, many of which were involved directly or indirectly in mass killing operations, finds that soldiers' beliefs in the necessity of the war and of its genocidal prosecution were shaped significantly by Nazi propaganda—both before and after the men entered the army. According to Bartov, a careful reading of soldiers' letters home reveals the "profound impact of indoctrination and propaganda on the soldiers' psyche."[96] Indeed, there is "remarkable similarity between their terminology, modes of expression, and arguments and those which characterize the Wehrmacht's propaganda."[97] He concludes that indoctrination and propaganda influenced soldiers in two related ways:

> First, it taught the troops totally to trust Hitler's political and military wisdom, and never to doubt either the morality of his orders or the outcome of his prophecies. . . . Second, it provided the soldiers with an image of the enemy which so profoundly distorted their perception that once confronted with reality they invariably experienced it as what they had come to expect. Indoctrination thus served the double purpose of strongly motivating the troops and greatly brutalizing them, for it legitimized both one's own sacrifices and the atrocities committed against the enemy. . . . This does not mean that every individual German soldier was a committed National Socialist; rather, it is to say that the vast majority of troops internalized the distorted Nazi presentation of reality.[98]

Browning, on the other hand, questions the degree to which the members of the police battalion he studied grasped the more esoteric aspects of Nazi propaganda. He acknowledges, however, that propaganda likely facilitated the killing by inspiring an abstract hatred of Jews and by incorporating Jews into the perpetrators' picture of the enemy. He writes: "If it is doubtful that most of the policemen [involved in the mass killing of Jews] understood or embraced the theoretical aspects of Nazi ideology as contained in SS indoctrination pamphlets, it is also doubtful that they were immune to . . . the incessant proclamation of German superiority and incitement of contempt and hatred for the Jewish enemy."[99]

It is conceivable, however, that Nazi propaganda would have fallen on deaf ears had it not been for the preexisting prejudices and negative stereotypes against Jews that were prevalent in German society even before the Nazis took power. In other words, if perpetrators' preexisting beliefs were not a cause of the Holocaust, perhaps they were a necessary precondition. Even scholars who have rejected German anti-Semitism as the sole or primary cause of the Holocaust have generally accepted this proposition.[100]

Preexisting prejudices and stereotypes do contribute to the explanation of many important patterns and processes of the Holocaust, including the brutal behavior of the relatively small group of committed Nazi fanatics and the passivity of most other Germans. A third kind of evidence, however, suggests that these attitudes may not have been even necessary preconditions for most rank-and-file perpetrators of the Holocaust. Perpetrators of the Holocaust killed not only Jews, against whom they clearly harbored preexisting prejudices, but also a wide array of defenseless civilians from nearly every country occupied by Germany during the war.[101] Jews were clearly the most important targets of Nazi violence. They were singled out for more complete, systematic annihilation and for more inhumane treatment than any other group. Yet German soldiers, police, and other functionaries proved willing to murder large numbers of non-Jewish civilians from countries including (but not limited to) Poland, the Soviet Union, Yugoslavia, Belgium, France, Greece, and Italy and from groups such as the Gypsies and the mentally and chronically ill within Germany itself. It could be argued that most Germans also possessed negative attitudes regarding many of these groups (especially the Poles and Russians), but other victims were drawn from nationalities or ethnic groups that were never singled out by Nazi ideology and against which Germans seem to have had no history of preexisting prejudice.

Mark Mazower, for example, describes an incident in which a German army unit received the order to assault the Greek village of Komeno in August 1943 in reprisal for an alleged partisan attack.[102] The soldiers surprised the village at dawn while most people were still asleep. They proceeded to massacre over half the population of the village — 317 men, women, and children, all of them civilians. Not only is there no evidence that these soldiers harbored preexisting prejudices against Greeks per se, many appear to have participated in the killing even though they felt that the action was immoral or even criminal. One soldier recalled that "almost none [of the men] agreed with the action."[103] Another told his commanding officer that this was "the last time I take part in something like that. This was an obscenity which had nothing to do with fighting a war."[104] A third soldier recalled that after the action, some men had considered deserting, but ultimately "we fell back on the conclusion . . . that we had just obeyed orders."[105]

A similar massacre took place in June 1944 during the notorious reprisal raid against the French village of Oradour-sur-Glane. There, SS troops brutally murdered 642 people, including 190 children.[106] Again, there is little reason to suspect that this behavior reflected preexisting prejudices against French people as such. Even Italy, Germany's close ally during the war, was not immune from Nazi reprisals. Indeed, as Michael Geyer has documented, Germany launched a "brutal war of annihilation [against much of occupied Italy], striking the civil population — men, women and children — in a frenzy of destruction" following Italy's surrender in 1943.[107] Thousands of Italian civilians and POWs were killed in cold blood by German soldiers during the course of this campaign.[108]

It should be emphasized that, unlike the Jews, these victims were not killed as part of a campaign of systematic extermination of an entire group of people. For the individual soldier tasked with carrying out the murders, however, the physical experience of killing defenseless men, women, and children must have been very similar. These kinds of operations against non-Jewish civilian populations were not confined to a few isolated incidents. Nor should they be attributed to the spontaneous actions of berserk soldiers driven to aggression by the psychological stresses of war. German forces perpetrated atrocities of this nature throughout occupied Europe.[109] The violence reflected an explicit German policy designed to deter partisan activity by carrying out reprisals against civilian populations.

According to some accounts, German perpetrators actually seem to have had less psychological difficulty in carrying out reprisals against suspected partisans than they did in exterminating Jews.[110] One Jewish survivor, who had extensive personal contacts with perpetrators while serving under a disguised identity as an interpreter for German forces in the Soviet Union, later recalled: "I think that the whole business of anti-Jewish moves, the business of Jewish extermination, they considered unclean. The operations against the partisans were not in the same category. For them a confrontation with the partisans was a battle, a military move. But a move against the Jews was something they might have experienced as 'dirty.'"[111]

These attitudes persisted despite the fact that, particularly on the eastern front, local Jewish populations were frequently singled out in partisan reprisals. Many perpetrators appear to have rationalized this contradiction by reasoning that Jews were likely to be communists and that communists, in turn, were likely to support the partisans.[112] Those who did not believe in an innate Jewish-communist connection simply assumed that, given Germany's official policies of anti-Semitism, Jews would have little choice but to join the partisans whether they were communists or not.[113]

Thus, if preexisting prejudices were a precondition for mass killing in Germany or elsewhere, Nazi atrocities against non-Jewish populations would seem to suggest that such attitudes need not be unusually severe to stimulate participation in violent acts. Prejudices and stereotypes of the kind that existed in Germany before the Nazi period unfortunately characterize relations between at least some groups in many, if not most societies. As noted in chapter 1, most historians agree that Jews in a number of other European countries suffered greater prejudice and discrimination than did Jews in Germany before the Nazi seizure of power. Likewise, while many Germans probably did harbor negative attitudes about their Polish and Russian victims, there is little evidence that these attitudes were more extreme than those between countless other historical antagonists who did not engage in mass killing. These observations suggest that hatred or ideological convictions alone are neither universally necessary nor sufficient to explain the behavior of most perpetrators.

Gratuitous Brutality and Unsupervised Compliance

If most Holocaust perpetrators were neither deeply committed Nazis nor fanatical anti-Semites, how can we account for the numerous acts of gratuitous brutality that Holocaust perpetrators visited upon their victims? How can we explain the fact that most perpetrators complied with orders to kill even in the absence of direct supervision or the threat of severe punishment? These behaviors would seem to represent a challenge to the explanations of perpetrator motivation offered in this chapter. Upon closer examination, however, such actions are entirely compatible with the selection effects and situational pressures described above.

Given the central importance assigned to the brutality of German killers in ideological explanations of Holocaust perpetrators, it is noteworthy that Goldhagen and others have offered little evidence to indicate that this behavior represented the actions of more than a minority of the participants. Goldhagen claims that German cruelty "was nearly universal" but he never attempts to quantify this assertion for any of the German units he studied.[114] Reliable evidence regarding the prevalence of brutality among Holocaust perpetrators is scarce, but there are significant indications that it was not nearly as common as Goldhagen suggests.[115] Many Auschwitz survivors have reported that there were relatively few pure sadists—perhaps 5 or 10 percent—among SS guards.[116] Indeed, one survivor went so far as to say that "nothing would be more mistaken than to see the SS as a sadistic horde driven to abuse and torture thousands of human beings by instinct, passion or some thirst for pleasure. . . . Those who acted in this way were a small minority."[117]

Other accounts of the very same police units that Goldhagen studied indicate that zealous killers may have been relatively few. Browning's research on several different German police units, for example, found only a minority (less than one third) of "enthusiastic killers" among the perpetrators.[118] Most killers fell into a middle group "who performed as shooters and ghetto clearers when assigned but who did not seek opportunities to kill (and in some cases refrained from killing, contrary to standing orders, when no one was monitoring their actions)."[119] Another group, perhaps somewhere between 20 and 30 percent of the men, consistently refused or evaded orders to kill.

Therefore, even if acts of gratuitous brutality reflected the deep anti-Semitism or fervent Nazi beliefs of those who committed them, the fact that such men appear to have been relatively few in number provides no evidence regarding the motivation of the majority of perpetrators or the attitudes of the broader public from which they were drawn. This level of brutality could simply be the result of a comparatively small group of sadists and true believers in the ranks. Such behavior might be expected from a minority of men even in units whose membership was not strongly influenced by selection for violence or fanaticism.

Another explanation for the gratuitous brutality exhibited by these perpetrators, however, suggests that, for at least some individuals, excessive cruelty toward victims may not reflect deep hatreds or ideological fanaticism at all. Rather, as evidence from the psychological research described above suggests, under the "right" circumstances gratuitous brutality and unsupervised compliance with violent orders is to be expected from a certain percentage of normal men. Indeed, this conclusion was the central finding of Zimbardo's prison experiment. Zimbardo's guards understood that their victims were simply college students like themselves and that, but for a toss of a coin, their roles might have been reversed. Neither direct supervision nor the threat of punishment can explain why Zimbardo's guards chose to torture their victims, since Zimbardo never gave the guards instructions to do so in the first place.[120] Goldhagen dismisses Stanley Milgram's findings, claiming that they cannot account for the gratuitous brutality and unsupervised compliance of many Holocaust perpetrators, but he fails even to address Zimbardo's research. Yet, according to Browning, the spectrum of behaviors exhibited by the perpetrators both he and Goldhagen studied bear "an uncanny resemblance" to the behavior of the guards in Zimbardo's prison experiment.[121]

The fact that excessive cruelty by German troops during the Second World War was not limited to actions against Jews also strongly suggests that gratuitous brutality can occur in the absence of ideological convictions or passionate hatreds. Extreme brutality appears to have been characteristic of many German actions against non-Jewish civilian populations. Mazower, for example, reports that "wanton cruelty—such as the deliberate mutilation of bodies" occurred during the massacre of Greek civilians at Komeno.[122] Indeed, one participant in the Komeno massacre recalled having realized for the first time after the episode that there were "sadists" in his unit.[123] Torture and brutality were also common in anti-partisan actions in France and Italy.[124] Even ethnic Germans were not always spared this kind of treatment. Rather, as Nikolaus Wachsmann found in his study of the Nazis' policy of "annihilation through labor" of state prisoners and so-called asocials in the Mauthausen concentration camp, even these predominantly ethnic German inmates were subjected to "unimaginable brutality" and "senseless labor" before they were murdered.[125]

This nonideological cruelty often seems to emerge from a gradual process of brutalization that transforms a certain percentage of seemingly normal individuals into gratuitously violent killers. As Roy Baumeister has documented, evidence from both psychological and historical research on sadistic behavior indicates that most sadistic individuals do not appear to have started out that way.[126] On the contrary, most sadists were initially reluctant killers, repelled by violence and blood. Only gradually did they come to take pleasure in hurting others. Engaging in violence changed them, and the more they did it the easier it became.

Participating in violence may have a transformative effect not only on the tendency to brutality but also on the perpetrators' beliefs about their victims. Milgram found evidence of this disturbing process while debriefing subjects of his experiment. He reported that "such comments as, 'he was so stupid and stubborn he deserved to get shocked' were common." Since the behavior of virtually all of Milgram's subjects indicated that they did not *want* to shock their victims, however, these statements were clearly post-hoc justifications. Thus, Milgram was drawn to conclude that "once having acted against the victim, these subjects found it necessary to view him as an unworthy individual, whose punishment was made inevitable by his own deficiencies of intellect and character."[127] The subjects of Milgram's experiments did not hurt their victims because they hated them; they hated their victims because they had hurt them.

This gradual transformation was readily apparent in the units studied by Goldhagen and Browning.[128] The majority were initially repelled by what they were ordered to do. Yet most became inured to the blood and violence, and some even came to relish it. As Browning concludes, "even if the 'ordinary Germans' who were conscripted as reserve policemen did not go to the east exuding ideological commitment to National Socialism and eager for the opportunity to kill Jews, when the deportations and killings began, most did as they were told and many were changed by the actions they undertook."[129]

Other Perpetrators

Although the scholarly debate regarding the role that hatred and ideological convictions play in motivating the perpetrators of mass killing has focused on the Holocaust, Goldhagen also speculates that these motivations may be common to most perpetrators of mass killing.[130] Few detailed accounts of the behavior of perpetrators of other cases of mass killing exist. Anecdotal evidence, however, strongly suggests that many of the same conclusions that apply to perpetrators of the Holocaust pertain to perpetrators of other cases of mass killing. Most such perpetrators need not be true believers to be efficient killers.

For example, in his research on the workers at the Khmer Rouge prison known as S-21, where thousands of Cambodians were brutally tortured and killed, David Chandler concludes that the situational pressures cited by Milgram and Zimbardo were largely responsible for motivating the perpetrators there.[131] Most workers at S-21 did not fit the profile of deeply committed communist ideologues. Indeed, most of them had joined the Khmer Rouge less than two years before they began their work at S-21. As Chandler observes, for the most part "their exposure to revolutionary discipline, to say nothing of Marxist-Leninist ideas, had been hortatory, brief and haphazard."[132] Yet these individuals quickly became capable torturers, inflicting indescribable and purely gratuitous cruelties on their victims.

Deep political convictions seem an especially poor explanation for the behavior of the young and largely illiterate soldiers who carried out most of the Khmer Rouge mass killings in the countryside. It is highly unlikely that these perpetrators could have grasped the abstruse political ideology that motivated Pol Pot and his associates. As one observer of the brutal evacuation of Phnom Penh by the Khmer Rouge noted: "The common soldier did not appear to be very concerned about politics, Cambodia's future or other ideological questions. I had the impression that a lot of them didn't know which group they belonged to. I felt that their fighting spirit and ability came more from rough discipline rather than from convictions. . . . [T]hey often seemed like animals being led into the field by the master."[133]

Preexisting prejudices and negative stereotypes cannot be ruled out as a motive for the murder of some Khmer Rouge victims, especially the Vietnamese, but most of those who lost their lives were drawn from the same class and ethnic or social group as their executioners.[134] Preexisting hatreds could hardly have played a central role in the Khmer Rouge murder of the so-called "new people," a derogatory term applied to a wide range of individuals including businessmen, city dwellers, foreigners, and virtually anyone with an education, since this group identity appears to have been manufactured out of whole cloth by Khmer Rouge ideologists.[135] As in the Holocaust, propaganda and indoctrination probably played an important role in facilitating the murder of these innocent victims. Thus, Chandler suggests that the young killers simply had "been trained to hate 'enemies of the Organization'—the Americans, who bombed the country, the traitors allied to the Americans, and the city dwellers who had refused to join the revolution."[136]

Situational factors and shallow beliefs also appear to have been sufficient motivation for many of the men who carried out the 1994 genocide in Rwanda. As Gérard Prunier argues: "If the notion of guilt presupposes a clear understanding of what one is doing at the time of the crime, then there were at that time . . . a lot of 'innocent murderers.'" For many of the perpetrators, he writes, "the political aims pursued by the masters of this dark carnival were quite beyond their scope."[137] To encourage participation in the killing, the organizers of the genocide orchestrated a campaign of propaganda and misinformation.[138] According to Helen M. Hintjens:

> State propaganda was designed to raise the hackles of the Bahutu [Hutu] population, and, during the early stages of the genocide there is little evidence of overt hostility from Bahutu towards their Batutsi [Tutsi] neighbors and relatives. Such hatred and fear was sometimes latent, and could be manipulated, but more commonly it was deliberately created in the context of well-prepared massacres . . . ethnic conflict was quite deliberately engineered in the run-up to the genocide.[139]

Such a campaign hardly would have been necessary if most Hutu killers were already firmly convinced of the righteousness of the genocide. This conclusion is reinforced by the numerous reports documenting that Hutu extremists often had to resort to force, including executions, in order to compel civilians to kill.[140] Indeed, a comprehensive inquiry carried out by the human rights group African Rights concludes that "most Hutu who complied [with orders to kill] were reluctant accomplices" and that "many [Tutsi] survivors readily admitted that [many Hutu] . . . were reluctant murderers."[141] The architects of the genocide apparently did not trust even Rwanda's regular army to play its part in the slaughter, sometimes deploying extremist militias behind army units to ensure the army's compliance during the genocide.[142]

Combat Motivation

Other compelling evidence for the influence of situational factors comes not from cases of mass killing, but from the behavior of soldiers in combat. If the willingness of human beings to kill others in the service of shallow ideas and beliefs seems inconceivable, one need only reflect upon the willingness of soldiers throughout history to offer up their own lives in pursuit of such goals.[143] Most scholars of combat motivation have concluded that soldiers are driven more powerfully by small-group dynamics — primarily the desires to protect fellow soldiers, conform to group expectations, and avoid the appearance of cowardliness — than by an ideological commitment to the goals of the war.[144] Some scholars have found a more central role for factors such as ideology, patriotism, and nationalism, but even these authors tend to stress that the origin of such attitudes often lies in systematic state propaganda, not deep, preexisting convictions.[145] Thus, as Gwynne Dyer concludes in his study of men in combat, although many soldiers "do feel the need for some patriotic or ideological justification for what they do . . . which nation, which ideology, does not matter: men will fight as well and die as bravely for the Khmer Rouge as for 'God, King, and Country.' Soldiers are the instruments of politicians and priests, ideologues and strategists, who may have high moral purposes in mind, but the men down in the trenches fight for more basic motives."[146]

History provides numerous examples of soldiers' willingness to risk their lives for political or military goals they barely comprehend, sometimes on distant battlefields in countries that, before the war began, they might not have been able to identify on a map. The behavior of soldiers during the infamous battles on the western front during the First World War is particularly illuminating in this regard. At bloody battles such as Verdun and the Somme, hundreds of thousands of French and British soldiers willingly walked into no-man's land and a wall of German machine gun and artillery fire. Members of the British cavalry adopted the motto "We'll do it; what is it?"[147]

There can be little doubt that these men believed in the justness of the allied cause, but after a few months at the front, the average infantryman understood that a frontal attack on German lines could not succeed and that he probably would be cut down within minutes of leaving his trench. Soldiers who may still have harbored hopes for success at the Somme were quickly disabused. More than twenty thousand British soldiers were killed on the first day of battle, most in the first hour of the attack.[148]

One British brigadier general described the participation of his troops in one such advance with a perverted sense of approval:

> They advanced in line after line, dressed as if on parade, and not a man shirked going through the extremely heavy barrage, or facing the machine gun and rifle fire that finally wiped them out. . . . [I] saw the lines which advanced in such admirable order melting away under the fire. Yet not a man wavered, broke the ranks, or attempted to come back. . . . [I] have never seen, indeed could never have imagined, such a magnificent display of gallantry, discipline and determination.[149]

A British sergeant, on the other hand, described a similar attack in quite different terms:

> That was a stupid action, because we had to make a frontal attack on bristling German guns and there was no shelter at all. . . . We knew it was pointless, even before we went over—crossing open ground like that. But you had to go. You were between the devil and the deep blue sea. If you go forward, you'll likely be shot. If you go back, you'll be court-marshaled and shot. . . . What can you do? Even before we went over, we knew this was death. . . . It was ridiculous. There was no need for it. It was just absolute slaughter.[150]

These surreal scenes led the military historian John Keegan to comment that "there is something Treblinka-like about almost all accounts of [the Somme], about those long docile lines of young men, shoddily uniformed, plodding across a featureless landscape to their own extermination."[151]

Perhaps this extraordinary level of compliance among the British soldiers would be easier to understand if these men were defending themselves or their homes. Yet these soldiers knew that they were relatively safe in their trenches. Britain itself never faced a serious threat of invasion during the First World War. In addition to more than 740,000 British soldiers killed in the First World War, tens of thousands of men each from Canada, Australia, India, and the United States, none of whom would have faced any immediate physical danger from the war raging thousands of miles away, also proved willing to die in a conflict that began over the assassination of a monarch in a tiny province of Austria-Hungary. If individuals are willing to give up their own lives under these circumstances, it is perhaps less remarkable to discover that they are also capable of killing others.

Moral Responsibility for Mass Killing

Some readers will undoubtedly find the conclusion that many perpetrators of mass killing manage to carry out their bloody work in the absence of deep personal convictions or hatreds of their victims a difficult one to accept. This reluctance may reflect a general human tendency to discount the effect of situational pressures in influencing the behavior of others. Indeed, so common is the failure to appreciate the power of these variables that social psychologists refer to this mistake as the "fundamental attribution error."[152] However uneasy it makes us feel, the "just following orders" defense so often advanced by perpetrators of mass killing may also be an accurate description of the behavior of many of these cold-blooded killers — although it is hardly an excuse for murder.

In light of these observations, it may be tempting to conclude that only a few powerful leaders deserve condemnation for mass killing and that participants in this violence, or bystanders in the societies in which it occurs, are somehow morally excused for their actions. This conclusion must be rejected. Mass killing would not be possible without the active participation of at least a small group of people in acts of brutal violence and, in most cases, without widespread public passivity or indifference to the killing. This behavior cannot be excused simply because it is commonplace.[153] Although compliance with authority and public passivity may be the rule, history also provides notable examples of individuals who have refused to carry out immoral orders or to stand by while killing took place — often at great personal risk. Human beings may be influenced by powerful situational pressures, but each of us remains individually responsible for his or her own actions.

Our reaction to the foregoing discussion, therefore, must not be to diminish our moral condemnation of those who participate in mass killing, or those who simply decline to resist it, on the grounds that they were following orders or that others likely would have acted same way in the same situation. Rather, we should take heed of the fact that the capacity for violence — or indifference to violence directed at others — exists in nearly all human beings and societies. This capacity can be a powerful and therefore tempting tool for those in a position to call upon it.

The Power of the Few

The evidence presented in the chapter indicates that mass killing does not require the active support of most people in the societies in which it takes place. The individuals charged with carrying out such violence may do so even in the absence of a deeply held prior commitment to its goals or a profound hatred of their victims. These findings have powerful implications for our understanding of mass killing. In particular, they highlight the decisive role that small groups or even individual leaders can play in the causal process of these episodes of violence. Although the goals and motives of political and military leaders sometimes closely reflect the societies they govern, often they do not. While democratic processes tend to select leaders who represent the broad interests of their societies, most regimes that have launched campaigns of mass killing did not attain power through democratic means.

Scholars have frequently remarked on the powerful influence that small groups or individual leaders have wielded over many of history's most infamous examples of genocide and mass killing.[154] Of course, these groups or individuals did not carry out mass killing on their own. Yet, in many cases, historians have argued convincingly that these bloody episodes would never have occurred without the instigation of specific leaders. The unique ideas, beliefs, strategies, and even personalities of these leaders, in other words, often constitute necessary conditions for mass killing. In this chapter and the preceding, I have tried to demonstrate that the remaining permissive conditions necessary for mass killing have been relatively common across states, cultures, and time. Even when leaders with an interest in violence have found such conditions absent, it has been remarkably easy to create them.

Most historians of the Holocaust, for example, seem to concur with Milton Himmelfarb's simple yet compelling thesis — "no Hitler, no Holocaust."[155] As Michael Marrus's review of Holocaust scholarship concludes:

> Hitler was the principal driving force of anti-Semitism in the Nazi movement from the earliest period. . . . Anti-Semitism was central because Hitler determined that it should be so. . . . Neither the existence of anti-Jewish traditions in Germany, the commitments of Nazi party leaders, nor the beliefs of the extensive Nazi following in the German population required the murder of the Jews. Put otherwise, anti-Semitism in Germany may have been a necessary condition for the Holocaust, but it was not a sufficient one. In the end it was Hitler, and his own determination to realize his anti-Semitic fantasies, that made the difference.[156]

Similarly, historians generally accept that the Great Terror in the Soviet Union would not have occurred without the personal influence of Stalin himself. As Robert Conquest concludes: "The nature of the whole Purge depends in the last analysis on the personal and political drives of Stalin. . . . The revolution of the Purges still remains, however we judge it, above all Stalin's personal achievement."[157] Nor have scholars found it easy to imagine China's bloody Cultural Revolution without the personal influence of Mao Zedong. Thus, Harry Harding writes: "it is no exaggeration . . . to conclude that the principal responsibility for the Cultural Revolution — a movement that affected tens of millions of Chinese — rests with one man. Without a Mao, there could not have been a Cultural Revolution."[158]

In the case of Rwanda, scholars generally agree that the impetus for the killing originated with a small group of fanatical Hutu leaders. Gérard Prunier, for example, holds that the organizers of the genocide were "on the lunatic fringes of radical Hutu extremism," part of "a small tight group, belonging to the regime's political, military and economic Élite who had decided through a mixture of ideological and material motivation radically to resist political change which they perceived as threatening."[159] By one estimate, no more than two dozen senior officials were responsible for orchestrating the genocide.[160]

Not only have leaders of such brutal regimes often conceived of and carried out their murderous policies without the active support of the majority of their societies, many have viewed the very idea that their policies ought to be responsive to the will of the people with utter contempt. Lenin, after all, was not only the father of Russia's bloody Red Terror but also the progenitor of the concept of the "vanguard of the proletariat." Writing in 1917, Lenin declared: "In times of revolution it is not enough to ascertain the 'will of the majority.' No — one must *be stronger* at the decisive moment, in the decisive place, and *win*. Beginning with the medieval 'peasant war' in Germany . . . until 1905, we see countless instances of how the better organized, more conscious, better armed minority imposed its will on the majority and conquered it."[161]

Even Hitler was willing to acknowledge that the Nazi party did not rely on popular support to accomplish its rise to power. On the contrary, the centerpiece of Hitler's political philosophy was the "Führer Principle," a doctrine that mandated unquestioning obedience to a single leader.[162] Throughout his political career, Hitler's explicit strategy had been to recruit the most radical elements in society and use them to lead public opinion and the nation down the path he had chosen. Thus, looking back on his rise to power in 1944, he reminded his generals: "I set up my fighting manifesto and tailored it deliberately to attract only the toughest and most determined minority of the German people at first. . . . [T]hen the moment will come where there'll be this minority on the one side and the majority in the other — but this minority will be the one that makes history, because the majority will always follow where there's a tough minority to lead the way."[163]

Enver Pasha, the leader of the "Young Turk" regime responsible for the Armenian genocide, suggested not only that he understood the powerful role that small groups had played in the rise of his regime but that his fear of the disproportionate power of such groups may actually have been one reason behind his decision to initiate the genocide. As he told the American ambassador Henry Morganthau: "You must remember that when we [the Young Turks] started this revolution in Turkey there were only two hundred of us. . . . It is our experience with revolutions which makes us fear the Armenians. If two hundred Turks could overturn the government, than a few hundred bright, educated Armenians could do the same thing. We have therefore deliberately adopted the plan of scattering them so that they can do us no harm."[164]

The power that small groups or individuals can wield over episodes of mass killing is perhaps no better illustrated than by the frequency with which such episodes have come to a halt when murderous regimes have been overthrown or individual leaders have died. Mass killings carried out by Nazi Germany, Japan, Cambodia, and Rwanda ceased practically overnight when the regimes that initiated them were overthrown by military force. Of course, bringing an end to mass killing by these particular regimes required war and extended military occupation by outside military forces. More revealing is the abrupt cessation of decades of mass killing in the Soviet Union and China following the deaths of Stalin and Mao. These two leaders were replaced not by foreign invasions but rather by high-ranking members of their own political parties. Nikita Khrushchev and Deng Xiaoping were hardly role models for democratic leadership. Each had played a supporting role in at least some of the violent episodes initiated by their predecessors. Neither man was afraid to use harsh methods to crush internal dissent. Nevertheless, their explicit criticisms of Stalin and Mao's brutal excesses, their reversals of many of their predecessors' radical policies, and the much less violent character of their own rule all strongly suggest that if these leaders had governed in the place of Stalin and Mao, the innocent people of the Soviet Union and China would have experienced far less suffering. The fact that no leader of the Soviet Union or China since the deaths of Stalin and Mao has sponsored violent campaigns on anything like the scale of these tyrants suggests that both men failed to represent the goals and interests of their respective regimes, let alone those of the broader societies over which they governed.

The powerful influence of individuals and small groups in mass killing not only diminishes the utility of broad social factors in predicting when and where this violence will occur, it also magnifies the role of idiosyncratic factors in the causal path leading to mass killing. The road to power of some of history's most brutal regimes was paved not by immutable historical processes or macro-level social structures but by serendipity, contingency, and historical fluke. As Henry Ashby Turner documents, the rise of the Nazi party in Germany was by no means preordained.[165] It would not have been possible without a great deal of luck and the repeated bungling of Weimar leaders. Just days before Hitler assumed the chancellorship, few of his contemporaries expected his bid for power to succeed. Even after it did, many doubted his ability to hold on to power for long. It is easy to imagine how events might have taken a radically different turn. If they had, Turner argues, a major war might still have occurred, but the Holocaust and many of the more terrible aspects of the Second World War almost certainly would have been avoided.[166] Impersonal historical forces may provide the conditions that make such events possible, but they do not make them inevitable or even likely.

These conclusions suggest that the search for the causes of mass killing should begin with the capabilities, interests, ideas, and strategies of groups and individuals in positions of political and military power and not with factors that predispose societies to produce such leaders. Powerful groups may achieve their influential positions because the public staunchly supports them, because the public is indifferent, or because other centers of political and military power in their societies are too weak or too inept to effectively oppose them. Whatever their path to power, groups that have managed to attain it have likely also achieved the prerequisite capabilities for mass killing.

Focusing on the goals and interests of groups already in or near positions of power, on the other hand, does not mean that it is impossible to anticipate mass killing. Groups with violent agendas often remain in or near power for extended periods before launching mass killing. Hitler governed Germany for more than eight years before he launched the Holocaust. His violent anti-Semitism was well known for years before he achieved power. Likewise, the Khmer Rouge began implementing their violent policies of "rural reform" in remote areas of Cambodia before they seized power over the entire country in 1975. Even Pol Pot's policy of emptying cities had been presaged in 1973 when the Khmer Rouge began to systematically burn rural villages in the effort to force peasants into new agricultural collectives.[167]

In Rwanda, the radical group of Hutu leaders responsible for the 1994 genocide was not in full control of the government and military until after the killing began. Nevertheless, Hutu extremists had occupied many high-ranking positions within the regime. Their radical political agenda was widely understood within Rwanda prior to the genocide. Some had even been openly calling for a policy of mass murder.[168] The Hutu militias responsible for much of the killing in 1994 had been carrying out small-scale massacres against Tutsi civilians for more than two years before the genocide began. In the months preceding the genocide, a wide range of warning signs suggested that massive violence, if not genocide, was imminent.[169]

Contemporary observers often have been aware of the violent ideas, plans, statements, and even actions of future perpetrators of mass killing, but too frequently they have failed to take these warnings seriously. As Michael Barnett writes of the failure of the international community to heed the warning signs in Rwanda: "Few dared to imagine the apocalyptic possibility of genocide. Genocide is not simply a low probability form of violence that ranks at the bottom of any list of violent alternatives. It resides outside the realm of human imagination."[170] Since threats of violence are far more common than mass killing, it is easy to dismiss them as mere bluster.[171]

By learning to recognize the specific kinds of goals, beliefs, and situations that make leaders likely to consider mass killing, however, we may be better able to discriminate between empty threats and those that indicate a more significant possibility of mass killing. The remaining chapters of this book, therefore, are devoted to identifying and understanding the factors and conditions that contribute to leaders' decisions to launch mass killing.

3. THE STRATEGIC LOGIC
OF MASS KILLING

To identify societies at high risk for mass killing, I have suggested, we must first understand the specific goals, ideas, and beliefs of powerful groups and leaders, not necessarily the broad social structures or systems of government of the societies over which these leaders preside. A few leaders cannot implement mass killing alone, but perpetrators do not need widespread social support in order to carry it out. A tiny minority, well armed and well organized, can generate an appalling amount of bloodshed when unleashed upon unarmed and unorganized victims. Levels of hatred, discrimination, or ideological commitment common to many societies are sufficient to recruit the relatively small number of active supporters needed to carry out mass killing and to encourage the passivity of the rest of society.

These conclusions suggest that we will best understand the causes of mass killing when we study the phenomenon from a "strategic" perspective. Rather than focusing on the social structures or psychological mechanisms that might facilitate public support for mass killing, a strategic approach seeks to identify the specific situations, goals, and conditions that give leaders incentives to consider this kind of violence. I contend that mass killing occurs when powerful groups come to believe it is the best available means to accomplish certain radical goals, counter specific types of threats, or solve difficult military problems. From this perspective, mass killing should be viewed as an instrumental policy calculated to achieve important political and military objectives with respect to other groups — a "final solution" to its perpetrators' most urgent problems.

Because mass killing is a means to an end, it is rarely a policy of first resort. Perpetrators commonly experiment with other, less violent or even conciliatory means in the attempt to achieve their ends. When these means fail or are deemed too costly or demanding, however, leaders are forced to choose between compromising their most important goals and interests or resorting to more violent methods to achieve them. Regardless of perpetrators' original intentions or attitudes toward their victims, the failure or frustration of other means can make mass killing a more attractive option.

It is important to emphasize that a strategic understanding of mass killing does not imply that perpetrators always evaluate objectively the problems they face in their environment, nor that they accurately assess the ability of mass killing to resolve these problems. Human beings act on the basis of their subjective perceptions and beliefs, not objective reality. Indeed, the powerful role that small groups and individuals play in the conception and implementation of policies of mass killing can amplify the influence of misperceptions in promoting such violence. The often misguided and sometimes outrightly bizarre ideas and beliefs of perpetrator groups can persist at least in part because they usually are shielded from the critical scrutiny of a wider audience. A profound obsession with secrecy, frequently engendered by years spent in political or military opposition, is common in perpetrator organizations and tends to exacerbate misperceptions.

A strategic approach to mass killing, therefore, suggests only that perpetrators are likely to employ mass killing when they perceive it to be both necessary and effective, not when it is actually so. In many cases, the threat posed by the victims of mass killing is more imagined than real. The Jews of Europe, after all, posed no conceivable threat to Germany in the 1930s. This reality mattered little, however, since Germany's leaders were steadfastly convinced of the contrary, and they possessed the power to act on their convictions. Perpetrators also frequently have overestimated the capacity of mass killing to achieve their goals, especially in the long term. While mass killing can be a powerful political or military strategy, it also can be decidedly counterproductive, even from the point of view of those who instigate it. In practice, the use of massive violence has often backfired, diverting scarce resources away from real threats, provoking increased resistance from victim groups, mobilizing third parties on behalf of the victims, or discrediting the ideologies in the service of which it has been employed.

Mass killing failed to achieve its perpetrators' objectives, at least in the long run, in all of the cases examined in this book. In the Soviet Union, China, and Cambodia communist leaders resorted to mass killing in an effort to force peasants to accept new, supposedly more productive means of agriculture. While the violence succeeded in coercing the peasantry, it also resulted in massive starvation, the near collapse of the economy, and eventually contributed to the decision to abandon radical communist agricultural methods. In Turkey, Nazi Germany, and Rwanda perpetrators used mass killing to eliminate perceived threats from ethnic minorities. In each case, the task of murdering defenseless civilians drew resources away from ongoing wars, contributing to major military defeats. During the civil war in Guatemala and the Soviet occupation of Afghanistan, mass killing was intended to destroy civilian support for insurgent movements. In Afghanistan, the violence simply drove millions to support the rebels and provoked increased international opposition to the Soviet occupation. In Guatemala, the tactic was more successful in the short run, but popular resentment of the military government remained high and the regime ultimately was forced to negotiate with the rebels and implement democratic reforms.

A Typology of Mass Killing

Rationality and Mass Killing

Many scholars have noted that mass killing and genocide can often appear rational from the perspective of the perpetrator. Peter du Preez, for example, contends that "there is a 'rationality of genocide' just as there is a rationality of business or athletics or war or science."[1] Likewise, Roger Smith writes that "genocide is a rational instrument to achieve an end."[2] More specifically, a number of scholars have pointed out that genocide can sometimes be motivated by the rational calculation that systematic violence will serve to counter real or perceived threats posed by victims or help to implement specific kinds of ideologies.[3]

Unfortunately, few scholars have gone beyond simply suggesting the potential rationality of genocide and mass killing to identify the specific conditions under which mass killing is most likely to appear necessary and effective to its perpetrators. Why, in other words, is mass killing a rational way to respond to some threats and implement some ideologies but not others? Helen Fein, for example, argues that many cases of genocide result from the violent repression of victim groups rebelling against severe discrimination.[4] Rebellion, however, is a far more common phenomenon than mass killing. Fein does not attempt to explain why mass killing is used to repress some rebellious groups and not others.[5] Without this knowledge, we can neither fully understand the "rationality" of genocidal repression nor anticipate with confidence where and when it is most likely to occur.

My research, like these authors', also suggests that perpetrators may view mass killing as a rational way to counter threats or implement certain types of ideologies. I argue, however, that perpetrators are likely to perceive mass killing as an attractive means to achieve these and other ends only in very specific circumstances and under very specific conditions. I have identified six specific motives — corresponding to six "types" of mass killing — that, under certain specific conditions, appear to generate strong incentives for leaders to initiate mass killing.

These six motives can be grouped into two general categories. First, when leaders' plans result in the near-complete material disenfranchisement of large groups of people, leaders are likely to conclude that mass killing is necessary to overcome resistance by these groups or, more radically, that mass killing is the only practical way to physically remove these groups or their influence from society. I refer to this general class as "dispossessive" mass killings. Second, mass killing can become an attractive solution in military conflicts in which leaders perceive conventional military tactics to be hopeless or unacceptably costly. When leaders' efforts to defeat their enemies' military forces directly are frustrated, they face powerful incentives to target the civilian populations they suspect of supporting those forces. I refer to this class of mass killing as "coercive" mass killings.

The specific real-world scenarios in which each type of mass killing occurs, as well as several selected historical examples of each scenario, are presented in table 1. I will briefly describe each of the types of mass killing in this table in subsequent sections of this chapter.

Of the six types mass killing, three have accounted for the majority of episodes of mass killing as well as the greatest number of victims in the twentieth century: communist mass killings, ethnic mass killings, and counterguerrilla mass killings. Chapters 4, 5, and 6 describe the general causes of these types of mass killing in greater detail and apply the strategic perspective to explain several prominent historical episodes of each type.

Conditionality

Although the scenarios described in this chapter generate powerful incentives for mass killing, they do not invariably provoke it. A variety of intervening variables may act to increase or decrease leaders' incentives or capabilities to launch mass killing and, consequently, the likelihood that

TABLE 1
A Typology of Mass Killing

Motive/Type	Scenario	Examples*
DISPOSSESSIVE MASS KILLING		
Communist	Agricultural collectivization and political terror	Soviet Union (1917–53) China (1950–76) Cambodia (1975–79) Turkish Armenia (1915–18)
Ethnic	Ethnic cleansing	The Holocaust (1939–45) Rwanda (1994)
Territorial	Colonial enlargement	European colonies in North and South America Genocide of the Herero in German South-West Africa (1904–7)
	Expansionist wars	German annexation of western Poland (1939–45)
COERCIVE MASS KILLING		
Counterguerrilla	Guerrilla wars	Algerian war of independence from France (1954–62) Soviet invasion of Afghanistan (1979–88) Ethiopian civil war (1970s and 1980s) Guatemalan civil war (1980s)
Terrorist	Terror bombing	Allied bombings of Germany and Japan (1940–45)
	Starvation blockades/siege warfare	Allied naval blockade of Germany (1914–19) Nigerian land blockade of Biafra (1967–70)
	Sub-state/insurgent terrorism	FLN terrorism in Algerian war of independence against France (1954–62) Viet Cong terrorism in South Vietnam (1957–75) RENAMO terrorism in Mozambique (1976–92)
Imperialist	Imperial conquests and rebellions	German occupation of Western Europe (1940–45) Japan's empire in East Asia (1910–45)

Note: This typology does not exhaust the entire universe of motives for mass killing in the twentieth century, but it does appear to account for the great majority of these episodes. At least two notable cases—the mass killing of between 250,000 and 1,000,000 people in Indonesia in 1965 and the mass killing of between 100,000 and 500,000 people in Uganda under Idi Amin from 1971 to 1979—do not appear entirely consistent with any of the motives described in this book.

*Selected examples only, not a complete list of all instances of mass killings within each category. Some examples combine aspects of more than one motive.

mass killing will occur. Although it is not possible to identify all of the factors and conditions that affect the likelihood of mass killing, I have attempted to identify some of the most significant intervening variables by analyzing the history of a number of less violent examples of the scenarios listed in table 1. I list these conditions at the end of each section below. It is important to note that these are not merely ad hoc lists of factors derived from specific historical cases. Rather, these conditions are influential precisely because each of them directly or indirectly influences the specific causal mechanisms implicated by the strategic theories described in this chapter — increasing or decreasing the availability of less violent strategies, or raising or lowering the impediments to mass killing.

Some of these conditions, such as the perpetrators' physical capability to carry out mass killing, the size of the potential victim group, and the ability of potential victims to flee to safety, are relevant to all types of mass killing. Other conditions apply only to specific scenarios. Conditions affecting the likelihood of communist mass killing, ethnic mass killing, and counterguerrilla mass killing are described in detail in chapters 4, 5, and 6.

DISPOSSESSIVE MASS KILLINGS

Dispossessive mass killings are the result of policies that, by design or by consequence, suddenly strip large groups of people of their possessions, their homes, or their way of life. These kinds of policies do not aim at mass killing as such, but in practice their implementation often leads to it.

My research identifies three major types of dispossessive mass killing in the twentieth century. First, regimes seeking to achieve the radical communization of their societies have forced vast numbers of people to surrender their property and abandon their traditional ways of life. Second, racist or nationalist regimes have forced large groups of people to relinquish their homes and possessions during the "ethnic cleansing" of certain territories. Third, the territorial ambitions of colonial or expansionist powers have often stripped preexisting populations of their land and means of subsistence.

A Note on the Role of Ideology in Dispossessive Mass Killing

Several of the cases categorized in this book as dispossessive mass killings have been described as ideological mass killings/genocides by other authors. Indeed, few scholars who have studied genocide and mass killing have failed to comment on the central role that ideology has played in some of the twentieth century's bloodiest mass killings. In particular, the ideology of ruling elites played a central role in the mass killings of communist states such as the Soviet Union, China, and Cambodia and of explicitly racist states such as Nazi Germany. Various authors have suggested that the most dangerous ideologies are those that seek national purification, dehumanize other ethnic groups, place national security above all other goals, or expound a political formula that excludes victim groups from the larger community or nation.[6]

From a strategic perspective, however, what the ideologies that lead to mass killing share is not their specific content but the magnitude, scope, and speed of the changes they force upon large groups of people. The desire to implement such radical changes may stem from ideological doctrines calling for a revolutionary transformation of the economic or demographic composition of society, but it may also stem from more "pragmatic" concerns, such as the effort to eliminate specific kinds of political or military threats, or the attempt to colonize and repopulate territories already inhabited by large numbers of people. Whatever its fundamental motivation, the effort to impose extremely radical changes on the lives of large numbers of people often results in the near-total material or political disenfranchisement of existing social groups.

Radical ends, however, require radical means. Leaders attempting to implement such sweeping agendas soon discover, or simply anticipate, that members of disenfranchised groups will not cooperate with the implementation of a new social order in which they stand to loose their livelihood, their homes, or their very way of life. Massive violence may be required to force such radical changes upon large numbers of people. Under these circumstances, leaders may simply decide that the victim group must be totally annihilated, or that killing large numbers of them is necessary to enforce compliance from the group and deter surviving members from mounting further resistance. Even if victim groups can be forced to submit, the process and aftermath of such radical changes, often involving the sudden relocation of vast numbers of people or the disruption of traditional modes of subsistence, can take a staggering toll in human life.

Despite the deadly consequences of the ideological, political, or territorial goals that motivate dispossessive mass killings, it is important to understand that these goals seldom, if ever, seek the killing of victim groups as an end in itself. This conception of the role of ideology in mass killing would simply lead to the tautological conclusion that groups engage in mass killing because they want to engage in mass killing. Rather, I contend that dispossessive mass killings occur when perpetrators conclude that this kind of violence is the most practical strategy to accomplish specific political or military objectives short of mass killing. These objectives may call for an open assault on the way of life of victim groups, for their segregation or even physical removal from society, but they do not amount to killing for killing's sake. In fact, as we shall see in chapter 4, mass killings in the Soviet Union, China, and Cambodia resulted from the effort to implement policies that communist leaders believed would ultimately improve the lives all citizens, including the social groups whose existence was most severely disrupted by them. In the eyes of communist leaders, violence became a necessary expedient because these groups failed to rise above their narrow "class consciousness" to appreciate the benefits of communist society.

Communist Mass Killing

The most deadly mass killings in history have resulted from the effort to transform society according to communist doctrine. Radical communist regimes have proven so exceptionally violent because the changes they have sought to bring about have resulted in the nearly complete material dispossession of vast numbers of people. Radical communist policies have extended well beyond the restriction of personal and political freedoms characteristic of authoritarian or dictatorial regimes. The most radical communist regimes have attempted to bring about the wholesale transformation of their societies, often including the abrupt destruction of traditional ways of life and means of production, and the subordination of personal choices and daily activities to the dictates of the state. Not surprisingly, many people have chosen to resist these drastic changes. Faced with the choice between moderating their revolutionary goals to allow for voluntary change and forcing change on society using whatever means necessary, communist leaders like Stalin, Mao, and Pol Pot opted for mass killing over compromise.

Mass killings associated with the collectivization of agriculture and other radical communist agricultural policies provide the most striking examples of this process. Communist agricultural policies like collectivization have tended to go hand in hand with mass killing because, more than any other communist program, these policies have stripped vast numbers of people of their most valued possessions — their homes and their way of life. The imposition of radical communist agricultural policies on the peasantry of the Soviet Union, China, and Cambodia resulted in millions of deaths. Many victims were executed outright in the effort to crush real or suspected resistance to the socialization of the countryside, but most died in the massive famines sparked by collectivization.

Communist leaders did not deliberately engineer these famines, as some have suggested, but they did use hunger as a weapon by directing the worst effects of the famines against individuals and social groups perceived to oppose collectivization.

In addition to violence associated with communist agricultural policies, communist mass killings have also taken the form of bloody intra-party purges and attacks on social and cultural elites, intellectuals, and members of opposition political parties. The Great Terror in the Soviet Union and the Cultural Revolution in China represent the most notorious examples of this kind of communist political terror.

Almost all governments face some form of domestic political opposition, so what explains the exceptional violence of these communist states? I argue that, like collectivization, these purges were motivated by the desire of leaders to eliminate perceived resistance to the communist transformation of society. Communist leaders feared opposition to their radical policies not only in the countryside but also among intellectuals and even members of the communist party itself. Indeed, the most savage political purges in the Soviet Union, China, and Cambodia were driven in large part by the effort to eliminate real and perceived opposition to the regimes' radical agricultural policies within the communist party. In the eyes of Stalin, Mao, and Pol Pot, the achievements of communism remained extremely fragile long after the revolution. Perhaps even more than they had in the collectivization campaigns in the countryside, however, communist leaders vastly inflated the extent and influence of their political enemies during the purges. The pseudo-Marxist belief that resistance to communism was motivated by one's class consciousness — an attribute that was difficult or impossible to change — lead to the prophylactic targeting of entire social groups and family members of suspects, a practice that massively expanded the scope of the terror.

Communist mass killing is more likely

- the higher the priority that communist leaders assign to the radical transformation of society
- the more the communization of society results in the dispossession of large numbers of people
- the more rapidly communist leaders seek to implement dispossessive policies
- the greater the physical capabilities for mass killing possessed by the regime
- the fewer and more difficult the options for victims of communist policies to flee to safety

TABLE 2
Communist Mass Killings in the Twentieth Century

Location-Dates	Description	Additional Motives	Deaths
Soviet Union (1917–23)	Russian Civil War and Red Terror	Counterguerrilla	250,000– 2,500,000
Soviet Union and Eastern Europe (1927–45)	Collectivization, Great Terror, occupation/ communization of Baltic states and western Poland	Counterguerrilla	10,000,000– 20,000,000
China (including Tibet) (1949–72)	Land reform, Great Leap Forward, Cultural Revolution, and other political purges	Counterguerrilla	10,000,000– 46,000,000
Cambodia (1975–79)	Collectivization and political repression	Ethnic	1,000,000– 2,000,000
POSSIBLE CASES*			
Bulgaria (1944–?)	Agricultural collectivization and political repression		50,000– 100,000
East Germany (1945–?)	Political repression by Soviet Union		80,000– 100,000
Romania (1945–?)	Agricultural collectivization and political repression		60,000– 300,000
North Korea (1945–?)	Agricultural collectivization and political repression	Counterguerrilla	400,000– 1,500,000
North and South Vietnam (1953–?)	Agricultural collectivization and political repression		80,000– 200,000

Note: All figures in this and subsequent tables are author's estimates based on numerous sources.
* Episodes are listed under the heading "possible cases" in this and subsequent tables when the available evidence suggests a mass killing may have occurred, but documentation is insufficient to make a definitive judgment regarding the number of people killed, the intentionality of the killing, or the motives of the perpetrators.

Ethnic Mass Killing

Ethnic, national, or religious groups may become preferential targets in any of the types of mass killing described in this book. In these pages, however, "ethnic mass killings" are distinguished from the other types of mass killing by the explicitly racist or nationalist motives of the perpetrators. Ethnic mass killing, I argue, is not simply the result of perpetrators' bitter hatred of other ethnic groups, or of a racist ideology that calls for the extermination of these groups as such. Ethnic mass killing has deeper roots in perpetrators' fears than in their hatreds. I find that mass killing is most likely to occur when perpetrators believe that their ethnic opponents pose a threat that can be countered only by physically removing them from society, in other words, by implementing a policy of ethnic cleansing. This perception may be shaped by perpetrators' ideological beliefs about other ethnic groups, as it was in Nazi Germany, but it may also be a reaction to real, if almost always misperceived or exaggerated, threatening actions of some victim group members, as it was in Rwanda in 1994. In many cases, a combination of ideological beliefs and real-world conflicts seem to shape perpetrators' perceptions of victim groups.

The decision to engage in ethnic cleansing, however, is not always a decision to perpetrate mass killing. Ethnic cleansing and mass killing are often conflated in popular parlance, but they are not synonymous. Ethnic cleansing refers to the removal of certain groups from a given territory, a process that may or may not involve mass killing. Nevertheless, like communist policies such as collectivization, large-scale ethnic cleansing frequently has been associated with mass killing because it often results in the near-complete material dispossession of large groups of people. Violence is often required to force people to relinquish their homes and their possessions. Even after victims have been coerced into flight, the process and aftermath of large population movements itself can be deadly.

The bloodiest episodes of ethnic mass killing, however, occur when leaders conclude that they have no practical options for the physical relocation of victim groups. In such cases, perpetrators may see violent repression on a massive scale as the only way to meet the perceived threat posed by their victims. The killing may be designed to deprive the victim group of its ability to organize politically or militarily by eliminating its elites, intellectuals, or males of military age. At the most extreme, perpetrators may conclude that systematic extermination is the only available means to counter the threat. Ethnic mass killing, therefore, is best seen as an instrumental strategy that seeks the physical removal or permanent military or political subjugation of ethnic groups, not the annihilation of these groups as an end in itself.

Ethnic mass killing is more likely

- the greater the threat that racist or nationalist leaders believe is posed by their ethnic, national, or religious adversaries
- the fewer and less practical the policies other than ethnic cleansing that racist or nationalist leaders believe will counter the perceived threat posed by their victims
- the more rapidly ethnic cleansing is carried out
- the greater the number of people subjected to ethnic cleansing
- the greater the physical capabilities for mass killing possessed by the racist or nationalist regime
- the fewer and more difficult the options for victims to flee to safety

TABLE 3
Ethnic Mass Killings in the Twentieth Century

Location-Dates	Description	Additional Motives	Deaths
Turkey (1915–18)	Genocide of Armenians	Counterguerrilla	500,000–1,500,000
Soviet Union (1941–53)	Deportation of nationalities	Counterguerrilla	300,000–600,000
Germany (1939–45)	Genocide of Jews and other Nazi race enemies		5,400,000–6,800,000
Yugoslavia (1941–45)	Ustasha violence against Serbs	Counterguerrilla	125,000–530,000
Eastern Europe (1945–47)	Post–WW II expulsion of ethnic Germans from Poland, Czechoslovakia, Yugoslavia, and elsewhere		2,000,000–2,300,000
India (1947–48)	Partition of India		500,000–1,000,000
Bangladesh (1971)	Partition of East Pakistan		500,000–3,000,000
Burundi (1972)	Genocide of Hutu	Counterguerrilla	100,000–200,000
Bosnia-Herzegovina (1990–95)	Ethnic cleansing of Muslims from Bosnia	Counterguerrilla	25,000–155,000
Rwanda (1994)	Genocide of Tutsi	Counterguerrilla	500,000–800,000

Territorial Mass Killing

The third general motive for dispossessive mass killing arises when powerful groups attempt to resettle territories already inhabited by large, preexisting populations. Unlike the ethnic mass killings described above, perpetrators of territorial mass killing do not seek to cleanse a given territory of its inhabitants because they believe these people themselves pose a threat, but rather because perpetrators want to populate (and usually cultivate) the land with their own people. As with ethnic mass killings, however, territorial mass killing occurs because the process and aftermath of rapidly removing large numbers of people from their homes often involves considerable violence.

Territorial mass killings have emerged in two closely related scenarios. First, mass killing can result when settler colonies attempt to expand their territory into regions already populated by indigenous people.[7] This scenario has occurred primarily in colonial settings, most notably in the European colonies of North and South America and to a lesser extent in Africa.

Not all colonists, however, have annihilated the indigenous peoples they encountered. Even states that have engaged in mass killing in some of their colonies have conducted themselves more humanely in others. What separates these "peaceful" colonies from the ones that have resorted to mass killing? The answer often seems to depend upon the nature of the colonial economy and its relationship to the indigenous population.

In agricultural economies, particularly those with an emphasis on grain production or herding, land is an extremely valuable asset. The economic structure of indigenous societies, however, may also depend heavily on access to large amounts of land. Many colonies do not encompass enough high-quality land to support both a land-hungry agrarian economy and the preexisting indigenous population. In such cases, the settlers' desire for more and more land has tended to push the colony into conflict with indigenous populations. Indigenous efforts to resist colonial expansion have prompted increasingly violent responses from the settlers, sometimes escalating to mass killing. Where surplus land is available, colonists have sometimes attempted to relocate indigenous people to distant or unwanted parts of the colony. Even in these cases, however, the outcome is often bleak. Violence commonly has been required to force indigenous people to abandon their homes and traditional territories. The displacement of large populations has often proved deadly, as the relocation of the Cherokee Indians in 1838 on the infamous "trail of tears" powerfully demonstrated.[8] Even those who have managed to survive relocation frequently have faced starvation, disease, and depredation by other groups in their new territories.

This deadly competition for land played a major role in the destruction of many indigenous tribes of America.[9] According to David Stannard, "since the colonizing British, and subsequently the Americans, had little use for Indian servitude, but only wanted Indian land . . . straightforward mass killing of the Indians was deemed the only thing to do."[10] Not all economies, however, are so economically dependent upon land. Non-agricultural forms of production require relatively little land but are often dependent on a cheap and plentiful source of labor. Indigenous people have often fulfilled this function. Indigenous people can also provide important markets for goods and have even provided soldiers for colonial armies.

Two French colonies in North America provide telling examples of how the economic relationship between colonists and indigenous peoples can influence the likelihood of mass killing.[11] In what is now Canada, the Huron people became an integral part of France's fur trade, serving as guides and skilled trackers for the French. French trappers relied on Huron villages for supplies and protection from other Indians. The

French and the Hurons maintained a relatively peaceful relationship until the Huron were decimated in a war with the Iroquois in 1649. The relationship between the French and the Natchez people of the lower Mississippi, on the other hand, ended in the annihilation of the Natchez by the French colonists. In the lower Mississippi, the French planned a large colony based on agriculture. They imported slaves from Africa for their servants and laborers. The Natchez people simply stood in the way of expanding French plantations. When the Natchez would not abandon their land peacefully, the French decided to remove them by force. By 1731 the Natchez had ceased to exist.[12]

The second major scenario of territorial mass killing results when states engaged in wars of expansion seek to resettle areas already densely populated and developed by others. Perhaps the most horrific example of this kind of mass killing occurred during the Second World War as Germany attempted to expand its territory into Poland, Russia, and other Eastern European states. This effort to acquire *Lebensraum* (living space) for Germany's population was one of Hitler's primary obsessions, rivaled in importance only by his interrelated campaign to rid Europe of the Jews. Hitler's plans called for physically removing many existing populations and repopulating the land with ethnic German farmers. In some places, German occupiers temporarily spared the conquered populations for use as slave labor during the war, but German plans called for the eventual relocation of tens of millions of Eastern Europeans.

German occupation had its most devastating effect in occupied Poland where colonization by German settlers began almost immediately following the German invasion in 1939.[13] Hitler designated vast swaths of Polish territory for near-total ethnic cleansing (of both Poles and Jews) and annexation by the Reich. Hitler never planned the systematic murder of all Poles, but the effort to subjugate and dispossess the entire nation nevertheless proved predictably violent. As Walther von Brauchitsch, the German army commander in chief, explained in a letter to a hesitant subordinate, "The solution of ethnic-political tasks, necessary for securing German living space and ordered by the Führer, had necessarily to lead to otherwise unusual, harsh measures against the Polish population of the occupied area."[14] Hitler ordered Polish political, military, and cultural leaders executed for fear that they would organize resistance to the occupation. At least 750,000 Poles and Jews were forced from the German-annexed territories of western Poland alone to make room for hundreds of thousands of German settlers from across Eastern Europe.[15] By the end of the war more than 22 percent of the prewar Polish population was dead.[16]

The German occupation of France and the Low Countries, on the other hand, reveals how different ends contributed to the utilization of different means. German military and police forces occupied French territory with the intention of exploiting its natural resources and labor as part of the effort to increase German war production. Hitler, however, never intended to colonize large portions of Western Europe. German violence in the west followed the more selective patterns associated with imperialism and the suppression of guerrilla resistance movements (I describe these motives for mass killing in subsequent sections). The German occupation in the west was hardly benevolent. The Nazis deported Jews and Gypsies to death camps as they did throughout Europe. German forces executed tens of thousands of non-Jews for resisting the occupation and deported hundreds of thousands for temporary forced labor in Germany, where many perished. Yet, compared to the near-complete devastation wrought by the German occupation in the east, Western European populations fared considerably better.

Territorial mass killing appears to have become much less common in the last hundred years than it was in previous centuries. Unfortunately, this trend is probably not the result of a general moral conversion among colonial or expansionist powers. Rather, it seems to reflect two historical trends. First, by the turn of the century, European violence and disease had already decimated many indigenous populations and European settlement had already expanded to the territorial limits of most major settler colonies. Second, especially since the end of the Second World War, the conquest of territory seems to have become less important for national security and economic prosperity, providing fewer incentives for expansionist wars.[17]

Territorial mass killing is more likely

- the higher the priority perpetrators assign to repopulating new territories
- the smaller the ratio of usable land per colonist resettled in new territories
- the greater the number of people already residing in colonized territories
- the more rapidly perpetrators seek to relocate existing populations
- the greater the physical capabilities for mass killing possessed by the perpetrators
- the fewer and more difficult the options for victims to flee to safety

TABLE 4
*Territorial (Colonial and Expansionist) Mass Killings
in the Twentieth Century*

Location-Dates	Description	Additional Motives	Deaths
Namibia (1904–7)	Genocide of Herero and Nama	Counterguerrilla	60,000– 65,000
Eastern Europe (1939–45)	Nazi territorial expansion	Counterguerrilla, imperialist	10,000,000– 15,000,000

COERCIVE MASS KILLINGS

Sometimes mass killing is simply war by other means. Coercive mass killings occur in major armed conflicts when combatants lack the capabilities to defeat their opponents' military forces with conventional military techniques. When such conflicts threaten highly important goals, leaders must search for alternative means to defeat their adversaries. Under such circumstances, military and political leaders may conclude that the most effective way to achieve victory is to target the civilians that they suspect of providing material and political support to their adversaries' military forces. Perpetrators of this kind of mass killing usually do not seek to exterminate entire populations; rather, they use massive violence and the threat of even greater violence to coerce large numbers of civilians or their leaders into submission. When more "selective" mass killing fails to dissuade civilian supporters or induce surrender, however, coercive mass killing can escalate to the genocidal targeting of suspect ethnic groups or the enemy populations of entire geographical regions.[18]

I divide coercive mass killings into three major types: counterguerrilla, terrorist, and imperialist.

Counterguerrilla warfare

Mass killing can become an attractive strategy for governments engaged in counterguerrilla warfare. Although many observers have characterized mass killing in counterguerrilla warfare as the result of the actions of undisciplined, frustrated, or racist troops, the strategic approach suggests that counterguerrilla mass killing is a calculated military response to the unique challenges posed by guerrilla warfare.

Unlike conventional armies, guerrilla forces often depend on the local civilian population for food, shelter, and supplies. Guerrillas also depend on the local population to reveal information about enemy outposts and troop movements and as a form of "human camouflage" into which guerrillas can blend to avoid detection. Thus, according to Mao Zedong's famous analogy, "the guerrillas are as the fish and the people the sea in which they swim."[19]

Civilian support can be a major source of strength for guerrilla armies, but it can also be a weakness. Regimes facing guerrilla opponents either at home or abroad have sometimes been able to turn the guerrillas' dependency on the local population to their own advantage. Unlike the guerrillas themselves, the civilian support network upon which guerrillas rely is virtually defenseless and impossible to conceal. Some regimes have found it easier, therefore, to wage war against a guerrilla army by depriving it of its base of support in the people than by attempting to target the guerrillas directly. In the terms of Mao's analogy, this strategy seeks to catch the fish by draining the sea. Not surprisingly, this strategy of counterinsurgency has frequently resulted in mass killing.

Theorists of counterguerrilla warfare have often advocated "selective" violence targeted only against those who provide active support for the guerrillas. In practice, however, such distinctions have been difficult to maintain. As I describe in detail in chapter 6, counterguerrilla warfare has often been characterized by reliance on indiscriminate tactics such as "free-fire zones," the intentional destruction of crops, livestock and dwellings, massive programs of population resettlement, and the use of torture and large-scale massacres designed to intimidate guerrilla supporters.

Guerrilla warfare, of course, has been one of the most common forms of combat in the twentieth century. Although it has seldom spared civilian populations, in most cases it has not provoked mass killing by counterinsurgent forces. As I document in chapter 6, when leaders believe that the guerrillas are not receiving significant support from the local population or do not pose a threat to the regime's critical goals or interests, they have little reason to order the killing of large numbers of civilians.

Counterguerrilla mass killing is more likely

- the greater the threat that perpetrators believe guerrillas pose to vital interests
- the more significant the support perpetrators believe that guerrillas receive from the civilian population
- the greater the difficulties the perpetrators encounter in defeating the guerrillas with less violent means
- the greater the numbers of people who reside in areas of guerrilla activity
- the greater the physical capabilities for mass killing possessed by the perpetrators
- the fewer and more difficult the options for victims to flee to safety

TABLE 5
Counterguerrilla Mass Killings in the Twentieth Century

Location-Dates	Description	Additional Motives	Deaths
Philippines (1899–1902)	US occupation of the Philippines		100,000–200,000
China (1927–49)	Nationalist repression in Chinese civil war		6,000,000–10,000,000
Spain (1936–43?)	Nationalist violence in Spanish civil war	Terrorist	185,000–410,000
Algeria (1954–63)	Algerian war of independence from France		70,000–570,000
Sudan (1956–71)	Suppression of southern Sudanese	Ethnic	250,000–500,000
Tibet (1959–60)	Suppression of Tibetan rebellion	Communist	65,000–90,000
Iraq (1963–91)	Suppression of Kurdish rebellions		85,000–265,000
Guatemala (1966–85)	Guatemalan civil war		100,000–200,000
Ethiopia (1974–91)	Ethiopian civil war	Communist	500,000–1,000,000
Angola (1975–2002)	Angolan civil war		60,000–375,000
Indonesia (East Timor) (1975–99)	Suppression of East Timorese secession		100,000–200,000
Afghanistan (1978–89)	Soviet invasion and occupation	Communist	950,000–1,280,000
El Salvador (1979–92)	Salvadoran civil war		40,000–70,000
Sudan (1983–2002)	Suppression of southern Sudanese	Ethnic	1,000,000–1,500,000
Somalia (1988–91)	Suppression of Isaaq clan/SNM	Ethnic	50,000–60,000
Burundi (1993–98)	Suppression of Hutu	Ethnic	100,000–200,000
Russia (Chechnya) (1994–2000)	Suppression of Chechen secession movement		55,000–60,000

POSSIBLE CASES

Tanzania (German Southwest Africa) (1905–7)	Suppression of Maji-Maji uprising		200,000–300,000
Vietnam (1945–54)	French suppression of Vietminh guerrillas		60,000–250,000

continued

TABLE 5
continued

	POSSIBLE CASES		
Colombia (1948–58)	"Conservative" violence against "Liberals" in Colombian civil war	Terrorist	50,000– 150,000
Vietnam (South) (1965–75)	U.S. and South Vietnamese suppression of NLF		110,000– 310,000
Cambodia (1969–73)	U.S. invasion-bombardment of Cambodia	Terrorist	30,000– 150,000
Uganda (1979–87)	Suppression of suspected NRA supporters		100,000– 300,000

Mass Killing as Mass Terror

A second scenario of coercive mass killing occurs when combatants engaged in protracted wars of attrition search for means to swiftly end the war. As in counterguerrilla killings, leaders may choose to target enemy civilians in the hopes of coercing surrender without having to defeat the enemy's military forces directly. During times of war, of course, civilians often become victims of famine, disease, and exposure or perish in the crossfire of opposing forces. These deaths, though tragic, do not qualify as mass killing as defined above because they are not intended by either party. Combatants may also target civilians intentionally, however, when leaders come to believe that bringing the conflict directly to the enemy civilian population will spread terror, break enemy morale, destroy enemy economic productivity, or spark rebellions inside enemy territory. The ultimate goal of this type of mass killing is simple — to speed the end of the war.

For lack of a better term, I refer to episodes of mass killing motivated by these kinds of goals as terrorist mass killings. Like most definitions of terrorism, this terminology focuses on the deliberate use of violence against civilian targets in the effort to coerce political change.[20] Unlike many conceptions of terrorism, however, this terminology encompasses terrorist violence conducted by states, and explicitly includes such violence when it occurs during war.[21]

The advent of strategic air and missile power in the second half of this century has rendered the strategy of terror during war an especially attractive and extremely destructive weapon. During the Second World War, Britain and the United States intentionally bombed German cities in an effort to weaken German public support for the war and force an early surrender. In the early stages of the war, British civilian and military leaders considered the possibility of using air power to attack Germany's military forces and industrial assets without targeting civilians, but they soon discovered that these techniques were not technically practical.[22] British strategic bombing planners ultimately decided that in order to crush the German will to fight, the Allies "must achieve two things: first, we must make [German towns] physically uninhabitable and, secondly, we must make the people conscious of constant personal danger. The immediate aim is therefore two-fold, namely to produce: (i) destruction; and (ii) the fear of death."[23] By 1942 the British government had directed the Royal Air Force to abandon its efforts to conduct precision bombing of military and industrial targets and stated that "a primary object" of RAF bombing raids should be "the morale of the enemy civil population."[24]

In public, of course, the allies were careful to justify their attacks by claiming that the raids were intended to destroy German war industries or military targets. The high proportion of incendiary bombs used by the allies, however, casts doubt on whether military targets were the first priority of these operations.[25] As for industrial targets, while the destruction of German industry was undoubtedly the primary objective of some attacks, many cities without significant industrial resources were also destroyed.[26] Arthur Harris, the head of the RAF Bomber Command, admitted in his memoirs that the destruction of several factories in the devastating 1943 raid on Hamburg—an attack that killed more than forty thousand people—had been "a bonus."[27] By the end of the war, British and American bombing probably killed between 300,000 and 600,000 civilians in Europe.[28]

Long-range bombers and missiles may have perfected the instruments of terror warfare, but the strategy of targeting enemy civilians in the effort to force a military surrender is probably as old as war itself. Military forces throughout history have relied on the practice of siege warfare and the use of starvation blockades to achieve the same effect. Famine is often an unintended consequence of war, but it too can be used as a military tool, like the bombing of cities, to induce capitulation without a conventional military victory.[29] During the First World War, for example, more than 250,000 people died of starvation and malnutrition when the British blockaded Germany and Austria-Hungary in an effort to starve them into surrender.[30] More recently, at least half a million people died in the late

1960s when Nigeria blockaded food supplies to the eastern part of the country, which was attempting to secede.[31]

In addition to strategic bombing and siege warfare, powerful sub-state insurgent groups have sometimes used coercive mass killing to terrorize their enemies, typically colonial governments and their loyalists among the native population. By killing large numbers of civilians from specifically targeted groups, these insurgents hope to achieve their political goals without directly engaging the superior military forces of their enemies. Algerian resistance groups relied heavily on this strategy during their war for independence from France, killing almost seventy thousand people—nearly all of them native Algerians.[32] Communist guerrillas in Vietnam also utilized mass terror in their fight for liberation against France and the United States.[33]

The incentives to resort to mass terror probably exist in most major conflicts, particularly for the weaker side. Yet terrorist mass killing has remained relatively rare compared to the number of conflicts waged in the last century. Three main factors seem to account for this pattern. First, many groups simply lack the physical capabilities needed to implement a military strategy of mass terror. While I have argued that mass killing does not require large or highly capable forces in the absence of organized resistance, terrorist mass killings take place during war and are often directed against civilian groups protected by substantial military organizations of their own. Large, expensive, and technologically sophisticated forces are often required to overcome or bypass enemy military defenses and kill civilians in large numbers. Few states throughout history, for example, have possessed the military forces necessary to carry out large-scale strategic bombing campaigns or to implement effective starvation blockades even if they wished to do so.

Sub-state groups, in particular, have seldom been able to muster the capabilities and organization necessary to carry out violence on the pace and scale of mass killing as defined in this book. Sub-state terrorism may be a "weapon of the weak," but mass killing through terrorism has eluded even the most determined international terrorist organizations. The increasing ease with which weapons of mass destruction, especially biological weapons, can be produced and delivered to their targets, however, seems likely to increase the capabilities of sub-state groups to carry out mass killing in the future.

Second, because mass killing can be a risky and costly strategy, even groups that possess the means to carry out mass terror have employed it only rarely. Mass killing can be counterproductive if it draws in concerned third parties, alienates important allies, or provokes international sanctions. Policies such as strategic bombing can backfire, stiffening the resolve of enemy populations and making surrender less likely.[34] As a result, most leaders would prefer to wage war with conventional means if possible. Combatants see mass killing as necessary and attractive only in the most desperate conflicts. In most wars, at least one combatant has the ability to win with means short of mass killing. Coercive mass killing becomes likely, therefore, only under the unusual circumstances in which the perpetrators' military forces are capable of killing large numbers of enemy civilians but incapable of conventional military victory. Paradoxically, then, groups that can marshal the forces to carry out a strategy of mass terror may actually have fewer reasons to utilize it, since groups with such formidable capabilities will often have the means to win without resorting to this kind of violence. While the weaker side in any major conflict may have an incentive to escalate to mass killing, it will seldom have the capabilities needed to carry it out against a militarily superior opponent.

Finally, when both parties to a conflict have the capability to wage a campaign of mass terror against each other, a state of mutual deterrence may prevail, further limiting the incidence of this kind of violence. Substate terrorist or guerrilla groups are particularly vulnerable to the threat of retaliation in kind, since they often lack the capability to defend their supporters from government repression.[35]

Terrorist mass killing is more likely

- the more the perpetrators believe the conflict threatens their vital interests
- the more the perpetrators believe that their enemies cannot be readily defeated with conventional means
- the greater the number of people who reside in territories engaged in conflict with the perpetrators
- the greater the physical capabilities for mass killing possessed by the perpetrators
- the less effective the capabilities for retaliation the perpetrators believe that victims possess
- the less the perpetrators believe that mass killing will provoke the intervention of other powers
- the fewer and more difficult the options for victims to flee to safety

TABLE 6
Terrorist Mass Killings in the Twentieth Century

Location-Dates	Description	Additional Motives	Deaths
Germany (1914–18)	Allied blockade of Germany in WW I		250,000– 425,000
China (1927–49)	Communist terror in Chinese civil war	Communist	1,800,000– 3,500,000
Spain (1936–39)	Republican terrorism in Spanish civil war	Communist	20,000– 55,000
United Kingdom (1940–45)	German bombardment of UK in WW II		60,000– 62,000
Germany (1940–45)	Allied bombardment of Germany in WW II		300,000– 600,000
Japan (1942–45)	American bombardment of Japan in WW II		268,000– 900,000
Algeria (1954–63)	FLN terrorism		70,000– 235,000
Vietnam (1954–75)	NLF (Viet-Cong) terrorism in Vietnam war	Communist	45,000– 180,000
Nigeria (1967–70)	Suppression of secession of Biafra	Counterguerrilla?	450,000– 2,000,000
Angola (1975–2002)	UNITA terrorism		125,000– 560,000
Mozambique (1975–1992)	RENAMO terrorism in Mozambican civil war		100,000– 700,000
Algeria (1992–2002)	Civil war/antigovernment terrorism		75,000– 150,000
POSSIBLE CASES			
North Korea (1950–54)	U.S./R.O.K. bombing and other killing in Korean War	Counterguerrilla	500,000– 1,500,000
Colombia (1948–58)	Liberal violence against conservatives in Colombian civil war		50,000– 150,000
Iraq (1990–97)	Economic embargo of Iraq by UN/U.S. (prior to "oil for food" program)		80,000– 170,000

Imperialist Mass Killing

The third scenario of coercive mass killing is closely linked to empire. Imperial powers have garnered a well-deserved reputation for the brutal treatment of civilian populations. The Roman empire, the Aztec empire in Central America, Nazi Germany's empire in Europe, and Japan's empire in China and Korea each perpetrated mass killing against at least some of their conquests. Like territorial mass killing, however, imperialist mass killing has declined in frequency in the twentieth century as the great European empires have steadily dissolved.

Much of the violence associated with imperialism seems to be motivated by the effort to diminish the costs of building and administering large empires.[36] The purpose of an empire is to extract wealth from conquests, but empires would be prohibitively expensive to maintain if each subject city, state, or province had to be defeated by force and then policed to a man. Imperial leaders, therefore, have strong incentives to adopt a strategy of mass killing as a means of deterring rebellions and resistance within their empire and as a method of intimidating future conquests into submission. The large-scale killing of rebellious subjects is intended to demonstrate to all others considering resistance the terrible fate awaiting those who refuse to accept imperial rule.

The Mongol empire ruled by Genghis Khan and his progeny was one of the earliest and most efficient practitioners of this strategy of mass killing. According to Paul Ratchnevsky, "Genghis Khan used terror as a strategic weapon in his military plans. . . . Terrible destruction was threatened in the event of resistance; bloody examples were designed to spread fear and reduce the populace's will to resist."[37] Because imperial powers intend mass killing to deter future resistance throughout the empire, they frequently employ it even after rebellious states or regions have capitulated. To ensure the greatest effect, the violence often is carried out in an exceptionally grisly and highly public manner. One of the bloodiest examples of this strategy in recent history occurred during the Japanese campaign to expand its empire into the Chinese mainland. In December 1937, Japanese troops descended on the city of Nanking in an orgy of rape, murder, and mutilation that ultimately left between 200,000 and 350,000 people dead.[38] Many explanations of the brutality of the Japanese empire in China have emphasized the racism, indiscipline, and vengefulness of Japanese troops.[39] However, the violence also represented a calculated strategy designed to terrify China's vast population into submission without a fight.[40] Indeed, it is likely that Nanking was singled out for especially harsh treatment because of the fierce resistance Japanese forces had encountered as they advanced on the city, and because of Nanking's symbolic value as the capital city of Nationalist China.

Of course, not all empires engage in mass killing, and even empires that have perfected this brutal strategy seldom unleash it against all of their conquests. The incentives for imperialist mass killing seem to be greatest when empires are relatively weak or overstretched, or when they make extreme demands on their subjects. Under these conditions, resistance to imperial rule is likely to be especially determined, and the empire's ability to police far-flung territories with conventional means will be heavily strained.

Imperialist mass killing is more likely

- the more the perpetrators perceive their empire as a vital interest
- the greater the numbers of people residing in areas resisting imperial rule
- the larger the size of the empire relative to the perpetrators' capabilities to police it
- the greater the physical capabilities for mass killing possessed by the perpetrators
- the fewer the capabilities for retaliation the perpetrators believe that victims possess
- the less the perpetrators believe that mass killing will provoke the intervention of other powers
- the fewer and more difficult the options for victims to flee to safety

TABLE 7

Imperialist Mass Killings in the Twentieth Century

Location-Dates	Description	Additional Motives	Deaths
East Asia 1937–45	Japanese occupation of East Asia (especially China)	Counterguerrilla	3,000,000– 10,600,000
Western Europe 1940–45	German occupation of Western Europe	Counterguerrilla	425,000– 625,000

4. COMMUNIST MASS KILLINGS: THE SOVIET UNION, CHINA, AND CAMBODIA

Communist regimes have been responsible for this century's most deadly episodes of mass killing. Estimates of the total number of people killed by communist regimes range as high as 110 million.[1] In this chapter I focus primarily on mass killings in the Soviet Union, China, and Cambodia — history's most murderous communist states. Communist violence in these three states alone may account for between 21 million and 70 million deaths.[2] Mass killings on a smaller scale also appear to have been carried out by communist regimes in North Korea, Vietnam, Eastern Europe, and Africa. Documentation of these cases in secondary sources, however, remains inadequate to render a reliable judgment regarding the numbers and identity of the victims or the true intentions of their killers.[3]

Communism has a bloody record, but most regimes that have described themselves as communist or been described as such by others have not engaged in mass killing. In addition to shedding light on why some communist states have been among the most violent regimes in history, therefore, I also seek to explain why other communist countries have avoided this level of violence.

Understanding communist mass killings is of vital importance not only because of the monumental death toll these episodes have generated. Communist revolutions are unlikely today, but past episodes of communist mass killing provide valuable lessons for our understanding of mass killing more generally. In particular, the history of communist mass killings underscores the difficulty of tracing the roots of this kind of violence to structural characteristics of society at large. On the contrary, communist mass killings highlight the decisive power that relatively small groups can exert over entire societies. As we have seen, communist regimes have often seized power with remarkably little public support. What support has been forthcoming for radical communist regimes has almost always been based on appeals to nationalism, wars of national defense or liberation, the promise of moderate economic reforms, or simply the lack of attractive political alternatives. The hard-line economic and social programs that distinguish communist states and that have been most closely associated with communist mass killings, on the other hand, usually have met with widespread resistance, even from those segments of society thought to benefit most from these policies.

Communist mass killings also demonstrate that neither preexisting differences, prejudices, discriminatory practices, nor long histories of conflict between victims and perpetrators are a necessary condition for even the most extreme levels of violence. Victims of communist mass killings have often been drawn from the same ethnic, social, and economic groups as their killers. In many instances, the victims have been members of the communist party itself. Real or suspected political differences, not preexisting social divisions, have defined the line between victims and perpetrators in communist states. This pattern of communist violence suggests that we should not simply assume that discriminatory social structures or intergroup prejudices are the prime causes or preconditions of mass killing, even in episodes of mass killing in which deep social cleavages between victims and perpetrators are readily apparent.

The remainder of this chapter is divided into six main sections. In the first section I describe the strategic perspective on communist mass killing. In the second, third, and fourth sections I apply this perspective to the mass killings in the Soviet Union, Cambodia, and China. In the fifth section I briefly explore the history of several nominally communist regimes that did not engage in mass killing. I conclude with a consideration of the implications of the decline in the global appeal of communism for the incidence of mass killing in the future.

A Strategic Approach to Communist Mass Killing

The effort to engineer utopia has been the justification for some of the world's most horrendous crimes.[4] It is no coincidence that the desire to create a radically different and better society has motivated the most deadly mass killings in human history. Isaiah Berlin describes the justification for mass violence in communism systems: If a "final solution" to the world's problems were possible, "surely no cost would be too high to obtain it: to make mankind just and happy and creative and harmonious forever—what could be too high a price to pay for that? To make such an omelet, there is surely no limit to the number of eggs that should be broken—that was the faith of Lenin, of Trotsky, of Mao . . . of Pol Pot."[5]

Why did the communist utopias of the Soviet Union, China, and Cambodia become history's greatest slaughterhouses? I argue that radical communist regimes have proven such prodigious killers primarily because the social changes they sought to bring about have resulted in the sudden and nearly complete material and political dispossession of millions of people. These regimes practiced social engineering of the highest order. It is the revolutionary desire to bring about the rapid and radical transformation of society that distinguishes radical communist regimes from all other forms of government, including less violent communist regimes and noncommunist, authoritarian governments.

The "dictatorship of the proletariat" is a dictatorship unlike any other. It is difficult to overstate the extent and the dispossessive impact of the social and economic transformation that leaders such as Lenin, Stalin, Mao, and Pol Pot imposed upon their countries. The social transformation sought by radical communist regimes has been far more extensive than the mere monopoly of political power and curtailment of individual liberties characteristic of authoritarian regimes. The latter have succeeded in maintaining power and suppressing internal political dissent with comparatively low levels of violence.[6] Radical communist policies, on the other hand, have often had the effect of completely dispossessing vast numbers of people, stripping them of their personal belongings, the products of their labor, their land, their homes, and their livelihood. The most radical communist visions have aimed at crushing all vestiges of individualism and creating a fundamentally new kind of human being.[7]

Social transformations of this speed and magnitude have been associated with mass killing for two primary reasons. First, the massive social dislocations produced by such changes have often led to economic collapse, epidemics, and, most important, widespread famine. Indeed, famine was one of the primary vehicles of mass killing in the Soviet Union, China, and Cambodia. Famines took the lives of perhaps seven million people in the Soviet Union, thirty million in China, and at least seven hundred thousand in Cambodia.[8] Although not all the deaths due to famine in these cases were intentional, communist leaders directed the worst effects of famine against their suspected enemies and used hunger as a weapon to force millions of people to conform to the directives of the state.

The second reason that communist regimes bent on the radical transformation of society have been linked to mass killing is that the revolutionary changes they have pursued have clashed inexorably with the fundamental interests of large segments of their populations. Few people have proved willing to accept such far-reaching sacrifices without the most intense levels of coercion. This fundamental dynamic of revolutionary change did not escape Machiavelli, whose insights into the nexus of violence and politics have survived almost five hundred years. In *The Prince*, Machiavelli cautioned that "nothing is more difficult to handle, more doubtful of success, and more dangerous to carry through than initiating changes in a state's constitution. The innovator makes enemies of all those who prosper under the old order, and only lukewarm support is forthcoming from those who would prosper under the new." Only those leaders who "can depend on their own resources and force the issue," he concluded, will succeed in bringing about a new order—"that is why all armed prophets have conquered and unarmed prophets have come to grief."[9]

Like Machiavelli, radical communist leaders have well understood that violence and terror can serve, in Marx's words, as the "the midwife of revolution." As Leon Trotsky explained, "the historical tenacity of the bourgeoisie is colossal. It holds to power, and does not wish to abandon it. . . . We are forced to tear off this class and chop it away. The Red Terror is a weapon used against a class that, despite being doomed to destruction, does not wish to perish."[10] Indeed, the attempt to impose communism has often led to violent uprisings, some on a truly massive scale.

As Alexander Dallin and George Breslauer conclude in their study of communist violence, a radical communist regime

> committed as it is to substantial transformations—whether for ideological or power related reasons—is bound to encounter and generate resistance and alienation, since the changes it is determined to carry out will necessarily clash with the values and perceived interests of some significant sectors of society. Anticipating such hostility, the authorities, in line with their preconceptions and images of class or group loyalties and grievances, may identify certain strata as requiring preemptive, or prophylactic, suppression, intimidation or removal.[11]

Communist leaders in the Soviet Union, China, and Cambodia did not set out with the goal of exterminating millions of people. They expected resistance from certain classes, but they hoped that most people would come to appreciate the superiority of the new way life they were trying to create, even if they suspected that this appreciation might require substantial "reeducation." Communist leaders did not shy away from violence, however, when they came to believe—sometimes in the wake of genuine opposition to their policies and sometimes because of their preconceived notions about the nature and sources of such opposition—that it was necessary to build and protect the revolutionary society they wanted to bring about.

In some cases, communist regimes have utilized "selective" killing to deter organized resistance and coerce active compliance with their policies. Specific individuals or groups accused of resistance were openly killed in the effort to intimidate many others. As Trotsky described it:

> Terror can be very efficient against a reactionary class. . . . Intimidation is a powerful weapon of policy, both internationally and internally. War, like revolution, is founded upon intimidation. A victorious war, generally speaking, destroys only an insignificant part of the conquered army, intimidating the remainder and breaking their will. The revolution works in the same way: it kills individuals, and intimidates thousands. In this sense, the Red Terror is not distinguishable from the armed insurrection, the direct continuation of which it represents.[12]

To ensure the greatest impact on the largest possible audience, communist perpetrators often have carried out such killings with studied brutality and in highly public places. The Chinese communists referred to this technique as "killing chickens to scare monkeys."[13] Historically, this kind of violence has proved highly effective in breaking organized resistance to both moderate communist and noncommunist authoritarian regimes. Communist leaders in the Soviet Union, China, and Cambodia, however, were not satisfied with the results of selective terror and political repression.

The ponderous death toll of communism in these states was driven not simply by the real threats posed by suspected counterrevolutionary groups and classes, but also by the adherence of communist leaders to a paranoid Marxist-Leninist or, perhaps more accurately, Stalinist worldview that vastly exaggerated the origin and scope of these threats. This worldview was characterized by the related beliefs that powerful opponents of the communist transformation of society were lurking everywhere and that certain social groups or economic classes were inescapably bound by their "class consciousness" to oppose communism through all available means. These beliefs led communist leaders to undertake massive prophylactic campaigns of violence and imprisonment designed to permanently subjugate or physically eliminate large social or political groups believed to stand in the way of the communization of society.

These fears were partly a consequence of the personal paranoia of individual communist leaders like Stalin, Mao, and Pol Pot. They also were powerfully shaped, however, by the same Marxist ideology that drove these men to seek the communist transformation of society in the first place. Marxist analysis suggested that a person's class background largely determined his or her behavior and attitudes. Marx himself put it most succinctly: "circumstances make men just as much as men make circumstances."[14] In its most radical interpretations, this ideology seemed to imply that class consciousness was somehow biologically determined and that individuals could never truly leave behind their social origins — an implication that Marx, a believer in the infinite malleability of human nature, almost certainly would have rejected.[15] This interpretation, in turn, led naturally, and fatefully, to the presumption that as long as members of supposedly reactionary classes survived, they would continue to pose a grave threat to the communist system.

Indeed, in the eyes of Stalin, Mao, and Pol Pot, the communist transformation of society remained surprisingly fragile even years after the revolution. They believed that resistance by reactionary classes would not end with the establishment of a communist state. Rather, the enemies of communism would continue organizing in secret for decades after the revolution, garnering support from capitalist forces abroad and infiltrating communist political organizations in the hopes of reversing the communist transformation of society. This ultra-paranoid vision led to its most murderous consequences under Stalin. As Stalin explained it to his fellow party members in 1929, "there have been no cases in history where dying classes have voluntarily departed from the scene. There have been no cases in history where the dying bourgeoisie has not exerted all its remaining strength to preserve its existence. . . . [T]hey feel their last days are approaching and are compelled to resist with all the forces and all the means in their power."[16]

These fears contributed to the belief that the only sure way to protect the communist system from its class enemies was to suppress these groups as a whole and prophylactically, not on the basis of individual involvement in known counterrevolutionary activities. Thus, Martin Latsis, the first deputy chairman of the Cheka, Lenin's internal police, instructed his comrades:

> We are not waging war against individual persons. We are exterminating the bourgeoisie as a class. During the investigation, do not look for evidence that the accused acted in deed or word against the Soviet regime. The first questions that you ought to put are: To what class does he belong? What is his origin? What is his education and his profession? And it is these questions that ought to determine the fate of the accused. In this lies the significance and essence of the Red Terror.[17]

In practice, communist notions of class have almost always failed to match the more complex realities of the societies upon which they have been imposed. Identifying members of supposedly parasitic groups such as landlords and kulaks has usually proved easier in communist propaganda than it has on the ground. Peasants themselves often failed to recognize communist theoretical distinctions between rural classes. Family, ethnic, or national loyalties repeatedly proved stronger than those of class. In the Soviet Union, China, and Cambodia these difficulties forced the communists to rely on simplistic and apparently arbitrary formulas and quota systems, often requiring that each village designate a certain percentage of its population as class enemies. Under such circumstances, nationality and race often became substitutes for the elastic notion of class, producing an ever longer list of victims.[18] The ensuing campaigns for the "liquidation" of entire social groups often resulted in violence on a massive scale. Because the paranoid communist worldview described above left little room for the reformation of individuals from suspect classes, many communist leaders concluded that execution or lifelong imprisonment were the only appropriate responses to the threat of counterrevolutionary subversion.

THE COMMUNIST SOCIOECONOMIC TRANSFORMATION AND POLITICAL TERROR

The strategic approach suggests that communist mass killings result from the effort to implement policies of radical social or economic transformation and to protect that transformation from real and perceived enemies. Communist regimes have also engaged in mass killing for a variety of other reasons mostly unrelated to communism itself. I will not describe these killings here, although one such case, the mass killing during the Soviet occupation of Afghanistan from 1979 to 1988, will be discussed in chapter 6.

Rather, in this chapter I will focus on violence associated with motives directly connected to the implementation of communism. This kind of mass killing has assumed two primary and related forms. The first and by far the most deadly form has been the systematic violence associated with the implementation of radical communist agrarian policies. Second, communist regimes have killed large numbers of people in sweeping political purges directed against suspected enemies in society at large and within the communist party itself.

Mass Killing and the Communist Transformation in the Countryside

The implementation of radical communist agrarian policies, especially agricultural collectivization, was the occasion for the most deadly instances of mass killings in the Soviet Union, China, and Cambodia. There are three primary reasons for the close association between mass killing and radical agrarian policies such as collectivization.

First, policies that entail the removal of large numbers of peasants from their land, the establishment of large collective farms, or the confiscation of most or all of the harvest have proven extremely difficult to implement in the absence of high levels of violent coercion. Peasants depend directly upon their land for their survival and their way of life. It is not surprising, therefore, that they usually place a very high value on it, along with the freedom to farm it as they see fit, and the right to benefit from the products of their labor. Even those agricultural workers who do not own farms themselves almost universally aspire to land ownership. The imposition of radical agrarian policies in the Soviet Union, China, and Cambodia was anathema to these fundamental peasant goals and interests, and peasants responded to them with multiple forms of resistance. In the Soviet Union, and to a lesser degree in China and Cambodia, peasants ultimately resorted to armed revolt to protect their freedom, property, and livelihoods. Communist leaders thus faced a stark choice between retreating from radical agricultural reforms and coercing the peasantry into accepting a deeply unpopular new way of life. The leaders of the Soviet Union, China, and Cambodia opted for communism over compromise. Because the peasantry constituted the most populous social class in all three countries, the number of victims of these policies was staggering.

The second reason that radical communist agrarian policies have been associated with such high levels of violence is that the architects of these policies have often perceived the social transformation of the countryside to require not only the elimination of preexisting forms of agricultural production but also the destruction of the institutions and traditions that supported the peasants' way of life. In the effort to gain the unprecedented degree of control over the day-to-day activities of millions of lives that their policies required, communist leaders often have sought the subjugation of all other local forms of power, organization, and loyalty. Radical communist agricultural campaigns, therefore, frequently have coincided with an assault on the other pillars of peasant life — religion, national, or ethnic loyalties, traditional systems of village leadership and political organization, and in some cases, even the family unit itself. The result of this assault has been simultaneously to increase resistance to communist policies and to multiply the number of potential targets of communist coercion and violence.

The third reason for the relationship between radical communist agrarian policies and mass killings is that such policies have often led to severely decreased agricultural productivity, especially in the period immediately following their implementation. When combined with the massive expropriation of agricultural products that has also been a hallmark of radical communist agrarian policies, even a moderate shortfall in the harvest can result in widespread starvation.[19] As noted above, collectivization sparked massive famines in each of the three states studied in this chapter. Not all of the deaths resulting from these famines represent mass killing as defined in this study. Communist leaders did not intend to cause many of these deaths. Nevertheless, in all three cases the famine was intentionally exacerbated by the regime, or directed against certain segments of the population. In all three cases, communist leaders refused to back away from their radical policies even after they had received credible reports that a major famine was taking place. Rather, leaders blamed food shortages on peasant grain hoarding or sabotage. They exported grain from famine-stricken regions and implemented internal passport systems designed to prevent peasants from fleeing to the cities or other areas where the famine was less severe. In the case of the Soviet Union, at least, there is strong evidence that Soviet authorities used hunger as a weapon to crush peasant resistance to collectivization. Deaths associated with these kinds of policies meet the criteria for mass killing because the regimes in question deliberately created conditions that they reasonably could have expected to result in widespread death.

Mass Killing, Terror, and Communist Political Purges

In addition to mass killings directly associated with the implementation of communism in the countryside, the communist regimes of the Soviet Union, China, and Cambodia each engaged in massive political purges of suspected enemies in society and in the communist party. The targets of these purges included current and former members of opposition political parties, moderates within the communist party, intellectuals, artists, religious, ethnic, or nationalist leaders, and a myriad of other suspected political opponents of the regime. These purges have often been portrayed as attempts by power-hungry communist leaders to gain absolute personal power for its own sake. I contend, however, that the purges were motivated primarily by leaders' efforts to protect and extend the communist transformation of their societies, a utopian project in which they genuinely believed.

In the Soviet Union, China, and Cambodia the most violent political purges were largely a response to political opposition that emerged during the communization of the countryside and were launched shortly after the spectacular failure of radical communist agrarian policies. The disastrous effects of these policies engendered opposition not only among their peasant victims but within the party itself. Communist party members began calling, in some cases openly, for a retreat from the most excessive communist policies.

If Stalin, Mao, and Pol Pot merely had been concerned with maintaining a grip on power, they could have easily reached a compromise with moderates in their party. Radical policies could have been rolled back. It is not possible to understand why these communist leaders reacted so violently to the prospect of political opposition without appreciating that they believed it threatened not merely their personal leadership, but their most deeply held goals. In order to ensure that these goals would be implemented even at the lowest levels of the party hierarchy, they sought to eliminate from their political organizations not only proven enemies but anyone lacking the proper revolutionary spirit.

Of course, communist leaders probably could have protected their vision for society with considerably less violence than they ultimately employed. The political purges in the Soviet Union, China, and Cambodia eventually assumed such massive proportions in large part due to communist leaders' perceptions that the opposition was far more widespread and potent than it was in reality. In particular, communist leaders in all three countries expressed fears that the party would be subverted from within by elements of the former ruling classes. These fears ultimately led to the repression of virtually anyone who expressed views that diverged even superficially from official communist doctrine. Individuals with only the flimsiest ties to the so-called reactionary classes came to be seen as implacable enemies of communism. It is tempting to dismiss the fantastically paranoid views of communist leaders as merely rhetorical justification for actions motivated by more objective or realistic concerns, but there are strong indications that these beliefs were sincerely held. Paranoid remarks pepper internal party documents as well as private communications.[20] Although this paranoia appears to have invaded even the personal lives of Stalin, Mao, and Pol Pot, it should not be attributed solely to their personal psychological aberrations. Rather, this mind set was intertwined deeply with the radical variant of Marxism to which each of these men subscribed.

THE SOVIET UNION

The Transformation of the Countryside

The collectivization of agriculture in the Soviet Union in the late 1920s and early 1930s was the world's first experiment with full-fledged communist agriculture. The socialization of agricultural production in some shape or form had been a central goal of the Bolsheviks ever since they attained power. Collectivization served two related purposes for the new regime. The first was essentially ideological. Private agriculture formed the basis of the Soviet economy at the time of the revolution. Until this vast reservoir of private property and production could be brought under the central control of the state, the Soviet Union would remain communist in name only.[21] The second purpose was more practical in nature, although many of the assumptions underlying it were also rooted in Marxist theory. Many Soviet leaders were convinced that the rapid industrialization of the economy was essential if the Soviet Union ever hoped to "catch up and overtake" the West. They also believed, however, that the resources needed for this massive effort could be obtained only through the exploitation of the country's vast agricultural resources. Food products collected from the countryside would be used to feed the burgeoning industrial work force at rock-bottom prices and the remainder sold for export. Collectivizing Russia's millions of individual peasant holdings into vast farms would dramatically increase agricultural productivity by rationalizing farming practices, achieving economies of scale, and facilitating the mechanization of agriculture. Centralizing agricultural production would also increase the state's ability to expropriate the surpluses of this expanded harvest. Thus, from the time of the revolution the question was not whether the state would seek to gain control of agriculture, but exactly when and how it would do so.

Soviet leaders had little love for the peasantry, whom most communists saw as hopelessly backward and uncivilized.[22] Nevertheless, for self-interested reasons, the regime hoped that the transition to communist agriculture would occur relatively peacefully. When external exigencies made industrialization seem a matter of great urgency and when the intensity of peasant opposition to collectivization became apparent, however, Soviet leaders did not hesitate to resort to violence on an unprecedented scale.

The First Socialist Offensive — War Communism

The communists' first efforts to wrest control of agriculture from the peasants began in 1918 in the midst of the Russian civil war. Under the banner of what would come to be known as "war communism," the Bolsheviks enacted a number of sweeping measures designed to bring the Soviet economy under the central control of the state. In the cities, the Bolsheviks nationalized industry, finance, and urban real estate. Private commerce and money were abolished and replaced by a state-run distribution system. War communism had its most powerful impact, however, in the countryside, where the vast majority of the Soviet population lived. War communism abolished the free market for agricultural products and replaced it with a system of forced grain requisitions. Peasants were per-

mitted to keep a small, predetermined amount of their harvest for subsistence, but they were forced to surrender the rest to the state in return
for currency or for industrial goods at fixed exchange rates well below
market values. Since inflation had rendered the ruble virtually worthless,
however, and since promised manufactured goods often failed to materialize, the policy frequently amounted to outright expropriation. Collective and state-run farms were also introduced on a small scale in this
period, but the fundamental aim of rural war communism was simply to
obtain as much of the peasants' grain as cheaply as possible to feed the
Red Army and the workers in the cities.

Historians contest whether Lenin and other Soviet leaders considered
war communism to be a temporary emergency measure mandated by the
exigencies of the civil war or whether it represented an ideologically motivated effort to apply Marxist principles to the economy. Both positions
probably hold some measure of truth. The war may have called for drastic measures, but the measures the Bolsheviks chose were determined
largely by their Marxist faith.[23] Many Bolsheviks would have preferred
to delay the confrontation with the peasantry until after the civil war
when the rural transformation could have been accomplished more gradually or, conversely, more rapidly and effectively, with the undivided resources of the state behind it. Ultimately, the war simply seems to have
accelerated the execution of policies that the Bolsheviks likely would have
instituted eventually even in the absence of war. From the point of view
of the peasantry, however, the rationale behind these policies was of little
interest, since the result, expropriation, was the same.

The Bolsheviks expected resistance to the policies of war communism
from the so-called kulaks, the richest strata of the peasantry. In fact, the
vast majority of the peasantry proved bitterly opposed to the expropriation of the products of their labor.[24] At first, peasants reacted to state
requisitioning with passive economic resistance. They decreased production, increased their private consumption, sold their produce on the black
market, and concealed their harvest from the authorities. When nonviolent requisitioning efforts failed to increase procurement of grain as much
as expected, however, the Soviet regime responded to peasant resistance
with higher quotas and increasingly brutal measures. Requisitioning
soon began to eat away at the peasants' subsistence crops and seed stocks,
contributing to a massive famine in 1921–22 in which as many as five million people may have perished.[25] In what would become a self-fulfilling
prophecy, many Bolsheviks viewed peasant resistance as the deliberate attempt to sabotage the revolution. Paramilitary "food detachments" and
units of the Red Army were dispatched to the countryside with orders to
gather food by whatever means necessary.[26] Lenin personally ordered

that those suspected of hoarding grain be subject to public execution.[27] Torture became common practice. Peasant families frequently were held hostage until grain quotas were delivered. What began as economic resistance rapidly developed into a full-scale civil war between the peasants and the Soviet regime.[28]

These peasant wars intensified following the defeat of the Whites in 1920. The rebellions drew on a much broader base of support than had the White armies. Lenin felt they posed a greater threat to the revolution than had the civil war itself.[29] Indeed, if not for the lack of political and military coordination between the diverse peasant opposition groups, these uprisings might well have toppled the regime.[30] Although Lenin did not hesitate to use the most violent means at his disposal to crush the rebellions, he ultimately decided that the only way to safeguard the new Soviet state was to appease the peasants by abandoning the policies of war communism. Nevertheless, so vehement had peasant opposition to the new regime become that unrest continued in some regions until 1924. As Orlando Figes sums up the situation in the early 1920s, "having defeated the White army, backed by eight Western powers, the Bolshevik government surrendered before its own peasantry."[31]

Retreat and Compromise: The NEP

The so-called New Economic Policy (NEP), introduced in March 1921, marked a significant retreat from both the ideological and pragmatic goals that had motivated the imposition of war communism. Excessive forced requisitions were replaced by a more moderate tax in kind, calculated as a percentage of the harvest. Peasants were permitted to sell the remainder of their harvest on the free market. Most Bolsheviks were prepared to accept the NEP as a tactical retreat, but many did so with deep reservations. Without firm state control over agriculture, the socialist ideals of the revolution remained largely unrealized. Worse yet, until the state could mobilize the agricultural surplus of the countryside for industrialization, they feared that the Soviet Union would lag behind the West in military production, rendering it vulnerable to "capitalist encirclement" and attack.[32] The intervention of foreign powers in Russia's civil war had made these fears even more pressing. In addition, the failure of other socialist revolutions to gain power in Europe in the wake of the First World War meant that the Soviet Union would have to rely on its own resources to industrialize and defend itself in a world that seemed increasingly hostile.

By the mid-twenties, following the death of Lenin, a serious split began to emerge within the Communist Party over the future of the NEP. The first camp, represented most prominently by Trotsky, argued that the concessions to the peasantry had gone too far and that the policies of the NEP were simply strengthening the forces most hostile to socialism. The time was ripe, they insisted, for a new "socialist offensive" in the countryside. The second camp, represented by Nikolai Bukharin, did not dispute the necessity of gaining state control over agriculture, but feared the country might not survive another all-out confrontation with the peasants. They contended that the countryside could be eased gradually into socialism through the application of market pressures rather than violence and coercion.[33] Stalin initially subscribed to the second view, although there are some indications that he was privately skeptical of the NEP from the outset, believing it represented a betrayal of the revolution's communist ideals.[34] Indeed, Stalin's public support of the NEP, among other differences, led Trotsky to brand him as "the gravedigger of the revolution" at a Politburo gathering in 1926.[35] Stalin's faction prevailed in the bitter internal debate over the issue. Trotsky was removed from the Politburo in 1926 and ultimately expelled along with his supporters from the party in 1927.

Two major developments, however, occurred between late 1926 and 1928 that appear to have persuaded Stalin that the Soviet Union should undertake a radical change of course. By mid-1929 he was embarked on a policy of rapid, forced collectivization far more radical and violent than Trotsky had ever imagined.

The first development concerned the growing reality of the Soviet Union's political and economic isolation and the renewed fears of attack from the West. In late 1926 and early 1927, the Soviet Union was gripped by a series of war scares based on rumors that Poland and Germany, with the support of Britain and France, were conspiring to redraw the map of Eastern Europe at the expense of the Soviet Union. These rumors proved to be baseless, but were lent further credence by several other significant setbacks for Soviet foreign policy during the same period. In April 1927, Chiang Kai-shek broke his fragile alliance with the Chinese communists with a brutal crackdown, dashing the possibility of a communist takeover or even a friendly regime in China. Great Britain terminated diplomatic relations with the Soviet Union in May. The Soviet envoy in Warsaw was assassinated in June. In September, France expelled the Soviet ambassador.

As many historians have pointed out, the Soviet regime seized upon and exaggerated these developments for domestic propaganda purposes.[36] Yet these events also seem to have reinforced real, long-standing fears of Soviet isolation and vulnerability and added greater urgency to the belief that something had to be done to address the Soviet Union's weakness vis-à-vis the West. Commenting on the timing of the collectivization drive many years later, V. M. Molotov, the former foreign minister of the Soviet Union, recalled, "We couldn't have delayed it any longer. Fascism was emerging. Soon it would have been too late. War was already looming on the horizon."[37] As John Sontag concludes, "There can be no doubt that belief in a foreign conspiracy had become a basic factor in Soviet calculations by 1928 and strongly influenced economic decisions taken in that and subsequent years."[38]

The second development was the severe grain crisis that struck the Soviet Union in 1927 and 1928. By the end of 1927 the amount of grain procured by the state fell to half of its 1926 level.[39] The shortfall was probably the result of a variety of factors including poor weather, widespread hoarding due to the war scare, and, most important, misguided Soviet economic policies that discouraged peasants from growing grain or selling what they did grow to the official state agencies.[40] Stalin and other party leaders were increasingly inclined to view peasant reluctance to sell grain to the state not as rational economic behavior but as deliberate attempts to undermine socialism and sabotage the regime.[41] By early 1928 Soviet leaders feared impending famine and workers' strikes in the cities and worried that they lacked the food necessary even to feed the Red Army. Once more, the regime appeared to be in critical danger.

The grain crisis seems finally to have convinced Stalin that economic incentives would not succeed in substantially increasing state grain procurements or productivity in the countryside.[42] Since the introduction of the NEP, a variety of tax and price incentives and efforts at political education had been tried in an attempt to increase grain procurements and encourage peasants to join collective farms. These efforts not only failed to achieve their desired effect, they resulted in a substantial decline in agricultural procurement by the state. The regime's efforts to encourage the formation of collective farms using economic incentives and educational programs had proved even less successful. Indeed, by 1927 state and collective farms still accounted for less than 2 percent of cultivated land. Peasant farming methods remained antiquated and far less productive compared to the highly mechanized forms of agriculture then coming into widespread practice in much of Europe and the United States.[43]

Ultimately, Stalin seems to have concluded that the state could not acquire more grain from the peasants without substantially raising the price it was willing to pay for it. Paying higher prices, however, would further delay the rapid industrialization that Stalin believed was critical for the survival and success of the regime. Given the urgent nature of the grain crisis and the growing perception of impending international conflict, Stalin felt that the Soviet Union could not afford the time to find out if Bukharin's socialism "at a snail's pace" would eventually succeed in increasing grain procurement or encouraging peasants to form collective farms. Moreover, raising prices would represent yet another concession to capitalism and to the independent political and economic power of the peasantry at the expense of the goals of the state. Ten years after the revolution, these compromises were increasingly difficult to reconcile with progress toward a communist society.

Thus, Stalin lashed out at those who said the regime "had no option but to make concessions to the peasants": "This is a defeatist attitude which betrays a lack of faith in socialist construction. What if the middle peasants went so far as to insist on concessions over the monopoly on foreign trade, or demanded a peasants' union? Would we have to give in over these too? This is defeatism. Our strength lies in the [collective farms], and in our efforts to activize the poor peasantry."[44]

Historians, like many within the Soviet leadership at the time, have disputed nearly all of Stalin's central assumptions during this period.[45] Was the grain crisis in fact as severe as it was made out to be? Had the NEP truly failed by the late 1920s, or could it have been repaired? Were large-scale collective farms actually more productive than existing farming methods might have been with only minor improvements? Was the regime's economic model of industrialization through the exploitation of agriculture a sound one to begin with? Whatever the objective reality of the situation facing the Soviet Union in the late 1920s, however, it is clear that Stalin and his followers had reached their own answers to these questions. These answers led them to conclude that the crash collectivization of agriculture was the only available means to simultaneously protect the Soviet state and advance its socialist ideals.

The Great Turn: Collectivization

Because Stalin felt that economic incentives and political education had failed, he believed that a certain degree of coercion would be necessary to meet the state's need for grain. Even Stalin, however, did not anticipate the need for violence on the massive scale that ultimately transpired during collectivization. Under the banner of "emergency measures," coercive methods began to be applied in some grain producing regions in January 1928. In many areas, free markets were closed. Peasants who refused to sell their surpluses to collectors at the state's price were subject to prison terms of up to five years and the confiscation of their property. For many peasants, these policies recalled the years of war communism. The harsh measures initially succeeded in increasing state procurements, but many peasants reacted as they had before — by decreasing their production of grain, hiding their harvest, and in some cases violently resisting Soviet authorities.[46] At least partly as a result, the harvest of 1928 continued to decline from its 1926 level, and procurements dropped even further in the winter of 1928–29. For Stalin, this latest round of resistance was only further evidence of intentional sabotage and the resilience of reactionary class-consciousness among the peasantry.

In a lengthy speech to the Central Committee in 1929, he attacked his former ally Bukharin and his supporters for their assertion that it was still possible to "persuade the class enemy to voluntarily forgo his interests and voluntarily deliver his grain surpluses to us": "Have they lost their senses? Is it not obvious that they do not understand the mechanics of the class struggle, that they do not know what classes are? Do they know how the kulaks jeer at our officials at village meetings called to promote procurements? . . . Try to persuade people like that. Class is class, comrades. You cannot get away from that truth."[47]

Stalin publicly blamed the procurement problems only on the kulaks, but he was increasingly convinced that any long-term reconciliation with an independent peasantry on terms favorable to the regime was impossible.[48] The experiences of the first half of 1928 had also made it clear that the party lacked adequate control in the countryside to coerce millions of individual peasant farmers to hand over their grain and that, in any case, doing so year after year would be a monumentally inefficient way to collect the agricultural surplus.[49] By the middle of 1928, therefore, Stalin appears to have concluded that even moderate levels of coercion could not be a permanent solution to the Soviet Union's agricultural problems without much deeper structural reforms. The regime needed to find a way to increase its ability to collect grain without decreasing agricultural productivity. The answer was large-scale collectivization.

Since Stalin believed that the survival of the regime depended on an immediate solution to the agricultural problem, and since the peasantry, who had violently resisted less intrusive state policies in the past, were certain to resist collectivization even more actively, the program would have to be carried out with utmost haste and virtually unlimited coercion. As Walter Lauquer concludes, "Had he seen another, less wasteful way to achieve his aim, he might well have adopted it. . . . But Stalin believed that the NEP no longer worked in agriculture, that agricultural cooperatives (based on foreign patterns) would probably not function in the Soviet Union, and that, in any case, there was no time for patient persuasion, for teaching peasants by trial and error."[50]

Stalin spent the last half of 1928 and the first part of 1929 planning the offensive against the countryside and overcoming the resistance from Bukharin and others to the newly proposed policy of crash collectivization. An official trip to Siberia in the winter of 1928 also seems to have persuaded Stalin that local party organizations were too closely aligned with peasant interests and would have to be purged before more radical measures could be adopted.[51] The final assault on the peasantry did not begin formally until the autumn of 1929.

It is difficult to fathom the magnitude and pace of the changes wrought by this policy on the peasantry of the Soviet Union. From 1929 to 1936, more than 130 million people were forced into 240,000 collectives, most in the three years between 1931 and 1934.[52] Collectivization completely transformed peasant life in the Soviet Union as the decision-making power of individuals and villages was suddenly replaced by the edicts of centralized state bureaucracies. Peasants were required to pool their land, farming implements, and livestock in large associations. New methods of farming were introduced. The peasants in effect became poorly paid laborers on what had once been their own farms. Even the poorest peasants complained to Soviet officials that "you turned us into worse than serfs."[53] The transformation was especially traumatic for the nomadic herding peoples of the steppe. For them, collectivization not only entailed the loss of land and imposition of state control over their economic production, but also submission to an entirely new, sedentary way of life. In Kazakhstan alone, nearly four hundred thousand households were forcibly settled between 1930 and 1936.[54]

As Lynne Viola describes it, the peasants believed that "collectivization was apocalypse, a war between the forces of evil and the forces of good. . . . They understood it as a battle over their culture and way of life, as pillage, injustice, and wrong. . . . Removed from the distorting lens of official propaganda, belief and perception, collectivization was a clash of cultures, a civil war."[55] It is hardly surprising that many Soviet peasants chose to fight this onslaught with virtually every means at their disposal. At first, the peasants resisted with largely nonviolent means. They refused to meet unreasonably high grain quotas. Many chose to slaughter farm animals or destroy their property before it could be turned over to the collectives. As communist pressure intensified, however, peasants increasingly turned to public anti-Soviet demonstrations, vandalism, arson, and violent attacks on local representatives of the Communist Party. In some regions, particularly the northern Caucasus and the Ukraine, the Soviet regime was faced with full-scale civil war as peasants fought back against local Soviet officials.[56]

The Soviet regime met all forms of peasant resistance with extreme brutality. Heavily armed units of the state political police and sometimes the Red Army were dispatched to the countryside to requisition grain, crush political resistance, and force the peasants into the collectives. Violence, however, was not reserved for individuals who had demonstrated active resistance to collectivization. Millions were targeted because their supposed kulak class background was simply assumed to have rendered them irreconcilably opposed to collectivization. Stalin believed that the experiences of the late 1920s had proven that a certain segment of the peasantry was essentially incapable of reform and would never submit to Soviet power. Indeed, it was during these years that Stalin had begun vocally propounding his theory that the class enemies of socialism would not retreat as the revolution progressed, but rather would resist even more fiercely as their property was expropriated and their prerogatives eliminated.[57] Pointing to the growing number of reports exposing kulak influence in so-called "false collectives"—farms that had been established during the NEP but had refused to hand over their grain during the grain crisis—party radicals concluded that if kulaks were admitted to the new collectives they would simply sabotage them from within.[58] Thus in December 1929 Stalin issued his infamous order calling for the "liquidation of the kulaks as a class" and proclaiming that "dekulakization is now an essential element in forming and developing the collective farms. . . . Of course it is wrong to admit the kulak into the collective farm. It is wrong because he is an accursed enemy of the collective farm movement."[59]

Various definitions of the term "kulak" were employed over the course of the campaign, and its interpretation was subject to vast differences at the local level. In some cases, having hired a single employee to help with the harvest or having owned a single cow was enough to make the difference between life and death. Status as a kulak before the revolution was enough to classify one as a kulak more than ten years later, since, as Robert Conquest notes, official policy during the campaign maintained that "a man's having at some time in the past fulfilled the conditions of a Marxist-devised class categorization is a matter of 'essence' which no later change can alter. . . . Thus, by a strange logic, a middle peasant could become a kulak by gaining property, but a kulak could not become a middle peasant by losing his. In fact the kulak had no escape. He was 'essentially' a class enemy, a sub-human."[60] Kulak family members, including young children, were subject to punishment through the same logic. Eventually the term came to be applied not only to supposedly rich peasants but to anyone suspected of resisting collectivization for any reason. Religious leaders, traditional village elites, former officers in the White armies and other "socially dangerous elements" were targeted in the effort to destroy all noncommunist sources of power in the countryside.

Stalin's call for the liquidation of the kulaks was not meant as a mandate for their systematic extermination, but in practice, dekulakization took an enormous toll in human life.[61] The most fortunate kulaks simply had their property confiscated or were exiled to the outskirts of their village. Others were permanently deported to Siberia, often with little or no provision made for their survival. Many were arrested or simply executed on the spot. In the first months of 1930, the pace and destructiveness of some local dekulakization drives appear to have exceeded Moscow's directives, resulting in such severe economic disruptions that the state was forced to retreat from collectivization temporarily until it could regain control over the campaign.[62]

From 1929 to 1936, between 8.5 million and 14.5 million people probably perished in the violence and famine associated with collectivization.[63] A third or more of the victims of collectivization were shot outright or died during deportation, in exile, or in labor camps.[64] In the years that followed, more died in forced labor camps and "special settlements" in the barren wastes of Siberia. The campaign was so violent that Leszek Kolakowski concludes it was "probably the most massive warlike operation ever conducted by a state against its own citizens."[65]

The majority of the victims of collectivization, however, died during the massive famine of 1932–33. Much of the shortfall in food production during these years was a result of unintended economic inefficiencies and dislocations produced by the rapid shift to the collective farming system. Drought also contributed to the abnormally small harvest. There is considerable evidence, however, that at least in certain regions, communist leaders intentionally exacerbated the famine with the intent of eliminating class enemies and crushing peasant resistance to collectivization. Soviet leaders, including Stalin, were well aware that a major famine had gripped the countryside in 1932.[66] Nikita Khrushchev later admitted that "we knew . . . that people were dying in enormous numbers."[67] Stalin believed that the peasants were simply hoarding grain and accused *them* of waging a "war of starvation" against the Soviet Union.[68] Yet the regime continued to confiscate large amounts of grain from famine-stricken regions and refused to release grain reserves. Harsh penalties, including execution, were levied against anyone caught stealing grain. A system of internal passports and police checkpoints was initiated which prevented starving peasants from seeking food or work elsewhere. Expropriation of grain was targeted against suspect classes or anyone who refused to join the collectives. Hunger was employed to coerce peasants — except the wealthiest kulaks, who were to be deported or executed — to join the collectives, where food was at least somewhat more plentiful.

Some scholars have argued that Stalin deliberately engineered the famine in an effort to crush nationalist movements in the Ukraine, Kazakhstan, and elsewhere.[69] It is true that these areas suffered the greatest loss of life during collectivization. Perhaps 5 million perished in the Ukraine and 1.5 million may have died in Kazakhstan.[70] In retrospect, however, the Communist Party's desire to eliminate nationalism in these regions appears to have been secondary to its desire to collectivize agriculture.[71] Large numbers of ethnic Russians also died in the famine.[72] Regions like the Ukraine suffered the most because peasants made up the overwhelming majority of the population there, and because these areas represented the major grain producing regions of the Soviet Union. Partly because of nationalist sentiments, and partly because these regions had the most to lose from the communization of agriculture, peasant resistance to collectivization and Soviet repression were greatest there.[73] As one party official explained to a subordinate during the campaign, "a ruthless struggle is going on between the peasantry and our regime. . . . It's a struggle to the death. . . . It took a famine to show them who is master here. It has cost millions of lives, but the collective farm is here to stay. We've won the war."[74]

Political Purges and Terror

Stalin's Great Terror gripped the Soviet Union from 1936 to 1939. Many authors have portrayed this brutal period as a consequence of Stalin's unrelenting drive to accumulate absolute power for himself and for the Soviet state. Stalin has often been portrayed, both by historians and by his contemporaries, as the consummate political opportunist, willing to espouse radically different ideas whenever it suited his agenda. Robert Conquest, for example, suggests that following the completion of the collectivization of agriculture in 1934, Stalin should have been ready to "consolidate and perhaps to relax, to reestablish the Party's links with the people, and to reconcile the embittered elements in the Party itself. Such were the ideas that seem to have entered the minds of many of the new Stalinist leadership. But they did not enter Stalin's. His aim remained . . . unchallenged power. So far he had brutalized the Party, but he had not yet enslaved it."[75]

This interpretation seems only partially accurate. There can be little doubt that Stalin's personality played a major role in both the initiation and course of the terror. He did seek virtually unlimited power. Stalin's ambition, however, was not simply to gain personal power for its own sake. Rather, the terror seems to have been motivated by Stalin's desire — shared by some other high-ranking radical party members — to protect the Soviet state and the radical transformation of society he had fought so hard to build from what he perceived to be vast numbers of enemies both inside and outside the party. Stalin's seemingly opportunistic moves were a means, not simply to personal power, but to his vision for Soviet society. When it was expedient, he was willing to compromise on his methods, but there is little to suggest that he ever lost sight of this central vision. Thus, like many Bolsheviks, he had supported the NEP when he believed the regime lacked the power to pursue any other course and when the NEP still seemed a viable road to socialism and industrialization. Later, when the regime was stronger and when he concluded that the NEP would not achieve these ends, he abandoned it for harsher methods. In the aftermath of collectivization, Stalin came to believe that this vision was once again threatened. The impetus for the terror was primarily his reaction — or more accurately, overreaction — to this perceived threat. Indeed, in his famous secret speech in 1956 Khrushchev concluded his scathing account of Stalin's terror by stressing that "we cannot say that these were the deeds of a giddy despot. He considered that this should be done in the interests of the Party; of the working masses, in the name of the defense of the revolution's gains. In this lies the whole tragedy!"[76]

The results of purges were so profound that some have argued the terror constituted a "second revolution from above."[77] On the other hand, the terror was so intimately connected with collectivization that it is difficult to disagree with Leonard Schapiro's conclusion that "Stalin's revolution in agriculture and industry and his assault on the party which consummated this revolution must be seen as integrated parts of one and the same process."[78] As described above, in the late 1920s Stalin had won a major battle with party opponents by securing support for his radical policy of crash collectivization. Opponents of the policy were forced to recant and were removed from their high-ranking positions, but many of them, including most notably Bukharin, remained in the party.

Nevertheless, the disastrous results of collectivization seemed to vindicate the so-called right opposition in the party. Even those who cared little about collectivization's human consequences worried about its long-term effects on the economy and on the ability of the regime to maintain even a modicum of popular support.[79] Others were concerned that Stalin had accumulated too much power over the party, encouraging the formation of a "personality cult" and silencing all voices opposed to him. Although the party held together through the crisis, in private many party members, particularly the Old Bolsheviks, attacked Stalin and his radical policies.[80] Criticism was also forthcoming from the old left. Trotsky, who had been exiled from the Soviet Union in 1929, continued to lash out at Stalin from abroad, arguing that his approach to collectivization would bring the country to ruin and urging opposition factions from both left and right to launch a coup against him.

In 1932, a group of moderates headed by Mikhail Riutin, a former Moscow district secretary and supporter of Bukharin, began harshly criticizing Stalin's policies during collectivization, denouncing his dictatorial leadership style and calling for his removal by force if necessary.[81] In a lengthy report distributed to a number of key party members, Riutin and his supporters concluded that "the right wing has proven correct in the economic field and Trotsky in his criticism of the regime in the Party."[82] The report went on to propose a retreat from the economic policies of collectivization and rapid industrialization and the restoration of party democracy including the reinstatement of Trotsky.

Stalin's policies also spawned serious discontent at lower levels of the party. During collectivization, large numbers of low-level cadres demonstrated their reluctance to push forward with collectivization as rapidly as Stalin had demanded.[83] Even the Red Army had proved hostile to collectivization, raising serious doubts about its loyalty.[84] Stalin had launched collectivization and dekulakization in the belief that certain segments of the Soviet population were simply not prepared to embrace the transition to full-fledged communism. Now, it seemed to him, the same was true of the Communist Party itself. What the Stalinist leadership referred to as "the new situation" had emerged.

Stalin believed that the experience of collectivization had taught the enemies of communism that an open attack on the regime or its policies was impossible. Instead, they would now seek to undermine it from within.[85] Stalin described this outlandish vision to the Central Committee in January 1933, warning them that:

> The remnants of the dying classes — industrialists and their servants, private traders and their stooges, former nobles and priests, kulaks and their henchmen, former White officers and NCOs, former gendarmes and policemen — they have all wormed their way into our factories, our institutions and trading bodies, our railway and river transport enterprises and for the most part into our collective and state farms. They have wormed their way in and hidden themselves there, disguised as "workers" and "peasants," and some of them have even managed to worm their way into the party.
>
> What have they brought with them? Of course they have brought their hatred of the Soviet regime, their feeling of ferocious hostility to the new forms of the economy, way of life, culture. . . . The only thing left for them to do is to play dirty tricks and do harm to the workers and collective farmers. And they do this any way they can, on the quiet. They set fire to warehouses and break machinery. They organize sabotage. . . . Some of them . . . go so far in their wrecking activities as to inject livestock . . . with plague and anthrax, and encourage the spread of meningitis among horses and so on.[86]

Opposition to Stalin's policies may have been real and growing, but it probably never posed a major threat to his continued rule. Riutin and his supporters were arrested a few weeks after their first meeting. Opposition to Stalin throughout this period remained almost exclusively political. If Stalin had simply wished to maintain his hold on power, he probably could have reached a compromise with the right wing of the party. Such a compromise, however, would have involved at least a partial rollback of the socialist transformation Stalin believed was crucial to the survival and prosperity of the Soviet Union.

Yet, as J. Arch Getty and Oleg Naumov explain, such a compromise would have been unthinkable because it was simply

> impossible for leading Bolsheviks within the Stalinist faction to accept that their policies were wrong. Everything in their background and intellectual baggage told them that . . . in Stalin's general line they had found the correct solution to Russia's backwardness, to class oppression, and to the problems of capitalism. . . . Aside from their desire to protect their privileged position, they really believed in socialism and their key importance in realizing it. It was genuinely impossible to imagine that their policies were wrong.[87]

Although serious concerns regarding the activities of opposition groups within the regime emerged in 1932, there is no evidence that Stalin was considering a major purge until 1934. It was not until 1936 or 1937 that the terror began in earnest. Relatively small-scale purges and political repression occurred throughout this period, but these were carried out primarily by expulsion from the party, or more rarely by arrest and imprisonment. The pattern of massive arrests and extrajudicial executions had not yet materialized. High-ranking party members were generally spared arrest. Bukharin himself was not expelled from the party until 1937, and he avoided execution until 1938. Historians continue to debate the significance of these years. Many scholars believe that Stalin simply lacked the political power to launch a frontal attack on the party during this period.[88] Indeed, Stalin did seek to have Riutin executed in 1932, but moderates in the party who opposed the death penalty for party members convicted of political offenses appear to have thwarted his efforts.[89] Other historians, however, contend that Stalin was genuinely willing to experiment with less repressive policies, hoping that the people and the party would fall in line. Thus, Getty and Naumov suggest that "Stalin and his Moscow intimates tried a variety of tactics to control their own far-flung machine. Membership purges, political jawboning, . . . delicate manipulation of texts to form or adjust alliances, investigations by police and control commissions, and various other tactics all failed to produce the results Stalin wanted." [90] Despite the apparent contradiction between Stalin's "hard" and "soft" policies, however, Getty and Naumov conclude that "both were means to an end: taking and maintaining control over the country in order to further the revolutionary program."[91]

Whatever the reasons for the comparative calm of this period, developments at the Seventeenth Party Congress in 1934 seem to have marked a turning point. The meeting was proclaimed the "Congress of Victors" in light of the revolutionary achievements of the previous years, especially collectivization. Party members rose to applaud Stalin as the genius behind these great "successes." Former opposition members, including Bukharin, made certain to be particularly lavish in their praise. On the last day of the meeting, however, when the secret ballots in the election for the position of general secretary were counted, Stalin was shocked to find that nearly three hundred No votes—almost a quarter of the total ballots—had been cast against him.[92] The apparent unanimity of the Congress had been a sham. Soon afterward, Stalin also learned that a group of Old Bolsheviks was seeking to replace him with Sergei Kirov, the popular Leningrad Party chief. If Stalin ever believed that soft measures would suffice to keep the opposition in check, these developments must have convinced him otherwise.[93] Fatefully, the duplicity revealed by the ballots also may have cemented Stalin's paranoid fears that the party had become infested with hidden enemies.

Scholars often date the inception of the terror to December 1934, when Kirov was assassinated. Many historians have implicated Stalin in the murder plot.[94] Although evidence of his responsibility remains mixed, he clearly used the assassination as the political pretext for the terror that came later. The period from 1935 to mid-1936 was consumed with show trials, purges, and bureaucratic reorganization as Stalin constructed the ideological and physical apparatus of the terror.[95] The terror reached its violent apogee, however, between 1937 and 1938. Stalin's enemies were no longer simply rebuked or expelled from the party but more often sent to the Gulag or executed.

The enemies that Stalin was most determined to crush were those who had any connection to opposition activity, past or present. An analysis of the fate of nearly nine hundred members of the Soviet political, military, and cultural elite, for example, determined that oppositionists were nearly five times more likely to become victims than other elites.[96] Of the 1,225 delegates to the "Congress of Victors" 1,108 were arrested. Only 41 of the 139 members and candidate members of the Central Committee elected at that meeting survived the terror.[97]

Yet the terror ultimately consumed vast numbers of individuals who had no links to opposition activity whatsoever. Two main processes seem to have contributed to the expansion of the terror. First, bureaucratic and personal dynamics from below probably caused the purges to snowball beyond what even Stalin had intended. Party cadre tried to demonstrate their devotion to Stalin, and thereby save their own necks, by gaining a reputation for ruthlessness. A cycle of escalating repression was set in motion as party members preemptively denounced anyone above or below who might be in a position to implicate them. Others sought to settle old grudges or even advance their careers by denouncing fellow citizens. Once arrested, the accused might denounce virtually anyone in an effort to diminish his own punishment.

Although these dynamics were understood at the highest levels, the desire to let no enemy go unmasked led to an acceptance of excesses. Molotov, who was one of Stalin's closest allies during this period, later admitted that he was well aware that people were slandering one another. "We would have been complete idiots if we had taken the reports at their face value," he told an interviewer. "We were not idiots." "It is indeed sad and regrettable that so many innocent people perished. . . . But I believe that the terror of the late 1930s was necessary. Of course had we operated with greater caution, there would have been fewer victims, but Stalin insisted on making doubly sure: spare no one, but guarantee absolute stability."[98] Indeed, arbitrary target figures for executions were established by province.[99] As Stalin told the Central Committee in 1937, "it does not take a big number of people to do harm and cause damage. . . . Thousands of people are required to build a big railway bridge, but a few people are sufficient to blow it up."[100]

Perhaps the most important reason for the massive expansion of the terror was the genuine belief of Stalin and his supporters that active opposition was far more extensive and dangerous than it was in fact. As scholars have often noted, Stalin's personal paranoia played a major part in sustaining this perception.[101] Stalin's dire evaluation of his situation, however, was also encouraged by his ideological conviction that political opposition was often motivated by the indelible mark of one's social origins. This principle led naturally to an even broader extension of violence and to the conclusion that only execution or lifelong imprisonment was adequate punishment for those suspected of opposition. This attitude is revealed chillingly in Stalin's reaction to a 1938 proposal that would have permitted the early release of certain Gulag prisoners for good behavior. "Can't we arrange things so that people stay on in the camps?" he suggested. "If not, we release them, they go back home and pick up again with their old ways. The atmosphere in the camp is different, there it's harder to go wrong."[102] The same principle helps to explain why the wives and children of many suspects were often arrested and executed along with the suspects themselves.[103]

Stalin's obsession with enemies also ensured that the terror would not remain limited to the party. "Class enemies" and "socially dangerous elements," including kulaks who had managed to escape death, deportation, or imprisonment during collectivization, once again became targets of mass arrest.[104] By the time the terror abated in 1939, at least five million people had been arrested and one million executed.[105] Many of the former would perish in the Gulag in the years to come.

CHINA

The task of assessing the causes of the mass killing in communist China is considerably more complicated than for the Soviet Union or Cambodia. Few scholars today dispute that tens of millions of people died in China under the leadership of Mao Zedong as a direct result of communist policies, especially during the Great Leap Forward between 1958 and 1962. In terms of absolute numbers, this toll almost certainly makes Mao's China the most deadly regime in history. Yet many scholars have concluded that these deaths were almost entirely the unintentional consequences of ill-conceived or poorly implemented social and economic programs, rather than systematic mass killing.

For reasons I will explore below, intentional killing does seem to have played a relatively smaller role in China's transition to communism than it did either in the Soviet Union or in Cambodia. Mao's legacy has long profited from the favorable contrast with these regimes, especially Stalin's. It would be difficult to apply a lower standard for comparison. Systematic violence was not at all uncommon in Mao's China. Evidence permitting a detailed estimate of the number of victims has yet to be disclosed.[106] Recent revelations, however, suggest that China was considerably more violent than earlier scholarship assumed and that Mao himself expressed a greater willingness to resort to brutal methods when they suited his purposes.[107] There can be little doubt that millions of innocent Chinese citizens lost their lives in episodes of officially sanctioned killing.

Throughout the years of Mao's rule, China vacillated between violent periods, marked by determined efforts to implement radical communist economic and social programs, and distinctly moderate interludes, characterized by a relaxation of the pace and scope of communist policies. This pattern was partly the result of an ongoing debate between Mao and more moderate members of the Chinese Communist Party (CCP) regarding the appropriate pace and methods of China's transformation.[108] The extent of these debates, however, particularly in first decade after 1949, should not be overstated. These vacillations also seem to reflect a process of genuine experimentation through which Mao and other party leaders sought to come to grips with the very real dilemmas of the communist transformation in Chinese society.[109] The eventual necessity of such a transformation was a proposition that virtually all CCP leaders accepted.

When domestic or international developments made rapid advances seem more readily attainable or more urgent, Mao promulgated radical programs. Mao was never willing to declare war on his own citizens as Stalin had done, but he approved of more selective terror and was prepared to countenance a significant amount of violence and suffering in the service of his goals. He was also prepared to terrorize the political opponents of these policies in the party and in society at large. When radical policies failed to achieve their objectives or threatened to devastate the economy, Mao would concede the necessity for at least a temporary retrenchment. Yet, following each retreat, he grew increasingly suspicious that enemies inside and outside the party had intentionally sabotaged his plans. It was seldom more than a year or two before Mao decided to purge his political opponents and begin a new, frequently more radical and devastating round of transformative campaigns. This cycle of violence was ultimately broken only by Mao's death.

The defense that Mao simply was unaware of the violence and devastation associated with his policies or was unable to control it becomes less and less persuasive with each successive political or economic campaign he launched. Mao may not have desired the violence and disruption his policies caused, but after years of experience he must have understood, as many of his party colleagues clearly did, what the consequences would be. It was Mao Zedong, after all, who famously reminded his followers that "revolution is not a dinner party."

The Transformation of the Countryside

The collectivization of agriculture was a central goal of the Chinese Communist Party long before it gained power. Mao had made it clear that he believed that China's future lay in the collectivization of agriculture as early as 1943.[110] The practical and ideological impulses for transforming agricultural production in China were similar to those of the Soviet Union. Indeed, Chinese leaders believed that Stalin had proved that collectivization could succeed, even if they hoped to avoid some of his worst excesses.

Chinese leaders saw the collectivization of agriculture as the key to China's economic development and industrialization. China's industrial base in 1949 was smaller than Russia's had been in 1917, and its farming practices were even more primitive. Collectivization would rationalize production, creating surpluses that could be used to develop Chinese industry. Like the other communist leaders studied in this chapter, Chinese leaders, especially Mao, also saw collectivization as a central aspect of their vision for a utopian socialist society.[111] The overwhelming majority of China's population and economic activity was located in the countryside.

China's revolution would remain a bourgeois affair until the means of production were fully socialized. Collectivization would also serve to build a new socialist consciousness among the masses, a goal that became increasingly prominent in the years after the revolution.

In the aftermath of victory, however, Chinese leaders seemed content to leave most of this to the future. Having spent decades organizing a peasant-based guerrilla movement in the countryside, the CCP achieved power in 1949 with far greater support from the peasantry and with a deeper understanding of peasant life than did the Bolsheviks or, later, the Khmer Rouge. Mao and other high party officials wished to avoid a violent conflict with China's peasants. Mao seems to have understood, much as Lenin did after the collapse of war communism, that a sudden assault on peasant interests ran the risk of economic disaster and perhaps open rebellion. Thus in 1950 he cautioned the party that "the view held by certain people that it is possible to eliminate capitalism and realize socialism at an early date is wrong, it does not tally with our national conditions."[112] He conceded that private ownership of land should be maintained for the time being and that peasants would have to be eased into socialism over a long period using economic incentives and political education.

Another factor contributing to the acceptance of a more gradual pace for the transition to communism was China's relationship with the Soviet Union. Chinese relations with the Soviets were far from perfect, but the existence of a powerful communist state across the border meant that China did not have to confront the dilemmas of "capitalist encirclement" or building "socialism in one country" that weighed so heavily on the Bolsheviks in the years after 1917. Chinese leaders hoped that Soviet economic assistance would help develop China's economy and that Soviet military aid would protect China from its enemies abroad.[113] As Mao frankly admitted in a speech in 1949,

> Just imagine! If the Soviet Union had not existed, if there had been no victory in the anti-fascist Second World War, if Japanese imperialism had not been defeated, if the People's Democracies [in Eastern Europe] had not come into being . . . if not for all these in combination, the international reactionary forces bearing down upon us would certainly be many times greater than now. In such circumstances, could we have won victory? Obviously not. And even with victory, there could be no consolidation.[114]

From Land Reform to Class Struggle

The first stage of the CCP's program to transform agriculture was known as the land reform campaign. Unlike collectivization itself, which Mao believed could be delayed, land reform had to be implemented immediately. In fact, land reform already had been launched in many communist-controlled zones before 1949. The party began to implement it in the rest of the country soon after the revolution. The stated purpose of land reform was to increase agricultural production and address rural inequality by redistributing land from so-called landlords to the rest of the peasantry. Communist leaders, however, also saw land reform as a powerful political tool. Land reform was designed to buy the support of the majority of peasants by handing out free land and, simultaneously, to crush those most likely to resist the imposition of communist power in the villages. Since peasants frequently did not prove as enthusiastic about land reform as the communists hoped, it seems likely that the latter goal eventually came to dominate the former. As Vivienne Shue observes, "land reform could be used to emasculate the traditional village elite, the entire old rural power structure; it could become the spearhead of a genuine social revolution to change the fundamental relations of power in the countryside."[115] Thus, although land reform left private ownership intact and even allowed it to expand, it also was seen as an integral step toward the socialization of the countryside that the party sought to achieve.

The party initially hoped that land reform could be carried out in an orderly fashion, with relatively little violence. Mao accepted that some landlords, local "despots," and "reactionaries" would have to be executed, but he seems to have believed that many of these enemies could be reformed.[116] He urged vigilance, but he was not obsessed with fears of counterrevolution in 1949.[117]

Two developments, however, soon contributed to a significant shift in tactics. First, the party quickly realized it had seriously underestimated the degree of peasant conservatism and resistance to even moderate CCP policies. Almost immediately after entering newly occupied areas, the party encountered resistance, not simply from landlords and former members of the Kuomintang, but from the lower strata of the peasantry as well. More than three thousand party cadres simply trying to collect the grain tax were assassinated by peasants in the regime's first year.[118] The regime's need to gain political control in the villages seemed increasingly urgent.

The second development, the Chinese intervention in the Korean War in the fall of 1950, reinforced these concerns. The economic benefits of land reform would have to be achieved more rapidly to contribute to China's economic and military development, and its political aims would have to be pursued more vigorously to consolidate political control at home. As Maurice Meisner concludes, Chinese leaders were suddenly "filled with fears over the survival of the new republic. . . . The essentially external threat to the survival of the revolution turned the initially moderate policies and practices of the new state into increasingly repressive ones and eventually to terror throughout most of the country."[119]

Indeed, in the last months of 1950 the CCP began shifting to a considerably more radical program for land reform, one meant to be implemented more rapidly and that extended the class struggle to a much wider set of enemies.[120] It proved to be an extremely violent affair. Since the party's more moderate efforts had already provoked some violent protest, there could have been no surprise that the intended victims of land reform would resist their dispossession. Most frequently their resistance was passive, as peasants tried to sell, conceal, or destroy their property rather than hand it over to the state.[121] Sometimes, however, they resorted to more violent means. In some regions, communist officials were assassinated and large-scale riots and armed rebellions erupted.[122] CCP cadres were dispatched to the villages with orders to identify landlords and other village "exploiters" and confiscate virtually all of their land, animals, and personal possessions. In an effort to incite "class struggle," landlords were dragged in front of village meetings where cadres encouraged poor peasants to "speak bitterness" against them. The meetings often culminated in brutal beatings or executions.

Most landlords survived the period, but torture and killing were common. The list of victims further expanded when land reform was combined with a "campaign against counterrevolutionaries" intended to eliminate other enemies of the regime both in the villages and in the larger towns and cities. Official party policy toward the counterrevolutionaries called for "executing some, imprisoning some and putting some under house arrest."[123]

Between one million and four million people were probably killed during the first years of the regime, and an additional four million to six million were sent to forced labor colonies, where many eventually perished.[124] It is often claimed that this level of violence exceeded what Mao and the party intended. It is probably true that Mao hoped to keep a tighter rein on the violence, but his previous experiences with land reform both before and after 1949 suggest that he probably understood it would be bloody.[125] Mao was reluctant to take any actions that would give the masses or the cadres an excuse to leave the rural power structure intact. Indeed, the party's most serious concern during the campaign against counterrevolutionaries seems to have been punishing cadres who tried to practice "peaceful land reform."[126] The party warned against "excessive lenience" and urged local cadres to "not fear executing people, only to fear mistakenly executing people."[127] Years later, Mao acknowledged that some people had been "unjustly killed" during the campaign, but he insisted that "basically there were no errors; that group of people should have been killed . . . if they had not been killed the people would not have been able to raise their heads."[128]

From Gradualism to the Socialist High Tide

China's land reform was largely completed by the end of 1952. From the point of view of the regime, it was largely successful. The distribution of land among the peasantry was significantly leveled, and government control in the villages was more firmly established. On the other hand, private ownership of land remained intact. Backward, small-scale peasant farming practices were still nearly universal. With end of the Korean War in 1953, the CCP could again turn its attention to the long-term project of building socialism in the countryside.

Chinese leaders planned a gradual, staged approach to achieving collectivization. Peasants would first be organized into mutual aid teams, where peasants would pool their labor but retain ownership of their land and other property. Next peasants would be formed into lower-level agricultural cooperatives, where they pooled land and animals but still received a share of the harvest and other farm produce according to the amount of land and equipment they had contributed. Only then would China proceed to full collectivization, a true socialist system in which virtually all property would become commonly owned and compensation would be based on labor alone. It was a process that Mao declared would take at least fifteen years to complete.

China followed this basic path until mid-1955 when, at Mao's behest, it was suddenly abandoned in favor of a far more ambitious schedule. At least two considerations seem to have contributed to this radical turn. First, although agricultural productivity had continued to increase after the revolution, it rose much more slowly than Chinese leaders had hoped.[129] Moreover, China's population and rates of grain consumption had increased during this period, further decreasing the surplus available to the state. The regime's plans for economic modernization, however, depended on substantial increases in agricultural productivity to fund industrialization. The party tried to make up the difference by increasing its control over the sale of surplus grain, but this move simply provoked peasant protest and aggravated the fundamental problem of low agricultural productivity as peasants increasingly resorted to hoarding food and to black markets.[130]

Second, the dilemma posed by the lower-than-expected agricultural surplus was further exacerbated by the growing realization that Soviet aid had not proved nearly as generous as Chinese leaders had hoped in 1949. Although Soviet advisors and technical assistance had been invaluable,

Soviet economic aid amounted to only 3 percent of China's development investment.[131] Most economic aid had come in the form of loans with relatively short repayment terms. By 1956 China would actually have a net foreign exchange deficit with the Soviet Union.[132] The death of Stalin in 1953 could only have cast further doubt on the future of Soviet aid.

These problems were widely recognized in the CCP in 1954. Not all leaders, however, advocated the same solutions. Party leaders such as Deng Zihui, the head of the Central Rural Work Department, and Liu Shaoqi, the party's second most powerful figure, saw the problems in the countryside as a reflection of general peasant conservatism and argued for reducing the pace of socialization. Mao, on the other hand, claimed that the majority of peasants actually desired more rapid collectivization. He blamed the problems in the countryside on hoarding by a relatively small group of rich peasants and insufficient enthusiasm and discipline among local party cadres.[133] Mao was convinced that immediate collectivization would simultaneously solve the problem of low productivity and overcome resistance by the rich peasants. In a major speech delivered in July 1955, Mao unveiled this radical turn to the party. He criticized his colleagues for "tottering along like a woman with bound feet" and proclaimed that a new "high tide of social transformation in the countryside" had arrived.[134] Mao was aware that some in the party were concerned that proceeding too rapidly with collectivization might result in the same kind of disasters encountered by the Soviet Union, but he brushed aside these fears declaring that "on no account should we allow these comrades to use the Soviet experience as a cover for their idea of moving at a snail's pace."[135]

Proponents of the more moderate line bowed to Mao's lead. From this point forward, peasants would no longer be eased into socialism in stages. On the contrary, many were ushered directly from their private, individual farms to full-scale collectives.[136] Their land and other assets were simply expropriated. Collectivization was implemented with extreme haste. By the middle of 1956, 90 percent of Chinese peasants had been moved into the collectives. Surprisingly, in light of the Soviet experience with collectivization, this extremely rapid and radical transformation appears to have been achieved with relatively little bloodshed. Scholars often have attributed this more peaceful process to the better organization of the CCP and a greater level of support for collectivization from the peasant masses.[137] These factors undoubtedly eased the transition to collectivization, but such observations neglect three important points.

First, many, perhaps even most peasants actually were opposed to collectivization. Various forms of coercion, including violence, were required to force them into the collectives.[138] Peasants accused of loosely defined counterrevolutionary activities were subject to arrest, and numerous instances of beatings and torture of peasants opposed to collectivization were recorded.[139]

Second, focusing only on the relative peace of 1955 and 1956 ignores the fact that collectivization was implemented only a few short years after the bloody land reform campaign of 1951 and 1952. The violence of land reform and the campaign against counterrevolutionaries had already demonstrated the consequences of open resistance to the party's policies. In many cases, this violence had been carried out in highly public settings, in the effort to ensure the largest possible audience.[140] As Thomas Bernstein concludes, "the Chinese regime, through its extremely effective application of violence during land reform, and the counter-revolutionaries' campaign, demonstrated its determination. . . . [C]ompliance during the upsurge [in collectivization] can be attributed to a sense of resigned inevitability."[141]

Third, the consequences of collectivization might well have been far more deadly if Mao had not quickly agreed to back away from the most radical elements of the program. By early 1956, it had become clear to many in the party that the rapid pace of collectivization was causing severe economic dislocations. As in the Soviet Union, some peasants slaughtered their livestock rather than turn it over to the collectives. Collectivization resulted in decreased productivity and, in combination with natural causes, contributed to major famines in some areas.[142] Party moderates prevailed upon Mao to relax the pace of the transformation.[143] He reluctantly agreed to a series of reforms instituted under the slogan of "opposing rash advance."[144] The size of collective farms was drastically reduced. Many peasants withdrew from the collectives and, in some cases, farms were completely disbanded. Unrealistic production targets were revised downward and compulsory government grain purchases were lowered. Some private markets were permitted to reopen. Peasants were allowed to keep small private plots and raise their own animals. These reforms may well have averted a much more serious catastrophe. Indeed, less than two years later, when Mao again embarked on a radical effort to transform China's agricultural production, he unleashed a wave of death and suffering unprecedented in human history.

From "Opposing Rash Advance" to the Great Leap Forward

Mao had agreed to retreat from his radical vision of collectivization, but according to Roderick MacFarquhar, "he never really accepted the necessity of this step backward and continued to yearn for rapid economic progress."[145] The policy of opposing rash advance had averted economic collapse in part by allowing the peasants to keep more of what they produced, but it had also reduced the surplus available to the state to finance industrialization. China's economic modernization seemed to be stagnating. As relations with the Soviet Union continued to deteriorate following the death of Stalin, it was becoming increasingly clear that China could no longer depend on assistance from abroad for its economic development or security.[146]

By the summer of 1957, however, Mao was coming to believe that the economic failures of collectivization had as much to do with resistance from the enemies of communism in society and in the party as they did with any inherent flaws in the policy itself or the pace of its implementation. Mao's conclusion stemmed in part from his experience with the Hundred Flowers Campaign of 1956, in which he had actively encouraged Chinese intellectuals and others to voice criticism of the party and its policies.[147] Before the campaign, Mao had estimated that not more than 3 percent of China's intellectuals were hostile to Marxism and that most of the criticism would be constructive and consistent with complete loyalty to the Communist Party.[148] In fact, the party and many of its most important socialist programs came under intense attack. Most of the criticism came from urban intellectuals, but in the countryside peasants and even some party members used the opportunity to express their opposition to collectivization.[149] One provincial party official complained that collectivization had "transformed people into beasts of burden."[150]

Opposition to communism clearly ran much deeper than Mao had expected. He became convinced that if the so-called right opportunists in society and the party could be reformed or eliminated, China's citizens would prove themselves capable of extraordinary productivity without the need for increased material incentives. To this end, Mao launched the "anti-rightist campaign," a major purge in which hundreds of thousands of people were arrested and sentenced to "reform through labor" in the Chinese prison camp system.[151] Scholars, writers, and journalists were the most prominent victims, but the campaign also extended to rural areas where it targeted surviving landlords, rich peasants, or their family members along with virtually anyone who had raised questions about collectivization.[152]

In early 1958, therefore, Mao decided that the time was ripe for one final push — a "Great Leap Forward" — that would simultaneously achieve the rapid industrialization of China's economy and complete the communist transformation of society. He dismissed the view that China's slow economic growth was the product of material constraints as nothing but a justification created by bourgeois intellectuals to conceal their opposition to communism. He lashed out at those in the party who had advocated the policy of opposing rash advance, accusing them of "pouring cold water on the masses." Mao believed that China's economy could rapidly and dramatically increase its productivity by tapping into the enthusiasm of the laboring masses and promoting radical communist forms of production. He confidently predicted that the Great Leap Forward would permit China's economy to overtake Britain's in a mere seven years and America's in fifteen.[153] It was a profoundly utopian vision, the pursuit of which suggests, in MacFarquhar's words, that in 1958 "Mao and many of his colleagues finally took leave of reality."[154]

The policies of the Great Leap Forward applied to all sectors of the economy, but they imposed the most radical changes on the countryside. All of the moderate rural reforms introduced in 1956 were swept aside and replaced by even more radical policies, implemented on an even more ambitious schedule. In a matter of months, 90 percent of the existing collective farms were grouped together into massive "people's communes," some with membership rolls comprising more than 100,000 people. The small private plots, privately owned livestock, and free markets that had helped stave off starvation in 1956 were completely collectivized. Peasants were no longer allowed the right, even in theory, to withdraw from the communes.[155]

The creation of the communes also facilitated the imposition of radical communist social policies and the unprecedented regimentation of peasant life by the state.[156] Families were not allowed to prepare their own meals, but rather were forced to eat in communal mess halls. In some communes, children were to be raised in communal nurseries. In others, money was abolished. All over the country peasants were organized into massive work brigades to construct dams, irrigation projects, roads, and bridges. Thousands died of exhaustion.[157] Traditional farming practices were done away with in favor of untested methods advocated by the state.[158] These schemes contributed to utterly unrealistic expectations regarding the amount of food that could be produced and therefore how much could be collected by the state.

The effort to force these radical changes on the Chinese countryside ultimately resulted in the most devastating famine in human history. Close to thirty million people are thought to have perished in the four terrible years between 1958 and 1962.[159] The famine claimed over 50 percent of the population in some villages. Despite the enormity of the disaster, there is no evidence to suggest that Mao or other Chinese leaders deliberately engineered the famine. Its primary causes were a combination of deeply flawed agricultural policies and the attempt by local cadres to meet or exceed the regime's preposterously high grain production goals.[160] At various times during the Great Leap Forward, Mao cautioned against excesses on the left as well as the right. The repressive political campaigns of previous years, however, had demonstrated repeatedly that leftist excesses usually would be excused with little more than a warning, while being labeled a rightist could mean expulsion from the party or imprisonment in labor camps. Most party officials concluded it was safer to err on the left than on the right.[161] In many regions, cadres confiscated nearly the entire harvest, leaving peasants with nothing.

Although Mao's intent was not to kill or starve peasants, when the famine struck his actions proved he was willing to pay a staggering price in human lives to achieve his radical goals. As in the Soviet Union, a system of household registration kept peasants from fleeing to the cities or other areas where the famine was less severe. Local granaries in some famine-stricken areas remained full, and peasants seeking access to them were shot. Grain exports to the Soviet Union actually increased by over 50 percent at the height of the famine.[162] Meanwhile Mao received numerous credible reports that a major famine was gripping the countryside, but he refused to change course.[163] Although he eventually accepted that the country was in the grips of a major famine — even giving up eating meat in symbolic solidarity with the starving masses — Mao blamed the famine on counterrevolutionaries: "we must recognize that there is a severe grain shortage because production teams are hiding and dividing grain and this is a common problem all over the country."[164] Following Mao's example, the Communist Party district secretary for Xinyang, a region containing ten million people, claimed that "the problem is not that food is lacking. There are sufficient quantities of grain, but 90 percent of the inhabitants are suffering from ideological difficulties."[165]

Mao's fears of opposition eventually engulfed the party as well. At a major party conference in Lushan in July 1959, some party members, most vocally Minister of Defense Peng Dehuai, expressed concerns about the consequences of the Great Leap Forward and urged a more moderate course. The criticism was intended to be constructive, but Mao interpreted it as a plot against his leadership and further evidence of "right opportunism" in the party.[166] Peng was accused of conspiring with the Soviet Union to overthrow Mao; he was stripped of his office and placed under virtual house arrest.[167] A broader "campaign against right opportunism" elsewhere in the party and society was launched. Large numbers of party members and ordinary peasants were sent to the camps where many would subsequently die in the famine.[168] Although no reliable estimates are available for the victims of this purge, years later the party would conclude that six million people had been wrongly punished in the campaign.[169] The purge only served to increase the already radical direction of the Great Leap Forward. High-ranking party members were fearful to suggest even the slightest deviation from Mao's preferred policies.

Local and regional officials desperately sought to protect themselves from the charge of rightism by promising to fulfill the most outlandish production quotas and racing to adopt the most radical socialist forms of production and social organization.[170]

Not all the suffering visited on China during the Great Leap Forward, however, was the result of the famine. The party officially proscribed coercion, but communist officials sometimes tortured and killed those accused of failing to meet their grain quotas.[171] According to Jasper Becker, as the famine grew worse, "Party cadres had increasingly to rely on force and terror to get the peasants to obey their orders. At the height of the famine, they wielded the power of life and death because they controlled the grain stores and could kill anyone by depriving them of food."[172]

As in the Soviet Union, the worst effects of the famine were specifically targeted at social groups suspected of hostility toward the regime. One local official remembered that during the famine "no one in a cadre's family died."[173] As Becker documents,

> The most vulnerable section of China's population, around five percent, were those whom Mao called "enemies of the people." Anyone who had in previous campaigns of repression been labeled a "black element" was given the lowest priority in the allocation of food. Landlords, rich peasants, former members of the nationalist regime, religious leaders, rightists, counter-revolutionaries and the families of such individuals died in the greatest numbers. During the Great Leap Forward many more people were placed in these categories and often imprisoned.[174]

Prisoners in China's labor camps may have suffered more than any other group since they were subject to hard labor and occupied the lowest position in the food distribution hierarchy. By one estimate, four million people may have perished in the camps during the Great Leap Forward.[175]

Unlike the formal period of collectivization, the radical communist agrarian policies of the Great Leap Forward and the hunger they produced eventually provoked a significant amount of active resistance and in some cases open revolt from the peasantry. The regime did not refrain from using violence to crush this resistance.[176] Secret Chinese military papers reveal that during the Great Leap Forward, "hunger and brutality precipitated widespread revolt and 'armed banditry.' . . . Challenged, the party launched an all-out military and political effort to 'suppress the counter-revolutionaries and pacify the countryside.'"[177] Nevertheless, direct violence did remain on a significantly smaller scale than in the Soviet Union. It seems likely, however, that both the degree of peasant resistance and the corresponding level of violent repression by the state would have been substantially higher if famine had not weakened or killed so many who might have opposed the policies of the Great Leap Forward.

Political Purges and Terror

Political purges and campaigns were a virtually constant feature of political life in communist China until the end of the Mao era. Political purges focused on a wide range of targets, but as in the Soviet Union, a recurring motive for the purges was the perceived need to eliminate opposition to the radical policies of social transformation favored by Mao and his followers.

The "campaign against the counterrevolutionaries" of 1950–1953, the "anti-rightist campaign" of 1957, and the "campaign against right opportunism" of 1959 have already been mentioned above. The most violent political terror in the history of communist China, however, was Mao's so-called Great Proletarian Cultural Revolution. The Cultural Revolution was far more than a mere purge, but at its heart lay a fundamental political conflict within the Chinese Communist Party. Like Stalin's Great Terror, the origins of the Cultural Revolution can be traced back to conflicts that emerged during the socialist transformation in the countryside. The catastrophe of the Great Leap Forward generated considerable opposition to Mao's radical policies, not only from peasants but also from moderate leaders within the party. At Lushan, Mao had pushed ahead with the Great Leap Forward over the opposition of Peng Dehuai and others, but by the summer of 1960, even Mao could no longer deny that it had been a disaster. At the Ninth Plenum of the Communist Party's Central Committee in January 1961, he grudgingly agreed to retreat from the radical policies of the last two years.

Nevertheless, Mao feared that the retrenchment might go too far, perhaps rolling back collectivization itself.[178] Several high-ranking communist leaders, most notably President Liu Shaoqi, seemed to be pushing in this direction. The events of the previous years, especially the Hundred Flowers Campaign and the resistance to the Great Leap Forward that Mao encountered at Lushan had left Mao deeply suspicious about the eagerness of the people and the party to follow through with the transition to communism.[179] Recent political developments in the Soviet Union, particularly the rise to power of Khrushchev and his policies of de-Stalinization, aggravated Mao's paranoia. Mao believed that the Soviet revolution had been betrayed from within by "bourgeois revisionists," and he feared a similar fate for China's revolution.

Mao's foremost concern does not appear to have been his personal hold on power itself. There is little to suggest that his position as leader was seriously threatened. Like Stalin, if Mao was concerned simply with maintaining his political power, he probably could have secured his future more easily through compromise with party moderates. Rather, Mao's behavior suggests that he was motivated more powerfully by the desire to protect what remained of his utopian vision of China's communist future from what he saw as a gathering reactionary momentum in the party and in society. In the years between 1962 and 1965, Mao fought to preserve at least some semblance of this vision — especially in the countryside — but he continued to suspect that the bureaucracy was frustrating his efforts. As Andrew Walder observes, "by the mid-1960s Maoists had concluded that the party itself had become corrupted by an ongoing, massive, yet largely hidden conspiracy of reactionary social classes and revisionist traitors who were consciously embarked on a plot to restore capitalism."[180]

This conspiratorial view was outlined in a political tract known as the Ninth Polemic, authorized by Mao in 1964. In a markedly Stalinist tone, the authors of the polemic argued that "in socialist society, the overthrown bourgeoisie and other reactionary classes remain strong for quite a long time. . . . They have a thousand and one links to the international bourgeoisie. They are not reconciled to their defeat." Instead, they "conduct open and hidden struggles against the proletariat in every field . . . they work to undermine socialism and restore capitalism . . . [they] sneak into government organs, economic departments, and cultural and educational institutions so as to resist or usurp the leadership of the proletariat."[181] Claiming that bourgeois forces, represented by Khrushchev, had already hijacked the Soviet state, the Polemic suggested that it was an open question "whether or not we can successfully prevent the emergence of Khruschov's [sic] revisionism in China. In short, it is an extremely important question, a matter of life and death for our party and our country."[182] Commenting on this passage, Roderick MacFarquhar writes that "here, unveiled, was the apocalyptic vision of a dark future which would eventually convince Mao of the need for the Cultural Revolution."[183]

Mao did not immediately resort to purges to meet this supposedly reactionary threat. He initially hoped to root out rightist attitudes in the party through campaigns encouraging the study of Marxism and the emulation of model Chinese citizens.[184] By 1965, however, it was clear to Mao that these efforts had failed to stem the tide of revisionism. He decided that yet another purge was his only recourse. The Cultural Revolution, as the campaign would come to be known, was a twin-pronged assault on the elements in the party and society that Mao believed stood in the way of the realization of true communism in China. The campaign commenced in the spring of 1966 with the purge of several high-ranking party members and expanded rapidly after that, eventually consuming as much as 60 percent of Communist Party officials.[185]

Since Mao felt that the CCP had been corrupted to the highest levels, he had to look elsewhere for the support he needed to carry out the Cultural Revolution. "When you are told to kindle a fire to burn yourselves, will you do it?" he asked.[186] Mao's principal instruments for implementing the Cultural Revolution were the infamous Red Guards. The Red Guards were large, loosely organized groups of young people composed primarily of radicalized urban university and middle school students.[187] As Mao and his supporters issued slogans urging the masses to "bombard the headquarters" and put "destruction before construction," the Red Guards set about terrorizing all elements of society suspected of representing bourgeois thinking or culture. Teachers and intellectuals, factory bosses, and suspected revisionist party officials were forced to submit to "struggle sessions" that frequently ended in savage beatings and sometimes in death. In Beijing during the height of the terror, trucks patrolled the streets collecting the dead. In the countryside, Mao sought to reintroduce some of the radical policies of the Great Leap Forward leading to another round of attacks on former landlords, their families, and cadres suspected of opposing collectivization.[188]

Real opposition to Mao's policies undoubtedly existed both inside the party and in the broader Chinese society, but Mao's understanding of the roots of the opposition vastly overestimated both its scope and intensity. As in the other communist states studied in this chapter, several related beliefs—that opposition to communism was motivated by class consciousness, that this consciousness was extremely difficult to rise above, and that class was a trait that could be passed from parents to children—contributed to the burgeoning scope of the violence.[189] Mao's conviction that "reeducation" through hard physical labor and psychological struggle was possible, at least in principle, may have averted the mass executions that characterized Stalin's Great Terror.[190] Nevertheless, between three and four million party members and cadres were eventually imprisoned.[191] Torture, overwork and inadequate nutrition were common in the Chinese prison system and ensured that many inmates, including Peng Dehuai and Lui Shaoqi, ultimately died there.[192]

Mao and his allies never had complete control over the violence of the Cultural Revolution. Fighting broke out between factions of the Red Guards. Eventually it escalated beyond what even they had envisioned. As with his previous campaigns, however, Mao probably understood that large-scale violence would be unavoidable in the Cultural Revolution. He did not seek violence or destruction for their own sake, but he was prepared to accept them as a means to achieve his goals. As Harry Harding concludes, the "costs of the Cultural Revolution were largely the predictable consequences of Mao's perception that China was on the brink of the restoration of capitalism and his prescription that the mobilization of urban youth was the best way to prevent it."[193]

Even the worst leftist "excesses" usually elicited little or no punishment, while the mere suspicion of "taking the capitalist road" could mean death. Indeed, the minister for public security instructed the police not to interfere with the Red Guards:

> Should Red Guards who kill people be punished? My opinion is that if people have died, well, they're dead; there's nothing we can do about that, and it isn't our problem. I am not happy with the idea that the masses are killing people, but if the masses hate bad people so much that we cannot stop them, then let's not bother trying to stop them. The people's police has to be behind the Red Guards. We must sympathize with them and pass information to them, particularly where the five [black] categories [the landlords, rich peasants, counterrevolutionaries, bad elements, and rightists] are concerned.[194]

In 1967, with China threatened by anarchy, Mao finally called in the army to restore order. In 1968, he ordered the demobilization of the Red Guards—a move that initially resulted in an increase in violence as the guards themselves became victims. The imposition of military authority did not end the Cultural Revolution, however, but merely reasserted central control over it. The purges and violence continued at lower levels until Mao's death in 1976. By then, between 400,000 and 1,000,000 people were dead, not including the multitudes that eventually perished in the camps.[195]

CAMBODIA

The struggle to achieve the communization of society reached its brutal apotheosis in Cambodia during the brief period from 1975 to 1979 under the rule of the Communist Party of Kampuchea (CPK), also known as the Khmer Rouge. Unfortunately, far less information is available regarding this chapter in the history of communism than exists for the Soviet Union or China. Comparatively few official government documents have been recovered from these years. Obsessed with secrecy, Khmer Rouge leaders rarely spoke in public or published information about the regime and its policies. The CPK refused even to reveal itself as the true governing body of Cambodia or to disclose the names of many of its leaders until September 1977, thirty months after it seized power.[196] Nevertheless, the limited documentation available on the ideology of the CPK leadership, along with the ample evidence regarding the implementation of Khmer Rouge policies, strongly suggests that the Cambodian mass killing was inspired by many of the same strategic considerations that motivated communist leaders in the Soviet Union and China.

As in the Soviet Union and China, most of the violence in Cambodia seems to have been the result of communist leaders' efforts to crush real and perceived resistance to the radical, dispossessive transformation that they sought to bring about in Cambodian society. The Khmer Rouge consciously set out to realize the transition to communism more rapidly and more completely than had their Soviet and Chinese predecessors.[197] Although the Khmer Rouge drew much of their inspiration from those revolutions, they ignored explicit warnings from other communist states regarding the dangers of this course. Khmer Rouge leaders bragged that they would "show the world that pure communism could indeed be achieved in one fell swoop. . . . We will be the first nation to create a completely communist society without wasting time on intermediate steps."[198]

Indeed, no drive to transform society has matched the scope, speed, and intrusiveness with which the Khmer Rouge thrust their peculiar brand of "pure communism" on the Cambodian people. Khmer Rouge leaders adhered to a particularly radical variant of Maoist Marxism—what Karl Jackson has described as "the ideology of total revolution"—that called for extraordinarily profound changes in the daily existence of Cambodians from all walks of life.[199] Agricultural production was transfigured. Major cities were emptied. Money, markets, and virtually all private property were eliminated. Former elites were stripped of power, and organized religion was abolished. Khmer Rouge leaders literally believed they were creating a completely new Cambodian society starting from "year zero." As Jackson concludes, "seldom has any regime sought so much change so quickly from so many."[200]

The Transformation of the Countryside

As in the other communist states examined here, the most significant changes in Cambodia under communism were directly related to the transformation of agricultural production. Approximately 85 percent of the Cambodian population worked in the agricultural sector. Although all CPK leaders probably favored some form of agricultural reform, many seem to have questioned the need for complete collectivization, its associated social and economic policies, and the furious pace at which these policies were ultimately implemented. For Pol Pot and his supporters, however, a policy of rapid and radical collectivization was seen as the key to achieving their most important economic, military, and ideological goals. Fatefully for the people of Cambodia, it was this faction — a faction that probably remained a minority in the CPK until 1973 or even later — that ultimately prevailed in the intra-party dispute.[201]

From a practical perspective, Pol Pot's faction was convinced that collectivization was the most efficient means to attain the economic and military independence that they believed was necessary to free Cambodia from the continuous ravages of foreign powers.[202] Unlike the Soviet Union, the Cambodian communist regime was not born alone into a world of capitalist states. Yet Pol Pot still perceived Cambodia to be surrounded by an extremely hostile world.[203] Some of these fears are easy to understand. When the Khmer Rouge seized power in 1975, Cambodia had only just emerged from a civil war against a regime backed directly by the United States — a war in which extensive American bombardment had killed as many as 150,000 Cambodian civilians.[204]

Pol Pot and his party allies, however, also seem to have viewed other communist states, particularly Vietnam, with at least as much suspicion as they did the "American imperialists." Although the Vietnamese had supported the Khmer Rouge during the civil war, long-standing tensions between the two states remained. By 1973 a serious rift had opened over disputed border regions and Vietnamese influence in the Cambodian Communist Party.[205] Military clashes between Vietnamese and Khmer Rouge forces broke out in 1975. The Soviet Union, for its part, could not be trusted as a reliable friend because it was too closely allied with the Vietnamese. Furthermore, Pol Pot believed that both countries were following a revisionist Marxist path, retreating from the ideals of socialism. Indeed, Khmer Rouge leaders suspected that the United States, the Soviet Union, and the Vietnamese were collaborating in an effort to overthrow the new regime.[206] Pol Pot hoped for continued support from China, but even Chinese friendship may have been in doubt following the death of Mao in 1976.

Pol Pot and his supporters believed that collectivization would contribute to the defense of their regime in two principal ways. First, collectivization would rationalize Cambodia's backward agricultural system. Small, privately owned peasant plots, which produced little more than a subsistence crop, would be organized into massive farming communities in which labor and resources could be pooled. An extensive system of canals and dikes would be constructed to irrigate Cambodia's water-hungry rice crop, further increasing productivity. Forests would be cleared to open up new fertile land. These reforms, they believed, would soon generate huge surpluses that could be harnessed to feed the military or be sold for export in return for the capital needed to speed the development of Cambodian industry and defense.[207] By centralizing production, collectivization would also facilitate the appropriation of the harvest by the state. Khmer Rouge planners believed that these policies would triple the harvest to three tons or more per hectare of land. As one party report put it, "striving for three tons has a very profound meaning. Three tons means national defense."[208]

Second, at least as important as protecting itself from external enemies, collectivization would help to control the large segments of the Cambodian population that the Khmer Rogue believed to be hostile to the regime.[209] Pol Pot had achieved power in Cambodia with far less popular support than Mao had, possibly even less than Lenin. The Khmer Rogue seem to have understood that they lacked support, at least among certain sectors of the population. Collectivization, they hoped, would win over much of the population by rapidly increasing their standard of living. The Khmer Rouge also suspected that some groups would probably never accept communism. Nevertheless, collectivization would provide an important weapon for dealing with these enemies by providing the organizational means to control them or, if necessary, to eradicate them.

Thus, only by increasing agricultural productivity, Pol Pot and his associates reasoned, could the regime develop the domestic resources needed to defend itself from its enemies abroad. Only by increasing the regime's ability to control and monitor the population could they defend it from enemies within. Collectivization solved both problems simultaneously.

CPK supporters of radical collectivization, however, also seem to have been moved by deeper, ideological impulses. Although rationalizing agricultural production and developing Cambodia's industry were vital goals, an equally important aim of collectivization and its related social policies was to contribute to the realization of their utopian vision for a new, egalitarian society.[210] The collective farms were seen as the means to produce not only an abundance of rice but also a radically new political and social consciousness among the people. Perhaps for this reason there is little evidence that Pol Pot and his followers, unlike other CPK members, ever seriously considered other possible routes to increased agricultural productivity. On the contrary, Pol Pot openly criticized other socialist countries for failing to stamp out all traces of individualism and private property in their societies. The dire lessons of the Soviet collectivization and even direct warnings from Chinese communist leaders regarding the possible dangers of such a course were dismissed out of hand.[211] Cambodia, Pol Pot claimed, must adopt a pure collectivist system. "The goal of our collectivism is to raise the living standards of the people," he told a meeting of high-ranking party members. But collectivism was also a goal in itself. "Our livelihood must improve, but it will do so along collectivist lines."[212]

The first Khmer Rouge experiments with collectivization actually began in 1973 in regions of Cambodia under communist control during the civil war. Prior to this period, the Khmer Rouge had instituted relatively moderate agricultural policies, including the small-scale redistribution of land and the organization of cooperative work teams.[213] Land remained in private hands and many peasants seem to have supported the reforms. In 1973, however, full-scale collectivization and an assault on other aspects of peasant life commenced in some Khmer Rouge zones under the banner of "Democratic Revolution." The shift in policy, which appears to have marked the increasing influence of Pol Pot's faction in the CPK, was launched on the heels of a major purge of cadres who supported more moderate economic plans and a closer relationship with the Vietnamese.[214] Most Cambodian peasants were opposed to the radical new policies.[215] According to Kenneth Quinn, "Cambodia's peasantry has a long history of ownership of its own land. . . . The history of the Pol Pot regime has been one of peasant resistance to the imposed changes, rather than active or even grudging support and involvement."[216] In many regions opposition was confined to passive resistance, but in some places peasants rose up and assassinated Khmer Rouge cadres.[217] The Khmer Rouge increasingly resorted to violence to gain compliance with their policies.[218]

Peasant resistance might have been expected to prompt a reevaluation or relaxation of these policies after the Khmer Rouge achieved national power in 1975. Unfortunately for the people of Cambodia, Pol Pot's faction believed there was simply no time to bring the population around to the idea of communism through patient persuasion or to acclimate them gradually to this alien way of life. They were convinced that, on the contrary, these radical changes had to be implemented immediately if the revolution and the regime were to survive.[219] The external and internal enemies that Khmer Rouge leaders so desperately feared would not stand idly by while Cambodia gradually developed its economy and consolidated its domestic political position. Pol Pot may well have looked to the extermination of the Indonesian Communist Party in 1965 as an example of what might happen to the CPK if it adopted a gradual course.[220] He explained the rationale behind his ambitious four-year economic plan to a meeting of his fellow party members in 1976: "Why must we move so swiftly? Because enemies attack and torment us. From the east and the west they persist in pounding and worrying us. . . . There is no time to wait for another occasion; waiting until 1977 . . . would be very slow. We won't wait. We must do it [now] even though we have only just emerged from war."[221]

Nationwide collectivization was launched in 1976. Because collectivization was not merely an instrument of economic production but the central organizational mechanism for building a pure communist society, Cambodia's collective farms assumed a more radical form than those in the Soviet Union.[222] The farms provided the organization necessary to transmit and enforce the regime's policies on virtually all aspects of life. The commune was the center for the political education of the masses where party propaganda could be efficiently communicated to a captive audience. Children were indoctrinated with Khmer Rouge political thought from a very early age. Villagers were forced to attend lengthy meetings where they were lectured by Khmer Rouge cadres and forced to denounce fellow citizens who failed to comply with the rules. The slightest deviation from the party line could be monitored and punished. Hair, clothing styles, and even language were subject to strict guidelines. To further the party's assault on all aspects of individualism, even the smallest private vegetable gardens were banned. All traces of capitalism, including money, were abolished. A policy of communal eating was established on the farms, and family members were routinely separated to ensure that alternate loyalties to the regime could not take root.[223]

By this time, Khmer Rouge leaders could have harbored no illusions about the necessity for violence and coercion in the implementation of these policies. On the contrary, the CPK reminded its cadres that "one hand is for production, the other for beating the enemy."[224] Full-scale rebellion broke out in at least one region.[225] In addition to genuine peasant opposition, however, Khmer Rouge ideology vastly exaggerated the scale and scope of the resistance. The regime's production schedules and quotas were profoundly unrealistic, but when peasants proved incapable of meeting them, Khmer Rouge leaders usually interpreted these failures as deliberate sabotage by class enemies and simply stepped up the repression.[226] The least signs of resistance to the regime's elaborate social policies were severely punished, often by death. State security services were explicitly told to proceed from the assumption that "wherever there are catastrophes or under-achievements in terms of building the country, defending the country or sorting out popular living standards, enemies exist in those places."[227] Even the famine that was triggered by the regime's policies was blamed on enemy agents and wreckers.[228]

Perhaps even more than their Soviet or Chinese predecessors, Khmer Rouge leaders seem to have believed that resistance to the revolution was rooted in a person's class and social origins.[229] As Jean-Louis Margolin notes, "for the Khmer Rouge . . . some social groups were criminal by nature, and this criminality was seen as transmittable from husband to wife, as well as an inherited trait. . . . We can speak of the *racialization* of social groups."[230] The Khmer Rouge targeted a wide range of groups that they believed constituted intractable foes of the communization of Cambodian society. These included not only traditional communist enemies such as rich peasants, landlords, and village political or religious leaders, but a host of other groups that appear to have been products of the unique brand of communist ideology advocated by the Khmer Rouge.

Cambodia's city dwellers were the most well known of these victims. The Khmer Rouge hoped that the collective farms would control their enemies in the countryside, but they were even more concerned about the urban population. The cities were the center of the capitalist way of life that the Khmer Rouge had set out to abolish. Urban areas were home to the elites of the old regime and to large concentrations of non-Khmer ethnic groups and nationalities. As Ben Kiernan writes, when "the Khmer Rouge applied their class analysis to the urban population, they found no allies."[231] Thus, immediately after seizing power the Khmer Rouge began forcibly emptying Cambodia's major cities and evacuating their populations to the countryside. In public, the Khmer Rouge claimed that they had taken this drastic step in an effort to bring the swelling city population closer to the food supply. Privately, Pol Pot admitted that he believed that forcing the bulk of the urban population into the countryside and exterminating their elites would render them easier to control.[232]

This policy subjected Cambodia's large urban population to the same kinds of life-shattering changes that had been reserved primarily for the peasantry in the Soviet Union and China. The Khmer Rouge forced nearly two million people out of the capital city, Phnom Penh, alone. Even the hospitals were emptied. Khmer Rouge cadres shot all those who resisted. Outside the cities, the expellees were sorted into groups based on Khmer Rouge ideological categories. Those suspected of any association with the Lon Nol regime or the military were executed immediately. The remainder faced a grueling journey to the countryside. By one estimate, 10,600 residents of Phnom Penh died during the trek, not including those executed at the outset.[233] Once they reached their rural destinations, former city dwellers were put to work in the fields. Many were unaccustomed to hard labor and soon perished from exhaustion. Even after relocation, city dwellers remained suspect and generally received lower food rations on the collectives. When famine struck, they suffered disproportionately. Perhaps four hundred thousand evacuees eventually died.[234]

The regime also targeted certain ethnic and national groups. The Khmer Rouge were deeply suspicious of the loyalty of Cambodia's large Vietnamese and Muslim Cham minorities. Members of these groups were represented disproportionately among the ranks of Pol Pot's victims.[235] Ethnic targeting was so pronounced that Kiernan suggests that "Khmer Rouge conceptions of race overshadowed those of class."[236] On the other hand, as Stephen Heder documents, in many ways Khmer Rouge ideology seems to have conflated the concepts of class and ethnicity.[237] Ethnic groups were singled out in large part because they were believed to be enemies of communism, and because their supposed group loyalties conflicted with the absolute allegiance demanded by the state. In the final accounting, members of the ethnic Khmer majority made up the largest absolute number of victims.

Because many of the regime's enemies were thought to be driven by their social backgrounds and consciousness to oppose communism, much of the violence under the Khmer Rouge was strictly preemptive.[238] No significant attempt was made to produce evidence of a person's individual guilt, beyond his membership in a suspect group, or to reform members of these enemy groups. Many simply were executed outright. Khmer Rouge slogans proclaimed that "it isn't enough to cut down a bad plant, it must be uprooted."[239]

The Khmer Rouge pursued their total revolution at a pace that matched their ambitions. Total collectivization was achieved less than two years after the revolution. The extraordinary pace and scope of the changes imposed by the Khmer Rouge resulted in extraordinary suffering for Cambodian society. Between 1,000,000 and 2,000,000 people perished during the forty-four terrible months the Khmer Rouge governed Cambodia.[240] This staggering loss represents approximately one eighth to one quarter of the country's population. By one estimate, 34 percent of Cambodian men aged twenty to thirty died, as did 40 percent of men aged thirty to forty and 54 percent of people of both sexes over sixty.[241] The Soviet collectivization of agriculture, which left roughly 5 to 6.5 percent of the Soviet population dead, was considerably less violent by comparison.

Half or more of the deaths caused by the Khmer Rouge appear to have been the result of executions or other violence.[242] Vast numbers of victims, however, also died, either of exhaustion while laboring in the fields or of starvation during the famine that gripped the country beginning in 1976. Despite allegations to the contrary, there is little evidence to suggest that the Khmer Rouge deliberately created the famine. Yet, as in the Soviet Union and China, there can be no doubt that the regime took actions that exacerbated it and directed its most deadly effects against suspect classes and other enemies of the regime. As Margolin notes, "the hunger that crushed so many Cambodians over the years was used deliberately by the regime in the service of its interests. . . . The games that were played with the food supply made forced evacuation easier, promoted acceptance of the collective canteens, and also weakened interpersonal relationships, including those between parents and children. Everyone, by contrast, would kiss the hand that fed them, regardless of how bloody it was."[243] The Khmer Rouge refused to relax the pace of the transformation or reduce their grain and rice quotas even after it was clear that a major famine was taking place. On the contrary, the regime continued to export rice in the effort to gain precious foreign capital. Survivors reported that Khmer Rouge cadres repeated the slogan "Losing you is not a loss, and keeping you is no specific gain."[244]

Political Purges and Terror

Documentation on the use of political purges by the Khmer Rouge is very limited, but it is evident that this kind of violence played a significant role in Cambodia.[245] In a pattern that bears a striking similarity to the Great Terror and the Cultural Revolution, these purges appear to have been part of an effort by Pol Pot and perhaps a few other like-minded Khmer Rouge leaders to protect the achievements of the revolution from what they perceived to be powerful and omnipresent enemies. As Jackson observes, "not only were the goals of the revolutionaries extreme . . . but in addition the revolutionaries lived in constant fear that their revolution would either be co-opted by the former ruling classes or crushed from without. The necessity of permanently eliminating all potential counterrevolutionary elites derived from a pervasive fear that revolutions are often betrayed, usually by their leaders."[246]

In fact, the radical nature of Pol Pot's goals and his fears of opposition were closely connected. Pol Pot's extremely radical policies generated opposition not only among the peasants it most directly affected but also within the Communist Party itself—much as collectivization in the Soviet Union and China had done. As noted above, opposition within the party to the radical course favored by Pol Pot and his followers emerged years before the Khmer Rouge launched their nationwide program of social and economic transformation in 1976. The party seems to have been deeply divided over a number of related issues, including Pol Pot's radical economic plans, his ideas for social transformation, and his insistence on complete independence from Vietnam. Even the party's principal expert on agriculture appears to have opposed Pol Pot's radical ideas concerning collectivization.[247] Pol Pot had managed to force his policies through during the war, but some regional party leaders had proved reluctant to implement them.

A series of purges beginning in 1971 had eliminated many suspected opponents in the party, particularly those with connections to Vietnam. When the Khmer Rouge emerged victorious in 1975, however, deep doubts persisted throughout the ranks of the party regarding the radical course that Pol Pot and his followers were plotting for Cambodia. These doubts appear to have emerged in intra-party debates over the shape of the regime's first four-year economic plan. Although many details of these debates are not known, David Chandler speculates that "many experienced cadres viewed with alarm the provisions of the Plan relating to collectivization . . . They knew the targets were impossible. . . . Some of them may also have thought the human consequences prohibitive. . . . There is no evidence that such views were welcomed by the Party Center. Indeed there is ample indirect evidence . . . that by the end of 1976, Pol Pot and his associates had become frightened and enraged by what they saw as widespread opposition to their policies."[248]

Driven by the belief that his radical policies were the key to the construction of his utopian social order, Pol Pot is unlikely to have considered compromise with party moderates as an acceptable solution to this dispute. Moreover, although it is still impossible to know for certain, it seems that opposition to Pol Pot may well have posed a threat not only to his grand schemes but also to his immediate hold on power. Testimony from several defectors indicates that some kind of plot against Pol Pot was launched in September 1976.[249] According to Quinn, an attempted coup "was organized and carried out by military leaders and senior party officials who were dismayed by the continuing level of violence in the country and the stark nature of the new society."[250] One Khmer Rouge defector explained that "all the soldiers wanted to create a rebellion that would allow people to go back to work as they did before the capture of Phnom Penh."[251]

Whatever the true nature of the opposition to Pol Pot, there is little doubt that he perceived his regime and his policies to be in serious jeopardy. Like Stalin and Mao before him, he responded with a series of brutal purges. High-ranking Khmer Rouge officials suspected of involvement in the coup were executed along with anyone voicing opposition to Pol Pot's radical designs. Five of the thirteen highest-ranking Khmer Rouge officials of 1975 were dead by 1978.[252]

Pol Pot's purges, like Stalin's during the late 1930s, rapidly expanded to include large numbers of people with little connection to opposition activity, including many people outside the party. Pol Pot, too, subscribed to a deeply conspiratorial worldview that motivated him to lash out in all directions at imaginary enemies. He accepted Stalin's notion that class struggle would intensify rather than abate after the revolution.[253] In 1975, following the evacuation of Cambodia's cities, a Khmer Rouge party journal warned cadres that the reactionary "classes have already collapsed, but *their views still remain, their aspirations still remain.* Therefore, they continue to conflict with the revolution. Whether they can carry out activities against us is the concrete condition which prompts us to continue the revolution."[254] Pol Pot believed that once the party had closed off the possibility of open opposition, enemies of the regime would be forced to seek to undermine it from within.[255] Indeed, the Khmer Rouge leadership became obsessed with the possibility of internal subversion.[256] In July 1978 a party publication declared that "there are enemies everywhere within our ranks, in the center, at headquarters, in the zones, and out in the villages."[257]

Falling back on the conviction that opposition to the regime was spawned by impure social backgrounds, party members with suspect "life histories" were purged and executed.[258] The same logic justified the practice of murdering victims' family members.[259] The Khmer Rouge are said to have murdered the entire population of the village where Lon Nol had once lived on the grounds that all were relatives or potential supporters of the former president.[260] Military organizations were purged. Intellectuals and all other potential sources of opposition were targeted. The purges also focused on anyone with foreign ancestry or connections abroad, especially the Vietnamese. One Khmer Rouge slogan counseled: "It is better to arrest ten people by mistake than to let one guilty person go free."[261]

No separate estimates have been produced for the death toll resulting from these purges, but the dead surely numbered in the tens of thousands and quite possibly much higher. Nearly fourteen thousand were executed in the infamous facility known as Tuol Sleng (or S-21) alone.[262] Ironically, some observers have suggested that it may have been the excessive brutality of these purges that led a group of Cambodian military officers to turn against the regime in 1978.[263] These officers forged an alliance with the Vietnamese, who ultimately succeeded in overthrowing the Khmer Rouge regime in January 1979.

Less Violent Communist Regimes

Understanding the reasons why the radical communist regimes described here proved to be so violent can also shed light on why many other nominally communist regimes have managed to avoid mass killing. Communist states such as Czechoslovakia, Cuba, Laos, and Nicaragua, among many others, never launched campaigns of mass killing against their citizens. Few of these states could be called pacific, but none experienced bloodshed to compare with the mass killings in the Soviet Union, China, and Cambodia.

A multitude of factors account for the differences between these less violent communist states and the brutal regimes discussed above. Many of these distinguishing characteristics are highly case specific, but I find that four general factors are particularly useful for understanding the less violent path of some communist states. These factors may operate alone, but more commonly they seem to function in combination. They may act to avert mass violence altogether or they may simply reduce its magnitude. It should be emphasized that these factors are not merely an ad hoc list of unrelated variables and conditions. On the contrary, they are significant across diverse cases precisely because they directly influence the causal processes identified in this chapter, decreasing the strategic incentives for mass killing facing communist leaders. The association of these factors with less violent communist regimes, therefore, provides further evidence for the validity of the strategic approach.

The first and most self-evident factor common to many less violent communist regimes is a relatively small population. One reason that the absolute death tolls in China and the Soviet Union were so staggering is that these countries happened to be two of the most populous states in the world. The population of the Soviet Union during the 1930s was over 160 million.[264] China's population at the start of the Great Leap Forward in 1958 was over 659 million.[265] By contrast, none of the communist states in Eastern Europe except for Poland had a population greater than twenty million people in 1946.[266] Although Cambodia's experience with communism — which left between 1,000,000 and 2,000,000 dead out of a total population of only 8,000,000 — demonstrates that even communist states with relatively small populations can produce monumental numbers of victims, it is axiomatic that less populous states must be relatively more radical and violent to generate the same absolute death tolls as larger ones. Indeed, as noted above, the Khmer Rouge consciously set out to surpass China and the Soviet Union in the speed and scope with which they implemented communism.

Because of the close connection between the implementation of radical communist agricultural policies and mass killing, the size of the population employed in the agricultural sector can be especially important. When peasants and farmers make up a relatively smaller percentage of the total population, radical agricultural policies such as collectivization become comparatively easier to implement. This appears to have been the case in East Germany, for example, where only 23 percent of the population was employed in agriculture in 1950, and in Czechoslovakia, where 39 percent were farmers.[267] In contrast, prior to collectivization, more than 80 percent of the populations of the Soviet Union, China, and Cambodia worked in agriculture.[268]

The mitigating effect of small population size is not simply an artifact of the high numerical threshold for mass killing utilized in this book. When the size of the population directly affected by radical communist policies is sufficiently small, the decrease in the amount of violence necessary to implement these policies may actually be greater than the proportional decrease in population relative to the states studied in this chapter. Small population size, especially in the agricultural sector, can open up an entirely different set of options for communist leaders. Dispossessed farmers may be able to find employment in the industrial sector or migrate to other countries. In Russia and China, communist leaders planned to exploit agricultural surpluses to finance industrial development. When the agricultural sector is sufficiently small, however, surpluses may flow in the opposite direction—from industry to agriculture. In these cases, collectivization may be facilitated by a greater reliance on positive economic inducements to convince farmers to join collectives or to compensate individuals for collectivized property.

A second factor that influences the likelihood of mass killing under communism is the degree of radicalism or moderation in the policies of social transformation adopted by these regimes. Less violent communist regimes have generally taken a more moderate, gradual, and incentive-based approach to the transformation of their societies. Compared to Stalin, Mao, and Pol Pot, leaders of less violent communist regimes have proved much less committed to transforming their societies into full-fledged communist utopias. For Stalin, Mao, and Pol Pot, the transformation of society in accordance with Marxist principles was the central goal of the revolution. Its attainment was an end that justified virtually any means. When faced with widespread popular resistance, economic dislocation, and even massive famines, these leaders refused to compromise their goals. Severe adverse consequences were seen not as indications that fundamental ideological assumptions needed to be rethought, or radical policies moderated, but as manifestations of an inevitable class struggle to be crushed without mercy.

Less violent communist leaders, often weaned on Stalinist doctrine, have frequently come to power with similarly radical ideas about the transformation of their societies. When confronted with the harsh realities required to bring about these changes, however, pragmatism has usually prevailed. When severe economic disruptions or widespread popular resistance to government policies have materialized, moderate communist leaders have been willing to compromise and, in some cases, completely abandon plans for the transformation of society. Sometimes these decisions, like Lenin's choice to discontinue war communism in favor of the more moderate NEP, have stemmed from the conclusion that the party simply lacked the capability to force communism on an unwilling society. In other cases, the lack of ideological commitment to the complete socialization of society has made it easier for leaders to suspend radical policies such as collectivization.

Although moderate communist regimes have not been afraid to use violence against political opposition and suppress individual liberties such as freedom of speech, press, and organization, they have generally imposed far fewer dispossessive changes on their societies than were forced upon the people of the Soviet Union, China, and Cambodia. Their more moderate policies have tended to generate fewer adverse affects on smaller numbers of people. As a result, they have also generated less resistance and consequently presented leaders with fewer incentives to contemplate large-scale violence.

Many communist regimes, for example, have focused their economic reforms primarily on the nationalization of major industries, financial institutions, or large estates — especially when foreign owned — and left small-scale agriculture and small businesses in private hands. The expropriation of property in the industrial sector usually is significantly easier to accomplish than it is in agriculture because industrial capital is typically concentrated in the hands of a relatively small number of individuals. The nationalization of industry need not dispossess the mass of industrial workers of their most valued possessions, nor does it impose upon them a fundamentally new way of life. Under communism, industrial laborers often continue to work in the same jobs, at the same factories, and in much the same ways as they had before. In some cases, the communization of industry actually can result in increased wages and improved working conditions for workers.

Even in the Soviet Union, China, and Cambodia, the nationalization of industry was accomplished with relatively little violence compared to the socialist transformation of the countryside. As Moshe Lewin points out, although the Bolsheviks nationalized all major industry and finance soon after they seized power,

> no one had demanded that the proletariat should change their way of life, or even their methods of production, which were the same as they had been before the revolution. Now [with collectivization] . . . the peasants were being urged to pool their property and to organize their production along totally new lines, to make an abrupt transition from a pre-capitalist phase of development to socialism, which was still for them an unknown quantity. It was unthinkable that the peasants could ever accept such a total disruption of their society of their own free will.[269]

Indeed, perhaps the most important aspect of policy moderation in less violent communist regimes has been their approach to the transformation of the agricultural sector, particularly their policies of collectivization. Less violent communist regimes often launched no major collectivization drives at all, or have opted to collectivize a relatively small number of farms. This pattern was particularly prevalent in nominally Marxist African states such as Benin, Cape Verde, Madagascar, and Mozambique, where true collective farms seldom accounted for more than 5 percent of the arable land.[270] In some countries, collectivization appears to have occurred in name only, with collective farms serving as a cover for the operation of private companies or for the traditional agricultural practices of individual farmers.[271] Other regimes have retreated from plans for large-scale collectivization after encountering practical difficulties or strong resistance from the peasantry. Such was the case in both Yugoslavia and Poland in the early 1950s.[272]

A few communist regimes, however, do appear to have succeeded in introducing widespread agricultural collectivization with relatively little violence or coercion. Often free from the real or perceived pressures for rapid industrialization and increasing military expenditures that impelled the Soviet, Chinese, and Cambodian collectivization programs, many of these states have felt less need to extract resources from agriculture and less urgency in achieving full collectivization. They have usually elected to implement collectivization with much greater freedom and flexibility for farmers, frequently by means of a gradual or staged approach. They have tended to rely on positive inducements, economic incentives, and political propaganda in order to encourage participation in collectives. They have permitted wealthier peasants to join collectives. Crucially, in contrast to the excessive and uncompensated seizures of grain and confiscation land that characterized collectivization in the Soviet Union, China, and Cambodia, less violent communist regimes have tended to demand less of their peasants' harvest and pay more for it. They have provided greater compensation for confiscated land and other property, especially from smallholders.

The collectivization of agriculture in Hungary illustrates both the violence associated with efforts to force a rapid transition to collectivization and the potential for a less violent transition when more moderate methods are employed. Hungary's first collectivization drive was launched under pressure from the Soviet Union and was heavily influenced by the Stalinist model. Peasants were forced to join collectives. Thousands of so-called kulaks were arrested, and cadres commonly resorted to violence to suppress opposition to collectivization.[273] These policies met with stiff resistance from the peasantry and provoked a major economic and political crisis for the new regime. Stalin's death in 1953, however, eased pressure from the Soviet Union for rapid collectivization and allowed a more moderate regime to come to power. Collectivization was largely abandoned, and many of the newly formed collectives were dissolved. A second collectivization drive was launched in 1958 by the regime installed by the Soviet Union following the suppression of the Hungarian revolution. As Joan Sokolovsky documents, however, the new regime adopted a considerably more moderate approach to collectivization.[274] State investments in agriculture, including aid from the Soviet Union and other Eastern European countries, were substantially increased. Peasants were compensated for the land, animals, and equipment that they contributed to the collectives. Subsidies for the purchase of equipment and livestock were provided to collective farms. Greater autonomy was granted to the collectives. Perhaps most importantly, the class struggle against the kulak was explicitly repudiated and all peasants were encouraged to participate in the collectives.[275] By the early 1960s, almost all of Hungary's arable land had been organized into state or collective farms with very little violence.

A third factor affecting the likelihood that communist regimes will engage in mass killing is the degree to which those groups and individuals liable to be dispossessed by the communization of society are capable of fleeing the country. The exodus of potential enemies of the regime limits the scope of the repression the regime must use to impose the transition to communism. It can also make available vital resources, especially land, that can used to entice the rest of the population into compliance. Under these circumstances, regimes may be able to make the transition to communism relatively peacefully—although seldom without any violence whatsoever. In Cuba, for example, approximately one million people out of a population of less than eight million fled the country in the aftermath of the 1959 revolution.[276] Among those who left were the owners of most of Cuba's major industries and large agricultural plantations. This exodus left Fidel Castro's regime with significant resources that might otherwise have required considerable violence to procure. Although several thousand people were killed as Castro cracked down on his remaining political opponents, over 85 percent of the land was ultimately consolidated in state and collective farms.[277] Robert Melson argues that the flight of "upper and middle classes" to the United States may have allowed Cuba to get "rid of its real and imagined enemies without having to resort to genocide."[278]

A similar pattern emerged in Vietnam after the Geneva Accords divided the country in 1954. More than nine hundred thousand residents of North Vietnam, or over 6 percent of the population, fled to the South.[279] Bernard Fall writes that as a result of this migration, "not only was land freed for redistribution by the Viet-Minh, but a vast reservoir of potential anti-Communist subversive elements was cleared from the area."[280] Between 1,500 and 50,000 people may have been killed in connection with the collectivization of agriculture in North Vietnam, but such figures pale in comparison to the massive violence experienced in the Soviet Union, China, and Cambodia.[281] The same may have been true in East Germany, where over 3,500,000 people, almost 20 percent of the population, fled the communist regime between 1950 and 1961, many as a direct response to collectivization.[282] Likewise, over one million Koreans, more than 10 percent of the population above the 38th parallel, made their way to the South between 1945 and 1947 following the communist takeover.[283] Hundreds of thousands of Japanese, including a major percentage of Korea's large landowners, also fled Korea after the Second World War. Estimates of the number of people killed by the North Korean regime vary widely, and it is very possible that mass killing did occur there, but several authors have noted that the exodus may have eased the process of communization in the North.[284]

The fourth reason that some communist regimes have avoided mass killing is that the leaders of these regimes do not seem to have shared the ultra-paranoid worldview held by Stalin, Mao, and Pol Pot. Leaders in less violent regimes have generally rejected, or at least placed less emphasis on, the Stalinist notions that individual behavior is determined by immutable class origins and that class struggle is destined to intensify following the victory of communist forces. Indeed, a shift in the mentality of the communist leadership goes a long way toward explaining why mass killing ceased virtually overnight in the Soviet Union and China immediately following the deaths of Stalin and Mao.[285] In his secret speech to the Twentieth Party Congress in 1956, for example, Khrushchev accused Stalin of being "sickly suspicious . . . everywhere and in everything he saw 'enemies,' 'two-facers' and 'spies.' " He explicitly rejected Stalin's notion that the class struggle would intensify as communism progressed. He attacked Stalin for using "mass repression at a time when the revolution was already victorious, when the Soviet State was strengthened, when the exploiting classes were already liquidated. . . . [H]e chose the path of repression and physical annihilation, not only against actual enemies, but against individuals who had not committed any crimes against the party and the Soviet government."[286]

Prior to Stalin's death in 1953, the distinction between the paranoid, Stalinist worldview and the more moderate views of less violent communist leaders was most clearly represented by the public split between Stalin and the Yugoslav leadership under President Josip Tito. Stalin attacked Tito over a wide range of issues, including Yugoslavia's more gradual, voluntary program for the collectivization of agriculture.[287] A major aspect of the dispute, however, focused on the Yugoslav attitude toward class struggle. Yugoslav leaders acknowledged that they would face enemies in the transition to communism, but unlike Stalin, they also believed that the former "exploitative classes" could be reformed and integrated into the rest of society. They rejected the Stalinist tactic of using terror as a prophylactic measure to suppress entire classes, focusing repression instead on specific individuals who resisted communist policies.[288] Stalin believed that the Yugoslav leadership's failure to launch an all-out assault on the capitalist classes, especially the kulaks, was a grave error that amounted to a repudiation of the policies he had fought so hard to implement in the Soviet Union. In a 1948 letter to the Yugoslav Communist Party, Stalin and Molotov attacked Yugoslav leaders for "their denial of the strengthening of capitalist elements, and in connection with this, the sharpening of the class struggle in the villages." They charged that "this denial arose from the opportunist contention that in the transitional period between capitalism and socialism, the class struggle does not become sharper, as taught by Marxism-Leninism, but dies out, as averred by opportunists of the Bukharin type, who postulated a decadent theory of the peaceful absorption of the capitalist elements into the socialist structure."[289]

Tito's comparatively moderate ideas about the nature of domestic opposition and the usefulness of repression also applied to the Yugoslav Communist Party itself. Tito did not subscribe to Stalin's theory that enemies of communism would infiltrate the party in vast numbers, seeking to destroy it from within. He proclaimed that "our revolution does not devour its children."[290] Although Tito was not afraid to crack down on the Cominformists in the party who had sided with Stalin during the Yugoslav-Soviet confrontation, Richard West stresses that "the persecution of Cominformists never became a witch-hunt, similar to the smelling out of 'Trotskyists' and 'saboteurs' in the Soviet Union during the 1930s. The great majority of people arrested in Yugoslavia really were Cominformists."[291] Perhaps twelve thousand were imprisoned, but there were few executions. Tito warned, "We mustn't allow petty suspicions to lead us, like the Russians, into destroying our comrades. We have to give our comrades a chance to correct their mistaken views."[292]

Reflecting on the violent history of the twentieth century, Robert Conquest observed that "humanity has been savaged and trampled by rogue ideologies."[293] As I have described in this chapter, radical communist ideologies savaged and trampled the Soviet Union, China, and Cambodia from top to bottom.

The mass killings carried out in these three countries were remarkably similar. Indeed, there can be little doubt that the younger regimes consciously studied, emulated, and sometimes attempted to outdo the ones that preceded them. All three regimes launched extremely radical campaigns to transform agricultural production. Each campaign ultimately resulted in massive violence, severe economic disruption, and famine. These catastrophes spawned increasing political opposition within the ruling parties of each state, which, in turn, provided the impetus for radical leaders to launch major political purges in order to protect their positions and their visions for society. Motivated by fantastically paranoid beliefs about the scope and nature of the opposition, each leader consequently broadened his purge until it swallowed a vast array of innocent victims in his own party and in society at large.

These were the acts of true believers. Stalin, Mao, and Pol Pot were radicals, even among members of their own radical political parties. Each sought more, faster, and deeper changes than almost all of his contemporaries. Each was convinced that his ends justified his means. Each ultimately sanctioned the use of massive violence because he believed it was the only "practical" way to achieve and protect his utopian vision for society.

Communism, especially the radical brand of communism preached by Stalin, Mao, and Pol Pot, today appears to be drawing its last breaths. These men may have subscribed to the maxim that one cannot make an omelet without breaking eggs, but as Richard Pipes has correctly pointed out, "apart from the fact that human beings are not eggs, the trouble is that no omelet has emerged from the slaughter."[294] The communist states of the Soviet empire have crumbled. With few exceptions, the remaining communist regimes in other parts of the world are steadily leading their societies closer to free markets, agricultural de-collectivization, and private property. The principles of communism have been widely discredited in the eyes of the world, and it seems highly unlikely that new revolutionaries will emerge to fight for them.[295] The single most important cause of mass killing in the twentieth century appears to be fading into history.

The strategic approach cannot help us foresee if or when similarly violent ideologies might emerge again. The history of communism in the Soviet Union, China, and Cambodia is a powerful demonstration of the degree to which historical accidents, serendipity, and the power of individual personalities can determine the rise of extremely radical and violent groups. The strategic approach, however, can help us recognize the general characteristics of ideologies, which, if deeply held by those with the power to act on them, may represent a significant danger of mass killing. As noted above, history's most savage ideologies have been those that called for the extremely rapid and radical transformation of society.

Such transformations almost always have come at great cost in human life.

It is impossible to rule out the advent of completely novel belief systems, but few contemporary ideological contenders seem ready to rival the bloody utopias of radical communism in their desire to rebuild society from the ground up. Radical racist ideologies remain a danger, but, with the possible exception of anti-Semitism, these ideologies have tended to remain localized to certain regions of the world and have been targeted against geographically localized ethnic groups. One reason why radical communism became history's most deadly ideology was its contention that it could, indeed that it must, be applied to every society on earth. No single racist ideology has attained the global appeal of communism, nor does any seem likely to do so.

Radical Islamist ideologies have sought a similar degree of control over society, and Islamist regimes in Sudan, Iran, and Afghanistan under the Taliban indeed have proved exceptionally violent. Yet these ideologies seem likely to remain restricted to the Muslim world. Perhaps more important, even the most radical Islamist regimes have not sought to completely dispossess the most populous groups in their societies, as the communist regimes described in this chapter did. This suggests that the violence associated with the attempt to foster Islamist societies may be less pervasive, although certainly not without bloodshed altogether. It may still be premature to celebrate the "end of history," but if no similarly radical ideas gain the widespread applicability and acceptance of communism, humanity may be able to look forward to considerably less mass killing in the coming century than it experienced in the last.[296]

5. ETHNIC MASS KILLINGS: TURKISH ARMENIA, NAZI GERMANY, AND RWANDA

Ethnic, national, and religious groups have been frequent victims of mass killing in the twentieth century. I distinguish ethnic mass killings from other instances of mass killing not simply by the distinct ethnic affiliation of the victims, but by the explicitly racist or nationalist ideologies and goals of the perpetrators. This terminology distinguishes cases of ethnic mass killing from other episodes of mass killing that are directed against specific ethnic groups but are motivated primarily by military considerations — as in cases of counterguerrilla mass killings targeted against an ethnically based insurgency movement — or by the desire for territory, as in the genocide of indigenous people or genocides during wars of territorial annexation.[1]

In this chapter I examine the genocide of Armenians in Turkey in 1915, the Nazi genocide of Jews in Germany and German occupied territories during the Second World War, and the genocide of Tutsi in Rwanda in 1994. These events represent three of this century's most violent episodes of ethnic mass killing. Racist or nationalist motives also appear to have played a prominent role in a number of other major mass killings in the last one hundred years, including, but not limited to, mass killings during the Soviet deportation to Siberia of Chechens-Ingush, Crimean Tartars, and various other nationalities from 1937 to 1953; the expulsion of ethnic Germans from Eastern Europe in 1945–47; the partition of India in 1947–48; the partition of East Pakistan/Bangladesh in 1971; and the civil war in Bosnia-Herzegovina between 1992 and 1995.[2]

Despite the extraordinarily violent record of these states, most racist and nationalist societies have not experienced mass killing. As I showed in chapter 1, the history of the twentieth century is replete with examples of deeply divided societies that have persisted for long periods without mass killing, although seldom without any violence whatsoever. Any effort to understand why some racist or nationalist regimes have proved so violent, therefore, must also seek to identify the factors and conditions that help to explain why others have not engaged in mass killing. Thus, in addition to the genocidal regimes of Nazi Germany, Turkey, and Rwanda, we must also consider racist and nationalist regimes that have not engaged in mass killing despite the presence of severe discrimination and lower levels of conflict between ethnic groups.

The remainder of this chapter is divided into five main sections. In the first section I describe the general strategic motivations for ethnic mass killing. In the second, third, and fourth sections I utilize this perspective to help explain the mass killings in Turkish Armenia, Nazi Germany, and Rwanda. In the fifth section I discuss the history of several "less violent" racist and nationalist regimes.

A STRATEGIC PERSPECTIVE ON ETHNIC MASS KILLING

Like the communist mass killings described in chapter 4, ethnic mass killings result from the effort to fundamentally reorganize society at the expense of certain groups. Both radical communist regimes and radical racist or nationalist regimes have been practitioners of social engineering on a monumental scale. Whereas the former have attempted to transform the economic and political organization of society, the latter have sought to transform its ethnic, national, or religious composition. From this perspective, at least, the oft debated comparison between Stalin and Hitler is justified.[3] As Alan Bullock's comparative study of the two leaders concludes, each man was committed to a "vision of a world which, however great the differences between them was equally inhuman."

> Hitler saw himself as called on by Providence to rescue the German people from the humiliation of defeat and the decadence of Weimar; to restore them to their rightful historic position as a master race, and to guarantee it for the future by creating a new Germanic empire in Eastern Europe. Stalin saw his mission as ending the centuries-old backwardness of Russia, turning a peasant society into a modern industrialized country and at the same time creating the first socialist state in the world. Nei-

ther task could be carried out without countless material and human sacrifices, but on the stage of world history on which they were actors the
cost had never counted.[4]

It might be argued that communist attempts at social engineering have
represented a "creative" program, in the sense that they have sought to
build new social structures, while racism and nationalism are purely destructive, seeking to change society simply by marginalizing or subtract-
ing some of its members. Although there is some truth to this view, in
practice both communist and racist/nationalist ideologies have contained
significant destructive as well as creative elements. Stalin, Mao, and Pol
Pot each believed that certain social groups or classes had no part to play
in the new society they were seeking to create, even if at times they were
willing to consider the possibility that these enemies could be reformed
rather than exterminated. Their ideology often seemed directed as much
against these groups as it was *toward* the creation of anything else. Conversely, each of the racist regimes studied in this chapter appears to have
viewed its mission not simply as the elimination of hated ethnic minorities but as the creation of a new, more harmonious society in which conflicts between groups would no longer occur and in which the dominant
group and its unique culture would be able to flourish.

The effort to eliminate supposedly alien ethnic or national elements,
therefore, has often been combined with ambitious projects to further the
cultural, material, and even biological prerogatives of favored groups.[5]
Nowhere was this revolutionary form of racist social engineering more
apparent than in Nazi racial and population policies. Hitler's crusade to
purge Germany of its Jews was only one part, albeit the centerpiece, of a
much broader program designed to reorganize the demographic composition of all of Europe.[6] Even the non-Jewish populations resident in vast
swaths of Eastern Europe were to be relocated to make room for farms
worked by ethnic Germans resettled from all over Europe. The foremost
aim of this plan was to insulate Germany from the threat of starvation
blockades like the one it had suffered under during the First World War,
but it was also intended to bring Europe's German minorities under the
direct protection of the Reich and concentrate the Aryan gene pool in a
single geographical area, thereby ensuring the biological purity and
strength of future Germans generations.

The Nazis' eugenic master plan was also pursued through a wide range
of fantastic schemes including the forced sterilization of "racially inferior"
Germans, the abduction of "racially valuable" children from occupied nations, the official promotion of large families for German women, and
even the creation of Aryan "stud farms" where supposedly racially supe-

rior men could pass along their genes to dozens of Aryan women.[7] Racial considerations were introduced into nearly every aspect of German life. These and other Nazi policies have led some scholars to conclude that Hitler aimed for a "racial revolution" in German society no less profound than the communist revolution in Russia.[8] Indeed, Heinrich Himmler, the chief of the Nazi SS, referred to his racial program as the "socialism of good blood."[9]

Although no other racist state has generated plans matching the scope and scale of Nazi social engineering, other regimes have attempted to achieve both creative and destructive goals through the process commonly known as "ethnic cleansing." Episodes of ethnic cleansing in the twentieth century have resulted from two primary motives. First, ethnic cleansing has been used in the effort to implement racist or nationalist ideologies calling for the ethnic, national, or religious purification of certain territories. Second, campaigns of ethnic cleansing have been utilized as a radical means to resolve political or military conflicts between ethnic groups over the control of territory. Most incidents of ethnic cleansing seem to be driven by a combination of these motives, although the latter has probably been more prominent, especially in recent years.

Ethnic mass killings, especially the Holocaust, have tended to be portrayed as little more than killing for killing's sake. From this point of view, the social transformation sought by racist or nationalist regimes is simply mass killing itself. The strategic approach, however, suggests that ethnic mass killing occurs when leaders come to believe that large-scale violence is the most practical way to accomplish a policy of ethnic cleansing. Although the terms "ethnic cleansing" and "mass killing" or "genocide" are often used interchangeably in popular discourse, I believe it is useful to maintain a clear distinction between them. Ethnic cleansing aims at forcibly removing large numbers of people from a given territory, a process that sometimes but not always involves mass killing.[10] The line between ethnic cleansing and mass killing can be a fine one, but mass killing remains a means to an end, not an end in itself.

Policies of large-scale, rapid ethnic cleansing have often gone hand in hand with mass killing because ethnic cleansing frequently results in the total material and political disenfranchisement of certain groups. Ethnic cleansing, like communist policies such as agricultural collectivization, is fundamentally a policy of social engineering. Like collectivization, it completely dispossesses vast numbers of people, forcing them to relinquish their possessions, livelihoods, and homelands. Even if leaders might prefer to carry out ethnic cleansing in a humane, orderly fashion, it is seldom long before they recognize that forcing changes of such magnitude on large numbers of people in a very short period can be difficult or impossible without resorting to the most extreme levels of violence. Both ethnic and communist mass killings, therefore, can be considered variations of "dispossessive" mass killing. Although the dispossessive consequences of ethnic cleansing tend to be more complete and devastating than communist policies such as collectivization, communist policies often have produced greater numbers of victims since they typically target the largest groups in their societies. Racist or nationalist policies, by contrast, usually are confined to minority groups.

Ethnic cleansing can lead to mass killing for three primary reasons. First, massive violence is often required to coerce large numbers of people to abandon their homes, belongings, and ways of life for what at best is usually a meager existence in a distant land. As Robert Hayden observes, "Physical slaughter enters the picture as an element of ethnic cleansing, since, after all, it usually takes a great deal of pressure to persuade people to leave their homes for 'homelands' that they might, in fact, never have seen."[11] This is the pattern of violence that characterized the mass killings in the former Yugoslavia from 1990 to 1995 when Serbian nationalists sought to rid contested territories of Muslims and Croats. For many observers, the extreme violence and seemingly gratuitous brutality of the war was difficult to comprehend. As Mark Danner observes, however, Serbian "officers were making rational, systematic use of terror as a method of war. Rather than being a regrettable but unavoidable concomitant of combat, rapes and mass executions and mutilations here served as an essential part of it. The Serbs fought not only to conquer territory but to 'clear' it of all traces of their Muslim or Croat enemies; or, as the notorious Serb phrase has it, to 'ethnically cleanse' what they believed was 'their' land."[12]

Second, rapidly relocating large numbers of people, some of whom may be sick, very old, or very young, can take a substantial toll in human life. The frequently inhospitable conditions prevailing in resettlement locations may result in further mortality. Many regimes seeking to implement ethnic cleansing simply lack the vast logistical resources necessary to carry out such transfers in a humane manner. Perhaps more importantly, because the organizers of ethnic cleansing usually view their victims as a substantial threat, they are rarely willing to devote scarce resources to ensuring their enemies' well-being. Perpetrators of ethnic cleansing may not actively seek to exterminate their victims, but seldom are they prepared to make significant sacrifices for their victims' welfare or survival. For example, tens of thousands of Jews died as a result of the harsh conditions imposed during deportation and ghettoization in the years between 1939 and 1941. Yet, as Christopher Browning has docu-

mented, during this period "ghettoization was not a conscious prepara-
tory step . . . to facilitate mass murder nor did it have the 'set task' of decimating the Jewish population."[13] As I will describe below, the Nazi
decision to physically annihilate the Jews does not appear to have been
reached until sometime in the summer or fall of 1941. Rather, the deaths
during deportation and ghettoization in this period resulted primarily
from the extremely low priority that the ghettos received in the Nazi al-
location of resources, especially food and medicine.

Finally, the desire to implement ethnic cleansing may lead to mass
killing when leaders conclude that the deportation and relocation of large
numbers of people is impractical or impossible. This conclusion may be
based on the belief that no territory is available to accept deported groups,
that relocating vast numbers of people would be prohibitively costly or
time consuming, or that refugees would continue to pose a cross-border
threat even after their deportation. Under these circumstances, leaders are
more likely to decide that straightforward mass killing of entire populations is the only practical means to remove ethnic groups from specific
territories. Alternatively, perpetrators may decide to accept the continued
presence of victim groups in society and seek instead to deprive them of
the ability to organize politically or militarily by killing and intimidating
the victim groups' elites, intellectuals, or men of military age on a mass
scale.

THE ARMENIAN GENOCIDE OF 1915

From 1915 to 1918, between 500,000 and 1,500,000 Armenians out of a
total population of less than 2,000,000 living in Turkey died in the first
ethnic mass killing of the twentieth century. Since the mid-sixteenth century, Armenian Christians had lived as one of many minorities in the
Ottoman empire, most in the eastern regions of what is now modern
Turkey. The Ottoman millet system granted the Armenians substantial
autonomy in their internal and religious affairs, but they remained officially subordinate to Muslims and enjoyed fewer rights and privileges under Ottoman law.[14] Despite this prejudicial relationship, Armenians and
Turks managed to live in relative peace until the last decades of the nineteenth century, when the Ottoman empire reached the verge of collapse.
The Armenian genocide was the final move in a long series of responses
by the Turks designed to halt the accelerating disintegration of their empire. When Turkish leaders became convinced that other solutions, some
involving violence, others offering accommodation and compromise,
had failed to counter what they perceived as a threat to the survival of

Turkey itself, ethnic cleansing and mass killing emerged as the preferred answers to the what the Turks referred to as the "Armenian question."

The "Armenian Question" and Early Attempts at Reform

The Ottoman empire had been in a state of decline since the late seventeenth century, losing important territories in Eastern Europe, Northern Africa, and the Balkans. In the nineteenth century the empire's territorial losses were increasingly the result of nationalist movements discontent with life as second-class citizens under Ottoman rule. Although the empire often responded to these rebellions with repression, it also undertook reforms designed to increase equality among imperial subjects and thereby decrease the impetus for further secessionist movements.[15] These reforms culminated in 1876 with the adoption of a new constitution that instituted greater democracy and proclaimed equality for all Ottoman subjects, including Armenians.

In practice, however, many of the new legal reforms remained unrealized. Moreover, by the late nineteenth century, many nationalist groups had decided that they had little interest in remaining part of the Ottoman empire under any conditions. These groups would be satisfied with nothing less than complete independence.[16]

The so-called Armenian question became a central issue in the collapse of the Ottoman empire during the Russo-Turkish War of 1877–78. Desperate to hold on to what remained of the Ottoman empire in Europe, the Turks increasingly resorted to violence against civilians in an effort to crush the rapidly multiplying separatist movements there. War erupted when Russia intervened to protect Christian populations in the Ottoman empire from this violent persecution, particularly the Slavic peoples of Bulgaria and Bosnia and Herzegovina. Russia routed Turkey in the war, occupying large areas of the empire and advancing to the outskirts of Constantinople. In 1878, the Western powers intervened to negotiate the Treaty of Berlin. Russia agreed to withdraw its army from Turkey, and in return the Ottomans agreed to grant several Balkan provinces autonomy or independence. The treaty also included clauses that pledged the empire to protect the rights of Christian minorities, specifically naming the Armenians.

Although the Turks resented the intervention by Western powers in their domestic affairs, the treaty provided no real means to enforce the protection of the Armenians or other minorities. Indeed, in the years after the treaty was signed, Armenians continued to be subjected to discriminatory policies. They suffered periodic depredations by Kurdish gangs, which went unpunished by Turkish authorities. Most Armenians had remained loyal to the empire during the war with Russia, but some of them began to organize politically and militarily.[17] Some groups appear to have wanted merely greater autonomy for Armenians within the empire, while others were clearly seeking independence. Some advocated reform through peaceful agitation, but others believed that violent means were necessary and justified.[18] Many seem to have concluded from the Russo-Turkish War that further intervention by Russia or the Western powers was Armenia's best hope for escaping Turkish domination.

From Reform to Repression

The Turkish regime under Sultan Abdul Hamid II saw Armenian political mobilization as a serious threat to the integrity of the Ottoman empire. Separatist movements in the Balkans had eroded the periphery of the empire, but the Armenian reform movement was perceived as a threat to the heart of Turkey itself. Furthermore, Muslims (primarily Turks and Kurds) actually outnumbered the Armenians in Anatolia, the region of Turkey that would have comprised the territory of a separate Armenian state. If the Armenians gained independence, these Muslims would have been forced to live under minority Christian rule.

The sultan is reported to have claimed that he would rather be beheaded than permit the formation of an independent Armenia.[19] He believed that the reforms of the first half of the century had failed to provide a solution to minority problems in the empire. Instead, he reacted to Armenian political agitation with increasingly severe political repression and violence, particularly during the early 1890s. The Western powers threatened to intervene to enforce the Treaty of Berlin if the Armenian reforms were not implemented. Finally, in response to an escalating number of Armenian political demonstrations, uprisings, and some acts of terrorism, the regime launched a wave of massacres that continued from 1894 to 1896 and that the sultan declared would deal with the Armenians "not by reform but by blood."[20]

Tens of thousands of Armenians, possibly over one hundred thousand, were slaughtered. Thousands more fled the country. For all their savagery, however, the massacres do not appear to have been intended to exterminate the entire Armenian population or to force them out of the country. Rather, they seem to have been carried out primarily in the effort to stamp out the Armenian independence movement.[21] As Vahakn Dadrian concludes:

> The resort to exterminatory massacres was viewed by the whole array of perpetrators as a problem-solving behavior. The Turko-Armenian conflict required a solution to be devised by central authorities. Since that conflict basically revolved around a system of reforms which, to these au-

thorities . . . were anathema, and since the pressure of the [European] powers to adopt these reforms was becoming intense and portentous, the option for a radical solution was considered and decided upon. . . . By substantially decimating the Armenian population in the provinces, the issue of Armenian reforms would erode, and, by the same token, through such punishment and terror, the Armenians would be reduced to an impoverished, cowed and even more submissive entity.[22]

For a time, the massacres and repression appeared to have been successful in "solving" the Armenian question. When the European powers failed to intervene to protect the Armenians as they had done for Christian minorities in the Balkans, many Armenians lost hope. Most Armenian revolutionary groups disbanded, moved underground, or scaled back their protests. Officially sanctioned repression and attacks against Armenians continued, but at much lower levels than the violence of 1894–96.

A Second Chance for Reform

The Sultan's violent solution, however, proved to be only temporary. The Armenian question resurfaced in Turkish politics in 1908 when a group of military officers representing the Committee of Union and Progress (Ittihad ve Terakki), also known as the "Young Turks" or Ittihadists, seized control of the government. The Young Turks came to power hoping to prevent the further decline of the empire by a return to the principles of Ottomanism and the 1876 constitution—suspended since the Russo-Turkish war—which promised greater equality, autonomy, and representation for all Ottoman subjects, including Armenians. The Young Turks specifically rejected the "despotic" style of governance practiced by the sultan. Indeed, many Armenians cheered the revolution in 1908. Two of the largest Armenian political parties had actively supported the Young Turks against the sultan.[23] The Young Turks provided arms to Armenian groups so that the Armenians could help in the fight against Islamic conservatives.[24] Once in power, the Ittihadists enacted a number of concrete measures designed to redress Armenian grievances.[25]

Like the earlier Turkish attempts to stave off the collapse of the empire through liberalization, however, the Young Turks' experiment with reform proved a failure. Christian minorities became disillusioned when the regime proved unwilling or unable to protect them from local Muslim groups opposed to the reforms. Rather than appeasing secessionist impulses, the new freedoms encouraged some minority groups to agitate for even greater autonomy and led others to conclude that the time was ripe to push for independence.[26] A series of disastrous defeats for the empire ensued. In 1908 Bulgaria proclaimed its independence, Austria officially annexed Bosnia and Herzegovina, and Albanian nationalists launched a major revolt against Ottoman rule. In 1911 the Italians occupied Libya. By the end of that year, the Young Turks had lost more than 35 percent of the empire's territory and 20 percent of its population.[27] The final humiliation occurred in October 1912 when a coalition of Balkan states, supported by Russia, launched a major offensive that succeeded in expelling the Ottoman empire from virtually all its remaining territories in Europe.

Nor did the Young Turks' reforms succeed in solving the Armenian question within Turkey itself. Many Armenians soon became disillusioned with the slow pace of reforms.[28] Locally organized attacks against Armenians continued. An especially brutal massacre occurred in the province of Adana in 1909. Although the regime sent army units to restore order and even prosecuted several Turks for their role in the violence, there were rumors that the military had participated in the massacres, prompting doubts about the government's commitment to protect Armenians.[29] The main Armenian parties remained opposed to secession until after the outbreak of the First World War, but in the intervening years some appear to have concluded that the chaos created by the Turkish defeats presented a political opportunity to increase their rights and autonomy within the empire.[30] A radical minority also may have seen the developments in the Balkans as proof of what a determined independence movement could accomplish and hoped to emulate these achievements.

From Integration and Reform to Ethnic Cleansing and Genocide

In January 1913 a small faction of radical Turkish nationalist officers within the Ittihadist Party, distressed by the political and military disasters of the previous years, seized control of the regime in a coup d'état and established a military dictatorship. The leaders of this group, the triumvirate of Talat Pasha, Ahmed Djemal (Cemal) Pasha, and Enver Pasha, were convinced that earlier policies of Ottomanism and reform had failed to prevent the collapse of the empire or preserve the peace within Turkey. They were determined to prevent any further disintegration of what remained of the once great Ottoman empire.

The leaders of the new regime were convinced that the empire's precipitous decline over the previous century had been the direct result of its multinational character. They believed they could save the Turkish homeland from a similar fate only by forging a homogenous Turkish national state. If separatist minorities had been the cause of the empire's disintegration, they reasoned, they could halt further losses only by ridding the state of its minorities altogether. As Richard Hovannisian argues, "The

Young Turk leaders were drawn to the newly articulated ideology of Turkism, which was to supplant the principle of egalitarian Ottomanism and give justification to violent means for transforming a heterogeneous empire into a homogeneous state based on the concept of one nation, one people."[31]

The leaders of the new regime believed that the Armenian minority represented the most critical threat to the creation of this new, more harmonious Turkish state. In 1913 Armenians were one of the largest remaining non-Turkish groups within the empire. The integration of the Armenians into Turkish society was perceived to be particularly difficult because, unlike other non-Turkish minorities such as Kurds and Arabs, the Armenians were also non-Muslim.[32] While the Young Turks believed that Muslim minorities could eventually be integrated into a Turkish state, they felt that Armenians would never make good Turkish citizens. As Bernard Lewis describes the mentality of the regime: "For the Turks, the Armenian movement was the deadliest of all threats. From the conquered lands of the Serbs, Bulgars, Albanians and Greeks, they could, however reluctantly, withdraw. . . . But the Armenians . . . lay in the very heart of the Turkish homeland — and to renounce these lands would have meant not the truncation, but the dissolution of the Turkish state."[33] The revelation in 1913 that members of an Armenian nationalist party had conspired to assassinate Talat Pasha, the minister of the interior, along with other high-ranking Turkish officials was seen as further proof that the Armenians could never be trusted.[34]

The new Turkish regime felt particularly threatened by the effort on the part of some Armenian groups to elicit support for their cause from foreign powers, especially Russia, Turkey's principal adversary. In the years between 1912 and 1914, Russia, largely for its own strategic and domestic political reasons, exerted increasing pressure on the Turks to grant autonomy to the Armenians.[35] Russia threatened to intervene militarily if the Turks refused to implement reforms or if they attempted to crack down on the growing Armenian unrest in eastern Turkey. In February 1914, as a result of these efforts, Turkey was forced to accept European administration of Turkish Armenia. The Turks blocked complete autonomy or independence for the Armenians, but the ultra-nationalist leaders of the regime were humiliated by yet another foreign intervention in Turkey's sovereign affairs.[36] Worse yet, the agreement seemed one step closer to Armenian secession, the outcome the Turks most desperately wanted to prevent.

Scholars disagree as to whether most Armenians at this time in fact sought an independent state or simply wanted greater autonomy within Turkey.[37] The leaders of the new regime, however, saw little difference between the two objectives. As Dadrian notes, "For the Turks it was not easy to forget that the Balkan nationalities' attainment of complete freedom and independence was traceable to the rudimentary demands for reform which eventually entailed some form of autonomy. . . . [A]ny kind of autonomy in any scheme of reforms for the Armenians was thus defined by the [Young Turk] leaders as a *non plus ultra* for Turkey."[38]

Events following the outbreak of the First World War appear to have provided the leaders of the Turkish regime with what they considered to be final proof that the Armenians constituted a mortal and immediate threat to the integrity of the Turkish homeland. After Turkey entered the war against Russia and the other Allied powers, many Armenians had remained loyal to the empire. Some even enlisted in the Ottoman army. Others, however, believed the outbreak of war was Armenia's best opportunity to gain independence.[39] Thousands of Armenians crossed the border and joined the Russian army. Armenians living abroad offered to raise a force of twenty thousand men to fight the Turks. Many Turks failed to appreciate that these acts represented only a minority of Armenians and were quick to brand the entire Armenian population as traitors.

Sporadic attacks on local Armenian populations began soon after Turkey entered the war, but it was not until the winter of 1914–15 that Turkish policy toward the Armenians seems to have escalated to one of systematic, genocidal deportation. This radicalization seems to have occurred in large part in response to the Turks' rapidly deteriorating military situation. In January 1915 the Russian armies dealt the Turks a series of major defeats, turning back the Turkish invasion at Sarikamis and pushing into Anatolia, the center of the Armenian population. Armenian guerrilla units sabotaged the Ottoman army from the rear. Several Armenian villages rose in open revolt against the regime, some in support of the Russian advance and some in self-defense against Turkish and Kurdish attacks. Again, it is difficult to determine how great a threat these Armenian actions actually posed to the Young Turk regime. The Armenian uprisings do appear to have contributed to the regime's military setbacks, if only by drawing Turkish forces away from the front.[40] Whatever the actual extent of the Armenian threat, however, there is little doubt that Turkish leaders perceived it to be substantial. Gwynne Dyer concludes that "there was a genuine, though mistaken, belief among the Ottoman leaders in Istanbul that there was a deliberate and coordinated Armenian uprising in the East, with empire-wide ramifications."[41]

With the beginning of the allied naval assault on the Dardanelles in February 1915, the empire appeared on the verge of collapse. Fears of impending military defeat increased the sense of urgency for dealing with the Armenians. Indeed, the decision to deport the Armenians was made shortly thereafter.[42] As Talat, one of the principal architects of the genocide, explained the decision at an Ittihadist Party gathering: "It was deemed necessary, in order to avoid the possibility of our army being caught between two fires, to remove the Armenians [from] all scenes of the war and the neighborhood of the railways."[43] Enver Pasha, the minister of war, told the American ambassador in 1915, "You must understand that we are now fighting for our lives . . . and that we are sacrificing thousands of men. While we are engaged in such a struggle as this, we cannot permit people in our own country to attack us in the back."[44] "In time of war," Enver claimed, "we cannot investigate and negotiate. We must act promptly and with determination."[45]

The Turks implemented their solution to the Armenian question swiftly and brutally. The decision was made to remove Armenians from the Turkish homeland immediately using whatever means necessary. Armenian soldiers had already been discharged from the Ottoman army following the military defeats of the winter of 1914–15, with many being forced into labor battalions. Arms were also confiscated from the Armenian civilian population. Armenian political and community leaders were arrested. In April, the regime ordered the deportation of the entire Armenian population of eastern Turkey to camps in the Syrian Desert. By autumn, most of eastern Turkey had been cleansed of its Armenian population. Eventually the deportations were expanded to include virtually all Armenians living in Turkey. The Turks made no effort to separate the small minority of Armenians who may have collaborated with the Russians from the majority who remained loyal. As Talat explained, this method was "utterly impossible," since "those who were innocent today might be guilty tomorrow."[46]

Turkish historians and even some Western scholars have suggested that the deportations were intended as a temporary military measure and that the massive death toll was the unintended result of famine, disease, or uncoordinated attacks by local Kurdish gangs.[47] Turkish actions, and the testimony of contemporary observers, including some Turkish officials, however, strongly suggest that the Turks saw the deportations as a permanent measure designed to solve the Armenian question once and for all. Indeed, many authors have concluded that the deportations were, in fact, intended to exterminate the Armenian population.[48] At a minimum, it appears that the Turks planned to expel the Armenians from the Turkish homeland and to reduce them to a state of permanent isolation and impotence. Able-bodied Armenian men were frequently shot immediately rather than deported, probably out of fear that they might later form the basis for an organized resistance. Armenian political and cultural elites were murdered. Armenian refugees were slaughtered in large numbers even after they had begun their forced march to the camps. The Turks made virtually no effort to provide supplies for the refugees either during their deportation or after they reached the camps.[49] Vast numbers of Armenians continued to perish from starvation and disease until the end of the war.

Documentary evidence of Turkish leaders' decision making during this period is extremely limited, but it seems likely that the regime decided on mass killing in the conviction that other potential options for dealing with the Armenian question had already failed or would not provide a permanent solution to Turkey's problems. Three considerations appear to have persuaded the Young Turks to conclude that ethnic cleansing was the most appropriate means to deal with the Armenian threat.

First, as described above, the leaders of the faction that seized power in 1913 were convinced that the efforts of earlier regimes to address Armenian separatism through reform and liberalization had failed. Vice Marshal Joseph Pomiankowski, who had close contacts with the Ittihadist regime through his position as the Austrian military plenipotentiary in Istanbul and military attaché at Ottoman General Headquarters during the war, noted in his memoirs that Turkish leaders believed that the collapse of the Ottoman empire had been due "to the overabundant humanity of the earlier Sultans who either ought to have had the conquered people forcibly embrace Islam, or ought to have exterminated them."[50] Indeed, even in 1913, the new regime may have been leaning toward some form of ethnic cleansing as the ultimate solution to the Armenian question, only awaiting the opportunity to act.

Second, although Turkish leaders may have considered another round of violent but non-genocidal repression, they knew that even the massive anti-Armenian massacres unleashed by Sultan Abdul Hamid in 1894–96 had failed to produce a long-term solution to the Armenian question. As one influential member of the regime cautioned the Ittihadist Central Committee in 1915:

If we remain satisfied with . . . local massacres . . . , if this purge is not general and final, it will inevitably lead to problems. Therefore it is absolutely necessary to eliminate the Armenian people in its entirety, so there is no further Armenian on this earth and the very concept of Armenia is extinguished. . . . Perhaps there are those among you who feel it is bestial to go so far. You may ask, for instance, what harm could children, the elderly or the sick do to us that we feel compelled to work for their elimination. Or you may feel that only those guilty should be punished. . . . I beg you, gentlemen, don't be weak. Control your feelings of pity. Otherwise these very feelings will bring about your own demise.[51]

Finally, the last remaining alternative — expelling the Armenians from the empire — likely would have appeared highly problematic for the Turks. Enver does seem to have entertained the possibility of expelling the Armenians to Russia, but he soon rejected this option.[52] One of the regime's primary concerns, after all, had been Armenian collaboration with the Russian invaders. Indeed, after the collapse of the Russian army in Turkey in 1917–18, Turkish forces pushed into Russian Armenia and began massacring Armenians who lived there along with the large number of Armenian refugees who had managed to escape across the border during the genocide.[53] Turkey's violent efforts to crush any possibility of an independent Armenia continued even after the First World War ended.[54] The surviving Armenian population was spared only by the intervention of the Red Army and the annexation of Armenia by the Soviet Union.

Nor was it likely that any of Turkey's Muslim neighbors would have been willing or able to accept over one million impoverished and discontented Christian refugees. Even if they had, the Turks might still have feared that the Armenians would simply regroup and attempt to return to reconquer their homeland. Since the Turks believed that the Armenian question had to be "solved" immediately if Turkey was to survive the war, the alternative of encouraging emigration to more distant states would surely have been deemed too time consuming. As one Turkish official declared: "There is no room for Armenians and Turks in our state, and it would be irresponsible and thoughtless for us if we didn't take advantage of this opportunity to do away with [the Armenians] thoroughly."[55]

The inhospitable Syrian Desert appears to have been chosen as the final destination for the deportees at least in part because the Turks wanted to avoid leaving Armenian populations near strategically important railways and roads.[56] This decision also had the effect of making the deportation more arduous, and ultimately more deadly, since it forced the refugees, including the old, young, and infirm, to travel long distances on foot through inhospitable terrain. Although it is possible that the Turks intended for some segment of the Armenian population to go on living in the desert indefinitely, the violent process of deportation and the harsh conditions awaiting the Armenians who survived the journey ensured that mass killing was the ultimate result.

THE HOLOCAUST

The Holocaust, which extinguished the lives of between five and six million Jewish men, women, and children, remains history's most infamous and bloody episode of ethnic mass killing. In many ways the horrors of the Holocaust are impossible to comprehend. Yet, in at least one fundamental sense, the most significant cause of the genocide is relatively transparent. Simply put, Hitler and a small group of radical anti-Semitic elites came to believe that the Jews posed a mortal political and racial threat to the German nation. Drawing on a bizarre combination of anti-Semitic Jewish conspiracy theories and pseudoscientific eugenic ideas, these men eventually concluded that the only way to save Germany was to rid it once and for all of Jewish influence. It was this desire to bring about the ethnic cleansing of German society, and ultimately all of Europe, that led to the Holocaust. As in the Armenian genocide, Nazi leaders did not initially believe that mass killing was the only way to accomplish their goals. Genocide emerged as the preferred response to the "Jewish question" only after the Nazis concluded that other means of expelling the Jews from Europe had proved insufficient to solve the problem as they defined it.

The "Jewish Threat"

Hitler and other radical anti-Semites believed the Jews posed two interrelated threats to Germany. The first threat was essentially political.[57] Hitler was convinced of the authenticity of the *Protocols of the Elders of Zion,* the anti-Semitic work of propaganda that claimed that the Jews were involved in a vast international conspiracy to destroy Germany and achieve world domination.[58] Central to the political aspect of Hitler's anti-Semitism was his belief that the Jews were responsible for the "stab in the back" that, he felt, had led to Germany's defeat in World War I. Hitler believed that during the war the Jews had coordinated the international coalition to isolate Germany and that they had fomented the collapse of the German war effort from within by seizing control of the economy and inciting Germans to revolution.[59] After the war, he believed, Jews continued to manipulate the governments of France, England, and the United States from behind the scenes.

Equally important to Hitler's political anti-Semitism was his belief that an unholy alliance bound Judaism to international Marxism.[60] Hitler was convinced that Marxism was the vehicle through which the Jews sought to dominate the world. He believed that the Jews had already engineered the Bolshevik revolution in Russia. Once in power, he claimed, the Jews had exterminated the Russian elite, whom Hitler believed were of German ancestry. He also noted, with some exaggeration, that the Bolsheviks had "killed or starved about thirty million people with truly fanatical savagery, in part amid inhuman tortures."[61] Hitler feared that the Jewish-Bolshevik alliance was planning a similar fate for Germany. "A victory of Bolshevism over Germany," he wrote, "would not lead to a [new] Versailles treaty, but to the final destruction, even the extermination, of the German people."[62]

In addition to the perceived political threat posed by the Jews, Hitler and other radical anti-Semites also believed that the Jews posed a biological threat to the German people. According to Hitler, the Jews were not a religious group but a biologically distinct race. This idea was rooted in a particularly pernicious variation of the social-Darwinist ideology that pervaded European thinking since the late nineteenth century.[63] In a perverted analogy to Darwin's theory of natural selection, proponents of this thesis argued that human beings belonged to unique races competing for survival. Racial purity was the most valuable asset in this struggle. In Hitler's eyes, of course, the Jews occupied the lowest position in the hierarchy of human races. They were a parasitic race and carriers of congenital diseases. Unable to win their own state or develop their own culture, the Jews lived off the labor and creativity of others, corrupting the purity and strength of other races through interbreeding. But the Jews, despite their supposed biological deficiencies, were not really a weak race in Hitler's eyes. He acknowledged that they had demonstrated a powerful instinct for self-preservation.[64] Through cunning and deception they had achieved positions of power in many of the world's great societies. If nothing was done to check Jewish influence, Hitler feared, the Aryan-German race would die out, the biological bases of its health and power corrupted from within.

Hitler's perception of the seriousness of the Jewish political-biological threat scarcely can be underestimated. In *Mein Kampf* he warned: "If, with the help of his Marxist creed, the Jew is victorious over the other peoples of the world, his crown will be the funeral wreath of humanity and this planet will, as it did thousands of years ago, move through the ether devoid of men."[65] Nor, according to Hitler, was the Jewish menace a matter that could be left to future generations. He believed the Jews posed an immediate threat to German survival.[66]

Despite the fanaticism with which Hitler and other radical anti-Semites believed in the Jewish threat to Germany, most did not immediately conclude that systematic mass killing was the best or only means to counter the Jews. Even Nazi anti-Semitism did not call for mass killing as an end in itself. Rather, the Nazis' primary aim was to purge Germany, and eventually all German-occupied territories, of Jewish influence. As Yehuda Bauer concludes, "the decision to kill Jews was one logical outcome of Nazi ideology, but not the only one."[67]

In contrast to the "intentionalist" interpretation of the Holocaust, which claims that the Nazis, or at least Hitler, had always intended to kill the Jews, the "strategic" interpretation offered here accords with those scholars who contend that the decision to exterminate the Jews was made only after the Nazis encountered a variety of practical problems in attempting to implement less bloody solutions.[68] Although these measures involved significant death, violence, and other inhumanities, they did not yet entail the systematic murder of every Jewish man, woman, and child.

Segregation and Coerced Emigration

Efforts to deal with the perceived threat posed by the Jews began almost immediately after the Nazis gained power in 1933. These efforts evolved through three different, albeit overlapping, phases before the Final Solution was launched. The first phase involved a variety of measures designed to protect Germany politically and biologically from Jewish influence while the Jews remained in Germany. One after another, Jewish economic and political rights were abolished. Jews were excluded from service in the government, medicine, law, academia, and other influential vocations. They were segregated from Germans in public places. Intermarriage between Jews and ethnic Germans was outlawed.

It is doubtful, however, that Hitler and other high-ranking Nazi racial experts ever believed that the Jewish threat as they defined it could be adequately addressed as long as the Jews remained in Germany. These early anti-Semitic policies probably were always intended as temporary measures or were designed to contribute to the second phase of Nazi anti-Jewish policy—the coerced emigration of Jews from Germany. Indeed, as early as 1934, a memorandum produced by the SS Security Service concluded: "the aim of Jewish policy must be the complete emigration of the Jews. . . . [T]he life opportunities of the Jews have to be restricted, not only in economic terms. To them Germany must become a country without a future, in which the old generation may die off with what still remains for it, but in which the young generation should find it impossible to live, so that the incentive to emigrate is constantly in force."[69]

Whatever the true goals of the Nazis' early anti-Jewish measures were, by 1937 at the latest coerced emigration seems to have become the preferred policy for dealing with the Jews. The Nazis imposed progressively harsher economic policies on the Jews, until it became nearly impossible for many to earn a living. Jewish citizenship was revoked. Organized attacks on Jewish individuals, businesses, and places of worship were sanctioned as part of the effort to force the Jews to emigrate.[70] The infamous Kristallnacht pogrom of November 1938 may have been conceived of, at least in part, for this purpose.[71]

Simultaneously, the Nazis undertook numerous actions designed to increase opportunities for Jewish emigration. German bureaucrats actively explored the possibility of cooperating with the British and Zionist organizations to create a Jewish state in Palestine.[72] Negotiations with other nations to facilitate Jewish emigration also were conducted.[73]

Emigration was delayed by the contradictory Nazi policy of confiscating the property of Jewish emigrants and by the reluctance of other countries to accept the subsequently impoverished Jews. Nevertheless, the regime's emigration policies proved very effective. By 1939, roughly 72 percent of Germany's five hundred thousand Jews had fled the country. William Rubinstein suggests that had the process been allowed to continue for a few more years, "it seems very likely that virtually every single Jew in the Nazi Reich would have emigrated to safety."[74]

From Emigration to Deportation

The invasion of Poland in September 1939 marked the beginning of the shift to the third phase of Nazi anti-Jewish policy. More than two million Jews lived in the German occupied areas of Poland. Since Hitler's grand plans for the demographic reorganization of Europe called for repopulating much of Poland with ethnic Germans, these Jews and eventually millions of Poles as well would have to go.[75] The conquest of France and the Low Countries in 1940 increased to over 3.7 million the number of Jews under German control.[76] Coerced emigration of the kind already under way in the Reich was clearly insufficient to deal with this vast population. The emigration process was slow, and the experiences of the previous years suggested that other countries would not be willing to accept such large numbers of refugees. By June 1940, Reinhard Heydrich, the head of the Reich Main Security Office, acknowledged that the "problem" of so many Jews could "no longer be solved by emigration alone."[77]

The outbreak of the Second World War also infused a new sense of urgency into Nazi anti-Jewish planning. Hitler's beliefs about the causes of the German defeat in the First World War led him to fear that Germany could not prevail in the new war as long as the Jewish influence was present in European society. "Before foreign enemies are conquered," he had concluded in *Mein Kampf,* "the enemy within must be annihilated. . . . Once so much as the shadow of defeat grazes a people that is not free of internal enemies [i.e., the Jews], its force of resistance will break and the foe will be the final victor."[78]

These new realities did not, however, immediately result in a decision to exterminate the Jews. Rather, they prompted more serious consideration of plans already being developed within the Nazi bureaucracy for the forced deportation of Jews to foreign territories.[79] This "territorial solution" evolved rapidly from 1939 to 1941.[80] Jews were to be concentrated in urban centers to facilitate their isolation, economic exploitation, and eventual deportation.[81] Early plans called for sending the Jews to the Lublin region of Poland, at the easternmost extremity of the German empire. The Nazis scrapped the Lublin plan, however, after it was decided that the region was needed to settle ethnic Germans from elsewhere in Europe. In some areas, Jews were expelled directly into the Russian-occupied zone of Poland.[82] In March 1940, Hitler was reported to have stated that

> the Jewish question is really a space question which was difficult to solve . . . since he [Hitler] had no space at his disposal. Neither would the establishment of a Jewish state around Lublin ever constitute a solution as even there the Jews lived too close together to be able to maintain a somewhat satisfactory standard of living. . . . He, too, would welcome a positive solution to the Jewish question . . . this, however, was not possible under present conditions when he had not even sufficient space for his own people.[83]

Before long, Europe began to appear too small for the regime's twin goals of attaining German Lebensraum and the creation of Jewish reservations. The Nazis began to consider deportation to more distant locales. Nazi bureaucrats developed fantastic plans to deport millions of Jews to Madagascar or to the wilds of Siberia. These plans were adopted as official policy at the highest levels. In May 1940, Heinrich Himmler, the man most directly responsible for Nazi deportation policies, drafted a memorandum stating that "I hope completely to erase the concept of the Jews through the possibility of a great emigration of all Jews to a colony in Africa or elsewhere. . . . [H]owever cruel and tragic . . . this method is still the mildest and best, if one rejects the Bolshevik method of physical extermination of people out of inner conviction as un-German and impossible."[84] Heydrich took up the same theme a few months later. Arguing that "biological extermination . . . is undignified for the German people as a civilized nation," he suggested that "after victory we will impose the condition on the enemy powers that the holds of their ships be used to transport the Jews along with their belongings to Madagascar or elsewhere."[85]

Tens of thousands of Jews died during deportation and upon arrival in the ghettos between 1939 and 1941. Many more surely would have perished if any of the plans for deportation had reached fruition. Nazi leaders made conflicting statements as to whether the deported Jews would be allowed to have their own state or whether they would remain quarantined in a reservation system policed by Germany. Although these policies were brutal and cruel, they did not seek the physical annihilation of the Jews. Indeed, while the Nazis were clearly willing to accept a significant amount of Jewish deaths during deportation and ghettoization and did little to ameliorate the harsh conditions, the possibility of using these "natural" processes to systematically exterminate the Jewish population was raised by some local authorities before 1941 and expressly rejected.[86]

While these deportation schemes may seem farfetched, the evidence is overwhelming that they were taken seriously by Nazi officials, including Hitler.[87] Significant human and material resources were devoted to these plans. Diplomatic efforts were launched to work out the details of the deportations with other countries.[88] Documentation of numerous secret discussions, meetings, and memoranda confirm that these plans were not simply a cover for the Nazis' ultimate genocidal aims, as some authors have suggested.[89] As Michael Marrus concludes, "It seems entirely possible that Nazi decision makers seriously intended such schemes and were prepared to live with insufficiencies that have been subsequently identified. . . . [I]nternal evidence and the context of these plans suggest that they were genuine efforts to deal with a Nazi-defined 'problem.'"[90]

From Deportation to Extermination

Scholars have fiercely disputed the exact timing of the fateful shift from Nazi planning for the deportation of the Jews to the policy of outright extermination.[91] Apart from those who believe that Hitler had been waiting for the opportunity to kill the Jews from the moment he gained power, most historians agree that the decision was made somewhere between the early spring and late autumn of 1941. Many scholars agree that this decision was based at least in part on the conclusion that the regime's earlier deportation schemes had failed and that deportation was no longer a practical solution to the "Jewish question."

It seems likely that several factors contributed to the perception that deportation was unworkable, although scholars differ as to which reasons were the most important in the minds of Nazi leaders. First, the Madagascar plan, the most seriously considered deportation scheme, had been predicated on the defeat of the British who controlled the sea-lanes between Germany and Madagascar. The Nazis were also counting on the cooperation of the French, who still controlled the island, and other allied powers that were expected to provide the ships needed to transport millions of Jewish refugees over such long distances. Germany's failure to triumph in the Battle of Britain undermined each of these assumptions, effectively ruling out the Madagascar plan by the early fall of 1940.[92]

Second, Germany's failure to knock Britain out of the war and Hitler's decision to launch the invasion of the Soviet Union made the purging of the Jews seem even more urgent than it had in 1939. Germany now found itself engaged in a two-front war — a predicament that Hitler had wished to avoid, and which he blamed largely on Jewish influence in Britain and the United States. Hitler's obsession with the danger of internal subversion and "fifth columnism" sponsored by Jews, and his fears of a repeat of 1918, meant that he could not delay action against the Jews. With the

Holocaust already under way in May 1942, he remarked: "Germans take part in subversive movements only when the Jews lure them into it. . . . Therefore one must liquidate the Jewish danger, cost what it takes."[93] He also believed that the Jews were behind the fierce guerrilla resistance German forces were encountering on the eastern front.[94] Hitler's grand plans for creating Lebensraum through the relocation of the non-Jewish populations of Poland and other Eastern European countries could be postponed or scaled back until the end of the war. Dealing with the Jews, on the other hand, was a prerequisite for victory. Until Jewish influence was eliminated from Europe, Hitler feared, Germany would face the constant threat of resistance abroad and subversion at home.

Third, Nazi population experts estimated that the conquest of the Soviet Union and the rest of Europe would swell the total number of Jews in the German sphere of influence to over eleven million people.[95] Officials in charge of deportation were hard pressed to find a suitable area to receive so many refugees and to provide the necessities of life for them in the midst of war.[96] The problem of providing food for this vast enemy population in a time of scarcity was a major concern for Nazi officials who were seeking desperately to avoid the mass starvation in Germany that had contributed to defeat in the First World War.[97] The Nazis, after all, by this time already had murdered tens of thousands of ethnic Germans suffering from mental or other chronic illnesses, the so-called "useless eaters" that Hitler feared would place an undue burden on Germany's resources during the war. Plans to deport the Jews to the barren wastes of Siberia remained under consideration as late as September 1941, but it is possible that at some point before then, the Nazis had begun to view these plans as a method of bringing about the destruction of the Jews through "natural means."[98]

Fourth, there are indications that Hitler worried that any plan for deportation that left the Jews encamped in an embittered mass just across the of border of the Reich would not completely eliminate the Jewish threat to Germany—especially after the war had begun. Indeed, before the Nazis officially decided to close the last doors to all Jewish emigration, they first banned the emigration of Jews of arms-bearing age, out of fear that they might become combatants against Germany.[99] Declaring that "the Jews are everywhere the pipeline through which all enemy news rushes with the speed of the wind into all branches of the population," Hitler suggested that deporting Jews to occupied Poland was not enough. They must be moved "straight away further to the east."[100] The additional logistical problems introduced by the perceived need to evacuate the Jews over such distances must have cast even further doubt on the practicability of deportation under wartime conditions. In January 1942, after the decision for genocide had already been made, Hitler explained: "It is entirely natural that we should concern ourselves with the [Jewish] question on the European level. It's clearly not enough to expel them from Germany. We cannot allow them to retain bases of withdrawal at our doors."[101]

Finally, if, as many historians have argued, the decision to systematically exterminate the Jews was not reached until sometime after the late summer of 1941, the military setbacks suffered by the German army in Russia during that time simply may have foreclosed the option of deportation to Siberia for the immediate future.[102] Although the German army did not suffer its first major defeats until December 1942, by late August the German offensive already was well behind schedule. Hitler seems to have concluded that the war could not be won until well into 1942 at the earliest. This was a very serious setback for Germany, since its military plans depended heavily on a quick victory.[103] The military delays also meant that Nazi planners would be faced with the more demanding problem of procuring food and shelter for large Jewish ghetto populations during the lean winter months.[104] As one SS officer had already suggested in a July 16, 1941, letter to Adolf Eichmann, "This winter there is a danger that not all of the Jews can be fed anymore. One should weigh earnestly if the most humane solution might not be to finish off those of the Jews who are not employable by some quick acting device. At any rate it would be more pleasant than to let them starve to death."[105]

These considerations appear to have led Hitler and other Nazi leaders to conclude that the most "practical" remaining option for ridding Europe of the Jews was systematic extermination. The precise contours of this policy, utilizing the combination of gas chambers and crematoria, probably did not crystallize until the late fall or winter of 1941. Once they did, Hitler's conviction that the Jewish question must be resolved before the end of the war ensured that the extermination would proceed at a terrible pace. Approximately 3.8 million Jews were dead by the end of 1942—roughly two-thirds of all the Jews who perished in the Holocaust.[106]

From this perspective, it can be seen that the Final Solution was "final" both in the sense that it was seen as a permanent solution to the Nazis' "Jewish question" and in the sense that it was the last in a series of Nazi efforts to deal with this question. As Yehuda Bauer argues, however, all these solutions "were based on the same principle . . . to 'remove' the Jews altogether. In prewar Germany, emigration suited the circumstances best, and when that was neither speedy enough or complete enough, expulsion—preferably to some 'primitive' place, uninhabited by true

Nordic Aryans, the Soviet Union or Madagascar — was the answer. When expulsion did not work, either, . . . the murder policy was decided on, quite logically on the basis of Nazi ideology. All these policies had the same aim: removal."[107]

As noted above, proponents of the intentionalist school have rejected this interpretation, arguing that the Holocaust was the result of Hitler's long-held plan to exterminate the Jews — a plan that he consistently pursued since as early as 1918. Hitler, they suggest, was merely awaiting the onset of war to provide the cover needed to carry it out. According to Lucy Dawidowicz, the annihilation of the Jews was "a central tenet in Hitler's ideology from which he never deviated . . . awaiting only the political opportunities for its implementation."[108] Intentionalist scholars invariably point to the numerous public and private statements by Hitler hinting at his desire for the destruction of the Jews. Most often cited is Hitler's infamous speech before the Reichstag on January 30, 1939, in which he warned: "If international Jewry within Europe and abroad should succeed once more in plunging the peoples into a world war, then the consequence will not be the Bolshevization of the world and therewith a victory of Jewry, but on the contrary, the destruction of the Jewish race in Europe."[109]

Although this and other statements by Hitler might seem to be straightforward indications of his desire to murder the Jews, there are two reasons to question whether genocide was truly Hitler's intent, or the intent of the Nazi regime, before 1941. First, many of Hitler's statements regarding the Jews remain open to interpretation. Most of Hitler's early remarks do not clearly call for systematic extermination. They call rather for the Jews to be "crushed" or to "disappear from Europe," for "the removal of the Jews altogether," or for "a solution to the Jewish question."[110] Some authors have speculated that Hitler issued these threats in an effort to intimidate Jews living abroad from using their supposed influence over Western powers to spark a global war against Germany.[111] In light of Hitler's later concerted efforts to keep the Holocaust a secret and his own refusal to speak of it openly, even within his inner circle, it seems unlikely that he would have declared his intentions so clearly even if he had been plotting genocide from an early date.

Moreover, in addition to the violent threats cited by intentionalist scholars, Hitler also made numerous statements in both public and private settings explicitly calling for Jewish emigration, resettlement, or deportation. As late as May 1940, Hitler wrote in the margin of a secret memorandum on Jewish deportation that Himmler's assertion that the "physical destruction of a people [was] un-German and impossible" was "very correct."[112] Even in his January 30, 1939, Reichstag speech, Hitler railed against France, Britain, and the United States for failing to accept more Jewish immigrants. "We will banish this people," he declared. "I believe the earlier this [Jewish] problem is resolved, the better. . . . There is more than enough room for settlement on this earth."[113]

Second, focusing on Hitler's often ambiguous and conflicting anti-Jewish threats neglects copious evidence regarding Nazi policies and actions that is simply incompatible with the intentionalists' assertion that a plan to systematically murder the Jews existed prior to 1941. There are no documents pointing to systematic planning for mass murder of Jews during this period. On the contrary, as described above, there is substantial evidence that high-ranking Nazis, including Hitler himself, fully approved of plans for coerced emigration and deportation. If Hitler had always intended to kill the Jews, why did he allow so many to flee to the safety of countries such as the United States, where he could never reach them?[114] Nor does the intentionalist assertion that Hitler was waiting for the onset of war to provide cover to launch a long-premeditated genocide withstand scrutiny. Rather, as Christopher Browning argues,

> If Hitler was merely awaiting the outbreak of conflict to pursue his "war against the Jews," why were the millions of Polish Jews in his hands since 1939 granted a thirty-month "stay of execution"? . . . If Hitler could kill at least seventy thousand Germans through the euthanasia program between 1939 and 1941, why was it not "opportune" to murder several hundred thousand German Jews who constituted an "internal menace" in wartime? It certainly would have occasioned far less opposition than euthanasia. Why was this period not used to make preparations and plans for mass extermination, avoiding the clumsy improvisations of 1941? In short, the practice of Nazi Jewish policy until 1941 does not support the thesis of a long-held, fixed intention to murder the European Jews.[115]

A Note on the Uniqueness of the Holocaust

Much has been written about the uniqueness of the Holocaust and its incomparability to other incidents of mass killing.[116] Although comparisons to the Holocaust (and Hitler) have frequently been abused for political purposes, I believe that at least some aspects of the Holocaust can be compared to other examples of genocide and mass killing and that such a comparison can produce meaningful insights into the more general causes of this kind of violence and into the Holocaust itself.

On the other hand, it cannot be denied that every historical event is unique in countless ways. History does not repeat itself, at least not exactly. Although proponents of the uniqueness of the Holocaust usually suggest a more comprehensive kind of incomparability, the Holocaust was clearly unique in any number of historical particulars, for example, in the Nazis' use of gas chambers to carry out much of the killing. At the most fundamental level, the Holocaust was unique because each of the millions of lives it extinguished was unique, never to lived again.

From the theoretical perspective described in this chapter, however, perhaps the most interesting singular attribute of the Holocaust is the peculiar pseudoscientific, eugenic concepts that informed the Nazi understanding of the Jewish threat. I know of no other example of mass killing driven so powerfully by the desire to eliminate a supposedly dangerous gene pool from society. The perverted logic of these ideas did not lead directly or inexorably to mass killing, but, as described above, it did rule out any possibility for the accommodation of Jews within Germany or German-occupied Europe. Because of the presumed biological nature of the Jewish threat, the Nazis could not tolerate nonpracticing or converted Jews, or even individuals with only one Jewish parent. When Nazi leaders concluded that less violent solutions for removing the Jews had proved unworkable, this ideology combined with the brutal efficiency of the Nazi state to produce a genocidal program that spared no Jewish man, woman, or child within its reach.

While the use of language by killers describing their victims as inferior, disease ridden, or subhuman is commonplace in the history of mass killing, these epithets almost always are secondary to deeper political and military conflicts. Most perpetrators of mass killing target entire ethnic groups for cleansing or extermination not because they believe that all members of these groups share the same tainted biology, but because perpetrators embrace the more traditional racist notion that all members of the victim group subscribe to the same political views or support the same military cause. When women and children have been targeted, it has not been because perpetrators consider them carriers of dangerous genes, but because the women are believed to be feeding the men and because it is feared that the children will grow up to avenge their fathers.

The ideological motivation for the Holocaust may have been unique, but its genocidal consequences were not. Contrary to popular belief, the Holocaust was not unique in the massive number of innocent lives it took, nor in the high percentage of the victim population it left dead. Between five and six million Jews perished in the Holocaust, a death toll representing between 57 and 67 percent of Jews in occupied Europe and between 30 and 36 percent of the world's Jewish population.[117] Other episodes of mass killing have surpassed this staggering toll in both absolute and proportional terms. If even a fraction of those who perished in the massive famines under Stalin and Mao are included, each of these tyrants is responsible for a greater absolute toll than Hitler, perhaps several times higher. In proportional terms, the Holocaust was surpassed by Rwanda's 1994 genocide, in which at least 75 percent of the Rwandan Tutsi population was murdered.[118] Likewise, if the higher estimates of the dead in the Armenian genocide are accepted, roughly three-quarters of the Turkish Armenian population perished in the genocide of 1915–18.[119]

Only by comparing the Holocaust to other episodes of genocide and mass killing can we assess its significance. Only by understanding its similarities and differences can we draw lessons from the Holocaust that might help us prevent or limit this kind of violence in the future. Indeed, the contribution that studying the Holocaust can make to the understanding of genocide and mass killing in general is one of the most important reasons why we must honor our obligation never to forget it.

RWANDA

The roots of the 1994 genocide in Rwanda can be traced to the political struggles between Hutu and Tutsi that emerged at the end of the Belgian colonial period in the 1950s.[120] Prior to European colonization, Hutu and Tutsi seem to have considered themselves more akin to castes or classes than to ethnic groups. Both groups spoke the same language and adhered to the same religion. Individuals occasionally moved between Hutu and Tutsi groups through intermarriage, clientage, or through the acquisition of wealth. In some regions of Rwanda the terms "Hutu" and "Tutsi" held little or no significance. Systematic violence between Hutu and Tutsi as such was unknown.[121]

The Belgian colonial administration of Rwanda, however, tended to racialize Hutu and Tutsi identities, rendering them exclusive and immutable. The Belgian administration heavily favored the Tutsi, who comprised less than 15 percent of the population, for positions of authority in the government. Eventually, European conceptions of Hutu and Tutsi groups seem to have been adopted by the Rwandans themselves, although many Rwandans appear to have defined the groups in relation to power and privilege rather than race.

Decolonization sparked the first violent conflict between Hutu and Tutsi in Rwanda in 1959. As independence approached, the Belgians began to promote democratization and an end to ethnic favoritism in Rwanda. Hutu leaders seized this opportunity to push for greater power, privileges, and representation. A struggle between Hutu and Tutsi for political control ensued that escalated to a series of violent attacks against the Tutsi. Hutu political leaders gained control of the government. The violence during this period forced thousands of Tutsi to flee the country, most seeking refuge in Burundi, Tanzania, and Uganda. The refugees made several efforts to fight their way back into Rwanda between 1961 and 1963, but each time they were repelled. In the winter of 1963–64, following the most serious refugee incursion, the Hutu government initiated a new wave of anti-Tutsi violence, resulting in the deaths of approximately ten thousand Tutsi. Another two hundred thousand, roughly half of the Tutsi population in Rwanda at that time, fled or were driven out of the country.[122] Tutsi incursions into Rwanda ended in 1967 (along with most anti-Tutsi violence inside Rwanda), but some refugees, especially those in Uganda, never gave up hope that they would eventually return. They spent much of the next thirty years organizing, training, and waiting for the moment to act.[123]

That moment came in October 1990, when the Rwandan Patriotic Front (RPF), the main Tutsi political organization in Uganda, decided to launch an invasion across the border into Rwanda.[124] The RPF made it clear that its goal was not simply the repatriation of Tutsi refugees but also the overthrow of the Rwandan Hutu regime led by President Juvenal Habyarimana.[125] The RPF invasion occurred at the same time that domestic and international forces were pressuring Habyarimana to democratize the Rwandan single-party political system. Both Tutsi and moderate Hutu within Rwanda had begun putting pressure on Habyarimana to dismantle the single-party state and allow the formation of new political parties. The concurrent RPF invasion and domestic upheaval sparked a political and military crisis in Rwanda that ultimately led to the genocide of 1994.

Confrontation and Repression

Habyarimana responded to this crisis with a variety of confrontational military and political measures. He refused high-level diplomatic contacts with the RPF. The Rwandan army, with the assistance of foreign troops, managed to turn back the RPF invasion. A wave of arrests targeted all potential sources of domestic opposition, both Tutsi and Hutu. Approximately thirteen thousand people were arrested.[126] Small-scale violent attacks on Tutsi civilians were carried out, especially in areas where the RPF had been active.

Neither Habyarimana's military strategies nor political maneuverings, however, proved effective for very long. The RPF invasion was repulsed but not defeated. Instead, it shifted to low-level guerrilla operations and repeated cross-border raids from Uganda into Rwanda.[127] Large numbers of Hutu civilians fled the northern areas of the country, where most of the fighting was taking place. The growing pool of internal refugees generated serious strains on Rwanda's economy. By early 1992, it was becoming evident that the Rwandan army lacked the capability to defeat the RPF.[128]

Habyarimana's domestic political crackdown also backfired. His ruthless methods actually increased internal opposition to the single-party system.[129] A number of political organizations were established to protest the policies of the regime and demand democratization. Pressures from Rwanda's foreign aid benefactors were also brought to bear on Habyarimana.[130] The French, who had contributed troops to repel the Tutsi invasion, made it clear to Habyarimana that their military assistance could not continue indefinitely and that a democratic political solution would ultimately be necessary.[131]

From Confrontation to Compromise

Having failed at political and military confrontation, Habyarimana reluctantly decided to try his hand at compromise. According to Joan Kakwenzire and Dixon Kamukama, by early 1991 Habyarimana seemed to have "realized the futility of using force in sorting out the political mess in the country."[132] In June 1991 he accepted a constitutional amendment allowing the formation of multiple political parties. In March 1992 he agreed to form a coalition government with the newly formed parties. Eleven out of twenty cabinet seats, including the post of prime minister, were awarded to opposition party representatives. The new government enacted policies designed to open the political process, fight corruption, ensure stronger civilian control over the military, and redress institutional discrimination against the Tutsi. Perhaps most importantly, the coalition government forced Habyarimana to agree to peace talks with the RPF. The agenda of the talks was to include not simply a negotiation of a cease-fire or the repatriation of Tutsi refugees, but also a comprehensive political agreement for power sharing with the RPF in Rwanda.

The formal peace talks began in July 1992 in Arusha, Tanzania. The two sides quickly agreed to a cease-fire and the broad outlines of a power-sharing agreement were in place by December. In early February 1993, however, the talks were derailed by a wave of local anti-Tutsi violence in Rwanda, which in turn prompted a new RPF military offensive. Although the offensive was partly a response to the anti-Tutsi violence, many observers believe that it was also part of an effort by the RPF to gain leverage in the final phases of the Arusha talks that were to address the crucial issue of the integration of RPF forces into Rwanda's national army.[133]

The offensive was remarkably successful. In less than two weeks, RPF forces advanced to within thirty kilometers of the capital city of Kigali. Hundreds of thousands of Hutu fled the fighting. Only the intervention of French troops prompted the RPF to halt its offensive and declare a uni-lateral cease-fire on February 20, 1993. Tanzanian and French intelligence services estimated that without continued French military support the RPF would defeat the Rwandan army.[134] France had already signaled that its troops would not stay in Rwanda forever. Perhaps realizing this, Habyarimana personally called for a resumption of the talks. The final accords were signed on August 4, 1993, and the United Nations agreed to oversee their implementation.

By nearly all accounts, the Arusha Accords were a triumph for the RPF. They granted the RPF a prominent role in both Rwanda's governmental institutions and its military organizations. The RPF received five cabinet seats in the transitional government, as many as Habyarimana's own party. Fifty percent of the command positions in the integrated army were to be filled by members of the RPF. The new political system substantially reduced the authority of Rwanda's president, emphasizing parliamentary politics and thereby increasing the RPF's power as a major opposition party. Bruce Jones suggests that the accords were made possible primarily by the RPF's military superiority and represented a "victor's deal which reflected RPF views much more than it did a true compromise."[135]

The "Tutsi Threat" and the Rise of Extremists

Scholars continue to disagree over how committed to the Arusha Accords Habyarimana actually was. At best, he was a reluctant partner. Throughout the talks, he publicly expressed reservations about many of the terms of the accords. It is possible that he never intended to implement the agreements in good faith. What is abundantly clear, however, is that a relatively small group of radical Hutu, both outside and within the Rwandan government and military, were convinced that the accords would have catastrophic results both for themselves and for the Rwandan Hutu population in general. Indeed, these extremists had been warning of the gravity of the Tutsi threat since the initial RPF invasion in 1990. As early as 1991, they had begun to organize Hutu militia groups, including the notorious Interahamwe ("those who stand or fight together") and Impuzamugambi ("those with a single purpose"). The militias terrorized the extremists' domestic political opponents and attacked RPF guerrillas and the Tutsi civilian "accomplices" believed to be providing the guerrillas with sanctuary, supplies, and information.[136] The extremists had also begun to coordinate radio and print media to use as outlets for their message. Many of these radical Hutu leaders were allied to the Coalition for the Defense of the Republic (CDR), an explicitly racist political party founded in early 1992 whose stated mission was to "defend the interests of the majority [i.e., the Hutu] publicly and consistently."[137]

Although extremist Hutu groups such as the CDR often collaborated with Habyarimana against the moderate Hutu opposition, they harshly criticized him for failing to take more forceful measures against the "Tutsi threat." Indeed, when Habyarimana agreed to resume negotiations after the RPF's February 1993 offensive, the CDR issued a statement arguing that the agreement "shows clearly that Mr. Habyarimana . . . does not care any more about the interests of the nation and is now defending other interests. . . . [Habyarimana's agreement to return to negotiations] constitutes an act of high treason."[138] Colonel Theoneste Bagosora, an extremist officer who would later emerge as one of the chief organizers of the genocide, took the floor at Arusha and warned that "if this system is implemented, there will be an apocalypse in Rwanda."[139]

The effort to understand precisely how Hutu leaders conceived of the Tutsi threat and why they believed it was so perilous in the context of post-1990 events must remain speculative. Relatively few internal documents or private statements from radical Hutu groups have become available, and many public remarks are clearly propaganda designed to incite Hutu to join the extremists or engage in violence. Nevertheless, scholars have pointed to at least three primary fears that seem to have contributed to Hutu perceptions of the Tutsi threat.

First, extremist Hutu leaders saw the Tutsi invasion, the rise of moderate Hutu political parties, and the subsequent power-sharing agreements as threats to their personal hold on power. The transitional government created by the Arusha Accords completely excluded the CDR. Many extremist Hutu politicians within Habyarimana's party would also have lost their positions and associated privileges under the accords. Hutu military officers perceived the accords to be particularly threatening since, as noted above, the agreement left half of the army's command positions in the hands of the RPF.[140] As a study conducted by the human rights group African Rights concluded, the Arusha Accords "introduced what the extremists dreaded: power-sharing, an end to privileges and the principle of accountability."[141]

Second, radical Hutu leaders saw the events of the early 1990s as a threat to the preservation of Hutu political and economic predominance more generally. They appear to have feared not only the loss of their personal privileges but a return to the system of Tutsi domination that had prevailed before 1959.[142] An internal Rwandan army memorandum issued in September 1992, for example, asserted that the regime was facing a severe threat from "Tutsi inside or outside the country, extremist and nostalgic for power, who have NEVER recognized and will NEVER recognize the realities of the 1959 social revolution and who wish to reconquer power by all means necessary including arms." The authors of the memorandum claimed that the Tutsi were motivated by "a single political will and a single political ideology, which is Tutsi hegemony."[143]

Although the RPF officially espoused a philosophy of ethnic unity, the conduct of their military campaign and their intransigence at the Arusha talks led many Hutu leaders to fear that the RPF never planned to share power. These fears were certainly exaggerated in Hutu propaganda, but they were not altogether fantastic. Anyone who doubted the potential for Tutsi domination needed only to look across the border to Burundi, where the Tutsi minority continued to repress the Hutu majority. Beginning in the late 1980s Burundi had attempted to democratize, but this experiment was brought to an abrupt halt in October 1993 when the newly elected Hutu president, Melchior Ndadaye, was assassinated by extremist Tutsi army officers. The assassination set off a massive wave of ethnic violence and a return to Tutsi domination. Eventually, these events led even some members of moderate Hutu political parties to share the extremists' fears of Tutsi domination.[144]

Finally, extremist Hutu leaders believed that the Tutsi posed a threat to the physical safety of Hutu in Rwanda. RPF forces had engaged in massacres of Hutu civilians on several occasions since the 1990 invasion.[145] Extremist Hutu politicians and ideologues continually warned that the RPF and their Tutsi "accomplices" within Rwanda would go on killing Hutu if nothing were done to stop them. Ndadaye's assassination and the subsequent violence in Burundi only intensified these fears. Hutu extremists began warning of Tutsi-RPF plans to systematically exterminate Rwandan Hutu, sometimes comparing the RPF to the Nazis or the Khmer Rouge.[146] It is difficult to determine the degree to which these fears were genuinely felt, or how much they were exaggerated in an effort to frighten ordinary Hutu civilians into supporting the extremists' agenda. References to the 1972 genocide in Burundi, which killed between 100,000 and 200,000 Hutu, however, were a constant theme in Rwandan Hutu political discourse. It seems plausible that at least some radical Hutu leaders truly feared a repeat of this kind of violence in Rwanda.[147]

From Compromise to Genocide

This understanding of the Hutu extremists' perception of the magnitude of the "Tutsi threat" may explain why the extremists felt they had to do something to protect themselves and their prerogatives from the Tutsi. As Gérard Prunier concludes, "When the political situation looked as if [the] Tutsi were going to come back to positions of power . . . such a desperate threat called for desperate remedies."[148] The perception of even the most desperate threat, however, cannot explain why genocide emerged as the extremists' preferred response. The scarcity of internal documents from the extremist groups that organized the genocide means that there can be no definitive answer to why the extremists settled on this bloody solution. In spite of these limitations, however, a largely deductive yet compelling explanation can be constructed that is consistent with what is known about the progression of events from 1990 to 1994 and with the limited evidence available from the extremists themselves. This explanation suggests that Hutu extremists arrived at the decision to launch a systematic genocide only after they had concluded that less violent options for dealing with the Tutsi threat had failed and that other potential solutions would be impractical or insufficient. Four factors may have contributed to this perception among the extremist groups.

First, as noted above, Habyarimana's confrontational strategy for dealing with the RPF invasion and domestic political opposition had failed by late 1991, or early 1992 at the latest. Sharing power with the RPF and domestic opposition may have been an acceptable if highly distasteful compromise for Habyarimana. Such a compromise, however, was precisely the outcome the extremists wished to avoid, since they feared it would simply result in the dreaded consequences described above. The RPF offensive of February 1993 and the assassination of Ndadaye in October of that year confirmed the extremists' conviction that power sharing with the Tutsi was impossible.

Indeed, many observers have speculated that Hutu extremists were responsible for shooting down the airplane carrying President Habyarimana immediately before the genocide began.[149] According to Francois Xavier Nsanzuwera, the former attorney general of Rwanda:

> They killed the President to be able to kill everybody else. My sense is that President Habyarimana was in favor of killing his political opponents but not the general public, that is women and children. . . . But this was the objective of the fanatics of the CDR whose language was to "clear the country of the internal accomplices of the RPF" after which they planned to engage the RPF in a fight to the death. Therefore they had to kill the President in order to kill everyone else who they considered an obstacle.[150]

Second, the extremists' own efforts to deal with the Tutsi threat had also failed. These efforts included significant violence but were not yet part of a systematic plan to exterminate the Tutsi. Since 1991, extremist militia groups had been conducting small-scale massacres of Tutsi civilians in Rwanda. Following the RPF offensive of 1993, the militias were expanded and massacres became more frequent. The massacres appear to have been intended to eliminate or intimidate the Tutsi civilian accomplices that the extremists believed were supporting the RPF invasion. They may also have been calculated to send a deterrent message to the

RPF itself. As one extremist politician announced on Rwandan radio, he had "a message for the RPF: Stop fighting this war if you do not want your supporters living inside Rwanda to be exterminated."[151] Extremist death squads also assassinated Tutsi elites and leaders of moderate Hutu political parties in the effort to crush domestic opposition and derail the Arusha talks. Despite these brutal methods, however, power-sharing negotiations continued and the RPF's military power continued to multiply. As Rwanda's minister of finance described the extremists' decision to launch the genocide: "They have resorted to massacres because they knew they could not win the war."[152]

Third, Hutu extremist groups tended to view the Hutu-Tutsi political and military conflict in quasi-racial terms, assuming that all Tutsi were enemies and that cooperation with them was impossible.[153] This view encouraged the conclusion that any effective response to the Tutsi threat must address all Tutsi living in Rwanda, not simply those who could be directly linked to the RPF or opposition activity. As a March 1993 article in an extremist newspaper explained: "A cockroach [a pejorative term for Tutsi] cannot give birth to a butterfly. It is true. A cockroach gives birth to another cockroach. . . . The history of Rwanda shows us clearly that a Tutsi stays always exactly the same, that he has never changed. . . . Who could tell the difference between the [Tutsi] who attacked in October 1990 and those of the 1960s. They are all linked . . . their evilness is the same."[154]

Unlike the Nazis' conception of the Jews, Hutu extremists do not appear to have felt that the Tutsi posed a biological threat to the Hutu. Rather, they simply argued that virtually all Tutsi were supporters of the RPF. As one suspected Hutu organizer of the mass killings in Rwanda remarked, "The Tutsis were not killed as Tutsis, only as sympathizers of the RPF . . . ninety-nine per-cent of Tutsis were pro-RPF. There was no difference between the ethnic and the political."[155] A former member of the Interahamwe explained that "we did not have a role of exterminating all Tutsi, but it was said that every Tutsi cooperates with the [RPF]."[156]

These perceptions were encouraged after the RPF began recruiting heavily from the Tutsi civilian population in Rwanda in late 1992. According to Prunier, "For the Habyarimana regime, and especially for the extremists elements in its ranks, this meant that the [RPF] was now a *direct* agent in Rwandan politics and that the whole Tutsi population inside the country could be viewed as potential 'fifth columnists.' . . . Killing civilians was promoted from the status of scare and intimidation tactics to the role of a major strategic concept. It was from that time on that the idea of the genocide . . . progressively began to be considered a 'rational' political project."[157] Although Tutsi men were the primary targets of the violence, even children would have to be dealt with somehow since they were destined to grow up to carry on the fight.[158] According to the investigation of the genocide carried out by African Rights, "As the militias were sent to kill, they were exhorted to kill the young children too — on the grounds that today's RPF fighters are yesterday's refugee children."[159] Likewise, Tutsi women had to be exterminated lest they give birth to more Tutsi children.[160]

Finally, extremist leaders seem to have believed that any solution that involved expelling or deporting the Tutsi from Rwanda would simply result in a perpetuation of the conflict. The current fighting, after all, was being carried out by the descendants of Tutsi who had fled or were driven from Rwanda in the years following the 1959 Hutu revolution. If expelling fully half of the Tutsi population had not solved the problem then, it made little sense to send more of them across the border now. Indeed, the desire of Hutu extremists not to repeat the "mistake of 1959" appears to have been one of the most important factors in motivating the decision for genocide. References to this "error" appear repeatedly in Hutu extremist political writings and speeches.[161] As Prunier described the extremists' logic: "It was a matter of survival and the mistake of 1959 could not be repeated: if the evil race had been thoroughly eradicated then, their children would not have been threatening us now. Simple but true."[162] Indeed, after the genocide began, extremist forces made every effort to prevent Tutsi from escaping to neighboring countries.[163]

This was the cold logic that led Colonel Bagosora to announce at a party two days before the genocide began that if the Arusha Accords were implemented, "the only plausible solution for Rwanda would be the elimination of the Tutsi."[164] It is impossible to determine the precise date, if indeed there was a single date, of the extremists' decision for genocide. It is evident that the slaughter was planned at least several months in advance of Habyarimana's assassination on April 6, 1994. The general idea of large-scale massacres, however, probably came under serious consideration in late 1992 and was finally adopted as an actual plan sometime soon after Ndadaye's assassination in Burundi in late October 1993.[165]

This timeline is largely consistent with the interpretation that the decision for genocide was reached when the extremists felt that all other solutions for dealing with the Tutsi threat had proved unworkable. By late 1992 it must have been apparent to the extremists that Habyarimana's efforts to defeat the RPF had failed and that the final outcome of the Arusha talks would be even more threatening to their interests than they had initially feared.[166] By October 1993 it should have been clear that the extremists' own violent efforts to crush the Tutsi by means of militias and death squads had failed as well. On the contrary, the Arusha Accords were beginning to be implemented under the supervision of the United Nations, and Habyarimana was coming under increasing international pressure to cooperate. The RPF offensive of February 1993 and Ndadaye's assassination probably convinced those extremists who still questioned the ethics of, or the need for, such a radical solution that genocide was both necessary and urgent. As Prunier concludes, in the history of the Rwandan conflict "killings were merely one of the means used in a broad spectrum of political tools which included war, bribery, foreign diplomacy, constitutional manipulations and propaganda."[167]

Once it began, the furious pace of the Rwandan genocide surpassed even the rate of the industrialized murder of the Holocaust. Because of their militarily inferiority to the RPF, the extremists probably concluded that their genocidal strategy could only succeed if they acted quickly. Although the killing was performed primarily with small arms and edged weapons, 500,000 to 800,000 people were murdered in less than three months. A quarter of a million people may have been killed in the first two weeks of the genocide.[168] Not all the victims were Tutsi. Between 10,000 and 30,000 Hutu suspected of sympathizing with the RPF were also murdered.[169]

Although the genocide exterminated more than 75 percent of Rwanda's Tutsi population, it did not defeat the RPF. The slaughter came to an end only when RPF forces routed the Rwandan army and seized control of the country. The extremists, along with between one and two million Hutu civilians, fled across the border to Burundi, Tanzania, and Zaire.

LESS VIOLENT RACIST AND NATIONALIST REGIMES

Racist and nationalist regimes have been a common feature in the history of the twentieth century. By definition, these regimes have engaged in overt or de facto economic, political, and cultural discrimination. They have often resorted to the violent repression of minority groups or subordinate majorities. Nonetheless, most racist or nationalist regimes have not engaged in mass killing as I define it. What separates these "less violent" racist and nationalist states from the openly genocidal regimes described above? The strategic approach suggests that the critical differences can be found in two sets of considerations. The first set encompasses the various considerations that contribute to leaders' perceptions that ethnic cleansing is the best available means to deal with ethnic, national, or religious adversaries. The second set consists of factors and conditions that render ethnic cleansing, once decided upon, more likely to escalate to mass killing.

Factors Influencing the Decision to Implement Ethnic Cleansing

The evidence presented in this chapter suggests that the likelihood that leaders will decide to implement a policy of ethnic cleansing is largely determined by their perceptions of two critical aspects of their environment: (1) the nature and degree of the threat posed by their ethnic opponents and (2) the availability and adequacy of policies other than ethnic cleansing for countering this threat. Ethnic cleansing becomes more likely when leaders perceive their ethnic opponents as threatening, not merely to the continued power and privileges of the regime, but to the integrity of the state or the physical safety of the dominant group, and when leaders simultaneously perceive that less violent policies have failed to meet these threats. In practice, of course, these perceptions are related closely, since the way leaders assess the severity of a threat often depends on their ability to counter it.

Why do some racist or nationalist leaders come to perceive other ethnic groups as such grave threats? Objective considerations, including any threatening actions by members of victim groups, clearly play a role in shaping leaders' perceptions. Leaders' perceptions also are shaped powerfully by their own unique sets of beliefs and values, however. These beliefs and values often do not correspond to objective realities. Indeed, sometimes they can be utterly bizarre and fantastic.

Nor is there any reason to expect that leaders' perceptions regarding victim groups will faithfully reflect the attitudes of the wider society or even the views of associates in their own regimes. After all, perpetrators of mass killing seldom achieve power through democratic means. In Turkey and Rwanda, the radical leaders who ultimately opted to implement mass killing came to power through coups, overthrowing leaders who also held racist or nationalist beliefs but apparently preferred compromise to ethnic cleansing. In Germany, although Hitler became chancellor through constitutional means, within less than a year he had dismantled Germany's democratic institutions and secured nearly complete dictatorial powers. There is little evidence that majorities in any of the three cases studied here actively supported policies of genocide.[170]

The strategic perspective presented here is not intended to identify when and where radical racist or nationalist organizations are likely to come to power. Factors such as wars, economic depressions, and weak domestic institutions almost certainly help to clear a path to power for some of these groups. Yet, as noted in chapter 1, these factors are relatively common. They rarely lead to the rise of genocidal regimes. In fact, even in Turkish Armenia, Nazi Germany, and Rwanda, the rise of extremist groups appears to have been highly contingent on idiosyncratic factors and unexpected events. In each case, scholars have suggested plausible alternate historical scenarios that might have precluded these groups from ever gaining power, thereby averting ethnic cleansing and genocide.[171]

South Africa's relatively peaceful transition from apartheid to a mul-
tiracial democracy in 1994 provides a striking example of how differently
events might have turned out in Turkey, Germany, and Rwanda. As in
each of these three states, South Africa in the late 1980s and early 1990s
was in the midst of a major national crisis, including a severe economic
depression and violent domestic uprisings. Extremist racist groups were
prevalent, including some within the ruling National Party and the South
African military.[172] Members of this so-called "third force" believed that
the policies of the previous forty years, including moderate political concessions, lower levels of violent repression, and even the regime's limited
use of ethnic cleansing had failed. While F. W. de Klerk reluctantly was
willing to compromise with Nelson Mandela's African National Congress (ANC) to avoid economic collapse and continued political isolation, the extremists believed that granting full democratic rights to the
blacks posed a serious threat to the Afrikaners' way of life and even their
survival. Indeed, in a nearly successful effort to derail the peace process,
supporters of the third force worked to foment clashes between the ANC
and other black groups that ultimately left thousands of people dead.[173]

Why then did not extremist groups come to power in South Africa as
they did in Turkey, Germany, and Rwanda? Given their prevalence in military and police organizations, it seems likely that extremist forces in
South Africa would have possessed more than enough physical capabilities to carry out mass killing if they had ever come to power. The answer
to this question lies beyond the scope of this book. A comparison with
Turkey, Germany, and Rwanda, however, suggests that perhaps the most
obvious answer — that most white South Africans simply did not support
systematic violence against blacks — is insufficient. After all, most Germans did not support such measures against the Jews in 1933, and most
Rwandan Hutu did not favor the extermination of the Tutsi in 1994. Indeed, it is instructive to note that the 68 percent of white South Africans
who voted in support of de Klerk's power-sharing negotiations in 1992 is
almost exactly the same as the percentage of Germans who voted *against*
Hitler in 1933.

The strategic approach is most useful, therefore, in assessing when
specific groups or leaders are likely to decide that ethnic cleansing is the
best available means to achieve their ends, not when or where these
groups will come to power. A brief comparison of the three genocidal
regimes studied in this chapter with the comparatively moderate regimes
that preceded them in each state reveals how leaders' differing perceptions
regarding the threats posed by Armenian, Jewish, and Tutsi minorities led
to radically different strategies for dealing with them. These within-case

comparisons are particularly illustrative because the abrupt transition between regimes in each of these three states makes it possible to examine
the independent impact of changes in leadership while broader social and
cultural factors remain relatively stable.[174]

Leaders of "moderate" regimes in Turkey before 1913, Germany before
1933, and Rwanda before April 1994 did harbor racist and nationalist attitudes regarding their respective Armenian, Jewish, and Tutsi minorities,
and they did see these groups as threats or problems. Nevertheless, these
leaders generally seem to have perceived their conflicts with minority
groups in political or economic rather than existential terms. Partly because of these perceptions, moderate leaders concluded that limited
forms of discrimination or repression, or even concessions, would be
sufficient to keep minority groups in check. The extremist regimes that
succeeded them, on the other hand, tended to see the Armenians, Jews,
and Tutsi as threats to the physical safety or even continued survival of the
majority, not simply its political and economic prerogatives. The belief
that previous moderate policies had failed to defuse these threats, combined with the outbreak of wars in which minority groups were implicated, simultaneously exacerbated these dire perceptions and ensured
that more radical solutions would be put into practice.

In Turkey, most members of the Young Turk regime that gained power
in 1908 seem to have believed — probably accurately — that the majority
of Armenians were interested simply in greater autonomy and equality
within the empire. As a result, they conceived of the "Armenian question"
primarily in political terms and saw the best hope for its resolution in policies of accommodation and integration. The rapid disintegration of the
empire under the pressures of secessionist movements, however, led to
the rise of an ultra-nationalist faction of the Young Turks in 1913. Following Turkey's entry into World War I, the suspected collaboration of
the Armenians with the Russian invaders convinced the extremists that
the Armenians posed more than a threat to Turkish dominance in domestic affairs. In fact, the Armenians were believed to be abetting the
dismemberment of the Turkish homeland itself. Since the extremists believed that previous policies of integration as well as limited repression
had failed, they concluded that Turkey would never be secure while a large
Armenian population remained within its borders.

In Weimar Germany, most center and left political parties explicitly
supported Jewish assimilation. Jews assumed prominent leadership roles
in the republic, including several cabinet ministries. Anti-Semitism, however, was rife within Germany's numerous conservative parties and in the
military. Yet even these racist elites typically held to traditional anti-Semitic beliefs that described Germany's "Jewish problem" in terms of the

supposed overrepresentation of Jews in high political, economic, and cultural positions.[175] Their preferred anti-Semitic measures usually aimed at the segregation of Jews in social life and their exclusion from German cultural and political institutions. Hitler and other radical anti-Semites in the Nazi party, on the other hand, saw the Jewish threat in nothing less than apocalyptic terms. The Jews were a biological threat to the strength of the Aryan race and, through their alleged ties to international communism and internal subversion, a threat to the survival of the German state. Segregation and exclusion were clearly insufficient to meet a threat so defined. Hitler's long-term strategy, therefore, probably always sought the physical removal of the Jews from Germany.

The contrast between the Rwandan regime under Juvenal Habyarimana and the Hutu extremist parties that replaced it at the outset of the genocide in April 1994 reveals a similar pattern. Habyarimana, who had governed the country since 1973, seems to have been concerned primarily with defending the power and privileges of his northern-based Hutu clan. He protected these privileges mainly through the restriction, although not complete exclusion, of Tutsi participation in the political process and access to public sector jobs. Even after the RPF invasion of 1990, Habyarimana still seemed to consider the domestic Tutsi threat largely in political terms. He did not shrink from engaging the RPF army militarily or using repression against his domestic political opponents, but he also was prepared to negotiate and grant limited political concessions to the Tutsi. The Hutu extremists, including many within Habyarimana's government and military, however, were convinced that the Tutsi were seeking to impose minority rule on Rwanda, possibly through the same kind of genocidal violence that sustained the minority Tutsi regime in Burundi. The perceived failure of Habyarimana's policies convinced the extremists that more radical solutions were necessary. As noted above, this internal conflict may well have led to Habyarimana's assassination in the opening act of the genocide.

Extremists in all three states came to believe that eliminating the threat posed by their ethnic enemies was the single most important issue on their agenda. Until this threat could be neutralized, they feared, nothing else was possible. Indeed, each group defined itself largely by its unwillingness to compromise on the issue of relations with minorities. The fact that each regime chose to divert scarce resources away from desperate ongoing wars to support their genocidal campaigns against minority civilian populations is an illustration of the intensity of these convictions. In Turkey and Rwanda, the extremists' fears had at least a small foothold in realty, since opposition groups claiming to represent minority populations in these states had organized militarily and used violence in the attempt to gain autonomy, secession, or the overthrow of the current regime. In Germany, on the other hand, the Jewish threat was purely a figment of Nazi ideology. Yet as the Holocaust itself ultimately demonstrated, this imagined threat proved at least as powerful a motivation for murder as any based in reality.

From Ethnic Cleansing to Mass Killing

As noted in the beginning of this chapter, ethnic cleansing and mass killing, though often conflated, are not one in the same. Ethnic cleansing almost always entails significant violence and coercion, but it has been accomplished without mass killing.[176] A comparison between the three genocidal regimes studied in this chapter and others that have implemented ethnic cleansing using lower levels of violence suggests three factors that can influence whether or not ethnic cleansing will lead to mass killing: (1) the size of the population subject to ethnic cleansing, (2) the speed with which ethnic cleansing is carried out, and (3) the availability of hospitable territories to receive refugee populations. These variables may operate individually or in conjunction. While many other factors undoubtedly play a role, these three are particularly significant because each of them directly influences the ability of perpetrators to relocate victims without resorting to massive violence.

The most obvious factor that can influence the likelihood that leaders will use mass killing to achieve ethnic cleansing is the size of the population subject to removal. All else being equal, the larger the population that must be relocated, the greater is the number of people likely to be subjected to violence. There were close to 2,000,000 Armenians in Turkey in 1915, 10,000,000 Jews in German-occupied Europe and the Soviet Union in 1941, and between 650,000 and 930,000 Tutsi in Rwanda in 1994. Several other of this century's most violent examples of ethnic mass killing also have been associated with the ethnic cleansing of vast numbers of people. Two million ethnic Germans died between 1945 and 1947 when nearly twelve million were expelled from Eastern Europe. Between 500,000 and 1,000,000 people perished during the partition of India in 1947–48 in which approximately 10,000,000 people forcibly were relocated. Over 10,000,000 Bengalis were forced from their homes and between 500,000 and 3,000,000 of them (mostly Hindus) died during the partition of Bangladesh in 1971.

The size of the victim population does not simply affect the degree of violence against victim groups in proportional terms. The practical difficulties associated with moving vast numbers of people over long distances can render less violent strategies of ethnic cleansing all but impossible. Larger populations are physically harder to move, more likely

to resist relocation, and less likely to be admitted for resettlement by foreign states.[177] The Nazis' policy of coerced emigration, for example, succeeded in forcing most of Germany's 500,000 Jews out of the country
between 1933 and 1939 without massive violence. This strategy was clearly
insufficient, on the other hand, for coping with the Jews living in Eastern Europe and the Soviet Union, as no other country was willing to accept such large numbers of Jewish refugees. The problems presented by
this vast population were partly responsible for the Nazis' shift to schemes
for deportation and ultimately genocide. Likewise, in 1972, Idi Amin was
able to deport nearly all of the seventy thousand Asians (most of Indian
descent) living in Uganda in a matter of months and with relatively little
violence.[178] Most of the refugees were evacuated by airplane and granted
asylum in Britain, Canada, the United States, and elsewhere. Such an operation would have been unthinkable had the population numbered in
the millions instead of the tens of thousands.

A second factor that seems to influence the likelihood that ethnic
cleansing will result in mass killing is the pace with which it is implemented. When perpetrators believe that they must carry out ethnic
cleansing rapidly, greater violence may be required to force people to
leave their homes. The lack of preparation can render it difficult or impossible for expellees to sell or take their personal belongings with them,
or to make their own arrangements for relocation. Under these circumstances, victims are more likely to resist relocation. In addition, when deportations are carried out in great haste, it is simply more difficult to
provide humane conditions for refugees during relocation or after resettlement, even if perpetrators were inclined to do so. As a result, the likelihood of mortality during and after relocation may also increase.

All three mass killings described in this chapter occurred in the midst
of war. In all three cases, perpetrators believed that they had to carry out
ethnic cleansing rapidly if their country hoped to survive the fighting.
Not all instances of ethnic cleansing, however, are propelled by such a
sense of urgency. When perpetrators are willing to allow more time for
relocation, less violent means become more practical. Both the perpetrators and the victims of ethnic cleansing have greater time to prepare for
relocation and resettlement, thereby decreasing the likelihood that victims will resist and reducing the likelihood of deaths resulting from harsh
conditions. With greater time, perpetrators may even be able to negotiate agreements with states willing to accept refugees.

As described above, the Nazi regime used economic and political pressures to encourage gradual Jewish emigration from Germany between
1933 and 1939. The process was by its nature cruel, but it occurred with
relatively little violence. Similarly, between 1960 and 1983, the white

regime of South Africa forcibly relocated approximately 3.5 million Blacks, Asians, and peoples of mixed race into segregated communities within the boundaries of the South African state.[179] The relocation was not without violence, but the removals took place over a period of more than twenty years, and at least some compensation could be paid to those who owned land or houses. In addition, although conditions in the homelands were harsh, South Africa devoted enough resources to their development to prevent widespread deaths from starvation and exposure — two of the most common causes of mortality during mass relocations.[180]

The third factor that can influence the violence associated with ethnic cleansing is the availability of territories for resettlement — territories that are acceptable to the sponsors of ethnic cleansing and capable of supporting the influx of refugees. The Nazi regime actively sought such a location for Jewish refugees in Palestine, Eastern Europe, Madagascar, and Siberia. In Turkey and Rwanda, the option of expelling refugees across the border was out of the question since leaders in both states were already facing cross-border incursions. Nevertheless, the fact that Turkish and Rwandan Hutu leaders had experimented with less violent domestic solutions before resorting to mass killing suggests that they might have sanctioned the deportation of their ethnic enemies to more distant locations if other states were willing to accept them. Indeed, in 1923 the new Turkish regime under Mustafa Kemal agreed to the internationally negotiated deportation of Turkey's Greek minority to Greece.[181]

The pattern of conflict in the former Yugoslavia illustrates how the availability of territories capable of accepting refugees can diminish — if not completely avert — the violence associated with ethnic cleansing. Large numbers of Muslims, Serbs, and Croats were forced to flee their homes during war, but Muslims suffered a disproportionate share of the violence. This pattern was due at least in part to the fact that unlike the Serbs and Croats, Muslims could not flee Bosnia to the protection of an independent state dominated by co-ethnic allies.[182] Indeed, unlike Serbian and Croatian leaders, Muslim leaders actively discouraged Bosnian Muslims from fleeing to safer areas as part of the effort to prevent the partition of Bosnia.[183]

Similarly, Serbian forces expelled at least 850,000 Kosovar Albanians from Kosovo in 1999, most of them in the course of just a few weeks in February and March. Between 2,100 and 11,000 people were killed as Serbs forced them from their homes, but it seems likely that the toll would have been much higher were it not for the well-supplied refugee camps established by NATO forces across the border in Albania and Macedonia.[184]

This perspective also suggests one reason why "stateless" groups have proven especially vulnerable to mass killing. Groups such as the Jews (prior to the establishment of Israel), Kurds, and Gypsies have been the repeated victims of mass violence, not simply because they have been historical objects of discrimination and hatred, but because they have had nowhere to run when threatened by conflicts with more powerful groups.

6. COUNTERGUERRILLA MASS KILLINGS: GUATEMALA AND AFGHANISTAN

The effort to defeat guerrilla insurgencies was the single most common motivation for mass killing in the last century. In this chapter I focus on two of the most significant episodes of counterguerrilla mass killing in recent history: the civil war in Guatemala from 1978 to 1996 and the Soviet occupation of Afghanistan from 1979 to 1988. Counterguerrilla motives have also been the driving force behind numerous other episodes of mass killing, including, but not limited to, the American occupation of the Philippines (1899–1902), the Chinese civil war (1927–49), the Algerian war of independence from France (1954–62), the French and American wars in Indochina/Vietnam (1945–75), the civil war in El Salvador (1979–92), the Ethiopian civil war (1974–91), the civil war in East Timor (1975–99), the suppression of Kurdish rebellions in Iraq (1961–91), the civil war in Sudan (1983 to present), the civil war in Burundi (1993 to present), and the Russian suppression of Chechen separatists (1994 to present).[1] Because radical communist states, racist or nationalist regimes, settler colonies, empires, and states engaged in wars of territorial expansion have often provoked guerrilla resistance movements, counterguerrilla motives have also played a significant but secondary role in many other cases of mass killing described in this book.

Counterguerrilla warfare seldom avoids violence against civilians altogether. Nevertheless, systematic mass killing remains relatively rare compared to the large number of guerrilla conflicts waged in modern times. To understand why this is so, in this chapter I will also analyze several notable counterguerrilla military campaigns that did not result in mass killing.

The remainder of this chapter is divided into five main sections. In the first section, I explain why perpetrators so often see mass killing as an attractive military strategy in counterguerrilla warfare. In the second and third sections, I employ this strategic perspective to help show why the conflicts in Guatemala and Afghanistan resulted in such high levels of violence against civilians. The fourth section explores the history of several counterguerrilla wars that did not result in mass killing. In the concluding section, I suggest some reasons why counterguerrilla mass killing has been so prevalent during the last one hundred years, and why, unfortunately, it seems likely to remain a common strategy of counterinsurgency in the future.

A Strategic Approach to Counterguerrilla Mass Killing

Although guerrilla tactics are probably as old as warfare itself, guerrilla wars have become especially prominent since the end of the Second World War.[2] Guerrilla warfare is notoriously difficult to define. The term, which means "small war" in Spanish, first appears to have entered military vocabulary during Napoleon's campaign against Spain in 1808–14. Since then, the term has come to signify almost any unconventional, revolutionary, or civil war.

In this book, however, I distinguish guerrilla wars from other forms of combat by three central characteristics. First, and most distinctively, clear lines of battle in guerrilla warfare are rare, and guerrilla forces frequently operate in territories that are technically under the military control of their adversaries. Second, guerrilla warfare relies primarily on irregular forces, organized in small, highly mobile units that operate mostly without heavy weaponry such as tanks, artillery, or aircraft. Third, guerrilla tactics seek to avoid decisive set-piece battles in favor of prolonged campaigns involving hit-and-run attacks, assassinations, terror bombing, and sabotage. These operations are designed to increase an opponent's political, military, and economic costs, as opposed to defeating his military forces directly.

A fourth characteristic of guerrilla combat, however, one common to many but not all guerrilla wars, is the most central for understanding counterguerrilla mass killing. Much more than conventional armies, guerrilla forces rely directly on local civilian populations for their logistical support, including food, shelter, supplies, and intelligence.[3] Guerrillas may also use civilian populations as a form of "human camouflage" into which they can disappear to avoid detection. As Mao Zedong, one of history's most influential strategists of guerrilla warfare, famously put it: "Because guerrilla warfare basically derives from the masses and is supported by them, it can neither exist nor flourish if it separates itself from their sympathies and cooperation. . . . Many people think it is impossible for guerrillas to exist for long in the enemy's rear. Such a belief reveals lack of comprehension of the relationship that should exist between the people and the troops. The former may be likened to water and the latter to the fish who inhabit it."[4]

Guerrilla warfare can be an extraordinarily powerful weapon. Skillfully applied, guerrilla tactics can provide even relatively small and weak groups with the capability to inflict significant military and political costs on regimes fielding vastly superior conventional forces. Determined guerrilla forces have proven extraordinarily difficult to defeat even by the most advanced Western armies. Conventional military tactics are poorly suited to combating an enemy that seeks to avoid direct military confrontations, has no permanent lines of supply or communication, and whose forces are often indistinguishable from the general population. Policing the vast spaces and large populations resident in areas of guerrilla activity requires resources beyond all but the largest armies. These dilemmas force regimes threatened by powerful guerrilla insurgencies to search for unconventional strategies capable of defeating their opponents. Unfortunately, the nature of guerrilla tactics has often led military and political leaders to conclude that the systematic targeting of civilian populations is the only "practical" solution to the seemingly intractable problems of guerrilla warfare.

As Mao understood, the close support of the civilian population is one of the great strengths of guerrilla warfare. This relationship, however, can also be a weakness. Rather than fighting the guerrillas on their own terms, regimes determined to defeat a guerrilla insurgency may adopt a strategy designed to sever the guerrillas from their base of support in the population. Unlike guerrilla forces themselves, this network of civilian support is largely immobile and nearly impossible to conceal. Since guerrilla warfare has no defined front lines separating contending forces, and since guerrillas seldom choose to commit large forces to the static defense of specific territories or population centers, counterguerrilla forces often have easy access to the guerrillas' civilian supporters. As such, these populations offer an obvious target for counterguerrilla operations. Roger Trinquier, a French counterinsurgency theorist and veteran of counterguerrilla wars in both Indochina and Algeria, gave this explanation:

It is the inhabitant who supplies the guerrilla with his food requirements on an almost day to day basis. . . . It is the inhabitant who also occasionally supplies him with ammunition. The inhabitant contributes to his protection by keeping him informed. . . . No troop movement can escape the inhabitant. Any threat to the guerrilla is communicated to him in plenty of time. Sometimes the inhabitant's home is the guerrilla's refuge, where he can disappear in case of danger. . . . But this total dependence upon terrain and population is also the guerrilla's weak point. We should be able, with our more powerful potential, to make him submit or to destroy him by acting upon his terrain and upon his support—the population.[5]

Likewise, Franklin Lindsay, a veteran of the U.S. Office of Strategic Services (the predecessor to the CIA) who advised the partisan movement against the German occupation of Yugoslavia during the Second World War, writes that "a guerrilla force is like the top of an iceberg; the supporting civilian organization, without which it cannot survive, is the much larger part that cannot be seen. Just as control of the air has become a prerequisite for successful frontal warfare, so control of the population is a prerequisite for successful unconventional warfare."[6]

The killing of civilians in counterguerrilla warfare has often been attributed to the conduct of overzealous, poorly disciplined, racist, or hate-filled troops. There can be little doubt that the frustration of waging a prolonged war against an opponent who refuses to stand and fight, along with the difficulty of distinguishing guerrillas from civilians, helps make atrocities more common in counterguerrilla warfare than in other forms of combat. The uncoordinated actions of uncontrollable or racist troops, however, are unlikely to generate the levels of violence necessary to meet the criteria for mass killing as I define it.

Counter-guerrilla forces do not engage in mass killing primarily because they lack discipline or because they hate their victims. On the contrary, I argue that mass killing in counterguerrilla warfare, including associated practices such as torture and public executions, often is viewed by its perpetrators in cold military terms, as one tactic among many used to respond to the unique threats posed by their guerrilla opponents. As I will document below, counterguerrilla forces have often combined mass killing with "positive" policies designed to improve the lives of the civilian population and draw support away from guerrillas. It is this understanding of counterguerrilla mass killing that explains the perverse logic behind the infamous comment of an American officer in Vietnam: "We had to destroy the village in order to save it."[7]

As political leaders and military commanders engaged in counterguerrilla warfare frequently have stated openly, if the civilian population is the "sea" in which the guerrilla "fish" swim, counterguerrilla mass killing is a strategy that seeks to catch the fish by draining the sea. Efforts to defeat guerrilla insurgencies by acting upon their support in the civilian population have led to the development of three related counterguerrilla tactics: counterterror, population resettlement, and scorched-earth warfare. Each of these tactics has often resulted in mass killing. In addition, counterguerrilla forces have also developed a range of nonviolent "civic-action" tactics designed to reduce or eliminate civilian support for guerrillas by addressing the root causes of the insurgency. These four tactics are often referred to collectively as "pacification." I will describe each of them in detail below.

Counterterror

Counterguerrilla forces have often sought to defeat insurgencies by terrorizing and intimidating the guerrillas' supporters among the civilian population. By killing individuals suspected of collaborating with the insurgents, often in public and sometimes in an especially gruesome manner, leaders seek to intimidate the rest of the population into shunning the guerrillas or revealing information about guerrilla activities. As Lindsay writes, "When two forces are contending for the loyalty of, and control over, the civilian population, the side which uses violent reprisals most aggressively will dominate most of the people, even though their sympathies may lie in the other direction."[8] Lindsay and most other Western theorists of counterguerrilla warfare are careful to point out that this tactic works best when it is applied in a selective manner, targeting only active participants in the insurgency and its most influential supporters. In practice, however, accurate discrimination in guerrilla warfare can be extremely difficult. Guerrilla organizations usually go to great lengths to conceal their membership and supporters. Counterguerrilla forces often lack the detailed intelligence necessary to distinguish between civilians and guerrillas.[9] Nor do they have the time or resources necessary to grant suspects the benefit of due process. Under these circumstances, the temptation to resort to violence and even torture to gather information from suspected guerrillas and their supporters can be substantial.[10]

The incentive to target civilians in counterguerrilla campaigns, however, is not solely the product of the practical difficulties of waging counterinsurgency warfare discriminately. Even if truly selective counterterror operations were possible, counterinsurgent forces would still face considerable incentives for mass killing. That is because most so-called guerrilla sympathizers are in fact civilians. They support the guerrillas with food, shelter, information, or political agitation but do not participate directly in acts of violence. The ability to determine who is a guerrilla combatant and who is a civilian guerrilla sympathizer, therefore, would not eliminate the incentives to target civilian populations. Furthermore, counterguerrilla forces frequently seek not simply to prevent civilians from actively supporting the guerrillas but also to force civilians to cooperate in the effort to defeat the insurgency. This kind of "cooperation" must often be elicited through violent coercion.

As a result of these problems and incentives, a strategy of counterterror can easily degenerate into an exercise in collective punishment involving the indiscriminate slaughter of large numbers of innocent civilians. As an American officer described the massacre of more than five hundred civilians in the Vietnamese village of My Lai: "It was really a good tactic when you stop to think about it. . . . if you scare people enough they will keep away from you. . . . I'm not saying I approve of the tactic. . . . I think it's an effective tactic."[11]

The German occupation of the Soviet Union and Eastern Europe during the Second World War provides one of the most savage examples of the strategy of counterterror in action. Facing widespread resistance from guerrilla partisans, German occupation forces adopted an explicit policy of "prophylaxis by terror" that Hitler vowed would "make the population lose all interest in insubordination."[12] The German High Command concluded that "a deterrent effect can be attained only through unusual hardness" and called for the application of "collective measures of force," even in cases of "passive resistance."[13] In many areas of German occupation, it became standard practice for Germans to execute between fifty and a hundred civilians for every German soldier killed by partisan guerrillas.[14] It was not unusual for entire villages, including women and children, to be exterminated in response to partisan attacks.[15]

Although it would be easy to attribute this kind of violence exclusively to the cruelty of the Nazi regime, even democratic states facing powerful guerrilla insurgencies have resorted to this tacit, albeit on a lesser scale. For example, terror was a common tactic of U.S. forces in the 1899–1902 counterinsurgency campaign in the Philippines. When they first arrived in the Philippines, U.S. military commanders were unused to guerrilla combat, but they soon grasped that "the unique system of warfare" utilized by the Filipinos "depended upon almost complete unity of action of the entire native population."[16] In response, General J. Franklin Bell, the commander of the U.S. Army in the province of Batangas, devised a strategy of terror and intimidation intended to separate the guerrillas from their supporters.[17] Describing his plans, Bell wrote that to "combat such a population it is necessary to make the state of war as insupportable as possible . . . by keeping the minds of the people in such a state of anxiety

and apprehension that living under such conditions will soon become unbearable. Little should be said. . . . Let acts, not words, convey the intention."[18]

Bell announced that "all consideration and regard for the inhabitants
of this place cease from the day I become commander." Lacking the information necessary to determine who supported the guerrillas and who
did not, a system of collective punishment was adopted. Bell argued that
even "neutrality should not be tolerated."[19] Only those who demonstrated active support for U.S. forces would be spared. A ruthless campaign was launched during which, according to one correspondent,
American soldiers killed "men, women, children, prisoners and captives,
active insurgents and suspected people, from lads of ten and up."[20] A
young lieutenant remarked that "the American soldier in officially sanctioned wrath is a thing so ugly and dangerous that it would take a Kipling
to describe him."[21]

Forced Population Resettlement

A second tactic frequently utilized in counterguerrilla warfare is the
forced displacement and resettlement of civilian populations. By relocating civilians from regions of intense guerrilla activity to "regroupment
camps" or "strategic villages" policed by government forces, regimes seek
to physically separate guerrilla combatants from the civilian support they
need to continue fighting.

Although in theory more humane than the terror tactics described
above, in practice population relocation often involves massive violence.[22] As with policies of ethnic cleansing, violence is often required to
force people to leave their homes and possessions for an unknown life in
a faraway location. The process of rapidly relocating large numbers of
people frequently leads to widespread mortality. The extraordinary expense of providing adequate sustenance, shelter, and sanitation for large
numbers of people means that starvation and disease often await refugees
in government camps.[23] Sometimes, in operations more accurately
termed "depopulation" than resettlement, counterinsurgent forces simply expel the entire population of guerrilla-active regions, making little or
no provision for their relocation.

To make maters worse, population resettlement has often been combined with the creation of so-called free-fire zones, in which any person
remaining in the evacuated area may be shot on sight on the presumption
of being a guerrilla or guerrilla supporter. As the American counterinsurgency theorist John McCuen explained the tactic:

> The concept is simple. The entire population is evacuated from an area,
> regrouped, and forbidden to re-enter it without special permission. By

so doing, the governing authorities remove the revolutionaries' only real important source of strength — the people. Without a population, the rebels are deprived of their protective screen, source of recruitment, food supply, intelligence network, and so forth. . . . Furthermore, the mobile forces [of the government] now have complete freedom of action, for they can attack as an enemy anyone remaining in the zone.[24]

One of the first experiments with the mass relocation of civilians in guerrilla war occurred during the Boer War of 1899–1902. In an effort to deprive the Boer guerrillas of support, the British forcibly removed over 150,000 people, almost all of them women and children, from their farms and interned them in squalid refugee camps.[25] Over 20,000 internees died of malnutrition and disease.[26]

The Ethiopian government also used large-scale resettlement in its battle to crush the guerrilla insurgency in Tigre. From 1984 to 1986, between 700,000 and 800,000 people were uprooted and relocated to government-controlled villages and camps. Between 50,000 and 200,000 are believed to have perished.[27] Although the Ethiopian government claimed the program was a famine relief measure, the relocated populations consisted primarily of those living in strategically significant regions, not the areas most severely stricken with famine or drought.[28] Most observers agree that the primary goal of relocation was to deprive the Tigrean rebels of their base of support.[29] Indeed, referring directly to Mao's writings, one cadre of the Workers' Party of Ethiopia plainly described the government's strategy for defeating the rebellion to a group of Tigrean peasants: "If you dry out the sea the fish will die. . . . We will dry out Tigre and force the bandits to give up. You are the backbone of the bandits, so we have to break you first; then we can also destroy the marrow."[30]

Scorched-Earth Warfare

A third counterguerrilla tactic, often employed in conjunction with population resettlement, is the systematic destruction of crops, livestock, dwellings, and other important infrastructure in areas of guerrilla activity. This "scorched-earth" strategy serves three primary functions.[31] First, it deprives guerrillas and their supporters of food and shelter, killing them or starving them into submission. Second, it can be used to force local populations into government-controlled resettlement camps and discourage refugees from returning to their homes. Finally, it can be used selectively as a severe punishment or deterrent for villages suspected of supporting the guerrillas.

Scorched-earth tactics have been a common feature of counterguerrilla warfare throughout this century. The U.S. Army employed them during the occupation of the Philippines following the Spanish-American War of 1898 to eliminate the source of supplies for the insurgents and to force the population into regroupment camps.[32] Hundreds of thousands of Filipino civilians died during the war, many of starvation directly attributable to the scorched-earth campaign.[33]

Scorched-earth tactics have been a central feature of the ongoing counterguerrilla war in Sudan as well, where they have also contributed to severe famines. According to a report by the human rights organization African Rights, the Sudanese regime hoped that the famine would break the will of the people and force them into government-controlled areas. The report concludes that "the creation of famine was a deliberate government military policy. The widespread burning of villages and food crops and stealing of livestock could have no other effect. There can be no doubt . . . that politicians and generals were fully aware of what they were doing when they launched the scorched-earth strategy."[34]

Perhaps nowhere were scorched-earth counterinsurgency tactics applied with greater ruthlessness than in the Japanese occupation of northern China during the early 1940s. In areas of intense guerrilla activity, Japanese tactics bordered on outright extermination. The army adopted what it called the "three all" policy—"kill all, burn all, loot all." Japanese brutality in China has often been attributed to anti-Chinese racism.[35] Racism was rampant in the Japanese army, but even in this case, strategic motives also seem to have been at work. In central China, where guerrilla resistance was not as strong, Japanese atrocities were less common—a pattern that cannot be explained by racism.[36] Rather, as Lincoln Li observes, Japanese violence against civilian populations was more directly the result of "a kind of scorched-earth policy in reverse. Indiscriminate devastation was designed to break the will of the populace from supporting the resistance cause, and to deprive the Chinese Communist military forces of sources of manpower and food supplies."[37] Likewise, Chalmers Johnson suggests that the policy "aimed at destroying the close cooperation that existed between the communists and the populace. The essence of the [three all policy] was to surround a given area, to kill everyone in it, and to destroy everything possible so that the area would be uninhabitable in the future."[38] Approximately nineteen million people in communist-controlled areas of northern China were rendered homeless by Japanese operations.[39] Eight million or more Chinese civilians may have perished under the Japanese occupation.[40]

Perpetrators have also implemented scorched-earth tactics in counterinsurgency warfare through the aerial bombardment of food crops and dwellings that provide sustenance and shelter for both guerrillas and civilians. For military organizations with sufficient air forces, the bombardment of guerrilla active areas can be an especially attractive strategy because it holds the promise of avoiding the high casualties often suffered by counterinsurgent forces in ground operations. This strategy is sometimes even more deadly for civilian populations, on the other hand, since the difficulty of distinguishing between guerrillas and civilians from the air and the inaccuracy of most aerial weapons means that targets are often selected at the village level or higher.

The Salvadoran air force used this counterinsurgency strategy to devastating effect. As a report by Americas Watch concluded, during the intense fighting of the early 1980s

> aerial power was being used extensively to drive *masas* [civilians suspected of supporting the guerrillas], or those designated in this way, from large sections of the country that were controlled by the guerrillas. The apparent purpose was to deprive the guerrillas of sources of food and information about troop movements. In the process many hundreds of civilians were killed in aerial attacks, and many more were injured. Villages were laid waste, farm animals were killed, peasants left their homes, often without any possessions.[41]

Civic Action

Violence and coercion are not the only means that counterinsurgent forces have employed to separate guerrillas from their civilian supporters. Indeed, counterinsurgency campaigns frequently combine the brutal tactics described above with policies designed to entice civilian supporters away from the guerrillas with the prospect of rewards including money, food, land, social and political reforms, or improved infrastructure. These strategies, commonly referred to as "civic action" or "winning hearts and minds," seek to address the root economic, political, or social causes of the insurgency and to convince the population that cooperation with the government is in their best interest.

Programs of civic action have been a common feature of counterguerrilla warfare, even in conflicts noted for their brutality. American forces in the Philippines, for example, combined violent reprisals against villages suspected of supporting the guerrillas with large-scale civic-action programs including sanitation projects, vaccination, education, and food distribution.[42] Similarly, the counterguerrilla war waged by the Chinese Nationalist regime against Mao's communist insurgency was characterized by "extermination campaigns" that killed millions of people. Yet, in some areas, the regime also implemented rent reduction, land reform, and affordable loan programs, which were designed to redress the peasants' grievances and to reward their loyalty.[43]

Unfortunately, civic-action programs can be extremely expensive to implement, especially when there are millions of hearts and minds to be won. Few regimes possess the resources or inclination to provide truly attractive rewards to very large numbers of people. Counterguerrilla forces facing a mass-based insurgency, therefore, have seldom relied on such tactics alone. The promise of positive incentives for cooperation usually has been buttressed substantially by threats of violent punishment for those suspected of supporting the guerrillas.

GUATEMALA

In the years between 1960 and 1996, Guatemala was ravaged by repeated waves of insurgency and counterguerrilla warfare. The insurgency began in 1960 when a small group of military officers launched a coup d'état against the Guatemalan regime. Although the coup failed, its organizers escaped capture, organized a small guerrilla force, and vowed to overthrow the government. From 1961 to 1978, however, the insurgency was unable to garner strong support from the rural population. Government-sponsored violence was pervasive, but killing remained at comparatively low levels. Beginning in 1978, however, the insurgents began to develop a significant following among the Guatemalan peasantry and adopted a mass-based guerrilla strategy. These fundamental changes in the nature of the guerrillas' tactics prompted equally fundamental changes in the regime's strategy for defeating them. The Guatemalan regime's effort to isolate the guerrillas from their newly won civilian supporters resulted in a devastating campaign of mass killing.

The Guerrillas' Foco Strategy and the Government Response

Following their failed coup in 1960, rebel military officers fled to the countryside in eastern Guatemala. There, they entered into an alliance with the military wing of the Guatemalan Communist Party, a faction that eventually came to dominate the insurgency. For the next several years the insurgent forces remained very small, probably numbering less than five hundred men.[44] They recruited approximately six thousand active supporters among the local peasants, but they did not develop a national, mass-based organization.[45] Most peasants had little interest in the conflict since they saw no reason to support one group of military officers against another. The guerrillas' communist program was at worst anathema to peasant interests and at best too abstract to motivate a national rebellion. In particular, the insurgency failed to achieve broad support among the indigenous Mayan Indians, who constituted the majority of Guatemala's population.[46] Rather, the insurgents operated according to the *foco* theory of guerrilla warfare famously advocated by Ernesto

"Che" Guevara. Robin Corbett describes this theory: "Denying the need for a mass movement or a vanguard party (and thus contradicting both Lenin and Mao Tse-tung), Guevara argued that a small, mobile, and hard-hitting band of guerrillas could act as the focus for the revolution . . . or *foco,* and go on to seize power."[47]

The *foco* theory suggested that a small number of daring guerrillas could spark a national revolution by staging highly visible raids and terrorist attacks on government targets. These attacks would serve to rouse the population into action by demonstrating the power and revolutionary spirit of the rebellion and by provoking an excessively repressive response on the part of government forces. Harsh government repression, in turn, would convince even more people of the need to join the revolutionaries and overthrow the regime. In its early years, therefore, the Guatemalan guerrillas focused on small-scale attacks and ambushes on police stations, military outposts, and patrols.[48] In urban areas they staged bombings, kidnappings, and assassinations of high-ranking officials.

The Guatemalan regime's response to the insurgency escalated with the severity of guerrilla attacks. Prior to 1965, government repression remained at relatively low levels. Indeed, guerrilla leaders remained in contact with their former friends in the army, sometimes even appearing in public in Guatemala City. In 1965 and 1966, however, the rebels launched a bold series of kidnappings, assassinations, and bombings that the Guatemalan government could not ignore.[49] From 1966 to 1967, the government waged a violent campaign to crush the rebellion. A state of siege was declared throughout the country.

The primary objective of this campaign was the destruction of the guerrillas' rural bases in eastern Guatemala. The army, backed by local militia units and government-organized death squads, killed anyone suspected of supporting the guerrillas. Entire villages were razed to the ground. Mutilated bodies were left in public places as a warning to others.[50] Between five and ten thousand people may have been killed over the course of the campaign.[51] Since there were no more than a few hundred guerrillas active at the time, however, most of the victims were undoubtedly innocent civilians. Many may actually have been government supporters.[52]

While the government's counterguerrilla campaign was shockingly brutal, its most violent effects remained localized to a few relatively isolated areas where the guerrillas received support from the population. The campaign largely succeeded in stamping out the guerrilla bases in the countryside.[53] Indeed, the guerrillas' failure to protect their civilian supporters probably hurt their cause among the masses for years to come.[54]

In 1967, the surviving rebels were forced to shift most of their operations to urban areas.[55] Others fled across the border to Mexico. For the next fifteen years various rebel groups carried out small-scale terrorist attacks and kidnappings. Government sponsored death squads waged a low-level war of counterterror against political opposition groups and anyone suspected of collaborating with the rebels. Amnesty International estimates that more than thirty thousand people were "abducted, tortured and assassinated" in the years between 1966 and 1981.[56]

Mass-Based Guerrilla War and Counterguerrilla Mass Killing

By 1976, disappearances and assassinations at the hands of government-organized death squads had become a way of life in Guatemala, especially in the cities. Although the repression took the lives of several hundred to over a thousand people each year, it never reached the level of mass killing. As in other Latin American countries such as Chile and Argentina, this level of violence proved sufficient to keep Guatemala's relatively small, primarily urban-based political opposition in check. Both the nature of the Guatemalan insurrection and the tactics the Guatemalan military used to counter it, however, began to change after a massive earthquake shook the country in February 1976, killing more than twenty thousand people.

The earthquake left more than one million people homeless. The government did little to help the victims, mostly the rural poor. On the contrary, corrupt public officials and army officers used their control over the distribution of international aid for their personal profit. The earthquake also brought thousands of international and domestic relief workers, missionaries, and labor unionists to Guatemala. They traveled throughout the countryside, spreading new ideas and promoting political organization.

The earthquake coincided with major changes in the economic organization of rural life in Guatemala. A serious economic downturn in the early 1970s, combined with a population explosion and a decline in traditional forms of agriculture, produced severe poverty throughout the countryside. Guatemala's large Mayan population, overrepresented among the rural poor, was particularly hard hit by the economic upheavals.[57]

These and other social, economic, and political developments dramatically increased dissatisfaction with the Guatemalan military regime during the 1970s. The guerrillas, in disarray or living in exile since the crackdown of the late 1960s, reemerged intent on taking advantage of these sentiments to build a national base of support among the peasants. Unlike the movements of the 1960s, the second generation of guerrillas intended to fight a prolonged, mass-based guerrilla insurgency. More important, the guerrillas set out to win the support of Guatemala's indigenous population as well as ladinos.[58] As Susanne Jonas notes, the insurgency abandoned the failed *foco* strategy of the 1960s and "transformed itself . . . into a force with broad popular support nationally, incorporating the indigenous population in massive numbers."[59]

The rebellion spread rapidly in the late 1970s. The government ruthlessly cracked down on all attempts at political organization, but the regime's violent tactics simply seem to have convinced more peasants to join the guerrillas. Indeed, David Stoll suggests that the majority of support for the guerrillas stemmed from the peasantry's reaction to overly harsh government repression, not from revolutionary ideological impulses or social or economic discontent.[60] The most powerful of the new generation of guerrilla groups, the Guerrilla Army of the Poor (EGP), swelled from just over a dozen men in 1972 to between four and six thousand regular fighters and ten thousand local irregulars by 1982.[61] The guerrilla's most powerful asset was its burgeoning support among the indigenous population, especially those living in Guatemala's western and central highlands. Between 250,000 and 500,000 native Americans are believed to have participated in the insurgency in one form or another — most providing food, clothing, shelter, and information to the guerrillas.[62]

This new organization constituted a formidable military force. Guerrilla operations posed a serious threat to the ability of the Guatemalan army, itself numbering only eighteen thousand men, to maintain control over the country.[63] In some areas, the guerrillas were carrying out attacks on an almost daily basis. By 1981 guerrillas virtually controlled nine of Guatemala's twenty-two provinces and had a significant presence in nine others.[64]

The Guatemalan regime could not fail to appreciate the significance of the changes in the nature of the insurgency. The regime's initial efforts to suppress the rebellion through a campaign of "selective repression" from 1978 to 1980 failed.[65] As Beatrice Manz notes, by 1981 "the Army sensed the guerrillas had tapped into a deep reservoir of popular discontent. . . . Unlike the 1960's, the guerrilla 'fish' were no longer in an isolated pond but rather swimming in a very large sea."[66] Indeed, the Guatemalan army estimated that the EGP alone had over 360,000 supporters in 1981.[67] The victory of the Sandinista insurgency in Nicaragua in 1979 served as a powerful warning to Guatemalan leaders of what a determined guerrilla resistance could accomplish. The Guatemalan defense minister recalled that "this was a great threat to Guatemala. The guerrillas were well entrenched and intended to declare a portion of the highlands liberated territory."[68]

By the early 1980s, the Guatemalan regime under President-General

Romeo Lucas realized that destroying the guerrillas directly would be all but impossible. Rather, defeating the insurgency would require crushing the guerrillas' civilian support and infrastructure. Eliminating the guerrilla's support, in turn, would require mass killing. Beginning in 1981, Lucas launched a major counterguerrilla campaign in both rural and urban locations. According to Michael McClintock, the army's policy "was to annihilate the guerrillas' social base across the board in the most seriously 'infected' areas."[69] Perhaps thirty-five thousand people, the vast majority of them civilians, were killed during the campaign.[70] Nevertheless, the army's tactics during this period remained disorganized and largely reactive.[71] Troops responded to guerrilla attacks by massacring local peasants and burning nearby villages, but the army had yet to formulate a systematic plan for defeating the insurgency. Indeed, the guerrilla resistance continued to grow under the Lucas regime.

Partly in response to Lucas's perceived inability to deal with the guerrilla threat, a group of young army officers deposed him in a coup in March 1982. The new regime, led by General Efraín Rios Montt came to power determined to crush the guerrillas by whatever means necessary. Montt, a military professional trained in counterinsurgency warfare in the United States, launched an exceptionally brutal counterguerrilla campaign that he publicly vowed would "dry up the human sea in which the guerrilla fish swim."[72] As Guatemala's deputy chief of staff General Alejandro Gramjo described the campaign, "here were the villages, here is the population supporting *la guerrilla* from behind, and the Army attacked everyone and we continued attacking, attacking until we cornered them and got to the point where the [the population] was separated from the subversive leaders. . . . Exactly in 1982 this strategy began."[73]

Jennifer Schirmer concludes that the "searing contradiction" of the Guatemalan army's strategy was that in order "to accomplish this 'separation,' certain areas are targeted for massive killings; that is, the military must treat the civilians they are to 'rescue' *as though they are combatants,* killing and burning all living things within the 'secured area.' . . . Nor are killings accidental 'abuses' or 'excesses'; rather, they represent a scientifically precise, sustained orchestration of a systematic, intentional massive campaign of extermination."[74]

Seventy-five thousand people, nearly all civilians, were slaughtered in eighteen months, most in the first eight months of the campaign.[75] In the area of highest guerrilla activity, known as the Ixil Triangle, approximately one-third of the local population may have been killed.[76]

Despite the massive violence associated with the campaign, the Guatemalan army's brutality was not primarily the result of bloodthirsty leaders, undisciplined troops, or racism directed against the guerrilla's indigenous supporters. Although each of these factors probably contributed to the violence, the actions of the Guatemalan military, as well as statements made by Guatemalan leaders, suggest that the brutality of the campaign is best understood as a calculated military response on the part of the regime to the exigencies of warfare against a mass-based guerrilla insurgency.

Guatemala's military leaders were not interested in killing for killing's sake. Indeed, at the same time that the regime massively stepped up its use of violence against the civilian population, it also launched a series of "positive" economic, social, and political projects designed to address the root causes of the insurgency and win the hearts and minds of the population. Atrocities were too widespread to reflect the uncoordinated actions of poorly disciplined troops. Rather, as Allan Nairn argued, the war in Guatemala was "a bloodbath not because the Guatemalan soldiers are irrational but because their enemy is a large portion of their own people, and to defeat them they must kill them."[77]

Racism also seems unlikely to be the main cause of the bloodshed. Violence against civilians targeted the areas of greatest guerrilla activity, not Indians specifically, and many Spanish-speaking ladinos were also slaughtered during the campaign.[78] Until the guerrillas expanded their support base to include Guatemala's vast indigenous population in the late 1970s, government terror was targeted primarily against the ladino peasants and political organizers suspected of sympathizing with the Left. As noted above, between five and ten thousand people, mostly ladino civilians, were killed in the counterinsurgency campaigns of 1966 and 1967. Because the guerrillas' support base at this time was relatively small, however, the scale of the killing did not reach the levels witnessed in the early 1980s.

Thus, as Schirmer contends, "without a structural analysis of violence as intrinsic to the logic of counterinsurgency, a regime that violates human rights seems to occur simply because of uncontrollable, bloodlusting commanders or poorly disciplined peasant recruits. . . . Rather than being irrational and out of control, many of these Latin American militaries are precisely in control and acting in their own best interests."[79]

Counterguerrilla Tactics in Guatemala

The Guatemalan regime employed each of the four tactics of counterguerrilla warfare described in the first section of this chapter.

Counterterror

The Guatemalan army under Rios Montt dramatically escalated the already brutal war of counterterror that it inherited from Lucas, killing more people in less than fifteen months than Lucas had in almost four years.[80]

Violence under the new regime focused even more intently on the insurgents' growing civilian support network. Indeed, Rios Montt himself frankly stated that "the problem of the war is not just a question of who is shooting. For each one who is shooting there are ten working behind him."[81] As Rios Montt's press secretary explained it, "The guerrillas won over many Indian collaborators. . . . Therefore, the Indians were subversives, right? And how do you fight subversion? Clearly, you had to kill Indians because they were collaborating with subversion. And then they [human rights advocates] would say, 'you're massacring innocent people.' But they weren't innocent. They had sold out to subversion."[82]

Beginning in 1982, therefore, the Guatemalan military developed a plan to apply counterterror with what it termed "scientific" precision specifically against those individuals and villages that army intelligence had determined were supporting the guerrillas. As General Gramjo described the strategy, "It was determined village by village if each was infiltrated and consciously or unconsciously involved [with the guerrillas]."[83] Another army officer explained that the offensive was "elaborated down to the last detail and the enemy, which had to be eliminated, very carefully defined."[84] Rios Montt rejected the practice of previous regimes of using death squads to secretly abduct and murder suspected leftists. On the contrary, he said he wanted to send a clear message to guerrilla supporters: "Whoever is against the . . . government, whoever doesn't surrender, I'm going to shoot. It is preferable that it be known that 20 people were shot, and not just that 20 bodies have appeared by the side of the road."[85]

Despite the widespread use of torture to extract information from captured guerrillas, in practice such careful discrimination proved nearly impossible.[86] Crude methods were used to identify guerrilla supporters. Labor organizers, community leaders, or educated persons frequently were executed without provocation. Troops simply assumed that anyone showing fear or attempting to flee advancing army units was a guerrilla supporter and therefore a legitimate target.[87]

In many cases, the army did not even attempt to determine individual guilt, instead targeting entire villages suspected of collaborating with the guerrillas. Villages were categorized into one of three color-coded zones. Villages in red zones were to be completely destroyed and their inhabitants killed. Villages in pink zones would be attacked but not leveled. Those in white zones were considered friendly and left untouched. As *Latin America Regional Reports* reported in 1983, "The killing is sometimes selective, with community leaders, such as teachers or church activists, and their families being singled out. In other instances whole villages have been wiped out. Everything depends on the Army's perception of the level of local support for the guerrillas."[88]

The difficulty of distinguishing civilians from guerrillas, however, was not the primary reason for the killing of noncombatants. Civilians were not merely unintentional victims of the army's counterterror operations. Rather, as James Morrissey observes, in many cases the "massive retaliation which followed guerrilla activities was deliberately aimed, not at the guerrillas, but at civilian populations anywhere near where the guerrillas had operated. . . . The intent was clearly not only to make the people reluctant to have anything to do with the guerrillas, but to make the consequences of the guerrillas' operations so repugnant that the guerrillas themselves would refrain from action rather that risk having people suffer such barbarism."[89]

The Guatemalan army believed that women and children contributed to supporting the guerrillas, so they too became legitimate targets. As the *Washington Post* reported, "Senior Army officials stated openly that they would have to wipe out what they called 'family nuclei,' including children, whom they considered essential to the revolutionary organizations in the countryside."[90] One army lieutenant justified his involvement in the massacre of women by arguing that "we have to finish them all off, to put an end to the guerrillas. The women are preparing their food. If we finish them off, things will soon calm down."[91] Children were killed because they were considered potential future recruits for the guerrillas.[92] The killing of women and children, often carried out in an exceptionally grisly manner, may also have been used to demonstrate to surviving individuals and villages the fate that awaited those who supported the guerrillas.

Population Resettlement

According to a secret Army General Staff document, a primary objective of the government's counterinsurgency strategy was to "deny the guerrillas access to the civilian population, from which it supports itself and within which it hides."[93] To help accomplish this goal, Rios Montt instituted a major new policy of relocating civilians from areas of high guerrilla activity to regions that the government could control more easily. Although the regime designed the resettlement policy as a less violent alternative to its military operations, implementing it ultimately involved extreme brutality. Villagers were far from enthusiastic about leaving their homes and belongings behind. The army often had to use violence to coerce them to relocate. Villages in areas of high guerrilla activity were typically burned to the ground, forcing their inhabitants to choose between fleeing to remote mountainous regions of the country—where they continued to be hunted by the army—or agreeing to relocate to government-controlled areas. Starvation, disease, and exposure took a great toll among those who chose to flee. As many as two hundred thousand people managed to escape across the border to refugee camps in Mexico, but the army sought to block this exodus, fearing that the camps would serve as protected bases for guerrilla operations.[94]

The counterguerrilla campaign displaced over one million people, fully half of the Indian population in the guerrilla-active areas, and far more than could be resettled in the government's "model villages."[95] Originally, the regime planned to build nearly fifty new villages capable of housing one hundred thousand people. This project, however, proved prohibitively expensive. Only half of the villages ultimately were built. Living conditions in the model villages were better than the meager existence available to those hiding out in the jungles and mountains, but most villagers still resented the loss of freedom and disruption of their traditional ways of life.[96] Although the government promised amnesty to guerrilla supporters if they agreed to settle in government-controlled areas, many refugees were summarily executed.[97] Many observers concluded that the government villages were little more than internment camps. As one reporter described them in 1988, "It is the firm threat of Army terror that makes the system work. The Army seldom needs to kill civilians nowadays; the Indians remember its pre-1982 massacres, and they know they will be killed if they fail to follow instructions or attempt to leave the hamlet."[98]

Scorched-Earth Warfare

The Guatemalan army's third and most devastating counterguerrilla tactic under Rios Montt was the extensive use of scorched-earth warfare. Rios Montt famously denied the existence of such a strategy in public, claiming, "We have no scorched-earth policy. We have a policy of scorched communists."[99] Nevertheless, in areas of suspected guerrilla activity, the army systematically torched entire villages, destroyed crops, and slaughtered livestock.[100] Soldiers returned to the same villages time and again to destroy any rebuilt homes or replanted crops.[101] The army intentionally burned vast swaths of forest in the effort to deny cover to the guerrillas. In some areas the devastation was so complete that climate and rainfall patterns appear to have been permanently altered.[102]

The army's scorched-earth policies served two strategic purposes. First, by burning villages and destroying crops and livestock, the army would deprive the guerrillas of the infrastructure they needed to continue fighting.[103] Second, scorched-earth tactics supported the regime's population resettlement program. By rendering large areas of the countryside uninhabitable, the army ensured that peasants who refused to relocate would face severe hardships, while those who agreed to move would have no incentive to return to their homes.[104] According to a 1982 Americas Watch report, this strategy represented "a deliberate policy of forcing peasants to near starvation," designed to drive villagers into government-controlled areas, the only places where food was available.[105]

Civic Action

In addition to the brutal counterguerrilla tactics described above, the Guatemalan regime under Rios Montt introduced a fourth strategy designed to reduce support for the insurgency. Rather than relying on violence and intimidation, this strategy sought to win the hearts and minds of the peasants with promises of security and economic development. These civic-action programs represented the "beans" in what Guatemalan officials referred to as their "guns and beans" counterinsurgency strategy. In many ways, Guatemalan military and political leaders considered this strategy even more important than the strictly military operations described above. Government officials claimed that only 30 percent of their efforts were devoted to the "guns" aspect of their strategy, with the remaining 70 percent devoted to "beans."[106] Beginning in 1982, the army created "civil affairs units" tasked with providing villages in government-controlled areas with food and clean water, medical care, improved roads, electrical power, and other community-oriented projects. The regime also implemented a number of political and social reforms. As a Guatemalan army officer described the strategy: "War is not only won with weapons. This [civic action plan] of ours means bringing life [and] revenue to a people, to a community. . . . There is a saying here in Guatemala: you get more with honey than with vinegar."[107]

Civic-action programs served two main purposes. First, they provided positive incentives to draw people into government-controlled areas. The model villages were designed to look attractive, with electric power and other modern amenities. One army officer explained that the model villages were intended to "fill [the refugees] up in the mountains looking down . . . with questions to put to [the guerrillas] who had told them that everything was abandoned after the massacres of the Army."[108] Another officer put it in simpler terms: "If you are with us, we'll feed you, if not, we'll kill you."[109]

Civic-action programs served a second, deeper purpose as well. They were designed to address what the army perceived to be the root causes of the insurgency and to move from simply separating the population from the guerrillas to enlisting them actively in defeating the insurgency. This strategy marked a major shift from the practices of the previous regimes. The 1982 civic-action plan concluded that the causes of subversion were "based on social injustice, political rivalry, unequal development, and the dramas of hunger, unemployment, and poverty; but it can be controlled if we attempt to solve the most pressing human problems."[110]

In addition to development programs, the Guatemalan army created a system of "civil defense patrols" in which the local population was required to assist the army in the war against the guerrillas. By mid-1983 Rios Montt claimed that over three hundred thousand people had been "recruited" into the patrols.[111] Five thousand Mayan Indians were also enlisted in the regular army. The patrols served several purposes. They facilitated closer cooperation between the population and the army. They forced the population to participate in its own defense. Perhaps most important, the army hoped the civil defense patrols would help bridge the cultural and social gap between Guatemala's indigenous people and the dominant Spanish-speaking population who controlled the government and the army.

The Guatemalan regime's civic-action and development programs ultimately proved far less appealing in practice then they did in theory.[112] As noted above, conditions in the model villages were far from idyllic. Although the villages had electricity and clean water, villagers often lacked sufficient land to provide subsistence for their families. Many became dependent on government aid. Although some indigenous people were successfully integrated into the war against the guerrillas, most appear to have participated in the patrols only under pressure from the army.

Despite these serious problems, Guatemala's civic-action programs appear to have been a genuine attempt by the regime to defeat the insurgency through methods other than violence. To be sure, these programs were not motivated by the altruistic desire to "elevate the population," as government propaganda portrayed it. Nevertheless, government documents and statements of high-ranking Guatemalan officials strongly suggest that the regime seriously intended civic-action programs to address poverty and inequality—the factors it perceived to be the root causes of the insurgency.[113] Lack of resources, rather than lack of commitment, was probably the most important reason for the deficiencies of civic-action in Guatemala.

Assessing the Effectiveness of Guatemala's Counterguerrilla Strategy

Most observers agree that the Guatemalan army's strategy after 1982 was remarkably effective at suppressing the insurgency.[114] The bloody counterguerrilla campaign succeeded in military terms, isolating the guerrillas almost completely from their base of support in the population. The government reestablished authority in most parts of the country. Guerrilla operations were reduced to sporadic hit and run attacks. The immediate threat of a guerrilla victory was squelched. Active guerrilla membership fell from 6,000 or more in 1982 to between 1,000 and 1,200 by 1988, with the majority of these having been pushed into the most remote regions of Guatemala or across the border into Mexico.[115]

The violent counterinsurgency campaign may have been successful in the short term, but its effectiveness in the longer term is more difficult to assess. The guerrillas, while severely weakened, were not completely defeated. By the early 1990s, they were showing signs of resurgence. The army's brutal tactics and suppression of political liberties had turned much of the Guatemalan population against the government and the military, including many who never supported the insurgents. Government repression continued into the 1990s, albeit at much lower levels than in the period from 1979 to 1983. Increasing international pressures for human rights and democracy were brought to bear on the regime. As Rachel McCleary notes: "Even though the military had won the war tactically, it had no clear criteria for ending state violence."[116]

Rios Montt was overthrown in a coup in 1983, and subsequent military regimes gradually accepted the need to yield political control to civilians. Elections were held in 1985, although only rightist and centrist parties were allowed to participate, and the first fully civilian government took office in January 1986. Initially, civilian control was largely a formality designed to appease international and domestic critics. The military continued to control its own operations and exerted substantial influence over many political issues from behind the scenes. Over the next decade, however, civilian control was consolidated. Despite resistance from some right wing politicians and army officers, including several coup attempts, military and civilian elites eventually seem to have accepted that continued violence could not end the fighting and would only exacerbate Guatemala's political and economic problems.[117] In 1994 the government agreed to allow refugees of the war to return to their homes — or what remained of them. In 1996 Guatemala signed a comprehensive peace accord with the guerrillas that abolished the civil patrol system and obliged the military to reduce its forces and orient itself for national defense rather than domestic operations.

Three decades of civil war in Guatemala were at an end. The terrible violence of these years concluded, not with an unconditional victory for the Guatemalan military but with their negotiated acquiescence to civilian authority and a government that included the participation of some of their former guerrilla opponents.

AFGHANISTAN

When Soviet leaders entered the war in Afghanistan in 1979, they neither desired nor expected to fight a bloody campaign against the country's civilian population. They hoped that the war would be quick and inexpensive, and that the main burden of the fighting would be born by their Afghan allies. Soviet leaders understood that the incumbent Afghan communist regime was unpopular with the Afghan population, but they believed that with some minor reforms, support for the resistance would dry up. Reforms, however, failed to produce the desired results, and the Afghan armed forces soon proved themselves completely unreliable. As the Soviets were drawn deeper into the military confrontation with the guerrilla resistance, Soviet commanders realized that their conventional military tactics were an inadequate response to the style of combat they faced in Afghanistan. In an effort to defeat the guerrillas while keeping their own costs—in both lives and Rubbles—to a minimum, the Soviets increasingly resorted to violent attacks against the civilian population. By 1988, when the Soviets decided to withdraw, between 1 and 1.5 million people, the great majority of them civilians, had died and nearly one-third of Afghanistan's population had fled the country.[118]

The assault on the civilian population was not primarily the result of frustrated or undisciplined Soviet troops or of racist Russian attitudes toward the Afghan people, as some authors have suggested.[119] These factors undoubtedly played a role in increasing the bloodshed, but three kinds of evidence suggest that they were the not most important reasons for the widespread violence against civilians. First, contemporary Soviet sources indicate a systematic policy of killing civilians. Second, such killings were too common and too methodical to have been primarily the result of unruly troops. Finally, the fact that the killing of civilians was concentrated in areas of high guerrilla activity, while other areas of Afghanistan were left untouched or even supplied with aid, strongly suggests that racist or nationalist attitudes were not the driving forces behind the killing. In fact, in the early stages of the war the Soviets attempted to decrease racial tensions with the population by drawing disproportionately on Soviet forces from the central Asian republics for duty in Afghanistan. A report of the Soviet General Staff indicated that the "High Command felt that Soviet Soldiers from these nationalities would be better accepted by their ethnically linked peoples of Afghanistan."[120]

The Soviet Union's choice of tactics in Afghanistan was motivated above all else by the tactics of their adversaries. As David Isby concluded in 1983, "It is the nature of the Afghan resistance that has resulted in some of the Soviet decisions about how to conduct operations and tactics. The Afghans are a nation in arms against the Soviets, but with no centralised command. The Soviets must therefore make war not just against the forces in the field but against the people as a whole."[121]

Background to the Soviet Invasion

In April 1978, the People's Democratic Party of Afghanistan (PDPA), an armed communist movement with only a few thousand members, seized control of Afghanistan, a country of between 15.5 and 17 million people, in a coup d'état.[122] The PDPA immediately launched a wave of violent repression, killing approximately 10,000 people linked to the former regime, including the president and seventeen members of his family, and imprisoning between 14,000 and 20,000 more.[123] The PDPA then established a variety of programs designed to rapidly socialize the Afghan society and economy. Many of these initiatives violated deeply held religious beliefs and cultural traditions of the great majority of the Afghans.[124]

Popular opposition to the regime spread quickly and soon took the form of a guerrilla insurgency waged by fighters calling themselves the Mujahideen (fighters for the faith). Opposition was particularly strong in highly conservative rural regions, where the regime's extremely unpopular agricultural policies affected large numbers of people.[125] Major uprisings erupted throughout the country. Large numbers of Afghan soldiers — perhaps more than 50 percent of the army by the end of 1979 — defected and joined the rebels. Factional fighting plagued the PDPA. By the spring of 1979, the survival of the Afghan regime appeared to be in jeopardy.

Leaders in the Soviet Union viewed the developments occurring just across its southern border with deep anxiety.[126] The Soviets had supported the PDPA regime from the start, but by the fall of 1979 they had completely lost faith in its new leader, Hafizullah Amin, who had assumed control of the party in a second coup in September of that year. The Soviets began to fear that the Afghan regime had been infiltrated by the CIA and soon might be replaced by a government hostile to the Soviet Union. Soviet leaders worried about the loss of international credibility they would suffer if a new communist regime so close to the Soviet Union were unseated by popular insurrection. They believed they had a commitment to support the fledgling communist movement in Afghanistan by whatever means necessary.

In early 1979 the Kremlin decided to send thousands of Soviet military advisors along with a large shipment of military equipment to Afghanistan in an effort to prop up the regime. Soviet pilots began flying bombing missions in support of Afghan ground forces. Despite this assistance, most members of the Politburo, including Premier Leonid Brezhnev, initially opposed sending Soviet ground troops into battle in Afghanistan.[127] By the end of 1979, however, growing popular resistance and Soviet distrust of Amin appear to have convinced Soviet leaders that direct military intervention was necessary to prevent the collapse of the Afghan regime. On December 25 the USSR invaded Afghanistan. Soviet forces helped to depose Amin and install Babrak Karmal, whose first official act was to request immediate Soviet "military assistance" for Afghanistan.

Soviet leaders hoped that Karmal, who vowed to repeal many of the more radical and violent policies of the previous two years, would secure greater support from the Afghan people. The result was precisely the opposite.[128] Most Afghans perceived the new regime as the puppet of a godless and anti-Islamic foreign power. Popular resistance multiplied. Many Afghans who had remained indifferent or had even supported the PDPA joined the opposition. Whole brigades defected from the Afghan army to the Mujahideen. Karmal was virtually impotent to suppress the massive insurgency. The rebels controlled much of the countryside and even some larger cities. Soviet military leaders realized that without a major intervention the Kabul regime would likely crumble.

The Soviet Union and the War against the Mujahideen

It appears that the Soviet Union did not originally plan to fight a counterinsurgency war in Afghanistan at all.[129] From 1980 until mid-1981, Soviet counterguerrilla operations remained tentative. The Soviets hoped to wage a short, low-cost war. Indeed, early Soviet plans called for withdrawing most military forces after only six months.[130] The Soviet army pursued a largely conventional strategy focused on securing major airfields, government centers, and roads.[131] The Soviets sought to leave direct confrontation with the rebels to the Afghan army. The strategy was poorly suited to the nature of the war in Afghanistan.[132] Since the Afghan army was too incompetent to mount serious operations of any kind during this period, the plan effectively gave the Mujahideen a free hand in many areas of countryside.

Relatively little direct evidence pertaining to the thinking of Soviet military leaders has been made public, even since the end of the cold war.[133] Nevertheless, numerous reports describing Soviet tactics and military operations are available. On the basis of these reports, most analysts surmise that sometime during the second half of 1980, Soviet military leaders recognized the deficiencies of their initial strategy and organization and began to adapt their forces and operations in response to their experiences.[134] In addition to technical and organizational innovations such as the greater use of air power and smaller, more independent fighting units, the new Soviet strategy also included increasingly violent attacks on the Afghan civilian population. By 1984, these so-called "special operations" had become the central focus of Soviet strategy. Soviet tactics took on the familiar pattern of counterguerrilla operations described in the introduction to this chapter.

The new Soviet strategy appeared to be based on the understanding that the Mujahideen depended on the support of the local population for food, shelter, and information. A Soviet General Staff report described the rebels' tactics: "When in danger [the] Mujahideen would melt into the local population where it was practically impossible to identify them. . . . Their main advantage was the active support of the local populace."[135] Hassan Kakar argues that the difficulty in fighting these forces directly led the Soviets to conclude that the "Mujahideen had to be detached from the people. As guerrilla fighters, they could not be a viable force without the support of local populations. Hence, the Soviets felt it necessary to suppress defenseless civilians by killing them indiscriminately, by compelling them to flee abroad, and by destroying their crops and means of irrigation, the basis of their livelihood."[136]

The Soviet strategy also seems to have been influenced by the desire of Soviet leaders to keep the costs of the war as low as possible.[137] The size of the Soviet contingent stationed in Afghanistan was relatively modest, reaching a peak of 115,000 troops in 1986.[138] By comparison, at the peak of its involvement in the Vietnam War, the United States stationed over 540,000 troops in South Vietnam, a country roughly one-fifth as large as Afghanistan. Soviet forces never sought to occupy or permanently control most areas of Afghanistan. As Alex Alexiev concluded in 1985, this strategy was "very likely due to the realization that such a military solution [a decisive defeat of the Mujahideen] is not obtainable short of a dramatic intensification of the Soviet effort entailing massive and perhaps intolerable personnel loss and economic and political costs."[139] Soviet forces also relied extensively on the use of air power in an effort to avoid the high casualties associated with ground operations in counterinsurgency warfare. The Soviet leadership's desire to limit the economic impact of the war also meant that costly but potentially less violent tactics such as population resettlement and civic action would play a relatively smaller role in Soviet strategy than in Guatemala.[140]

Soviet Counterguerrilla Tactics in Afghanistan

Counterterror

Soviet troops and pro-Soviet Afghan forces frequently employed counterterror tactics against civilians suspected of supporting guerrillas. As Jeri Laber and Barnett Rubin have documented, "The strategy of the Soviets and the Afghan government has been to spread terror in the countryside so that villagers will either be afraid to assist the resistance fighters who depend on them for food and shelter or be forced to leave."[141] Executions often were carried out with extreme savagery and in full public view, presumably to further intimidate the population. Since the Soviets

generally lacked the information necessary to identify guerrilla supporters on an individual basis, they often slaughtered entire villages, including women and children. Two defectors from the Soviet army claimed
that these atrocities were not merely the actions of out-of-control troops.
In a typical operation, rather, "an officer decides to have a village searched
to see if there are any rebels in it. . . . What usually happens is we found
a cartridge or a bullet. The officers said: 'This is a bandit village; it
must be destroyed.' . . . The men and young men are usually shot right
where they are. And the women, what they do is try to kill them with
grenades."[142]

The frequent use of air power in reprisal attacks on Afghan villages exacerbated the toll of Soviet counterterror operations. According to one
estimate, aerial bombardment was the most common cause of civilian casualties during the war, accounting for 46 percent of all deaths and in-
juries.[143] Although the evidence remains inconclusive, numerous sources
reported that the Soviets used chemical weapons in some aerial attacks.[144] A certain number of deaths resulting from aerial bombardment
were undoubtedly the unintentional "collateral damage" of inaccurate
Soviet weapons—especially high-altitude bombers. There is strong evidence, however, that bombardment was also employed intentionally to
punish entire villages suspected of aiding the guerrillas.[145] Indeed, comparatively slow and low-flying helicopter gun ships probably carried out
the majority of aerial attacks. As Rubin concludes, "Bombing conveyed
to a village and its neighbors *as collectives* the message that supporting the
resistance had a cost."[146]

Alexander Rutskoi, a Soviet fighter pilot in Afghanistan who would
later become the vice president of Russia under Boris Yeltsin, reportedly
acknowledged the use of these tactics. Viktor Ivanenko, the head of the
KGB, told a reporter that during a conversation with Rutskoi regarding
the Russian war in Chechnya in 1995, Rutskoi suggested that Russia
should use the same approach he had employed in Afghanistan: "A *kishlak* [village] fires at us and kills someone. I send a couple of planes and
there is nothing left of the *kishlak*. After I've burned a couple of *kishlaks*
they stop shooting."[147]

While Soviet military operations focused on the countryside, the
Afghan secret service (the KHAD) waged its own war of counterterror
in the cities. Suspected political opponents of the regime were subjected
to arbitrary arrest, torture, and execution.[148] After the Russian withdrawal a former representative of the KHAD estimated that 150,000
people had been arrested during the Soviet occupation.[149] Although executions appear to have decreased after Amin's ouster, and most were
conducted with at least some legal process, one former Afghan judicial

official stated that over eight thousand people were put to death from 1980 to 1988.[150]

Population Resettlement or Depopulation?

The pattern of Soviet military operations strongly suggests that population relocation was a significant part of Soviet counterinsurgency strategy in Afghanistan. Although direct evidence of Soviet intentions is limited, most analysts and observers of the war have concluded that the Soviets adopted an intentional policy of attacking villages in areas of high guerrilla activity in the effort to force the population into flight.[151] Free-fire zones were established in depopulated areas, permitting Soviet troops to shoot anything that moved.[152] In addition to killing tens of thousands in attacks on villages, this policy eventually produced one of the most massive refugee movements in modern history. Approximately 5 million people out of a total prewar population of between 15.5 and 17 million had fled the country by the early 1990s, the great majority across the border to Pakistan. Two million more were displaced within Afghanistan.[153] Many refugees died during the difficult journey over mountain passes to Pakistan.[154]

The exodus was most significant in areas of intense guerrilla activity. Claude Malhuret, the executive director of the Paris-based human rights group Doctors without Borders, estimated in 1983 that the Soviets already had killed or expelled nearly half of the population in areas controlled by the Mujahideen.[155] According to Edgar O'Ballance, "The Soviets were reversing conditions conducive to the operation of Mao Tse-tung's theory of guerrilla warfare, based on the 'guerrilla fish' swimming and hiding in the 'sea of the people.' The Soviets were draining away the 'sea' by removing the inhabitants, and so making it harder for the Mujahideen . . . to operate, as they were being deprived of shelter, food and information."[156] A postwar study commissioned by the U.S. Marine Corps concluded that the massive flight of the Mujahideen's rural support base ultimately forced the guerrillas to develop their own fixed logistic bases in many areas.[157]

During the first several years of the war, the Soviets made virtually no effort to direct the flow of refugees. Although so-called "displaced persons camps" were established outside major cities, the Soviets did not seem to have an organized plan for relocating refugees within Afghanistan. For this reason, analysts of the war often refer to the Soviet strategy in Afghanistan as "depopulation" rather than resettlement.[158] Some observers suggested that the Soviets hoped to encourage refugee flows across the border to the massive camps in Pakistan, where the burden of their care would fall on others. This seems unlikely, however, since the Soviets knew that the camps in Pakistan served as bases for the guerrillas and were a major source of Mujahideen recruits. Indeed, the Soviets often attacked or turned back refugee columns heading for the border.[159] It seems more likely, therefore, that the Soviets — lacking the resources necessary to provide for domestic relocation programs or to seal off the long border with Pakistan — simply hoped that refugees would relocate to government-controlled areas within Afghanistan, especially in and around the major cities.

As the war dragged on, at least some efforts were made to provide for the relocation of displaced populations. In 1986, for example, the Afghan government launched a project to deport over three hundred thousand people from several eastern provinces under control of the Mujahideen to Afghanistan's barren Western deserts. As O'Ballance notes, "The ostensible reason was to take people from overcrowded areas to develop the economy in south-western parts of the country by bringing virgin land under cultivation. The real reason was to drain off people from some of the Mujahideen 'liberated zones.'"[160]

Scorched-Earth Warfare

Scorched-earth tactics also played a significant role in Soviet counter-guerrilla strategy.[161] In regions of high guerrilla activity, Soviet forces systematically burned crops and dwellings, reducing vast swaths of territory to wasteland. Soviet aircraft employed incendiary weapons, including napalm and phosphorous cluster munitions, to burn crops from the air. Entire herds of livestock were slaughtered or confiscated. Irrigation systems were intentionally destroyed, rendering agriculture in Afghanistan's arid climate all but impossible. Some reports suggest that Soviet forces deliberately poisoned village grain stores and water supplies. Houses and agricultural fields were heavily mined. By 1984 these tactics and the ensuing exodus of the rural population resulted in a 75 to 80 percent decline in agricultural production compared to pre-1979 levels.[162]

Direct evidence of Soviet intentions is once more lacking, but analysts and scholars have suggested three possible functions of scorched-earth tactics in Soviet-Afghan counterguerrilla strategy. First, these tactics may simply have been another way of punishing villages suspected of supporting the Mujahideen. Second, scorched-earth warfare, particularly the use of mines, supported the policy of depopulation by rendering certain areas of the country permanently uninhabitable, thereby discouraging refugees from returning to their homes.[163] Finally, these tactics seem to have been intended to destroy the infrastructure upon which guerrilla forces relied for food and shelter.[164]

Civic Action

The counterinsurgency strategy of the Soviet Union and the Afghan communist regime did not rely exclusively on violence. It also utilized positive inducements in the effort to gain the support or at least neutrality of the population, and to address the root causes of the rebellion. Winning the hearts and minds of the Afghan population was never the primary objective of Soviet-Afghan counterinsurgency strategy, but such policies did constitute an increasingly important complement to strictly military operations in the later years of the conflict.

Soviet-Afghan policies in the early stages of the conflict aimed less at providing new benefits to the population than at reversing the unpopular policies of 1978–79 that had provoked the rebellion in the first place. For example, the government repealed or ceased to enforce many of its antireligious laws. The Kabul regime also rebuilt damaged mosques and constructed over a hundred new ones.[165]

Land reform had been one of the communist regime's most detested policies, generating powerful enemies among the religious and village leaders whose land was confiscated and garnering little support even from those who received land.[166] In 1981 the Karmal regime, under pressure from the Soviets, substantially revised the land reform program in an effort to regain popular support in the countryside. The government returned confiscated land or paid compensation to key groups including religious and village leaders, officers in the Afghan military, and farmers who agreed to sell their harvest to the state. These groups were also exempted from the acreage ceilings imposed by the land reform. The redistribution of land gave priority to peasants with sons in the Afghan military. The government granted beneficial treatment to peasants who grew cash crops rather than food crops that could be used to feed the Mujahideen. As Rubin argues, these changes "effectively transformed land reform into a counterinsurgency measure. Ownership of land became a privilege that the state would protect in return for allegiance."[167]

When these efforts failed to win back a significant portion of the population, more direct inducements were employed. Money and even weapons were offered to village leaders who supported the regime.[168] Political reforms were instituted, allowing for greater representation at the local level. Government jobs and economic development projects were awarded in an effort to win the support of key villages or ethnic groups. The Afghan government also implemented a program designed to lure refugees back from Pakistan with the promise of land and monetary rewards.

The Soviets and the Afghan regime, however, continued to combine these positive measures with more violent counterinsurgency operations designed to bring increasing pressure on the rural population to cease their support for the guerrillas. As Anthony Cordesman and Abraham Wagner describe the strategy, Soviet and Afghan forces utilized a "mix of carefully targeted attacks, bribes, and other activities designed to win political control rather than defeat the Mujahideen in battle. The mix of ruthless 'carrot and stick' tactics was more successful than the largely military tactics the USSR had used earlier, but it still could not win control of the countryside."[169]

Assessing the Effectiveness of the Soviet-Afghan Counterguerrilla Strategy
As in Guatemala, the overall success of the Soviet's counterinsurgency strategy is difficult to assess. Although the Soviet Union agreed to withdraw its forces from Afghanistan in 1988, many analysts do not attribute the withdrawal primarily to a Soviet military defeat. Despite the fact that the Soviets never devoted their full resources to the war, they prevailed in almost every military confrontation with the Mujahideen. The provision of Stinger antiaircraft missiles by the United States to the Mujahideen made Soviet air operations more difficult, but contrary to popular belief, the missiles do not appear to have been a decisive factor in ending the war.[170] The Soviet Union probably could have continued to shoulder the economic burden of the war for at least several more years.[171] As late as 1986, Mark Urban suggested that "in purely military terms the Soviets and their Afghan allies are winning."[172]

While the Soviets may not have lost the war, neither were they able to win it. The Soviet Union paid a high price in human life for the war, losing between fifteen thousand and twenty-six thousand soldiers during the course of the conflict.[173] They were never able to completely seal off the border with Pakistan from which the Mujahideen received supplies and recruits. Perhaps more important, Soviet-Afghan operations were unable to destroy completely the guerrillas' civilian support network within Afghanistan. Thus, Cordesman and Wagner's analysis of the war concludes:

> The Soviets repeated many aspects of the American experience in [Vietnam]. They were able to win most military encounters, but they were not able to occupy the countryside, and they faced an insuperable military problem: they could not defeat an aroused people and were committed to backing a government that lacked popular support. . . . Nothing short of the destruction of the people could allow Soviet forces to defeat the enemy in the countryside and outside major urban areas and strong points. Nothing short of a truly massive Soviet military presence five to six times the forces the USSR deployed could have allowed them to occupy the territory they gained temporary control of through tactical victories.[174]

It appears that some Soviet leaders understood these fundamental issues, perhaps as early as 1983.[175] In 1986, Marshal Sergei Akhromeyev, chief of the General Staff of the Soviet Armed Forces, told the Politburo that it was time to recognize that "we have lost the struggle for the Afghan people. A minority of the people supports the government."[176] For some time after Soviet leaders had grasped the futility of the situation in Afghanistan, however, they continued to deem withdrawal politically impossible. Most assumed that such a retreat would seriously undermine Soviet credibility with the West. Only after Gorbachev and other "new thinkers" — who believed in the necessity of reducing the USSR's foreign commitments and favored greater security cooperation with the West — had secured control of the Soviet regime did withdrawal from Afghanistan become a reality. As Diego Cordovez (the principal UN negotiator of the 1988 Geneva Accords, which provided for the Soviet withdrawal from Afghanistan) and Selig S. Harrison conclude:

> Despite the widespread stereotype of a Soviet military defeat, Soviet military forces were securely entrenched in Afghanistan when the Geneva Accords were finally signed on April 14, 1988. The Red Army did not withdraw in the wake of a Waterloo. . . . Confronted by a military and political stalemate, Gorbachev decided to disengage because the accords offered a pragmatic way to escape from the growing costs of deadlock and to open the way for improved relations with the West.[177]

LESS VIOLENT COUNTERGUERRILLA WARFARE

Perhaps because guerrilla warfare can be such a powerful weapon, it has also been one of the most common forms of combat in the twentieth century. As a result, counterguerrilla mass killing also has been all too common. Nevertheless, most guerrilla wars have not resulted in mass killing.[178] Few counterguerrilla wars have been prosecuted without any violence against civilian populations, but many regimes have waged counterguerrilla warfare without the kind of large-scale, systematic killing of civilians that occurred in Guatemala and Afghanistan.

My research identifies two main factors that appear to influence government incentives to target civilians during counterguerrilla warfare. These factors do not exhaust the variables that can affect the likelihood of mass killing during guerrilla wars, but they do appear to be the most powerful determinants of this kind of violence.

The Guerrilla-Civilian Relationship

The most significant factor that can influence the likelihood of mass killing in counterguerrilla warfare is the way that leaders confronting a guerrilla adversary perceive the relationship between the guerrillas and the civilian population. As I have tried to demonstrate, mass killing in counterguerrilla warfare is usually the result of a military strategy that seeks to destroy or deny guerrillas access to their civilian support network. The greater the number of supporters and the more extensive the assistance that leaders believe the guerrillas are receiving from the civilian population, therefore, the greater will be the incentives to target this population.

Not all guerrilla forces, however, depend so heavily upon the local civilian population for support. Whether out of necessity or for strategic reasons, some guerrilla forces have rejected Mao's strategy of "people's war" and attempted to wage an insurgency with relatively little support from the local population. These kinds of forces, which often bear a greater resemblance to what are commonly thought of as terrorist organizations, may receive the majority of their support from foreign powers or they may simply choose to carry out low-level operations without the need for extensive civilian participation. Whatever the reason, if leaders believe that their adversaries are not receiving substantial support from local civilian populations, they have little incentive to target large numbers of civilians in counterguerrilla operations. This conclusion is supported by Timothy Wickham-Crowley's comparative study of guerrilla conflicts in Latin America from 1956 to 1976, which found that "the deeper and more thorough the overlap between the guerrilla combatants and the civilian population, the more likely that the government would engage in terror against the civilian population."[179]

The importance of the relationship between the guerrillas and the civilian population is powerfully illustrated by the way regimes confronting guerrilla opponents react to changes in this relationship. As described above, for the first fifteen years of the Guatemalan civil war, the insurgency lacked broad-based civilian support, adhering instead to the *foco* theory of guerrilla warfare. As a result, government repression during this period, while extensive, focused primarily on the regime's urban political opponents and never reached the level of mass killing. Only after the guerrillas adopted a rural, mass-based strategy in the late 1970s did the Guatemalan military respond with a systematic violence against the civilian population.[180]

Attacks on civilians during the civil war in El Salvador in the 1980s reflect a similar logic. During the first half of the decade, Salvadoran guerrillas relied heavily on civilian support. The Salvadoran military responded with brutal tactics designed to destroy the guerrillas' civilian support system.[181] Perhaps fifty thousand people were killed between 1980 and 1983.[182] As a report by the human rights group Americas Watch documents, however, by the mid-1980s government attacks on civilians grew less frequent. The shift away from overt attacks on civilians was due in part to diplomatic pressure from the United States, El Savador's most important benefactor, but Americas Watch concluded that "the largest factor in their discontinuation was a shift in strategy by the guerrillas. . . . Their new strategy involved a greater reliance on the dispersal of their forces throughout the country. . . . They continued to obtain food from civilians in the areas in which they operated. . . . Yet for the armed forces to bomb and strafe these civilians would have been counterproductive, because many were not supporters of the guerrillas."[183]

Support for guerrilla forces is sometimes limited to small or isolated segments of the civilian population. In Europe and the United States, for example, a number of small urban guerrilla/terrorist groups such as the Red Brigade, Direct Action, and the Weather Underground emerged in the late 1960s. Yet, as Richard Rubenstein argues, no "dirty war" was launched against these groups because "no European or North American government has felt compelled to choose between unleashing a full-scale counterterrorism campaign and submitting to radical destabilization." The fact that no such campaign was instigated, Rubenstein claims, "is attributable not so much to liberal restraint as to . . . [the terrorists'] own inability to spread rebellion far beyond a narrow circle of alienated intellectuals and oppressed workers. As a result of political weakness, terrorists could be singled out for very harsh treatment . . . without rending the entire fabric of legality."[184] Lack of popular support for insurgent groups may also help explain the absence of mass killing in counterguerrilla wars in Peru and Bolivia in the 1960s.[185]

The British defeat of the 1948–58 communist insurgency in Malaya (now known as Malaysia) is often touted as an illustrative example of a successful yet generally humane counterguerrilla campaign. The British ability to defeat the insurgency, however, was greatly assisted by the failure of the guerrillas, known as the Malayan Races Liberation Army (MRLA), to win the support of the largest segments of the Malayan population. Despite their name, the guerrillas drew their support almost entirely from a group of approximately one million Chinese squatters who had fled the cities during the Japanese occupation of 1939–45 and had been eking out a living on the fringes of the Malayan jungle.[186] Ethnic Malays, who constituted the majority of the population, overwhelmingly opposed the insurgency, which they feared would lead to Chinese domination and whose communist ideology they rejected. Even among the squatters, support for the guerrillas was surprisingly thin.[187] The guerrillas often had to resort to terror and intimidation to gain their cooperation, or even neutrality.[188] The squatters' impoverished condition and loose attachment to the land also greatly facilitated Britain's population resettlement strategy, as the "New Villages" constructed for the squatters actually represented an improvement in their standard of living.[189] Deprived of support, the insurgency dwindled to a few hundred men by 1960.

Guerrilla forces sometimes receive their support primarily from foreign powers rather than domestic civilian populations. The Contra guerrillas of Nicaragua, for example, received the great majority of their support from the United States and were based principally in camps across the border in Honduras. Largely dependent on external support, the Contras seldom operated for long periods deep in Nicaraguan territory. The Sandinista regime could not launch major attacks against the bases in Honduras without risking direct American intervention.[190] While many Nicaraguans came to oppose the Sandinistas, only a limited number supported the Contras, who engaged in frequent atrocities against civilians and who continued to be associated with the highly unpopular Somoza regime.[191] For the most part, therefore, the Sandinistas had little incentive to target Nicaraguan civilians in counterinsurgency operations. The main exception to this general pattern occurred along Nicaragua's northern border and Atlantic coastal region, where the Contras did enjoy significant support from dissatisfied indigenous groups. The Sandinista regime sought to pacify these regions with a campaign of forced population resettlement combined with at least limited use of scorched-earth warfare and free-fire zones.[192] While several hundred people may have died as a result of these operations, the relatively small number of relocated individuals (approximately 30,000 over the course of the war) meant that the violence remained at comparatively low levels.[193]

A similar situation developed in Rhodesia (now known as Zimbabwe) where guerrilla forces operated primarily out of bases in neighboring Zambia and Mozambique. What support the guerrillas received from the civilian population inside Rhodesia they appear to have obtained largely through coercion.[194] Because of this, even the racist Rhodesian regime had little reason to target civilians in large numbers. Between six and twelve thousand civilians may have been killed from 1972 to 1979, but the guerrillas themselves seem to have been responsible for much of this violence.

Less violent counterguerrilla strategies may also succeed when popular support for guerrillas is broad but not deep. Such appears to have been the case in the successful suppression of the so-called Huk rebellion in the Philippines from 1947 to 1953. During the first three years of the rebellion, the communist Huks dominated the countryside of the Philippine island of Luzon. Perhaps two million people lived in Huk-controlled areas, and many willingly paid taxes to the rebels or provided them with food, shelter, or information.[195] Early efforts by the U.S.-backed Philippine army to crush the insurgency involved repeated attacks on civilians that ultimately drove even more people into the hands of the guerrillas. In 1950, however, the new Philippine secretary of defense, Ramon Magsaysay, introduced a new, less violent counterinsurgency strategy based on a different understanding of the nature of the Huks' civilian support base. Although the Huks received significant support from peasants, most Huk supporters simply sought moderate economic reforms and an end to government repression—not the vision of a communist society offered by the Huks.[196] As Michael Shafer argues, the "insurgency was thus vulnerable to even minor government concessions targeted to the [Huk] rank and file. . . . As a result, the insurgency's longevity depended on government intransigence. If the government could manage the effort, even minimal reforms could undo it."[197] Grasping this crucial weakness in the insurgents' support, Magsaysay discouraged large-scale violence against civilians in military operations and introduced a number of moderate political and economic reforms targeted at the Huks' rural supporters. The new strategy worked, and within two years the rebellion had all but died out.[198]

The Nature of the Guerrilla Threat

Mass killing in counterguerrilla warfare may also be averted when insurgent military operations remain at levels that do not pose a major military threat to the government. As noted above, the operations of fringe organizations such as the Red Brigade or Direct Action were constrained primarily by their small size and lack of popular support. Other guerrilla/terrorist organizations, however, have demonstrated considerable restraint in the scale and targets of their operations despite potentially formidable capabilities and relatively broad popular support. In these cases, the pattern of restraint may be the result of the insurgents' calculation that massive violence would damage their movement politically, or it may simply reflect the fear of massive government reprisals. Whatever the reason, many regimes choose to let very low-level insurgencies persist indefinitely rather than devote the resources, risk the casualties, or incur the domestic and international political consequences necessary to defeat the insurgency unconditionally.

Perhaps the most notable example of this pattern occurred between South Africa's apartheid regime and the African National Congress (ANC) during the 1970s and 1980s. Although the ANC enjoyed the support of the majority of the black African population, and its military arm comprised twenty-seven thousand members, it generally limited its operations to acts of sabotage, demonstrations, strikes, and economic boycotts.[199] Systematic attacks on white civilians were never adopted as official ANC policy despite the fact that South Africa's segregated buses, schools, and restaurants would have made easy targets. In 1998, South Africa's Truth and Reconciliation Commission attributed thirteen hundred killings, including many black victims, to the ANC for the entire period between 1960 and 1994. ANC leaders probably decided against a more violent strategy because it would have risked undermining political support for the movement, especially internationally. Moreover, as Nelson Mandela explained during his trial in 1964, "experience convinced us that rebellion would offer the government limitless opportunities for the indiscriminate slaughter of our people."[200] As a result, the white regime was never threatened militarily by black violence.[201] The South African regime violated human rights on a massive scale and did not shy away from selective political murders, but it never resorted to mass killing. Since the threat from the ANC was more political than military in nature, and since most white leaders understood that widespread attacks against black civilians would increase their political problems, violent repression remained at low levels compared to conflicts like Guatemala and Afghanistan.[202]

The conflict in Northern Ireland followed a similar pattern. The Irish Republican Army (IRA) received significant public support from Catholics in Northern Ireland, but like the ANC it never escalated its attacks to a level that directly threatened British rule. Unlike the ANC, the IRA did sanction attacks on civilian targets, but these attacks remained at comparatively low levels. The IRA and related paramilitary organizations were responsible for approximately 1,800 total deaths, including 640 civilians, in thirty years of fighting in Northern Ireland.[203] By way of comparison, in 1984, the conflict killed a total of sixty-four people on all sides — about one-third the number who died in traffic accidents in Ulster that year.[204] The IRA's strategy put political pressure on the British government but gave it little incentive to resort to systematic killing of civilians.

The evidence strongly suggests that mass killing in counterguerrilla warfare is motivated primarily by the nature of guerrilla warfare itself. The mass killings in Guatemala and Afghanistan were not the result of frustrated or racist troops, but rather of military strategies specifically designed to eliminate the civilian support network upon which Guatemalan and Afghan guerrilla forces depended.

Mass killing can be a powerful military tool, at least in the short term. From a political perspective, however, it also can backfire, increasing public support for guerrillas and generating powerful international pressures against regimes that engage in it. As a counterinsurgency strategy, mass killing in both Guatemala and Afghanistan produced decidedly mixed results—even from the point of view of its perpetrators. In Guatemala, although the guerrilla insurgency was largely suppressed, it was not eliminated. Popular resentment of the regime remained high. Successive Guatemalan regimes were forced to introduce political reforms and negotiate with the guerrillas. In Afghanistan, although the Soviets remained dominant militarily through the end of the war, popular support for the Mujahideen was virtually total. The availability of outside support for the guerrillas severely limited the effectiveness of Soviet pacification efforts. Soviet leaders ultimately chose to withdraw rather than continue fighting. Neither the Guatemalan nor the Soviet regime truly "lost" its war with the guerrillas. In the long run, however, only the indefinite continuation of large-scale violence could keep the insurgents at bay. Neither regime proved willing or able to incur the military and political costs associated with this course of action.

If the long-term results of mass killing as a counterinsurgency strategy in Guatemala and Afghanistan are representative of the effectiveness of this strategy more generally, why does mass killing remain so common in guerrilla warfare? Why haven't military and political leaders learned from the past failures or limitations of this strategy? Indeed, even the Soviet Union's experience with guerrilla warfare in Afghanistan did not deter Russia from resorting to similar tactics only a few years later in its brutal counterinsurgency campaign in Chechnya.[205]

I believe that regimes facing determined guerrilla opponents have continued to gravitate toward mass killing because less violent counterguerrilla strategies have proven extremely costly, time consuming, and at least equally prone to failure. Although some counterinsurgency theorists have touted the effectiveness of less violent strategies in places like Malaya and the Philippines, the evidence presented above suggests that lack of strong civilian support for guerrillas was the primary reason for the success of less violent counterguerrilla strategies in these conflicts. In Vietnam, on the other hand, where popular support for the insurgents was stronger, the United States expended vast resources in a self-conscious attempt to emulate these more humane strategies, but achieved few results.[206]

Regimes facing well-organized guerrilla opponents with strong support from the civilian population have few attractive options for meeting this threat. For leaders determined to avoid defeat, and frustrated with the failure of conventional military strategies, mass killing may appear to offer the last chance for victory at an acceptable cost. As long as guerrilla warfare remains a common form of modern combat, therefore, counterguerrilla mass killing is likely to remain common as well.

CONCLUSION: ANTICIPATING AND PREVENTING MASS KILLING

The evidence presented in this book points to three central conclusions about the causes of mass killing. First, small groups often play an important role in instigating and carrying out this kind of violence. Mass killing is usually conceived of and organized by a relatively small number of powerful political or military leaders acting in the service of their own interests, ideas, hatreds, fears, and misperceptions — not reacting to the attitudes or desires of the societies over which they preside. Indeed, in the Soviet Union, Nazi Germany, China, and Cambodia — the four bloodiest mass killings I investigated — there are strong reasons to believe that, but for the influence of a single dictatorial leader, the violence might have been averted or at least substantially diminished. Perpetrators do not need widespread social support to carry out mass killing. Compliance with authority or simply passivity and indifference to the suffering of victims, what I have called negative support, is more important than active support or participation in the killing itself. In each of the eight cases I examined, relatively small military or paramilitary groups, acting under direct orders from political and military authorities, carried out the majority of the actual killing. Civilians did play a significant role in the violence in Rwanda and the Chinese Cultural Revolution, but even in these cases the killers represented only a small fraction of society, and military or paramilitary forces killed many or most of the victims.

Second, because small groups can play such a central role in causing mass killing, I find that characteristics of society at large, such as preexisting cleavages, hatred and discrimination between groups, and nondemocratic forms of government, are of limited utility in distinguishing societies at high risk for mass killing. There is substantial evidence of preexisting hatreds or discrimination directed against at least some victim groups in each of the cases examined in this book — especially the genocides in Turkey, Nazi Germany, and Rwanda. There is little indication, however, that these attitudes were more severe than they were in many other countries that never experienced mass killing. In Guatemala and Afghanistan, perpetrators made efforts, albeit halfhearted ones, to minimize the extent of social differences and ameliorate discrimination against victims in an effort to draw support away from insurgent movements. In the Soviet Union, Nazi Germany, China, Cambodia, and Rwanda, on the other hand, leaders deliberately promoted hatred and discrimination through propaganda and indoctrination in the effort to increase public support for attacks on victim groups. Preexisting animosity between groups is a particularly weak explanation for the communist mass killings described in chapter 4, since many victims of these regimes were never objects of intense hatred by society at large. In fact, in all three countries, the perpetrators directed much of the killing against the communist party itself.

Third, mass killing usually is driven by instrumental, strategic calculations. Perpetrators see mass killing as a means to an end, not an end in itself. None of the cases of mass killing considered here can be accurately described as killing for killing's sake. Indeed, mass killing was never the only strategy that leaders considered to achieve their ends. Mass killing has not always been a policy of last resort, but rarely has it been a policy of first resort either. With the possible exception of Cambodia, leaders in all eight cases examined in this book appear to have seriously considered or actively experimented with options short of mass killing to achieve their ends. Leaders adopted mass killing in frustration, only after they came to believe, although often mistakenly, that other strategies for achieving their goals were impossible or impractical.

The history of all eight cases suggests that leaders conceived of mass killing as a instrumental strategy designed to achieve their most important political or ideological goals, counter their most dangerous threats, or solve their most difficult military problems. Leaders saw mass killing as a bloody but effective solution to such problems. I have also tried to demonstrate, however, that leaders are likely to perceive mass killing as an attractive strategy only in a few, relatively uncommon situations. Three specific historical scenarios — the implementation of radical communist policies, large-scale ethnic cleansing, and counterguerrilla wars — have generated the incentives for the majority of episodes of mass killings in this century. Even in these situations, however, mass killing is not inevitable. A variety of factors and conditions, including the size of the targeted civilian population, the pace with which dispossessive changes are implemented, and the ability of victim groups to flee to safer areas can impact the incentives and ability of perpetrators to carry out mass killing.

Root Causes

As I described in the chapter 1, prevailing explanations of genocide and mass killing tend to focus on broad social variables such as highly fragmented or discriminatory societies, dehumanizing attitudes between groups, or nondemocratic forms of government as the root causes or preconditions for this kind of violence. Such theories would seem to suggest, therefore, that societies with these characteristics must remain in constant danger of mass killing — perhaps only awaiting the trigger of a war or crisis to spark the return of violence. If this perspective is accurate, only a fundamental change in the structure of the society, its form of governance, or the character of intergroup relations can eliminate the risk of mass killing in the long run.

Ervin Staub, for example, argues that preventing genocide should include efforts to increase cultural exchanges between groups, encourage people to help one another, provide basic needs for all members of society, and change the way parents raise and educate children.[1] Helen Fein concludes that "the best way to avoid . . . genocides is to promote nonviolent change in states (and occupied regions) based on ethnoclass domination."[2] Rudolph Rummel's research on democracy and mass violence, on the other hand, suggests that "the way to end war and virtually eliminate democide [the murder of any person or persons by a government] appears to be through . . . *fostering democratic freedom*."[3]

Political leaders have often endorsed similar strategies for preventing genocide. President Clinton, for example, argued in 1996 that while the United States should strongly support the international tribunals established to punish perpetrators of genocide in places such as Rwanda and the former Yugoslavia, "our commitment to punish these crimes against humanity must be matched by our commitment to prevent them in the first place. . . . Accountability is a powerful deterrent, but it isn't enough. It doesn't get to the root cause of such atrocities. Only a profound change in the nature of societies can begin to reach the heart of the matter. And I believe the basis of that profound change is democracy."[4]

Reducing stratification in society, increasing understanding between groups, and encouraging the spread of democracy are worthy goals. There are many good reasons to pursue these efforts even if they did nothing to prevent mass killing. Nevertheless, I believe that this "root cause" approach to the prevention of mass killing is limited in at least two significant ways.

First, the research presented here suggests that while these efforts might help reduce the incidence of mass killing, they would not eliminate it. Perpetrators of mass killing have proved capable of inventing entirely new victim groups even in relatively homogenous societies. Although democracies seldom if ever commit mass killing against their own citizens, as Rummel acknowledges, democracies do kill noncitizens living within their borders and foreign civilians during wars. Eliminating social cleavages or spreading democracy, therefore, would not necessarily prevent mass killing.

In fact, if not carefully managed, the effort to promote these changes might actually make matters worse. As Jack Snyder has suggested, the process of democratization may increase the likelihood of violence by creating incentives for elites to foster nationalist, racist, or revolutionary ideas in the effort to win public support.[5] Until democratic institutions are strong enough to guarantee the free flow of information and the protection of minority rights, even comparatively harmonious societies may be vulnerable to such appeals. Indeed, three of the episodes examined in this book—the mass killings in the Soviet Union, Germany, and Rwanda—followed close on the heels of failed democratization efforts. In the case of Rwanda, international efforts to introduce democratic reforms may have contributed inadvertently to the genocide by threatening the Hutu extremists' hold on power.[6]

Of course, efforts to eliminate social cleavages and promote democracy, assuming they could be properly administered, would still be well worth pursuing even if they could not prevent all instances of mass killing. Unfortunately, a second serious limitation of these strategies suggests that whatever promise they may hold in theory is unlikely to be widely achieved in practice. Because the number of societies characterized by these social ills is so large, and because the practical tasks of remedying them are so demanding, the cost of intervening preemptively to ameliorate these problems wherever they occur could be prohibitive.

If, as I have argued, mass killing can occur in the absence of unusually severe cleavages between social groups, then most societies also contain at least some groups that could potentially become victims of this kind of violence. International actors interested in reducing anti-Semitism in the 1920s, for example, would have had to focus their efforts not only on Germany but also on several other European states in which discrimination against Jews was at least as severe, and in which the Jewish populations were many times larger. Such efforts would have been laudable, but highly impractical. Eliminating anti-Semitism in Europe, of course, still would have done nothing to protect the hundreds of other minority groups around the globe suffering from similar levels of discrimination.

The problems of fostering democratization may be even more daunting. Even today, most states lack stable democratic governments. Many of the least democratic regimes are also the most deeply entrenched in power and therefore the most resistant to reform. The international community simply lacks the resources to bring about democratic change everywhere it is needed.

Even if the list of states threatened with mass killing could be effectively narrowed, perhaps by focusing only on the most highly discriminatory or authoritarian regimes, influencing the basic structures or attitudes of societies from the outside remains an extraordinarily difficult task. Social scientists and policy makers are ill prepared for this challenge. Regardless of the resources available for the endeavor, international actors do not yet understand how to build democracies or foster more harmonious relations between groups. Moreover, these efforts are likely to prove far too time consuming to be useful in preventing imminent violence.

Most scholars of genocide and mass killing have recognized these practical limitations and endorsed more immediate solutions, including international military intervention, economic sanctions, or the provision of humanitarian assistance to halt or limit mass killing.[7] If the theoretical propositions forwarded by many of these same scholars are accurate, however, such measures would fail to address the root causes of the violence. They would be short-term solutions at best. Until the social and political structures responsible for the violence could be transformed, mass killing would remain a constant risk.

Unfortunately, these conclusions have also served as a ready excuse for inaction for international actors in a position to intervene.[8] If only fundamental changes in states and societies can prevent mass killing in the long run, and if such changes are difficult or impossible to effect from the outside, it is all too easy to dismiss calls for intervention as futile or shortsighted.

In the early 1990s, for example, American officials employed this logic repeatedly to justify their reluctance to intervene more forcefully to halt the violence in the former Yugoslavia.[9] In 1992 Acting Secretary of State Lawrence Eagleburger described the conflict in these terms: "This war is not rational. There is no rationality at all about ethnic conflict. It is gut, it is hatred; it's not for any set of values or purposes; it just goes on. And that kind of warfare is most difficult to bring to a halt."[10]

President Clinton's national security advisor, Anthony Lake, used the same rationale to explain America's hesitancy to intervene in Rwanda. Speaking at a White House press briefing in May 1994, at the height of the genocide, Lake introduced the Clinton administration's new policy on peacekeeping. Referring to Somalia, Bosnia, and Haiti as well as Rwanda, Lake explained: "These kinds of conflicts are particularly hard to come to grips with and to have an effect on from outside because, basically, of course, their origins are in political turmoil within these nations. And that political turmoil may not be susceptible to the efforts of the international community. So, neither we nor the international community have either the mandate, nor the resources, nor the possibility of resolving every conflict of this kind."[11]

The former secretary of state Henry Kissinger opposed sending ground troops to Kosovo in 1999 for similar reasons: "Ethnic conflict has been endemic in the Balkans for centuries. Waves of conquests have congealed divisions between ethnic groups. . . . [T]hese conflicts have been fought with unparalleled ferocity because none of the populations has any experience with — and essentially no belief in — Western concepts of toleration. The principles of majority rule and compromise that underlie most of the proposals for a solution have never found an echo in the Balkans."[12]

The argument appeared again during the 2000 U.S. presidential campaign. In numerous speeches and debates, the then candidate George W. Bush repeatedly referred to the futility of "nation building" as the main reason why he believed America's military interventions in the former Yugoslavia and Somalia had been mistakes, and why the Clinton administration's decision not to send troops to try to halt the killing in Rwanda had been fundamentally correct.

A Strategic Perspective on Preventing Mass Killing

The perspective on mass killing proposed here paints a discouraging picture of our world. Yet, while it emphasizes the frightening ease with which mass killing can be carried out, it also suggests that the practical problems of preventing or limiting this violence will be different, and in at least some respects less daunting than other theories might lead us to expect. The strategic approach suggests two major implications for intervention to prevent or limit mass killing.

Anticipating Mass Killing

First, the strategic approach identifies a relatively narrow set of situations, conditions, and events that might serve as warnings that mass killing is imminent. The regimes most likely to resort to mass killing are those attempting to implement radical social changes that materially dispossess large numbers of people in a short period of time, those seeking the physical expulsion of large groups of people, or those trying to defeat mass-based guerrilla insurgencies.[13] When situational factors render less violent strategies for achieving these ends difficult or impossible, mass killing becomes a significant possibility.

Of these three scenarios, we should expect counterguerrilla mass killing to remain the most common, as it was during the last fifty years. Ethnic mass killings have been considerably less frequent, although they have often claimed more victims. Future communist mass killings are highly unlikely given the declining appeal of communist ideology since the end of the cold war. Nevertheless, we should remain vigilant of groups espousing similarly radical social changes, as this form of mass killing can have the bloodiest consequences of all. Focusing our attention on these three scenarios and conditions undoubtedly will still result in oversights and false warnings, but I believe it should be substantially more reliable than the "root causes" approach.

Significantly, once we know what to look for, even outside observers should be able to identify many of the risk factors for mass killing, often well in advance of the onset of violence. Because mass killing is rarely a policy of first resort, careful observers may receive warning of the potential for mass killing when leaders attempt to achieve their goals through other means. The Soviet regime, for example, spent nearly twelve years openly trying to socialize agricultural production using tax and price incentives and low levels of violent repression before Stalin declared an all-out war on the peasantry in 1929. In Germany, more than seven years passed between the Nazis' seizure of power and the initiation of the systematic murder of the Jews. Throughout this period, the Nazis did not attempt to conceal their racist ideology or their efforts to cleanse Germany of Jews through emigration and deportation. Likewise, Guatemala's military regime struggled for more than three years to crush the guerrilla opposition in the countryside before it resorted to full-scale mass killing in 1981.

Although the strategic approach emphasizes the murderous potential of small groups, it does not suggest that we need to monitor the statements and activities of every radical racist or nationalist organization or political fringe movement in every society around the globe. Rather, we should focus our attention and resources on understanding the ideologies, goals, and interests of groups in or near political and military power—particularly in societies with weak or unstable political institutions. Fringe movements advocating radical social changes or discrimination and violence against other groups pose little threat of mass killing if they lack the power to act on their beliefs. Groups lacking broad popular support stand a much better chance of seizing power if they possess organized military or paramilitary forces and if other political and military actors are too weak or lack the will to prevent them from seizing control and carrying out their plans.

The Khmer Rouge, for example, seized power in Cambodia with relatively small military forces and without widespread public support thanks in large part to the military weakness and unpopularity of the Lon Nol regime. Although the Nazis received a much higher degree of public support than the Khmer Rouge, no less than two-thirds of Germans voted against the Nazis in Germany's last free election. The Nazi rise to power in the face of this political opposition was greatly facilitated by Germany's economic instability and by the frailty of the Weimar political system.

In the United States, on the other hand, racist groups such as the Ku Klux Klan failed to achieve national power despite membership estimated at between 1.5 and 5 million during the heyday of the Klan in the 1920s.[14] The fact that the Klan and other racist groups were responsible for at least 4,700 lynchings between 1882 and 1944 attests to their violent ambitions and their powerful political influence, especially in the South.[15] That the Klan failed to kill a greater number reflects more than the refusal of the vast majority of Americans to support this kind of violence — even though less violent forms of racism were pervasive in both the North and the South. It also reflects the ability of America's political institutions to ensure that the preferences of the majority were enforced, if only to the extent of preventing full scale mass killing.

Identifying the places where mass killing is most likely to occur is a critical task. Effective intervention seldom can wait for clear evidence that systematic killing is under way. Because killing is easier when victims are deprived of time to organize resistance, or do not even recognize that mass killing is under way, perpetrators usually do their utmost to ensure that the violence proceeds with maximum haste. The killers can work at a terrible pace. In Rwanda, Hutu perpetrators murdered between 500,000 and 800,000 people in less than four months, most in the first thirty days.[16] Although the Holocaust continued until the end of the Second World War, the Nazis killed 3.8 million Jews in the first eighteen months of the genocide between the summer of 1941 and the end of 1942.[17] Even if intervention could halt mass killing within a few weeks of its onset — a decidedly optimistic assumption — in many cases this would be too late to save tens or even hundreds of thousands of victims.

The difficulty of anticipating impending mass killing has often impeded effective intervention. Few people are prepared to imagine the possibility of something as unusual and terrible as mass killing. Warning signs that appear obvious in retrospect may be seen by contemporary observers only as indications of "normal" conflict, or dismissed altogether as the racist or nationalist blustering of a fanatical few. In Rwanda, for example, UN and American officials failed to anticipate the genocide despite numerous warnings from well-placed Rwandan sources and foreign observers.[18] Even reports from the commander of UN peacekeeping forces in Rwanda, which warned of the potential for mass violence against civilians in the weeks and months before the genocide, did not move UN officials. Indeed, the steady stream of warnings may have had the opposite effect. As the U.S. State Department's political-military advisor in the Bureau of African Affairs recalled, he "tended to discredit" such reports "because we had heard allegations of genocide, or warnings of genocide, pertaining to Rwanda dating back at least to 1992."[19]

The Hutu extremists' politics were by no means secret. Some extremist party members had been calling openly for genocide for several years. Although the extremists did not gain control of the Rwandan state until the genocide began, it was widely known that they occupied positions of authority within the government and military. They had been steadily increasing the size of their militia forces over the past several years. Although these groups remained small in absolute terms, the Rwandan political system was plainly too weak to keep these groups in check. The extremists had the means, the motive, and the opportunity for mass killing. Most observers interpreted the relatively low-level violence in the years before the genocide as an indication that the violence was likely to remain limited in the future.[20] Had they recognized that the failure of low-level violence to secure the extremists' goals might prompt this small but powerful group to consider more drastic solutions, perhaps the world would not have been taken so much by surprise when the genocide erupted in 1994.

Even high-level Rwandan officials could not make this intellectual leap. As Marc Rugenera, a moderate Hutu who served as minister of finance in Habyarimana's cabinet recalled:

> The idea that anyone could conceive of another war seemed crazy to me, plain crazy. Because it was so self-evident to me that no rational person could contemplate war, especially as peace seemed within our grasp, I did not think that those who wanted war constituted a significant threat. At most I thought they would continue assassinating individual political opponents. But never, never did I think even for a second that they would mount the operation whose results we see today. . . . How could we imagine that they would kill women, children and old people? Unfortunately, we believed that most of the opponents of the Arusha [peace]

process would end up seeing reason. But as you can see, we were horribly wrong.[21]

The strategic perspective on mass killing suggests that if we hope to anticipate mass killing, we must begin to think of it in the same way its perpetrators do. Mass killing becomes imaginable, even rational, for its perpetrators when they come to believe that the slaughter of civilians could be an effective means to their most important ends, when they become frustrated with other methods to achieve these ends, and when they have marshaled the capabilities to carry it out. When these conditions apply, the possibility that mass killing may occur must become imaginable for those seeking to prevent it as well.

Intervention to Prevent or Limit Mass Killing

The second set of implications of the strategic perspective for preventing mass killing relate to what international actors can do to prevent or limit the violence if they believe it is likely to occur, or once it has already begun. Because the strategic perspective finds that the impetus for mass killing usually lies with high political and military leadership, not in social or governmental structures, it suggests that effective intervention to prevent mass killing need not seek the fundamental transformation of foreign societies. Rather, intervention to prevent mass killing should focus on disarming and removing from power the small groups and leaders responsible for instigating and organizing the killing. This kind of intervention would take the form of relatively traditional military operations designed to defeat the perpetrators' military forces, protect victim groups on the ground, and provide humanitarian assistance to refugee populations.[22] Western states and military organizations have had a great deal more experience and success with these kinds of operations than they have had with efforts to foster democracy or end hatred and discrimination in foreign societies.

Intervention of this kind need not constitute merely a Band-Aid solution to deeper problems. If those responsible for the killing can be stripped of power, social groups should be able to live together without mass killing indefinitely. Short-term military intervention cannot erase long-standing prejudices or establish democracy in foreign societies, although it might help create conditions more conducive to these outcomes. Unless large numbers of forces remain to carry out long-term policing operations, it cannot ensure that conflict between political or ethnic groups will not continue at lower levels.[23] In at least some cases, however, it does have the potential to stop the systematic murder of large numbers of unarmed men, women, and children.

This does not mean that preventing mass killing necessarily will be cheap or easy. I have suggested that we should think of mass killing not as a fundamentally different form of conflict but as a strategy used by groups seeking to prevail in military or political conflicts under certain extreme conditions. For the same reason, we should avoid conceiving of military intervention to prevent mass killing as an alternative to war. Preventing mass killing will often require nothing less than war, albeit war for humanitarian purposes. If mass killing can be war by other means, preventing it must be war for other ends.

Waging war against a determined adversary is always a costly course of action. It requires large and expensive military forces. It carries with it the substantial risk that interveners will suffer substantial casualties and that they will inflict casualties on others. War usually makes things worse before it can make them better. Although mass killing seldom receives the active support of the societies in which it occurs, these same societies may vigorously oppose foreign interventions seeking to end the killing. For example, while most Germans probably did not actively support the Holocaust, many did support the broader German war effort, and millions of them were willing to fight in Hitler's armies against the allies. The allied victory in 1945, an achievement that undoubtedly saved millions of lives, proved that unseating even the Nazi regime was possible. Unfortunately, it ultimately required the most destructive war in world history. Similarly massive and violent undertakings almost certainly would have been required to overthrow the murderous but deeply entrenched regimes of the Soviet Union and China.

Not all wars, on the other hand, are comparable to World War Two. Not all intervention to prevent mass killing, therefore, is likely to confront such determined resistance. As John Mueller has observed, perpetrators of ethnic conflict and mass killing have relied less and less on professional military organizations, especially in recent years.[24] Perpetrators of mass killing often lack well-disciplined military forces and rely instead on poorly trained and ill-equipped militias and paramilitary groups. These irregular forces may be sufficient for the task of murdering unarmed civilians, but without broad-based support from local populations, they are no match for professional Western militaries.

This is one reason why many observers have suggested that a relatively modest military intervention could have prevented or at least limited the genocide in Rwanda. Roméo Dallaire, the Canadian general in command of UN peacekeeping forces in Rwanda in 1994, has argued that a force of five thousand men, promptly deployed, would have been sufficient to prevent most of the killing.[25] A subsequent analysis by a panel of military experts largely supported Dallaire's claim.[26] Although other analysts have been less sanguine about how much an intervention in Rwanda might have accomplished, few have suggested that interveners would have faced stiff military resistance and few have disputed that intervention could have saved many lives. Alan Kuperman, for example, contends that Dallaire's claims are based on several unrealistic assumptions, including how quickly outsiders could have recognized the genocide and transported an intervention force to the region, how rapidly the genocide progressed, and how many troops would have been required to suppress the violence.[27] Nevertheless, even utilizing more conservative assumptions, Kuperman estimates that a force of 15,000 U.S. troops, arriving relatively late in the genocide, might have saved 125,000 lives in Rwanda.[28] This force would have been large only in comparison to the hypothetical interventions suggested by Dallaire and others. Compared to the forces utilized in traditional military operations such as the 1991 Persian Gulf War, in which the United States deployed over half a million troops, it would have been extremely small. The rapid victory of the Tutsi-dominated Rwandan Patriotic Army—a lightly armed force of between twenty and twenty-five thousand men—over the Hutu perpetrators suggests that, once on the scene, a well-equipped Western military force would have faced relatively light opposition and suffered relatively few casualties.[29]

THE ROLE OF THE UNITED STATES IN PREVENTING MASS KILLING

The United States is one of few countries capable of independently conducting large military operations far from its borders, so it is natural that the question of preventing mass killing has fallen to it before all others. Americans and their leaders have frequently expressed the conviction that the United States and other international actors have a responsibility to intervene to prevent genocide or other large-scale atrocities whenever possible. Every American president from Jimmy Carter to Bill Clinton has publicly reaffirmed America's commitment to the prevention of genocide.[30] Indeed, when asked in the last year of his presidency whether there was such a thing as a "Clinton Doctrine" to guide foreign policy, President Clinton responded that he believed that "whether within or beyond the borders of a country, if the world community has the power to stop it, we ought to stop genocide and ethnic cleansing."[31]

The American public also seems broadly to support intervention to prevent genocide. For example, a July 1994 poll found that when Americans were asked, "If genocidal situations occur, do you think that the U.N., including the U.S., should intervene with whatever force is necessary to stop the acts of genocide?" 65 percent responded "always" or "in most cases."[32] In 1999, another poll showed that 58 percent of Americans agreed that the United States has a moral obligation to use force to prevent genocide even in Africa, where the United States has few traditional security interests.[33]

America's record of international interventions over the past fifty years seems sharply at odds with these sentiments, however. During the cold war, military interventions for primarily humanitarian purposes were virtually nonexistent. This reluctance to intervene stemmed in part from legitimate concerns about the potential for military interventions to ignite larger wars with the Soviet Union or others. The refusal of the United States to ratify the United Nations Genocide Convention until 1986, on the other hand, also suggests a deeper ambivalence about humanitarian intervention.[34] Since the end of the cold war, the United States has intervened with force for humanitarian purposes more frequently. Nevertheless, America's post–cold war policies have failed to reflect a strong commitment to preventing genocide and mass killing.

Rather, America's record of intervention during the 1990s suggests that while the United States supports action to prevent mass killing in principle, it has not been willing to make even small sacrifices to uphold this principle in practice. The distinction between our convictions and our actions has been particularly stark when the sacrifices have included the possibility of American casualties. At the outset of the U.S.-led intervention in Somalia in 1992, for example, polls showed that between 73 and 81 percent of Americans supported the action.[35] Although the intervention saved tens or even hundreds of thousands of lives, support for the operation started to drop as soon as American troops expanded their mission from the provision of food to the more dangerous task of disarming local militias.[36] After eighteen American soldiers were killed in a fierce fire fight in Mogadishu in October 1993, support declined even further. A few days after the battle, 60 percent of Americans polled agreed with the statement that "Nothing the U.S. could accomplish in Somalia is worth the death of even one more soldier."[37] The American experience in Somalia would prove to be one of the most important factors in preventing a more serious consideration of military intervention in Rwanda, less than six months later, in response to perhaps the most unambiguous example of genocide since the Holocaust. As a former U.S. Defense Department official described the government's reaction to reports of the Rwandan genocide, "Everybody was partially traumatized by Somalia. . . . They did not want an intervention."[38]

One of the most significant consequences of the desire to keep casualties to a minimum has been that when the United States has opted to intervene with force, it has been extremely reluctant to place ground troops in combat. This often has meant delaying the introduction of ground forces until all the parties to the conflict can reach an agreement and, to minimize the possibility of being drawn into the fighting, defining narrowly the rules of engagement under which these forces can operate. In the former Yugoslavia, for example, the United States resisted sending ground troops to Bosnia until 1995, when the Serbs finally agreed to a peace plan. By then, most of the killing and ethnic cleansing had already been accomplished. The largely European UN forces on the ground in Bosnia prior to the agreement were not empowered to protect civilians and could only stand by and watch as large-scale massacres unfolded before their eyes.

The recognition that the United States and other international actors are unwilling to suffer even small numbers of casualties in humanitarian interventions has led many human rights advocates and policy makers to endorse policies that avoid placing ground troops in combat altogether. A wide range of options have been suggested or employed, including the withholding of foreign aid, the establishment of war crimes tribunals, the imposition of diplomatic or economic sanctions, arms embargoes, economic blockades, and the use of air strikes.[39] These strategies seek to prevent mass killing, not by physically preventing perpetrators from killing their victims, but by deterring the use of violence in the first place or compelling its cessation through the threat of punishment.

Thus, Human Rights Watch has argued that unequivocal international political condemnation, the withdrawal of economic aid, and the imposition of an arms embargo might have halted the 1994 genocide in Rwanda by turning the population and mid-level government functionaries against the Hutu extremist regime.[40] Likewise, many have credited NATO's air campaign against Serbia with preventing mass killing in Kosovo in 1999 without the need for a risky ground invasion.

Unfortunately, while these strategies avoid many of the risks of ground combat, the findings of this book provide little reason to believe that they will be widely effective in preventing mass killing. Like the decision to go to war, leaders do not take lightly the decision to embark upon a policy of mass killing. On the contrary, leaders order mass killing in an effort to achieve their most important goals or counter what they perceive to be their most dangerous threats. They usually do so only after other alternatives have failed to achieve these goals or defeat these threats. Since states threatening punitive actions are generally less committed to preventing mass killing than perpetrators are to carrying it out, such threats often lack credibility.

Even when punitive threats are actually carried out, the costs imposed by these measures simply may not be great enough to persuade perpetrators to abandon their most important goals. Decades of Western political and diplomatic sanctions and of economic and military embargoes, for example, failed to force the Soviet Union and China to alter their policies.[41] Nor did international sanctions or the threat of prosecution for war crimes deter Serbian-sponsored violence in Bosnia or Kosovo. Although both the Young Turks and the Nazi regime were threatened with international sanctions, including comprehensive economic blockades, both Turkey and Germany chose to wage total war rather than surrender to external pressures.

The threat of air strikes holds greater potential for increasing the costs facing perpetrators of mass killing, but even this weapon has not proved widely effective.[42] Allied strategic bombing of Germany and Japan leveled entire cities and killed hundreds of thousands of people, yet it did not compel either nation to cease mass killing.[43] Many scholars question whether the strategic air campaign proved a decisive contribution to the German or Japanese surrenders at all.[44] In Kosovo, the seventy-eight-day NATO bombing campaign may well have contributed to the Serbian withdrawal, but it could not have prevented mass killing if this had been the Serbs' intention.[45] The air strikes did not stop the Serbs from killing between 2,000 and 10,000 Kosovar Albanians and expelling almost 850,000 more.[46] Indeed, America's extreme aversion to casualties meant that NATO aircraft were forced to operate at high altitude, a policy that may have contributed to several incidents of mistaken attacks on Kosovar Albanian civilians.

Perhaps more important than the practical limitations of punitive policies such as sanctions or air strikes, however, is the significant risk that they may actually incite the very violence they seek to prevent.[47] Sanctions and air strikes may succeed in increasing the costs of mass killing for perpetrators, but if perpetrators simply blame the victims for the setbacks and suffering inflicted by these policies, the incentives to engage in mass killing, and possibly even popular support for it, may rise. Since punitive policies cannot physically protect potential victims, these policies leave an open door to mass killing.

History provides several examples of this perverse dynamic. International diplomatic pressure to end the abuse of Armenians in Turkey, for example, appears to have increased the Young Turks' perception that Armenians were a foreign, treacherous group that posed a mortal threat to the integrity of Turkey.[48] In Rwanda, the threat of foreign aid cutbacks and diplomatic pressure on the Hutu-dominated regime to end human rights abuses and negotiate with the Tutsi rebels may have helped convince Hutu extremists, and even some moderates, that the Tutsi minority posed a grave threat.[49] The small UN force eventually deployed to oversee the implementation of the peace agreement between Hutu and

Tutsi forces was neither equipped nor authorized to protect the Tutsi after the genocide began. Likewise, the NATO bombing campaign in Kosovo appears to have hardened Serbian opinion against the Kosovar Albanians and rallied public support behind Milosevic, at least initially.[50]

Once a truly total campaign of genocide is under way, of course, neither public condemnation nor sanctions nor air strikes could make things any worse. These options would then be justified even if they saved only a few lives. Before the slaughter has begun, however, the lessons of these cases suggest much greater attention to the potential for unintended consequences of punitive measures.

FACILITATING ESCAPE

If international actors are unwilling or unable to intervene directly to defeat the perpetrators of mass killing, therefore, they should be cautious about seeking to punish perpetrators without providing protection to defenseless victim groups. A more effective strategy to protect victims from mass killing without placing ground troops in combat would be to help potential victims of mass killing escape to safer areas. Indeed, the history examined in this book demonstrates that the ability of potential victims of mass killing to flee across borders often has been a critical factor in limiting or averting mass killing. This conclusion might seem self-evident, but explanations that locate the prime causes of mass killing in hatred between groups, in scapegoating behavior, or the desire to kill for killing's sake seem to suggest that the perpetrators of mass killing would generally seek to prevent victims from fleeing to safety. If perpetrators are willing to permit the flight of victim groups, however, then intervention designed to facilitate escape might offer some hope of preventing or limiting the violence.

Of course, intervention to assist the escape of potential victims is not without its own set of serious problems and costly side effects. These problems can be especially acute when the exodus of refugees leads, as it often has, to permanent population relocation or to the political or ethnic partition of states.[51] Many critics have pointed out that providing international support for these policies simply rewards ethnic cleansing; moreover, they claim that these policies may simply set the stage for future conflicts, when refugees try to fight their way back to their former homes.[52] For my part, I have argued here that the notion that physical separation is the only way to prevent a continuing cycle of violence between groups consumed by mutual hatred and fear — the premise of at least some arguments in favor of partition or population transfers — is flawed. If the groups responsible for mass killing can be removed from power, even a long history of enmity and violence need not portend repeated waves of mass killing in the future.

On the other hand, critics of partition and population transfers often seem to ignore the reality that international actors are seldom willing to pay even modest political and military costs to support more aggressive forms of intervention to prevent mass killing. If no state or coalition of states is willing to intervene directly to confront perpetrators bent on mass killing, the remaining choice is no longer between abetting ethnic cleansing and fostering a multiethnic society, but between ethnic cleansing and mass killing. Critics of partition and permanent population relocation see little difference between ethnic cleansing and mass killing because, as the history presented in this book confirms, major involuntary population movements often are associated with massive violence and death. Critics often point to the bloody history of unregulated or poorly regulated partitions and relocations, such as the partition of India and Pakistan in 1947 or the expulsion of ethnic Germans from Eastern Europe following the Second World War, to illustrate this point.

The very purpose of international intervention during population relocation or partition, however, would be to reduce the severity of these consequences for the affected populations. If more careful preparation and greater resources were devoted to facilitating transportation and resettlement, displaced populations might leave their homes with less coercion, and the hardships of relocation could be significantly eased.[53] The serious human costs attendant to even the most carefully executed program of population relocation or partition mean that international actors should support these policies only as a last resort, when mass killing (not simply violent conflict) is imminent or in progress, and only if international support for intervention to protect victims where they live cannot be mustered.

These shortcomings, however, should not be allowed to serve as an excuse for doing nothing in the face of mass murder. The ability of potential victims of mass killing to flee across borders probably has averted millions of deaths in this century. While NATO air strikes could not prevent Serbs from killing Kosovar Albanians, the construction of well-supplied refugee camps across the border in Albania probably did encourage many victims to flee rather than fight, and ensured that those who did escape would survive. Similarly, as I noted in chapter 4, the massive exoduses following the communist revolutions in Korea, Cuba, and Vietnam may have saved vast numbers of lives.

These relocations were dependent on the willingness of neighbors to accept large numbers of refugees. More frequently, however, attempts to escape from mass killing have met with international indifference or even opposition. It is possible that greater international openness to refugees could have helped reduce the toll of many of this century's bloodiest mass killings, including the genocides in Turkish Armenia, Nazi Germany, and Rwanda. As described in chapter 5, Nazi Germany actively encouraged the emigration of its Jewish population between 1933 and 1939, which ultimately resulted in the exodus of more than 70 percent of Germany's Jews. Had Western nations put up fewer barriers to Jewish immigration, they might have saved many more lives.[54] Some scholars have argued that greater openness to Jewish refugees from Germany before the war would not have prevented the Holocaust because the great majority of Holocaust victims resided in Eastern Europe.[55] This is correct, but even after the war began in 1939, the Nazis continued to search for ways to deport Jews from conquered territories. Tens of thousands of Jews managed to emigrate from Austria and Czechoslovakia after Germany occupied these states. Had other nations shown a greater willingness to facilitate Jewish emigration, not only might thousands more Jews have escaped before the war, but it is possible that the Nazis would not have been so quick to abandon their policy of encouraging Jewish emigration after hostilities began.

Unlike Nazi Germany in the thirties, neither the Young Turks nor Rwanda's Hutu extremists attempted to deport or expel their victims in large numbers. On the contrary, each regime actively sought to prevent victims from fleeing to neighboring countries. These policies, however, should not be interpreted as evidence that the perpetrators would countenance nothing less than complete extermination or that they simply wanted to kill their victims for the sake of killing. Rather, Turkish and Hutu perpetrators rejected expulsion because situational factors made it appear a counterproductive solution to the central problems they were trying solve. In Rwanda, the extremists probably decided against expulsion because they looked back on the de facto ethnic cleansing of the late 1950s and early 1960s as the prime cause of their current predicament. Indeed, the Tutsi forces attempting to fight their way back into the country in the early 1990s were descendants of those who had fled more than thirty years earlier. Similarly, although Turkish leaders do appear briefly to have considered the possibility of expelling the Armenians into Russia, they ultimately rejected this option for fear that Armenian refugees would simply join forces with the invading Russian army.

Nevertheless, despite the efforts of Turkish and Hutu perpetrators, thousands of Armenian and Tutsi refugees did manage to escape from Turkey and Rwanda. Relatively small military interventions designed to protect refugee columns and keep borders open might have facilitated the escape of many more. Indeed, American officials appear to have considered a plan to establish protected zones on Rwanda's borders during the genocide. Kuperman estimates that such a strategy, combined with the use of helicopters to protect major escape routes, might have saved seventy-five thousand lives.[56] It is not clear how serious the United States was about this proposal, but the UN rejected it at least in part because it could not have saved the vast majority of Rwandans who never could have made it across the border.[57] Since the UN's member states lacked the willingness to implement a more robust intervention, however, the alternative saved no one at all.[58] If more distant states had been willing to accept Armenian or Tutsi refugees, it is possible that Turkish and Hutu leaders would have actually encouraged them to leave, since these refugees would not have been perceived to pose an immediate threat of cross-border attack.

The possibility of escape for refugees might also have reduced the death toll in Guatemala. Throughout the war, the Guatemalan regime feared that refugee camps across the border in Mexico were being used as secure bases for the insurgency. As a result, the Guatemalan army sought to prevent refugees from fleeing to Mexico and even engaged in cross-border attacks against refugee camps there. Yet the regime also seemed willing to consider less violent solutions to the refugee problem. In fact, the Guatemalan regime actively pressured Mexico to move the refugee camps farther away from the border, where they would no longer pose a threat to Guatemala. Mexico initially resisted relocating the refugees because it did not want to assume permanent responsibility for them, but in 1984 and 1985 it agreed to move about seventeen thousand refugees to camps farther away from the border.[59] Unfortunately, this move came too late to have much effect, since the most severe period of violence in Guatemala had ended in 1983. If this strategy had been implemented earlier, and had greater international aid been provided to Mexico for relocation, however, the Guatemalan government might actually have encouraged refugee flows to Mexico, and many more lives might have been saved.

FACING MASS KILLING

Scholars dispute whether America's failure to intervene more resolutely to uphold its commitment to prevent genocide and mass killing stems from the attitudes of the general public or reflects the failure of political leaders to shape those attitudes.[60] Whatever the origins of this hesitancy, however, the research presented in this book shows that Americans must reject the comfortable notion — shared by many leaders and the public — that the root causes of this kind of violence render intervention futile.

It is possible to prevent or limit mass killing and genocide if we are willing to pay a price for our convictions. In some cases, that price will be modest in comparison with the number of lives we will save. In others, the costs may be prohibitive. The United States alone cannot prevent this kind of violence everywhere it occurs. Yet, the lesson of the Holocaust, perhaps the defining episode of violence in a century marked by bloodshed, is not that preventing mass killing and genocide is easy. The pledge "never again," issued in the wake of that tragedy, did not include the qualification "so long as there is virtually no risk of casualties." Deciding where and how to intervene to avert such violence in the future will require hard choices about the potential costs and benefits of action. By failing to face the causes of mass killing, we have avoided facing these hard choices for too long.

NOTES

Introduction

1. Shepard Krech, "Genocide in Tribal Society," *Nature,* September 1994, pp. 14–15.

2. Estimate based on numerous sources. See tables 2–7 in chapter 3. The term "mass killing" is defined below. Using a more expansive definition, Rudolph Rummel estimates that between 76 million and 360 million people were killed in "democides" from 1900 to 1987 — with a "prudent or conservative midrange estimate" of 169,198,000 deaths. Rummel's estimates tend to be considerably higher than those of most other scholars. See Rudolph Rummel, *Statistics of Democide: Genocide and Mass Murder Since 1900* (Charlottesville, Va.: Center for National Security Law, 1997), p. 355; and Rudolph Rummel, *Death by Government* (New Brunswick, N.J.: Transaction, 1994), pp. xviii–xx. Zbigniew Brzezinski estimates more than 80 million politically motivated deaths from 1900 to 1993, not including civilian or military deaths during war. See Zbigniew Brzezinski, *Out of Control: Global Turmoil on the Eve of the Twenty-First Century* (New York: Charles Scribner's Sons, 1993), p. 17. Matthew White estimates 83 million deaths from "genocide and tyranny" and an additional 44 million in "man-made famines" during the twentieth century. See Matthew White, "Historical Atlas of the Twentieth Century" http://users.erols.com/mwhite28/warstat8.htm [June 2003]. Using a more restricted definition, Barbara Harff estimates that between 8.9 and 19.8 million people were killed in forty-eight episodes of genocide and "politicide" between 1945 and 1994. See Barbara Harff and Ted Robert Gurr, "Victims of the State: Genocides, Politicides and Group Repression from 1945 to 1995," in Albert Jongman, ed., *Contemporary Genocide: Causes, Cases, Consequences* (Leiden: Den Haag, 1996), pp. 49–51.

3. Rummel, *Death by Government,* p. 15. Rummel's estimate is for the period between 1900 and 1987. William Eckhardt estimates 85,527,000 war-related deaths between 1900 and 1988, of which approximately 50 percent were civilians. Estimates of civilian war-related deaths by Eckhardt appear to include many episodes of intentional killing and therefore overlap considerably with geno-

cide and mass killing. See William Eckhardt, "Civilian Deaths in Wartime," *Bulletin of Peace Proposals* 20, no. 1 (1989): 90.

4. For a more detailed description of process tracing, see Alexander L. George and Timothy J. McKeown, "Case Studies and Theories of Organizational Decision Making," *Advances in Information Processing in Organizations* 2 (1985): 21–58.

1. *Mass Killing and Genocide*

1. Raphael Lemkin, *Axis Rule in Occupied Europe: Laws of Occupation, Analysis of Government, Proposals for Redress* (Washington, D.C.: Carnegie Endowment for International Peace, 1944), p. 79.

2. For the complete text of the genocide convention, see Lawrence J. LeBlanc, *The United States and the Genocide Convention* (Durham, N.C.: Duke University Press, 1991), pp. 245–249. For a description of Lemkin's efforts to draft and ratify the convention, see Samantha Power, *"A Problem from Hell": America and the Age of Genocide* (New York: Basic Books, 2002), pp. 17–85.

3. *Oxford English Dictionary,* 2d ed., 6:445.

4. For one example, see Robert Johnson and Paul S. Leighton, "American Genocide: The Destruction of the Black Underclass," in Craig Summers and Eric Markusen, eds., *Collective Violence: Harmful Behavior in Groups and Governments* (Lanham, Md.: Rowman and Littlefield, 1999), pp. 95–140. The use of the term "holocaust" has generated a similar political debate. See Samuel G. Freedman, "Laying Claim to Sorrow beyond Words," *New York Times,* December 13, 1997, p. A19.

5. For reviews of the debate on the definition of genocide, see Scott Straus, "Contested Meanings and Conflicting Imperatives: A Conceptual Analysis of Genocide," *Journal of Genocide Research* 3, no. 3 (November 2001): 349–375; Helen Fein, *Genocide: A Sociological Perspective* (London: Sage, 1993), pp. xi–xix, 1–31; Eric Markusen and David Kopf, *The Holocaust and Strategic Bombing: Genocide and Total War in the Twentieth Century* (Boulder: Westview, 1995), pp. 39–64; and Frank Chalk and Kurt Jonassohn, *The History and Sociology of Genocide* (New Haven: Yale University Press, 1990), pp. 12–23.

6. This definition is similar in some respects to Rummel's concept of "democide." Rummel's definition, however, includes the killing of any number of civilians, no matter how small. In addition, Rummel specifies that democide must be carried out by government groups, while the perpetrators of mass killing can belong to any kind of group. See Rudolph Rummel, *Death by Government* (New Brunswick, N.J.: Transaction, 1994), pp. 31–43.

7. Disease can also be spread intentionally as part of an effort to exterminate large numbers of people. European colonists, for example, appear to have made deliberate efforts to spread fatal diseases among native American populations, although it remains unclear whether these early experiments with biological warfare proved "successful." See William H. McNeill, *Plagues and Peoples* (Garden City: Doubleday, 1976), p. 222; and Russell Thornton, *American Indian Holocaust and Survival: A Population History since 1492* (Norman: University of Oklahoma Press, 1987), pp. 78–79.

8. Raul Hilberg, *The Destruction of the European Jews* (New York: Holmes and Meier, 1985), p. 338. This estimate does not include those who died of privation, rather than execution, in German labor and concentration camps.

9. Gerald Reitlinger, *The Final Solution: The Attempt to Exterminate the Jews of Europe 1939–1945* (London: Vallentine, Mitchell, 1968), p. 545; and Arno J. Mayer, *Why Did the Heavens Not Darken?: The "Final Solution" in History* (New York: Pantheon, 1988), p. 365.

10. Steven Katz, for example, argues that "the concept of genocide applies *only* when there is an actualized intent, however successfully carried out, to physically destroy an *entire* group." Steven Katz, *The Holocaust in Historical Context: The Holocaust and Mass Death before the Modern Age* (New York: Oxford University Press, 1994), p. 128; italics in original.

11. If an episode of mass killing continues for more than five years, all deaths resulting from it are included as long as at least 50,000 civilians were killed in any five-year period during the episode. For example, approximately 80,000 civilians were intentionally killed during the civil war in El Salvador from 1979 to 1992. Although this figure represents an average of less than 50,000 deaths every five years, more than 50,000 of these occurred in the five-year period from 1980 to 1985. All intentional civilian deaths resulting from the civil war are therefore included as mass killing.

12. The Nazis may well have *wished* to kill American Jews, but for obvious reasons they took no concrete steps to do so. If such unactualized ambitions were sufficient to establish genocide, the term would be stretched beyond all meaning. Members of numerous racist groups around the world undoubtedly harbor similar, and similarly unrealizable, desires today.

13. Quoted in LeBlanc, *The United States and the Genocide Convention,* p. 245.

14. Barbara Harff's definition of genocide and politicide, for example, focuses on the "the promotion, execution, and/or implied consent of sustained policies by governing elites or their agents—or in the case of civil war, either of the contending authorities—that are intended to destroy, in whole or in part, a communal, political, or politicized ethnic group." Harff, however, does not define the phrase "in part" with a specific numerical percentage. See Barbara Harff, "No Lessons Learned from the Holocaust? Assessing the Risks of Genocide and Political Mass Murder since 1955," *American Political Science Review* 97, no. 1 (February 2003): 58.

15. The populations of many indigenous tribes of Central and South America, for example, comprise only a few thousand individuals.

16. See Bryan Mark Rigg, *Hitler's Jewish Soldiers* (Lawrence: University Press of Kansas, 2002).

17. This definition is generally consistent with the definition of "civilian" adopted by the two 1977 additional protocols of the Geneva Convention. See Michael Bothe, Karl Josef Partsch, and Waldemar A. Solf, *New Rules for Victims of Armed Conflicts: Commentary on the Two 1977 Protocols Additional to the Geneva Conventions of 1949* (The Hague: Martinus Nijhoff Publishers, 1982), pp. 274–318. For more on the history and evolution of the international legal protection of civilian populations during war, see Yvonne van Dongen, *The Protection of Civilian Populations in Time of Armed Conflict* (Amsterdam: Thesis Publishers, 1991).

18. For example, of the forty-nine episodes of genocide and politicide identified by Barbara Harff from 1945 to 2000, thirty-one (approximately 63 percent) qualify as episodes of mass killing as defined here (several of Harff's cases are grouped together into single cases in this book). The remaining eighteen of Harff's cases do not meet the definition of mass killing because none was estimated to have taken more than fifty thousand lives in five or fewer years. Applying the criteria for mass killing identifies approximately eighteen additional cases (including possible cases) not included in Harff's list for the same period. Most of these cases, despite very high absolute death tolls, probably did not meet Harff's criterion that the perpetrators "eliminate or intend to eliminate so many people that the group ceases to function as a social or political entity." See Harff, "No Lessons Learned from the Holocaust?" p. 58; and Barbara Harff and Ted Robert Gurr, "Victims of the State: Genocides, Politicides and Group Repression from 1945 to 1995," in Albert Jongman, ed., *Contemporary Genocides: Causes, Cases, Consequences* (Leiden: Den Haag, 1996), pp. 33–58. For a complete list of cases of mass killing in the twentieth century, see tables 2–7 in chapter 3.

19. See Fein, *Genocide,* xi–xii; and Lucy S. Dawidowicz, *The Holocaust and the Historians* (Cambridge: Harvard University Press, 1981), p. 17. Other scholars, most notably Jean-Paul Sartre, have argued for the study of cases of aerial bombardment and other wartime mass killings alongside more widely accepted cases of genocide. See Jean-Paul Sartre, *On Genocide* (Boston: Beacon, 1968). For other proponents of this view, see Leo Kuper, *Genocide* (New Haven: Yale University Press, 1981), p. 46; and Markusen and Kopf, *The Holocaust and Strategic Bombing.*

20. Chalk and Jonassohn, *History and Sociology of Genocide,* p. 24. This definition leads Chalk

and Jonassohn to the perplexing conclusion that the civilian deaths caused by the use of siege warfare against cities such as Carthage qualify as genocide, while civilian deaths due to aerial bombardment do not.

21. Fein, *Genocide,* pp. xi–xii.

22. Dawidowicz, *The Holocaust and the Historians,* p. 17.

23. See Gar Alperovitz, *The Decision to Use the Atomic Bomb* (New York: Knopf, 1995), esp.
p. 673.

24. For a review of the literature on mass killing and genocide, see Fein, *Genocide,* pp. 32–50.
A useful if somewhat dated review can be found in Kuper, *Genocide,* pp. 40–56.

25. These three families are, of necessity, artificial. Authors referred to within each family are
not necessarily in complete agreement with each other, and many authors combine factors and explanations from more than one category.

26. Kuper, *Genocide.* The concept of a plural society does not originate with Kuper, although
he appears to be the first to apply it specifically to the study of genocide. For a brief review of the
origins and problems of plural society theory in the study of ethnic conflict more generally, see
Donald L Horowitz, *Ethnic Groups in Conflict* (Berkeley: University of California Press, 1985),
pp. 135–139. Helen Fein similarly asserts that "ethnic stratification" is an important predisposing
factor for some types of genocide. See Helen Fein, "Accounting for Genocide after 1945: Theories
and Some Findings," *International Journal on Group Rights* 1 (1993): 88–92.

27. For example, see Israel W. Charny, *How Can We Commit the Unthinkable? Genocide: The Human Cancer* (Boulder: Westview, 1982), esp. pp. 206–207; Herbert C. Kelman, "Violence without
Moral Restraint: Reflections on the Dehumanization of Victims and Victimizers," *Journal of the
Social Issues* 29, no. 4 (1973): 25–61; Chalk and Jonassohn, *History and Sociology of Genocide,* pp. 27–
28; and Herbert Hirsch and Roger W. Smith, "The Language of Extermination in Genocide,"
in Israel Charny, ed., *Genocide: A Critical Bibliographic Review* (New York: Facts on File, 1988),
pp. 386–403. Some proponents of the plural society theory have expressed reservations about the
explanatory power of theories that focus on dehumanization. See Kuper, *Genocide,* pp. 91–92; and
Fein, *Genocide,* pp. 36–37. These theories are included here because, like the plural society theory,
they suggest that the root causes of mass killing can be found in unusually bad relations between
social groups.

28. Kuper, *Genocide,* pp. 57–58.

29. See James D. Fearon and David D. Laitin, "Ethnicity, Insurgency and Civil War," *American
Political Science Review* 97, no. 1 (February 2003): 75–90); Matthew Krain, "State Sponsored Mass
Murder: The Onset and Severity of Genocides and Politicides," *Journal of Conflict Resolution* 41, no.
3 (June 1997): 346; Rudolph J. Rummel, "Democracy, Power, Genocide and Mass Murder," *Journal of Conflict Resolution* 39, no. 1 (March 1995): 21. Barbara Harff examined numerous indicators
of ethnic and religious cleavages but found that the occurrence of genocide and politicide was significantly more likely only in states in which the ruling elite represented a minority ethnic group.
See Harff, "No Lessons Learned from the Holocaust?" pp. 66–67.

30. Benjamin Valentino, Paul Huth, and Dylan Balch-Lindsay, "Draining the Sea: Mass Killing
and Guerrilla Warfare," *International Organization* 57, no. 1 (Winter 2004).

31. See Steve Heder, "Class, Nationality and Race in Communist Crimes against Humanity:
Theoretical and Historical Reflections on Marxist Racism and Violence," in Alexandre Kimenyi
and Otis L. Scott, eds., *Anatomy of Genocide: State Sponsored Mass-Killing in the Twentieth Century*
(Lewiston: Edwin Mellen, 2001), pp. 129–185. On the Soviet Union, see Robert Conquest, *The
Nation Killers: The Soviet Deportation of Nationalities* (New York: Macmillan, 1970), p. 12; and Terry
Martin, "The Origins of Soviet Ethnic Cleansing," *Journal of Modern History* 70 (December 1998):
813–861. On Cambodia, see Steve Heder, "Racism, Marxism, Labeling, and Genocide in Ben Kiernan's *The Pol Pot Regime,*" *South East Asia Research* 5, no. 2 (1996): 101–153; and David Chandler,

The Tragedy of Cambodian History (New Haven: Yale University Press, 1991), p. 285. For the argument that race was more important than class in Cambodia, see Ben Kiernan, *The Pol Pot Regime: Race, Power and Genocide in Cambodia under the Khmer Rouge, 1975–1979* (New Haven: Yale University Press, 1996).

32. David. P. Chandler, *Voices from S-21: Terror and History in Pol Pot's Secret Prison* (Berkeley: University of California Press, 1999), p. 36.

33. J. Arch Getty and William Chase, "Patterns of Repression among the Soviet Elite in the Late 1930s: A Biographical Approach," in J. Arch Getty and Roberta T. Manning, eds., *Stalinist Terror: New Perspectives* (Cambridge: Cambridge University Press, 1993), pp. 225–246.

34. Robert Conquest, *The Great Terror: A Reassessment* (Oxford: Oxford University Press, 1990), pp. 179–180, 279.

35. It has often been suggested that inequality in land ownership was a primary basis of class cleavages in these societies. Indices of the concentration of land ownership reveal that, although far from equitable, inequality in the Soviet Union, China, and Cambodia prior to their revolutions was not unusually high compared to other nations. A survey of land inequality in forty-seven nations in 1964 reveals an average Gini coefficient of land concentration of 71.6. Prior to their revolutions, estimates for the Gini coefficients for Russia, China, and Cambodia are 44–73, 38–64.6, and 50–54 respectively. Figures calculated from Bruce Russet, "Inequality and Instability: The Relation of Land Tenure to Politics," in James Chowning Davies, *When Men Revolt and Why: A Reader in Political Violence and Revolution* (New York: Free Press, 1971), pp. 210–211, 347 n. 16; and Frederic L. Pryor, *The Red and the Green: The Rise and Fall of Collectivized Agriculture* (Princeton: Princeton University Press, 1992), pp. 455–465.

36. See Robert Conquest, *Harvest of Sorrow: Soviet Collectivization and the Terror-Famine* (New York: Oxford University Press, 1986), pp. 97–98, 133–135; Lynne Viola, *Peasant Rebels under Stalin: Collectivization and the Culture of Peasant Resistance* (New York: Oxford University Press, 1996), pp. 67–99; Edward Friedman, Paul G. Pickowicz, and Mark Selden, *Chinese Village, Socialist State* (New Haven: Yale University Press, 1991), pp. 81–82; Jasper Becker, *Hungry Ghosts: Mao's Secret Famine* (New York: Free Press, 1996), pp. 28–34; and Chandler, *Tragedy of Cambodian History*, pp. 238–239.

37. Jean-Louis Margolin, "China: A Long March into Night," in Stéphane Courtois et al., *The Black Book of Communism: Crimes, Terror, Repression* (Cambridge: Harvard University Press, 1999), p. 477. See also Friedman, Pickowicz, and Selden, *Chinese Village, Socialist State*, pp. 81–83, 95–98; and Lucien Bianco, "Peasant Responses to CCP Mobilization Policies, 1937–1945," in Tony Saich and Hans van de Ven, eds., *New Perspectives on the Chinese Communist Revolution* (Armonk: M. E. Sharpe, 1995), pp. 175–187.

38. Conquest, *Harvest of Sorrow*, pp. 45–46, 74; and Viola, *Peasant Rebels under Stalin*, p. 35.

39. Quoted in Maurice Hindus, *Red Bread* (New York: Jonathan Cape and Harrison Smith, 1931), p. 22.

40. David P. Chandler, *Brother Number One: A Political Biography of Pot* (Boulder: Westview, 1992), p. 108; and Karl D. Jackson, "The Ideology of Total Revolution," in Karl D. Jackson, ed., *Cambodia 1975–1978: Rendezvous with Death* (Princeton: Princeton University Press, 1989), pp. 37–78.

41. See Jack Snyder, *From Voting to Violence: Democratization and Nationalist Conflict* (New York: W. W. Norton, 2000); Human Rights Watch, *Slaughter among Neighbors: The Political Origins of Communal Violence* (New Haven: Yale University Press, 1995); Michael Freeman, "The Theory and Prevention of Genocide," *Holocaust and Genocide Studies* 6, no. 2 (1991): 189; and James D. Fearon and David D. Laitin, "Violence and the Social Construction of Ethnic Identity," *International Organization* 54, no. 4 (autumn 2000): 845–877.

42. Susan L. Woodward, *Balkan Tragedy: Chaos and Dissolution after the Cold War* (Washington, D.C.: Brookings Institution, 1995), p. 228; and V. P. Gagnon Jr., "Ethnic Nationalism and In-

ternational Conflict: The Case of Serbia," *International Security* 19, no. 3 (winter 1994–95): 133–134.

43. Lena H. Sun, "For Refugees, a Lament for Loss and Vigil for Peace," *Washington Post*, December 9, 1995, p. B7.

44. Gagnon, "Ethnic Nationalism and International Conflict," p. 134; and Steven A. Holmes, "Number of Black-White Couples is Rising Sharply, Study Says," *New York Times*, July 4, 1996, p. A16. Thanks to John Mueller for providing these citations.

45. See Gagnon, "Ethnic Nationalism and International Conflict"; Woodward, *Balkan Tragedy*, pp. 225–228; John Mueller, "The Banality of Ethnic War," *International Security* 25, no. 1 (summer 2000): 42–70; Laura Silber and Allen Little, *Yugoslavia: Death of a Nation* (United States: TV Books, 1996), pp. 25–26; Human Rights Watch, *Slaughter among Neighbors*, pp. 114–125; Robert M. Hayden, "Imagined Communities and Real Victims: Self Determination and Ethnic Cleansing in Yugoslavia," *American Ethnologist* 23, no. 4 (November 1996): 783–801; and David Rieff, *Slaughterhouse: Bosnia and the Failure of the West* (New York: Touchstone, 1996), pp. 111–113.

46. Michael Burleigh and Wolfgang Wippermann, *The Racial State: Germany 1933–1945* (Cambridge: Cambridge University Press, 1991), p. 153. Burleigh and Wippermann note that at least 5,200 were killed in the "children's euthanasia" program (p. 144), but is not clear whether these are included in the larger figure. Elsewhere, Burleigh estimates that as many as 200,000 people were killed as part of the Nazis' euthanasia campaign between 1939 and 1945, a figure that probably includes non-German victims. Michael Burleigh *Death and Deliverance: "Euthanasia" in Germany 1900–1945* (Cambridge: Cambridge University Press, 1994), cover page.

47. Burleigh, *Death and Deliverance*, pp. 183–219. Negative public reactions to the euthanasia program, especially from the church, may have played a role in speeding the end of the official program in 1941. Burleigh, however, claims that "the 'euthanasia' programme was not halted because of some local difficulties with a handful of bishops, but because its team of practiced murderers were needed to carry out the infinitely vaster enormity in the East" and because the organizers of the euthanasia campaign "had slightly exceeded their initial target of killing one chronic patient per thousand inhabitants of Germany" (p. 180). As Burleigh documents, an unofficial euthanasia program continued after 1941 both inside Germany and in the greater secrecy provided by remote concentration camps (pp. 238–266).

48. See Kuper, *Genocide*, pp. 189–209. Helen Fein concludes that although she could find "no linear or other clear relationship between discrimination and genocide," deep discrimination and political exclusion between groups may nevertheless play an important role in provoking genocide by increasing the likelihood of rebellion by repressed groups and, in turn, the likelihood of a genocidal response by the state. See Fein, "Accounting for Genocide," p. 88.

49. Michael R. Marrus, *The Holocaust in History* (New York: Meridian, 1989), p. 93. See also Saul Friedländer, *Nazi Germany and the Jews*, vol. 1, *The Years of Persecution, 1933–1939* (New York: HarperCollins, 1997), pp. 80–87.

50. Sarah Gordon, *Hitler, Germans and the "Jewish Question"* (Princeton: Princeton University Press, 1984), p. 48.

51. Norman Finkelstein, for example, concludes that "there was much less popular participation in and support for violent racist incitement in Nazi Germany than in the American South." See Norman G. Finkelstein and Ruth Bettina Birn, *A Nation on Trial: The Goldhagen Thesis and Historical Truth* (New York: Holt, 1998), p. 46.

52. René Lemarchand, "Managing Transitional Anarchies: Rwanda, Burundi, and South Africa in Comparative Perspective," *Journal of Modern African Studies* 32, no. 4 (1994): 588.

53. These two explanations are not exclusive, and some authors suggest that elements of both may be valid.

54. See Ervin Staub, *The Roots of Evil: The Origins of Genocide and Other Group Violence* (Cam-

bridge: Cambridge University Press, 1989), pp. 13–50; Charny, *How Can We Commit the Unthinkable?* esp. pp. 107–110, 186–192; and Florence Mazian, *Why Genocide? The Armenian and Jewish Experiences in Perspective* (Ames: Iowa State University Press, 1990), esp. pp. 243–247. Mazian's work does not emphasize explicitly the psychological mechanisms of scapegoating. René Girard proposes similar theories of "collective persecution," based on an analysis of theological texts and mythology. See René Girard, *The Scapegoat* (Baltimore: Johns Hopkins University Press, 1986).

55. Specifically, many scholars draw on "frustration aggression theory," which suggests that humans respond aggressively when they feel threatened or are unable to achieve important goals. This hypothesis was originally proposed by John Dollard and his colleagues in the late 1930s. See John Dollard et al., *Frustration and Aggression* (New Haven: Yale University Press, 1939). For more recent examples and refinements of frustration aggression theory, see R. A. Baron, *Human Aggression* (New York: Plenum, 1977); and Leonard Berkowitz, *Aggression: A Social Psychological Analysis* (New York: McGraw-Hill, 1962).

56. Robert C. Tucker, *Stalin in Power: The Revolution from Above, 1928–1941* (New York: Norton, 1992); Conquest, *The Great Terror*; and Dimitri Volkogonov, *Stalin: Triumph and Tragedy* (New York: Grove Wiedenfeld, 1988), pp. 308–309.

57. Daniel Jonah Goldhagen, *Hitler's Willing Executioners: Ordinary Germans and the Holocaust* (New York: Knopf, 1996). Similar, although less categorical, views are offered in James M. Glass, *Life Unworthy of Life: Racial Phobia and Mass Murder in Hitler's Germany* (New York: Basic Books, 1997); Dawidowicz, *The Holocaust and the Historians*, pp. 11–12, 41–42; Lucy S. Dawidowicz, *The War against the Jews 1933–1945* (New York: Bantam Books, 1986), pp. 164–167; and Michael H. Kater, "Everyday Anti-Semitism in Prewar Nazi Germany: The Popular Bases," in Michael R. Marrus, ed., *The Nazi Holocaust: Historical Articles on the Destruction of the European Jews in Nazi Europe*, vol. 5, *Public Opinion and Relations to the Jews in Nazi Europe*, vol. 1 (Westport, Conn.: Meckler, 1989), pp. 151–181. For a convincing, if somewhat combative critique of Goldhagen's argument, see Finkelstein and Birn, *Nation on Trial*. More measured criticism as well as Goldhagen's reply and some sympathetic commentary can be found in Robert R. Shandley, ed., *Unwilling Germans: The Goldhagen Debate* (Minneapolis: University of Minnesota Press, 1998); and Christopher R. Browning, "Ordinary Germans or Ordinary Men? A Reply to the Critics," in Michael Berenbaum and Abraham J. Peck, eds., *The Holocaust and History: The Known, the Unknown, the Disputed, and the Reexamined* (Bloomington: Indiana University Press, 1998), pp. 252–265.

58. See Ian Kershaw, *Popular Opinion and Political Dissent in the Third Reich: Bavaria 1933–1945* (Oxford: Clarendon, 1983), pp. 274–277; David Bankier, *The Germans and the Final Solution* (Oxford: Basil Blackwell, 1992); Gordon, *Hitler, Germans and the "Jewish Question,"* pp. 56, 207–208; Marlis G. Steinert, *Hitler's War and the Germans: Public Mood and Attitude during the Second World War* (Athens: Ohio University Press, 1977), pp. 132–147; Friedländer, *Nazi Germany and the Jews*; Martin Broszat, "The Third Reich and the German People," in Hedley Bull, ed., *The Challenge of the Third Reich: The Adam von Trott Memorial Lectures* (Oxford: Clarendon, 1986), pp. 77–94; Otto Dov Kulka, " 'Public Opinion' in Nazi Germany: The Final Solution," in Marrus, *The Nazi Holocaust*, pp. 139–150; and Eric H. Johnson, *Nazi Terror: The Gestapo, Jews, and Ordinary Germans* (New York: Basic Books, 1999), pp. 483–484.

59. Marrus, *The Holocaust in History*, p. 94.

60. Kershaw, *Popular Opinion and Political Dissent*, p. 274.

61. See David Bankier "The Use of Antisemitism in Nazi Wartime Propaganda," in Berenbaum and Peck, eds., *The Holocaust and History*, p. 44; and Kershaw, *Popular Opinion and Political Dissent*, p. 371.

62. See Roger Manvell and Heinrich Fraenkel, *Himmler* (New York: Putnam's, 1965), p. 197; and Steinert, *Hitler's War and the Germans*, pp. 141–142. Steinert suggests that the efforts of Nazi leadership to keep the genocide secret may have stemmed in part from the negative reaction of the

German public to the "euthanasia" killings of the incurably sick and mentally ill from 1939 to 1941 (p. 83). It should be noted that Nazi efforts to keep the genocide secret ultimately failed. By the end of the war, most Germans appear to have surmised that Jews were being killed in large numbers. For more detailed accounts of what contemporary Germans knew about the Holocaust, see Lawrence D. Stokes, "The German People and the Destruction of the European Jews," *Central European History* 6 (1973): 167–191; Johnson, *Nazi Terror,* pp. 431–459; Bankier, *Germans and the Final Solution,* pp. 101–115; and Walter Laqueur, *The Terrible Secret: Suppression of the Truth about Hitler's "Final Solution"* (Boston: Little, Brown, 1980), pp. 17–40.

63. Quoted in Michael Burleigh, *The Third Reich: A New History* (New York: Hill and Wang, 2000), p. 660.

64. Quoted in Manvell and Fraenkel, *Himmler,* p. 197.

65. Michael Mann, "Were the Perpetrators of Genocide 'Ordinary Men' or 'Real Nazis'? Results from Fifteen Hundred Biographies," *Holocaust and Genocide Studies* 14, no. 3 (winter 2000): 341.

66. For a review of these theories, some quite bizarre, see Ron Rosenbaum, *Explaining Hitler: The Search for the Origins of His Evil* (New York: Random House, 1998).

67. See Barbara Harff, "The Etiology of Genocides," in Isidor Wallimann and Michael Dobkowski, eds., *Genocide and the Modern Age* (New York: Greenwood, 1987), pp. 41–59; Krain, "State Sponsored Mass Murder"; and Robert Melson, *Revolution and Genocide: The Origins of the Armenian Genocide and the Holocaust* (Chicago: University of Chicago Press, 1992). It should be noted that Melson's work seeks to explain only a small set of what he calls "total domestic genocides": the Armenian genocide, the Holocaust, the genocide of the Gypsies, the mass killing during the Soviet collectivization of agriculture, and the Cambodian mass killing.

68. See Ben Kiernan, "Roots of Genocide: New Evidence on the U.S. Bombardment of Cambodia," *Cultural Survival* 14, no. 3 (1990): 20–22.

69. Krain's research, for example, finds that even societies experiencing both civil and international wars during the same four-year period (an approximation of the factors emphasized by Melson) have only approximately a 3–8 percent chance of experiencing genocide/politicide during that time. Krain's strongest result finds an increase of between 17 percent and 19 percent in the probability of genocide/politicide when decolonization and civil war occur in the same five-year period. Krain, "State Sponsored Mass Murder," pp. 346–355. Melson likewise acknowledges that his theory does "not imply that circumstances of revolution and war will invariably produce total domestic genocide. . . . [R]evolutions that lead to wars create conditions that are potentially genocidal. Whether such conditions in fact lead to genocide depends on the ideology of the perpetrators, the identity of the victims, and the other options that may be open or closed to ideological vanguards that have seized power following a revolution." Melson, *Revolution and Genocide,* pp. 278–279.

70. For a notable exception, see Harff, "No Lessons Learned from the Holocaust?"

71. Rummel, *Death by Government,* pp. 1–2.

72. See also Harff, "No Lessons Learned from the Holocaust?" p. 66; Steven C. Poe and C. Neal Tate, "Repression of Human Rights to Personal Integrity in the 1980s: A Global Analysis," *American Political Science Review* 88, no. 4 (December 1994): 853–872; and Fein, "Accounting for Genocide," pp. 92–93.

73. Robert B. Asprey, *War in the Shadows: The Guerrilla in History* (New York: William Morrow, 1994), p. 133. For more on the war, see Stanley Karnow, *In Our Image: America's Empire in the Philippines* (New York: Random House, 1989), esp. pp. 139–195.

74. Michael Sherry, *The Rise of American Air Power* (New Haven: Yale University Press, 1987), pp. 260, 314.

75. Alistair Horne, *A Savage War of Peace: Algeria 1954–1962* (New York: Viking, 1977), p. 538; and Bernard B. Fall, *The Two Vietnams: A Political and Military Analysis* (New York: Praeger, 1967),

p. 129. For a firsthand account of France's brutal tactics in Algeria, see Paul Aussaresses, *The Battle of the Casbah: Terrorism and Counter-Terrorism in Algeria, 1955–1957* (New York: Enigma Books, 2002).

76. See David Stannard, *American Holocaust: The Conquest of the New World* (Oxford: Oxford University Press, 1992).

77. Quoted in Mireya Navarro, "Guatemalan Army Waged 'Genocide,' New Report Finds," *New York Times,* February 26, 1999, p. A1. For more on U.S. direct and indirect involvement in mass killings in Latin America and elsewhere, see Michael McClintock, *Instruments of Statecraft: U.S. Guerrilla Warfare, Counterinsurgency, and Counterterrorism, 1940–1990* (New York: Pantheon, 1992).

78. Kathy Kadane, "U.S. Officials' Lists Aided Indonesian Bloodbath in '60s," *Washington Post,* May 21, 1990, p. A5; and George Lardner, "Papers Show U.S. Role in Indonesian Purge," *Washington Post,* July 28, 2000, p. A8.

79. Rummel, *Death by Government,* p. 16.

80. A public opinion poll taken after the bombing of Hiroshima and Nagasaki indicated that less than 5 percent of Americans felt America should not have used the bomb and 23 percent felt America actually should have dropped *more* bombs before permitting Japan to surrender. Cited in Elliot Aronson, Timothy D. Wilson, and Robin M. Akert, *Social Psychology: The Heart and the Mind* (New York: HarperCollins, 1994), p. 483.

81. See Gar Alperovitz, *The Decision to Use the Atomic Bomb* (New York: Knopf, 1995), p. 673.

82. Rummel, *Death by Government,* p. 20.

83. Krain, for example, finds "power concentration by itself has little effect on the probability of onset" of genocides and politicides. Krain, "State Sponsored Mass Murder," p. 347.

2. The Perpetrators and the Public

1. The description of this incident is drawn from Christopher R. Browning's account in *Ordinary Men: Reserve Police Battalion 101 and the Final Solution in Poland* (New York: HarperCollins, 1993), pp. 55–77.

2. See Israel W. Charny, "Genocide and Mass Destruction: A Missing Dimension in Psychopathology," in Israel Charny, ed. *Toward the Understanding and Prevention of Genocide* (Boulder: Westview, 1984), pp. 154–174; and Ronald Aronson, "Social Madness," in Isidor Wallimann and Michael Dobkowski, eds., *Genocide and the Modern Age: Etiology and Case Studies of Mass Death* (New York: Greenwood, 1987), pp. 125–141.

3. Nadezhda Mandelstam, *Hope against Hope* (New York: Atheneum, 1970), p. 108.

4. See Rudolph J. Rummel, *Death by Government* (New Brunswick, N.J.: Transaction Publishers, 1994). Although I have not conducted a systematic study of this question, it appears that the relatively few episodes of mass killing carried out by democracies have indeed received a comparatively wide degree of popular approval. Since almost all mass killings by democratic states have targeted foreign civilians or noncitizens, often during times of war, this level of support may reflect a more general tendency (in both democracies and undemocratic regimes) toward wider public approval of mass killing of foreigners or war-related mass killing.

5. For the first view, see Richard Pipes, *The Russian Revolution* (New York: Random House, 1990). For the latter view, see Ronald Grigor Suny, "Toward a Social History of the October Revolution," *American Historical Review* 88, no. 1 (February 1983): 31–52; and Ronald Grigor Suny, "Revision and Retreat in the Historiography of 1917: Social History and Its Critics," *Russian Review* 35, no. 2 (April 1994): 165–182.

6. Orlando Figes, *A People's Tragedy: A History of the Russian Revolution* (New York: Viking Penguin, 1997), p. 493.

7. Martin Malia, *The Soviet Tragedy: A History of Socialism in Russia, 1917–1991* (New York: Free Press, 1994), p. 134.

8. Quoted in ibid., p. 93.

9. Sarah Gordon, *Hitler, Germans and the "Jewish Question"* (Princeton: Princeton University Press, 1984), p. 72.

10. James Diehl, *Para-Military Politics in Weimar Germany* (Bloomington: Indiana University Press, 1977), pp. 295–296. The SA eventually grew to over 2 million or perhaps even 3 million members, but since much of this growth occurred after the Nazi seizure of power and the subsequent banning of other political organizations and paramilitary groups, it is impossible to know whether the ranks of non-Nazi paramilitaries also would have expanded during this period.

11. The numbers of people killed by the various parties in Yugoslavia during the Second World War (the Germans, the Ustasa, Tito's Partisans, and Serbian Chetniks) are fiercely disputed. Various estimates for Serb victims of the Ustasa can be found in Aleksa Djilas, *The Contested Country: Yugoslav Unity and Communist Revolution, 1919–1953* (Cambridge: Harvard University Press, 1991), p. 126. Djilas claims that the figure of 125,000 Serb victims in Croatia is from "the most systematic and objective study so far." More estimates for Serb victims, along with the cited estimate for Jewish victims can be found in Marcus Tanner, *Croatia: A Nation Forged in War* (New Haven: Yale University Press, 2001), p. 152.

12. Branimir Anzulovic, *Heavenly Serbia: From Myth to Genocide* (New York: New York University Press, 1999), p. 107. See also Tanner, *Croatia*, pp. 153–157; and Djilas, *Contested Country*, pp. 122, 124.

13. Anzulovic, *Heavenly Serbia*, p. 107.

14. Vladimir N. Brovkin, "Introduction: New Tasks in the Study of the Russian Revolution and the Civil War," in Vladimir N. Brovkin, ed., *The Bolsheviks in Russian Society: The Revolution and the Civil Wars* (New Haven: Yale University Press, 1997), p. 3.

15. See Norman G. Finkelstein and Ruth Bettina Birn, *A Nation on Trial: The Goldhagen Thesis and Historical Truth* (New York: Henry Holt, 1998), p. 31; Ian Kershaw, *Popular Opinion and Political Dissent in the Third Reich: Bavaria 1933–1945* (Oxford: Clarendon, 1983), pp. 230–231; Gordon, *Hitler, Germans*, pp. 67–71, 82–83; Henry Ashby Turner Jr.,*Hitler's Thirty Days to Power: January 1933* (Reading, Mass.: Addison-Wesley, 1996), pp. 177–178; and Michael R. Marrus, *The Holocaust in History* (New York: Meridian, 1989), pp. 11–13.

16. See Kershaw, *Popular Opinion and Political Dissent*, pp. 274–277; Marrus, *The Holocaust in History*, p. 94; David Bankier, *The Germans and the Final Solution* (Oxford: Basil Blackwell, 1992); Gordon, *Hitler, Germans*, pp. 56, 207–208; Marlis G. Steinert, *Hitler's War and the Germans: Public Mood and Attitude during the Second World War* (Athens: Ohio University Press, 1977), pp. 132–147; Martin Broszat, "The Third Reich and the German People," in Hedley Bull ed., *The Challenge of the Third Reich: The Adam von Trott Memorial Lectures* (Oxford: Clarendon, 1986), pp. 77–94; Otto Dov Kulka, " 'Public Opinion' in Nazi Germany: The Final Solution," in Michael R. Marrus, ed., *The Nazi Holocaust: Historical Articles on the Destruction of the European Jews in Nazi Europe,* vol. 5, *Public Opinion and Relations to the Jews in Nazi Europe,* vol. 1 (Westport, Conn.: Meckler, 1989), pp. 139–150; and Eric H. Johnson, *Nazi Terror: The Gestapo, Jews, and Ordinary Germans* (New York: Basic Books, 1999), pp. 483–484.

17. Saul Friedländer, *Nazi Germany and the Jews,* vol. 1, *The Years of Persecution, 1933–1939* (New York: HarperCollins, 1997), p. 4.

18. Chalmers A. Johnson, *Peasant Nationalism and Communist Power: The Emergence of Revolutionary China, 1937–1945* (Stanford: Stanford University Press, 1962). See also Walter Laqueur, *Guerrilla: A Historical and Critical Study* (Boston: Little, Brown, 1976), pp. 272–273. Similarly, Thomas J. Christensen argues that Mao exploited the 1958 crisis in the Taiwan Straits in an effort to drum up nationalistic support for the Great Leap Forward. See Thomas J. Christensen, *Useful Adversaries: Grand Strategy, Domestic Mobilization and the Sino-American Conflict, 1947–1958* (Princeton: Princeton University Press, 1996), pp. 217–225.

19. Ben Kiernan, *The Pol Pot Regime: Race, Power and Genocide in Cambodia under the Khmer Rouge, 1975–1979* (New Haven: Yale University Press, 1996), pp. 19–25.

20. Karl D. Jackson, "Introduction: The Khmer Rogue in Context," in Karl D. Jackson, ed., *Cambodia 1975–1978: Rendezvous with Death* (Princeton: Princeton University Press, 1989), p. 9. See also Kate G. Frieson, "Revolution and Rural Response in Cambodia: 1970–1975," in Ben Kiernan, ed., *Genocide and Democracy in Cambodia* (New Haven: Yale University Southeast Asia Studies, 1993), pp. 33–50.

21. Tim Judah, *The Serbs: History, Myth and the Destruction of Yugoslavia* (New Haven: Yale University Press, 1997), p. 238.

22. Human Rights Watch, *Leave None to Tell the Story: Genocide in Rwanda* (New York: Human Rights Watch, 1999), pp. 65–85. See also African Rights, *Rwanda: Death, Despair and Defiance,* rev. ed. (London: African Rights, 1995), pp. 69–85; and Bruce D. Jones, *Peacemaking in Rwanda: The Dynamics of Failure* (Boulder: Lynn Rienner, 2001), pp. 35–36.

23. Adam Hochschild, *The Unquiet Ghost: Russians Remember Stalin* (New York: Penguin, 1994), pp. 58–59; and Jasper Becker, *Hungry Ghosts: Mao's Secret Famine* (New York: Free Press, 1996), pp. 285, 309–310.

24. Daniel Jonah Goldhagen, *Hitler's Willing Executioners: Ordinary Germans and the Holocaust* (New York: Knopf, 1996), pp. 164, 167. Goldhagen's estimate is not limited to individuals who took part in acts of actual violence or killing. Goldhagen notes that "it would not be surprising if the number turned out to be five hundred thousand or more" (p. 167). Even this undocumented figure, however, amounts to only about 3 percent of the adult male population in Germany in 1938, or one German perpetrator for every ten to twelve Jewish victims.

25. B. R. Mitchell, *European Historical Statistics: 1750–1975* (New York: Facts on File, 1980), p. 47. The adult population was defined as all individuals between twenty and forty-nine years of age. If Goldhagen's figures include German women and non-German perpetrators, of course, the percentages of participating populations would become even smaller. Approximately three hundred thousand Eastern Europeans were serving in SS-organized police formations tasked with various aspects of policing, "pacification," and the extermination program in late 1942. See Christopher Browning, "The Euphoria of Victory and the Final Solution: Summer–Fall 1941," *German Studies Review* 17, no. 4 (fall 1994): 475.

26. Raul Hilberg, *The Destruction of the European Jews* (New York: Holmes and Meier, 1985), p. 126. Hilberg estimates that over 1,300,000 people were ultimately killed in these operations (p. 338).

27. The estimate for SS guards is from Aleksander Lasik, "Historical-Sociological Profile of the Auschwitz SS," in Yisrael Gutman and Michael Berenbaum, eds., *Anatomy of the Auschwitz Death Camp* (Bloomington: Indiana University Press, 1998), p. 274. Lasik notes that SS guards accounted for 75 percent of camp personnel. As a result of personnel turnover, approximately seven thousand SS men and women served in Auschwitz throughout the war. The estimate of the Auschwitz death toll is from Franciszek Piper, "The Number of Victims," in Gutman and Berenbaum, *Anatomy of Auschwitz,* p. 62.

28. These organizations also forced thousands of Poles, Russians, Jews, and members of other captive or victim groups to help carry out the killing.

29. Michael Burleigh, *Death and Deliverance: "Euthanasia" in Germany 1900–1945* (Cambridge: Cambridge University Press, 1994), pp. 147, 160.

30. Edwin Bacon, *The Gulag at War: Stalin's Forced Labour System in the Light of the Archives* (New York: New York University Press, 1994), p. 178 n. 49.

31. For a detailed discussion of the debate over the Gulag population, see ibid., pp. 23–41.

32. The estimate of Khmer Rouge strength is from William Shawcross, *Sideshow: Kissinger, Nixon and the Destruction of Cambodia* (New York: Simon and Schuster, 1979), p. 373. Elizabeth

Becker estimates that the Khmer Rouge army numbered 68,000 and the party 14,000 in April 1975. See Elizabeth Becker, *When the War Was Over: Cambodia and the Khmer Rouge Revolution* (New York: Public Affairs, 1986), p. 165. For a history of the Khmer Rouge rise to power, see Timothy Carney, "The Unexpected Victory," in Jackson, *Cambodia 1975–1978,* pp. 13–35.

33. Seth Mydans, "Cambodian Killers' Careful Records Used against Them," *New York Times,* June 7, 1996, p. A1.

34. David P. Chandler, *Voices from S-21: Terror and History in Pol Pot's Secret Prison* (Berkeley: University of California Press, 1999), pp. 17–29.

35. Gérard Prunier, *The Rwanda Crisis: History of a Genocide* (New York: Columbia University Press, 1995), pp. 3, 245; Philip Gourevitch, *We wish to inform you that tomorrow we will be killed with our families: Stories from Rwanda* (New York: Farrar, Straus and Giroux, 1998), p. 243; and Human Rights Watch, *Leave None,* pp. 222–223.

36. Quoted in Mahmood Mamdani, *When Victims Become Killers: Colonialism, Nativism, and the Genocide in Rwanda* (Princeton: Princeton University Press, 2001), p. 6. See also Gourevitch, *We wish to inform you,* pp. 244–245.

37. Quoted in Mamdani, *When Victims Become Killers,* p. 7.

38. See Jones, *Peacemaking in Rwanda,* p. 41; and Alan Kuperman, *The Limits of Humanitarian Intervention: Genocide in Rwanda* (Washington, D.C.: Brookings Institution, 2001), pp. 15–16.

39. John Mueller, "The Banality of Ethnic War," *International Security* 25, no. 1 (summer 2000): 61; Prunier, *Rwanda Crisis,* p. 342 n. 60; and Jones, *Peacemaking in Rwanda,* pp. 39–41.

40. Mueller, "Banality of Ethnic War," p. 61. The preliminary findings of a new research project conducted by Scott Straus, including extensive surveys and interviews with perpetrators and survivors of the genocide, suggests roughly similar numbers. Personal communication with author.

41. Mueller, "Banality of Ethnic War," p. 61.

42. Kuperman, *Limits of Humanitarian Intervention,* p. 18.

43. See John P. Sabini and Maury Silver, "Destroying the Innocent with a Clear Conscience: A Sociopsychology of the Holocaust," in Joel E. Dimsdale, ed., *Survivors, Victims, and Perpetrators: Essays on the Nazi Holocaust* (Washington, D.C.: Hemisphere Publishing, 1980), pp. 338–343. For discussions of the various psychological mechanisms that make such behavior possible, see Albert Bandura, "Moral Disengagement and the Perpetration of Inhumanities," *Personality and Social Psychological Review* 3, no. 3 (1999): 193–209; Stanley Milgram, *Obedience to Authority: An Experimental View* (New York: HarperCollins, 1974), p. 122; and W. Kilham and L. Mann, "Level of Destructive Obedience as a Function of Transmitter and Executant Roles in the Milgram Obedience Paradigm," *Journal of Personality and Social Psychology* 29 (1974): 696–702.

44. James J. Sheehan, "National Socialism and German Society: Reflections on Recent Research," *Theory and Society* 13, no. 6 (November 1984): 866–867.

45. On the general problems of collective action, see Mancur Olson, *The Logic of Collective Action: Public Goods and the Theory of Groups* (Cambridge: Harvard University Press, 1965).

46. Kershaw, *Popular Opinion and Political Dissent,* pp. 226–228.

47. For a review of the literature on Jewish resistance, see Marrus, *The Holocaust in History,* pp. 133–155.

48. See Roy F. Baumeister, *Evil: Inside Human Cruelty and Violence* (New York: W. H. Freeman, 1997), pp. 223–237.

49. Roy F. Baumeister and W. Keith Campbell, "The Intrinsic Appeal of Evil: Sadism, Sensational Thrills and Threatened Egoism," *Personality and Social Psychological Review* 3, no. 3 (1999): 210–221.

50. Ibid., pp. 211–213.

51. Dave Grossman, *On Killing: The Psychological Cost of Learning to Kill in War and Society*

(Boston: Little, Brown, 1995), pp. 178–185; and Gwynne Dyer, *War* (New York: Crown Publishers, 1985), pp. 117–118.

52. Joanna Bourke, *An Intimate History of Killing: Face to Face Killing in 20th Century Warfare* (New York: Basic Books, 1999), pp. 18–21; and John Mueller, "Hatred, Violence and Warfare: Thugs as Residual Combatants" (paper presented at the annual meeting of the American Political Science Association, San Francisco, September 2001), pp. 5–6.

53. Released prisoners appear to have been utilized to fill out the ranks of killing organizations in (among other cases) the Armenian genocide of 1915, the former Yugoslavia, and Rwanda in 1994. See Vahakn Dadrian, "The Role of the Special Organization in the Armenian Genocide during the First World War," in Panikos Panayi, ed., *Minorities in Wartime* (Providence: Berg, 1993), p. 58; Susan L. Woodward, *Balkan Tragedy: Chaos and Dissolution after the Cold War* (Washington, D.C.: Brookings Institution, 1995), p. 238; Gourevitch, *We wish to inform you,* p. 242.

54. By way of comparison, roughly two million adults — including more than 2 percent of the total male population between the ages of twenty and thirty-five — were incarcerated in America's prisons and jails at the end of 2000. See *Bureau of Justice Statistics Bulletin: Prisoners in 2000* (Washington, D.C.: U.S. Department of Justice, 2001), pp. 1, 11.

55. See Richard Rhodes, *Masters of Death: The SS Einsatzgruppen and the Invention of the Holocaust* (New York: Alfred Knopf, 2002), pp. 206–214.

56. Mueller, "Banality of Ethnic War," pp. 42–70.

57. Ibid., p. 54. See also David Rieff, *Slaughterhouse: Bosnia and the Failure of the West* (New York: Touchstone, 1996), pp. 131–132.

58. Judah, *Serbs,* p. 233.

59. This pattern of violence was also apparent during the fighting in Kosovo in 1999, see Tim Judah, *Kosovo: War and Revenge* (New Haven: Yale University Press, 2000), pp. 245–246.

60. Mueller, "Banality of Ethnic War," p. 43.

61. Quoted in Rhodes, *Masters of Death,* pp. 152–153. These difficulties led the Nazis to search for more "sanitary" methods of killing, a search that eventually culminated in the development of the gassing/incineration system.

62. Michael Mann, "Were the Perpetrators of Genocide 'Ordinary Men' or 'Real Nazis'? Results from Fifteen Hundred Biographies," *Holocaust and Genocide Studies* 14, no. 3 (winter 2000): 359.

63. John M. Steiner, "The SS Yesterday and Today: A Sociopsychological View," in Joel E. Dimsdale, ed., *Survivors, Victims, and Perpetrators: Essays on the Nazi Holocaust* (Washington, D.C.: Hemisphere Publishing, 1980), pp. 431–434.

64. Quoted in Mueller, "Banality of Ethnic War," p. 49.

65. Quoted in Finkelstein and Birn, *Nation on Trial,* p. 62.

66. Victor Serge, *Memoirs of a Revolutionary, 1901–1941* (London: Oxford University Press, 1963), p. 80.

67. Charles W. Sydnor Jr., *Soldiers of Destruction: The SS Death's Head Division, 1933–1945* (Princeton: Princeton University Press, 1977), pp. 14–19.

68. Ibid., pp. 16–17.

69. Ibid., p. 17.

70. Browning, *Ordinary Men,* pp. 164–169.

71. See Milgram, *Obedience to Authority.* For excellent reviews of Milgram's findings and related research, see Arthur G. Miller, *The Obedience Experiments: A Case Study of Controversy in Social Science* (New York: Praeger, 1986); and Alan Elms, "Obedience in Retrospect," *Journal of Social Issues* 51, no. 3 (fall 1995): 26.

72. See Miller, *The Obedience Experiments,* pp. 67–87; W. H. J. Meeus and Q. A. W. Raaijmakers, "Obedience in Modern Society: The Utrecht Studies," *Journal of Social Issues* 52, no. 3 (fall 1995):

155–175; and Kenneth Ring, Kenneth A. Wallston, and Michael Cory, "Mode of Debriefing as a Factor Affecting Subjective Reactions to a Milgram-Type Experiment: An Ethical Inquiry," *Representative Research in Social Psychology* 1 (1970): 67–85.

73. See Lee D. Ross, "Situationist Perspectives on the Obedience Experiments," *Contemporary Psychology* 33, no. 2 (1988): 101–104; Lee Ross and Richard Nisbet, *The Person and the Situation: Perspectives of Social Psychology* (Philadelphia: Temple University Press, 1991), esp. pp. 52–58; and Phillip Zimbardo, "The Psychology of Evil: A Situationist Perspective on Recruiting Good People to Engage in Anti-Social Acts," *Research in Social Psychology* 11, no. 2 (1995): 125–133.

74. Philip Zimbardo et al., "The Psychology of Imprisonment: Privation, Power and Pathology," in David L. Rosenhan and Perry London, eds., *Theory and Research in Abnormal Psychology,* 2d ed. (New York: Holt, Rinehart and Winston, 1975), pp. 270–287. For a study replicating Zimbardo's results, see S. H. Lovibond, M. Adams, and W. G. Adams, "The Effects of Three Experimental Prison Environments on the Behavior of Nonconflict Volunteer Subjects," *Australian Psychologist* 14 (1979): 273–285.

75. Zimbardo et al., "Psychology of Imprisonment," pp. 270–287.

76. See Elms, "Obedience in Retrospect," p. 30.

77. Dyer, *War,* pp. 102–129.

78. Milgram did perform a variation of his basic experiment in which he found that when two "peers" (actually confederates of the experiment) were present and *refused* to obey orders to administer the shock, only 10 percent of subjects continued to obey the experimenter to the maximum voltage level. When the two peers obediently followed the experimenter's instructions, 72.5 percent of the subjects proved willing to administer the highest level of shock—not significantly higher than the 65 percent compliance in the baseline experiment with no peers present. Milgram did not attempt to test the effect of peer pressure independently of the effects of authority. See Miller, *Obedience Experiments,* pp. 58–65. In both variations of the experiment, however, the "peers" were introduced to the subject only minutes before the experiment began. In real-world situations in which peers have well-established relationships, it seems likely that the effects of peer pressure, both positive and negative, would be much greater.

79. Browning, *Ordinary Men,* pp. 184–186. For a further argument stressing the power of situational factors over anti-Semitism, see Jürgen Matthäus, "What about the 'Ordinary Men'? The German Order Police and the Holocaust in the Occupied Soviet Union," *Holocaust and Genocide Studies* 10, no. 2 (fall 1996): 134–150.

80. Miller, *Obedience Experiments,* p. 203.

81. See Goldhagen, *Hitler's Willing Executioners*; and James M. Glass, *Life Unworthy of Life: Racial Phobia and Mass Murder in Hitler's Germany* (New York: Basic Books, 1997). Thomas Blass argues that a combination of situational and ideological convictions motivated most perpetrators of the Holocaust. See "Psychological Perspectives on the Perpetrators of the Holocaust: The Role of Situational Pressures, Personal Dispositions, and their Interaction," *Holocaust and Genocide Studies* 7, no. 1 (spring 1993): 30–50.

82. Goldhagen, *Hitler's Willing Executioners,* pp. 393, 185, 402; italics in original.

83. Milgram, *Obedience to Authority,* p. 10. See also Ross, "Situationist Perspectives," p. 103.

84. Browning acknowledges that most perpetrators he studied expressed their revulsion to the killing in physical rather than ethical terms, but he also notes that "given the educational level of these reserve policemen, one should not expect a sophisticated articulation of abstract principles. The absence of such does not mean that their revulsion did not have its origins in the humane instincts that Nazism radically opposed and sought to overcome." See Browning, *Ordinary Men,* p. 74.

85. See Omer Bartov, *Hitler's Army: Soldiers, Nazis and War in the Third Reich* (Oxford: Oxford University Press, 1991), pp. 147–178.

86. Quoted in Ernst Klee, Willi Dressen, and Volker Riess, eds., *"The Good Old Days": The Holocaust as Seen by Its Perpetrators and Bystanders* (New York: Konecky and Konecky, 1988), pp. 168–171.

87. See Goldhagen, *Hitler's Willing Executioners,* pp. 385–389; Blass, "Psychological Perspectives," pp. 35–37; and Klee, Dressen, and Riess, "Good Old Days," esp. pp. 1–135.

88. Browning, *Ordinary Men,* pp. 170–171; Klee, Dressen, and Riess, "Good Old Days," pp. 76–86; and Goldhagen, *Hitler's Willing Executioners,* pp. 379–381.

89. Goldhagen, *Hitler's Willing Executioners,* p. 385.

90. Browning, *Ordinary Men,* pp. 55–77.

91. Christopher R. Browning, *Nazi Policy, Jewish Workers, German Killers* (Cambridge: Cambridge University Press, 2000), pp. 155–156.

92. Matthäus, "What about the 'Ordinary Men'?" pp. 144–145.

93. Milgram, *Obedience to Authority,* p. 10.

94. Albert Bandura, Bill Underwood, and Michael E. Fromson, "Disinhibition of Aggression through Diffusion of Responsibility and Dehumanization of Victims," *Journal of Research in Personality* 9, no. 4 (December 1975): 253–269. Of course, unbeknown to the subjects (as in the Milgram experiments) no actual shocks were delivered.

95. On the role of dehumanizing propaganda in military units and society during war, see Sam Keen, *Faces of the Enemy: Reflections of the Hostile Imagination* (New York: HarperCollins, 1991), esp. pp. 24–26.

96. Bartov, *Hitler's Army,* p. 147.

97. Ibid.

98. Ibid., pp. 118, 144.

99. Browning, *Ordinary Men,* p. 186.

100. For example, see Finkelstein and Birn, *Nation on Trial,* pp. 53–54; and Ian Kershaw, "German Public Opinion during the Final Solution: Information, Comprehension, Reactions," in Asher Cohen et al., *Comprehending the Holocaust* (Frankfurt am Main: Verlag Peter Lang, 1988), pp. 146–147.

101. See Michael Berenbaum, ed., *A Mosaic of Victims: Non-Jews Persecuted and Murdered by the Nazis* (New York: New York University Press, 1990); and Christopher R. Browning, "Ordinary Germans or Ordinary Men? A Reply to the Critics," in Michael Berenbaum and Abraham J. Peck, eds., *The Holocaust and History: The Known, the Unknown, the Disputed, and the Reexamined* (Bloomington: Indiana University Press, 1998), pp. 252–265.

102. Mark Mazower, "Military Violence and National Socialist Values: The Wehrmacht in Greece 1941–1944," *Past and Present,* no. 134 (February 1992): 129–158.

103. Quoted in ibid., p. 130.

104. Quoted in ibid., p. 131. It is difficult to judge the sincerity of these statements, since they were given in the context of an inquiry conducted thirty years after the event. The former soldiers may well have been trying to diminish the extent of their own responsibility. Mazower suggests, however, that there may be substantial truth to the statements since the former soldiers voluntarily admitted much incriminating evidence and since the investigation never resulted in a trial. In any case, what is most relevant for this discussion is that Germans agreed to kill Greek civilians against whom they held no preexisting prejudices.

105. Quoted in ibid., p. 131.

106. Martin Gilbert, *The Second World War: A Complete History,* rev. ed. (New York: Henry Holt, 1989), p. 537.

107. Michael Geyer, "Civitella Della Chiana on 29 June 1944: The Reconstruction of a German 'Measure,'" in Hannes Heer and Klaus Naumann, eds., *War of Extermination: The German Military in World War II, 1941–1944* (New York: Berghahn Books, 2000), p. 184.

108. See ibid.; and Gilbert, *Second World War*, pp. 461–462, 475.

109. Bartov, *Hitler's Army*, pp. 90–94. See also Geyer, "Civitella Della Chiana," pp. 199–204; Richard Overy, *Russia's War: A History of the Soviet War Effort, 1941–1945* (New York: Penguin, 1997), p. 144; and Alexander Dallin, *German Rule in Russia 1941–1945*, 2d, rev. ed. (Boulder: Westview, 1981), pp. 74–76.

110. See Matthäus, "What about the 'Ordinary Men'?" pp. 143–144; and Browning, *Nazi Policy*, pp. 152–154, 167.

111. Quoted in Matthäus, "What about the 'Ordinary Men'?" p. 144.

112. Hannes Heer, "Killing Fields: The Wehrmacht and the Holocaust in Byelorussia, 1941–42," in Heer and Naumann, *War of Extermination*, pp. 64–68; Christian Streit, "The German Army and the Policies of Genocide," in Gerhard Hirschfeld, ed., *The Policies of Genocide* (London: German Historical Institute, 1986), p. 9; Christopher R. Browning, *Fateful Months: Essay on the Emergence of the Final Solution* (New York: Holmes and Meier, 1985), pp. 39–56; and Bartov, *Hitler's Army*, pp. 89–95.

113. Browning, *Fateful Months*, p. 49.

114. Goldhagen, *Hitler's Willing Executioners*, p. 402.

115. For a critique of the evidentiary basis for this aspect of Goldhagen's thesis, see Finkelstein and Birn, *Nation on Trial*, pp. 67–75.

116. Ibid., p. 67.

117. Quoted in ibid.

118. See Browning, *Ordinary Men*, p. 168; and Browning, *Nazi Policy*, p. 166. For a similar estimate, see Matthäus, "What about the 'Ordinary Men'?" p. 141.

119. Browning, *Ordinary Men*, p. 168.

120. Nor can the threat of punishment explain the behavior of subjects in Milgram's experiment, since Milgram never threatened them with any form of punishment for noncompliance.

121. Browning, *Ordinary Men*, p. 168.

122. Mazower, "Military Violence," p. 155.

123. Ibid.

124. See Max Hastings, *Das Reich: The March of the 2nd SS Panzer Division through France* (New York: Holt, Rinehart and Winston, 1981); and Gilbert, *Second World War*, p. 550.

125. Nikolaus Wachsmann, "Annihilation through Labor: The Killing of State Prisoners in the Third Reich," *Journal of Modern History* 71 (September 1999): 650–652.

126. See Baumeister, *Evil*, pp. 223–237.

127. Milgram, *Obedience to Authority*, p. 9.

128. Note that this process of brutalization does not explain why the men participated in the killing in the first place, but it may explain why some killed with gratuitous brutality.

129. Browning, *Nazi Policy*, p. 169.

130. Goldhagen, *Hitler's Willing Executioners*, pp. 14–15.

131. Chandler, *Voices from S-21*, pp. 143–155.

132. Ibid., p. 34.

133. Quoted in Laqueur, *Guerrilla*, p. 272.

134. Chandler, *Voices from S-21*, p. 147. On anti-Vietnamese prejudices, see Kiernan, *Pol Pot Regime*.

135. David P. Chandler, *Brother Number One: A Political Biography of Pot* (Boulder: Westview, 1992), p. 108; and Karl D. Jackson, "The Ideology of Total Revolution," in Jackson, *Cambodia 1975–1979*, pp. 37–78.

136. David P. Chandler, *The Tragedy of Cambodian History* (New Haven: Yale University Press, 1991), p. 253.

137. Prunier, *Rwanda Crisis*, pp. 247, 232.

138. See Human Rights Watch, *Leave None*, pp. 65–85; and African Rights, *Rwanda*, pp. 69–85.

139. Helen M. Hintjens, "Explaining the 1994 Genocide in Rwanda," *Journal of Modern African Studies* 37, no. 2 (1999): 248.

140. African Rights, *Rwanda*, pp. 993–1002.

141. Ibid., pp. 994, 999.

142. Jones, *Peacemaking in Rwanda*, p. 38.

143. Psychological experiments have also found evidence that individuals are willing to engage in acts that are potentially dangerous and painful to themselves when ordered to do so by authority figures. See Miller, *Obedience Experiments*, pp. 78–80.

144. See Richard Holmes, *Acts of War: The Behavior of Men in Battle* (New York: Free Press, 1985), pp. 270–359; Anthony Kellett, *Combat Motivation: The Behavior of Soldiers in Battle* (Boston: Kluwer, 1982), pp. 167–213; E. A. Shils and Morris Janowitz, "Cohesion and Disintegration in the Wehrmacht in World War II," *Public Opinion Quarterly* 12, no. 2 (summer 1948): 280–315; and S. L. A. Marshall, *Men against Fire* (New York: William Morrow, 1947).

145. See Bartov, *Hitler's Army*.

146. Dyer, *War*, p. 104. Dyer finds that small-group dynamics are the most important among these motives.

147. Quoted in Holmes, *Acts of War*, p. 286.

148. John Keegan, *The Face of Battle: A Study of Agincourt, Waterloo and the Somme* (New York: Penguin, 1976), p. 260.

149. Quoted in Tim Travers, *The Killing Ground: The British Army, the Western Front and the Emergence of Modern Warfare, 1900–1918* (London: Allen and Unwin, 1987), p. 158.

150. Quoted in Lyn Macdonald, *Somme* (London: Michael Joseph, 1983), p. 157.

151. Ibid., p. 260.

152. See Lee Ross, "The Intuitive Psychologist and His Shortcomings," in Leonard Berkowitz, ed., *Advances in Experimental Psychology*, vol. 10 (New York: Academic, 1977); and Ross and Nisbet, *Person and Situation*.

153. See Sabini and Silver, "Destroying the Innocent," pp. 338–343. On the psychological tendency to conflate the explanation of an act with the condoning of it, see Arthur G. Miller, Anne K. Gordon, and Amy M. Buddie, "Accounting for Evil and Cruelty: Is to Explain to Condone?" *Personality and Social Psychological Review* 3, no. 3 (1999): 254–268.

154. On the power of individual leaders to shape world events more generally, see Daniel L. Byman and Kenneth M. Pollack, "Let Us Now Praise Great Men: Bringing the Statesman Back In," *International Security* 25, no. 4 (spring 2001): 107–146.

155. Milton Himmelfarb, "No Hitler, No Holocaust," *Commentary* 77, no. 3 (March 1984): 37–43. On support among other scholars for Himmelfarb's thesis, see Ron Rosenbaum, *Explaining Hitler: The Search for the Origins of His Evil* (New York: Random House, 1998), esp. pp. 281–282, 292.

156. Marrus, *The Holocaust in History*, pp. 17–18. As noted above, the willingness of Germans to murder millions of non-Jewish victims casts doubt onto whether anti-Semitism, at least unusually severe anti-Semitism, was even a necessary condition for the Holocaust.

157. Robert Conquest, *The Great Terror: A Reassessment* (Oxford: Oxford University Press, 1990), pp. 53, 70. See also Robert C. Tucker, *Stalin in Power: The Revolution from Above, 1928–1941* (New York: Norton, 1992); and Dimitri Volkogonov, *Stalin: Triumph and Tragedy* (New York: Grove Wiedenfeld, 1988), pp. 308–309. Other scholars have questioned the degree of Stalin's premeditation and control over the Terror and have suggested that certain segments of the Soviet elite may have voluntarily supported it, at least initially. Even in these accounts, however, the original impulse for the Terror rests with a small group of powerful political leaders, and Stalin remains the

single most important figure behind it. See J. Arch Getty and Oleg V. Naumov, *The Road to Terror: Stalin and the Self-Destruction of the Bolsheviks, 1932–1939* (New Haven: Yale University Press, 1999), esp. pp. 569–586.

158. Harry Harding, "The Chinese State in Crisis, 1966–9," in Roderick MacFarquhar, ed., *The Politics of China* (New York: Cambridge University Press, 1993), p. 235. Harding notes that Mao was a necessary but not a sufficient condition for the Cultural Revolution. See also Roderick MacFarquhar, *The Origins of the Cultural Revolution*: vol. 3, *The Coming of the Cataclysm, 1961–1966* (New York: Columbia University Press, 1997), esp. pp. 466–473.

159. Prunier, *Rwanda Crisis,* pp. 142, 242. See also Human Rights Watch, *Leave None,* pp. xvii–xx, 44–45; and Human Rights Watch, *Slaughter among Neighbors: The Political Origins of Communal Violence* (New Haven: Yale University Press, 1995), p. 23.

160. Filip Reyntjens cited in Jones, *Peacemaking in Rwanda,* p. 39.

161. Quoted in Richard Pipes, *Three "Whys" of the Russian Revolution* (New York: Vintage, 1997), p. 32; italics in original. According to Pipes, neither Lenin nor Trotsky "ever claimed . . . that the Bolsheviks emerged victorious because they had the masses behind them" (pp. 31–32). For a similar statement made by Lenin in 1922 referring to the early Communist Party as "a minuscule handful of people" and "a negligible kernel," see Dimitri Volkogonov, *The Rise and Fall of the Soviet Empire: Political Leaders from Lenin to Gorbachev* (London: HarperCollins, 1998), p. 71.

162. See Eberhard Jäckel, *Hitler's World View: A Blueprint for Power* (Cambridge: Harvard University Press, 1972), pp. 82–83.

163. Quoted in David Irving, *Hitler's War* (New York: Avon Books, 1990), p. 31.

164. Quoted in Ronald Grigor Suny, *Looking toward Ararat: Armenia in Modern History* (Bloomington: Indiana University Press, 1993), p. 113.

165. Turner, *Hitler's Thirty Days to Power,* esp. pp. 163–183.

166. Ibid., pp. 172–176. See also Henry Ashby Turner, "Hitler's Impact on History," in David Wetzel, ed., *From the Berlin Museum to the Berlin Wall* (Westport, Conn.: Praeger, 1996), pp. 109–126.

167. Kenneth M. Quinn, "The Pattern and Scope of Violence," in Jackson, *Cambodia 1975–1978,* p. 181.

168. See Human Rights Watch, *Leave None,* pp. 141–179.

169. Samantha Power, *A Problem from Hell: America and the Age of Genocide* (New York: Basic Books, 2002), pp. 329–389; and Prunier, *Rwanda Crisis,* p. 169.

170. Michael Barnett, *Eyewitness to Genocide: The United Nations and Rwanda* (Ithaca, N.Y.: Cornell University Press, 2002), p. 156.

171. This also appears to have occurred in Rwanda. See Kuperman, *Limits of Humanitarian Intervention,* pp. 104–105.

3. The Strategic Logic of Mass Killing

For a discussion of the definition of terrorism see Bruce Hoffman, *Inside Terrorism* (New York: Columbia University Press, 1998), pp. 13–44.

This definition is similar to the one suggested by Caleb Carr: "terrorism is simply the contemporary name given to . . . warfare deliberately waged against civilizns with the purpose of destroying their will to support either leaders or policies that the agents of such violence find objectionable." Caleb Carr, *The Lessons of Terror: A History of Warfare against Civilians* (New York: Random House, 2002), p. 6.

1. Peter du Preez, *Genocide: The Psychology of Mass Murder* (London: Boyars/Bowerdean, 1994), p. 3.

2. Roger W. Smith, "State Power and Genocidal Intent: On the Uses of Genocide in the Twen-

tieth Century," in Levon Chorbajian and George Shirinian, eds., *Studies in Comparative Genocide* (New York: St. Martin's, 1999), pp. 3–14.

3. In addition to du Preez and Smith, see Frank Chalk and Kurt Jonassohn, *The History and Sociology of Genocide* (New Haven: Yale University Press, 1990), pp. 29–40; and Barbara Harff and Ted Robert Gurr, "Toward an Empirical Theory of Genocides and Politicides," *International Studies Quarterly*, no. 32 (1988): 363.

4. Helen Fein, "Accounting for Genocide after 1945: Theories and Some Findings," *International Journal on Group Rights* 1 (1993): 88–92.

5. Nor does Fein attempt to explain why severe discrimination leads to rebellion in some cases but not others.

6. See Chalk and Jonassohn, *History and Sociology of Genocide*, pp. 37–40; Helen Fein, "Revolutionary and Antirevolutionary Genocides: A Comparison of State Murders in Democratic Kampuchea, 1975–1979, and in Indonesia, 1965–1966," *Comparative Studies in Society and History* 35, no. 4 (October 1993): 796–823; du Preez, *Genocide*, pp. 28–47; and George A. Lopez, "National Security Ideology as an Impetus to State Violence and State Terror," in Michael Stohl and George A. Lopez, eds., *Government Violence and Repression* (New York: Greenwood, 1986), pp. 73–95.

7. Settler colonies should be distinguished from imperial possessions. Settler colonies are territories intended to be permanently inhabited by large numbers of people from the colonizing state. Imperial possessions are not densely settled. Rather, subjects of empire are required to provide goods and services for the empire. Empires have also been frequent perpetrators of mass killing, although for very different reasons that will be described below.

8. Between 4,000 and 8,000 of 17,000 Cherokees died during the 1,200-mile forced march to Oklahoma. See David E. Stannard, *American Holocaust: The Conquest of the New World* (Oxford: Oxford University Press, 1992), pp. 122–125.

9. In many instances, the ravages of European diseases so decimated native populations that settlers were capable of expropriating native lands without resorting to mass killing. See William H. McNeill, *Plagues and Peoples* (Garden City: Doubleday, 1976), pp. 176–207; Alfred W. Crosby Jr., *The Colombian Exchange: The Biological and Cultural Consequences of 1492* (Westport, Conn.: Greenwood, 1972), pp. 35–65; Thornton Russell, *American Indian Holocaust and Survival: A Population History since 1492* (Norman: University of Oklahoma Press, 1987), pp. 44–47; and Jared Diamond, *Guns, Germs and Steel: The Fates of Human Societies* (New York: Norton, 1997), pp. 210–214.

10. Stannard, *American Holocaust*, p. 246.

11. The relationship between the French and Native Americans in these two colonies is described in Gary B. Nash, *Red, White, and Black: The Peoples of Early America* (Englewood Cliffs, N.J.: Prentice Hall, 1974), pp. 99–109. Nash asserts that the nature of the economic relationship between Native Americans and colonists was also a major determinant of Native American survival elsewhere in America (pp. 67, 87, 92). See also Chalk and Jonassohn, *History and Sociology of Genocide*, pp. 173–193. For similar arguments regarding the importance of the economic relationships between colonists and indigenous people, see Wilbur R. Jacobs, "The Fatal Confrontation: Early Native-White Relations on the Frontiers of Australia, New Guinea, and America — a Comparative Study," *Pacific Historical Review* 40, no. 3 (1971): 306–307; and Paula Mitchell Marks, *In a Barren Land: American Indian Dispossession and Survival* (New York: William and Morrow, 1998), pp. 2–4.

12. As with most individual Native American tribes, the Natchez population was too small to qualify as a mass killing as defined in this book. This example is intended to illustrate the motives behind numerous instances of violence against Native Americans, which, when considered together, account for a much higher death toll.

13. On the German resettlement program during the war, see Götz Aly, *Final Solution: Nazi*

Population Policy and the Murder of the European Jews (London: Arnold, 1999); and Anna C. Bramwell, "The Re-Settlement of Ethnic Germans, 1939–41," in Michael R. Marrus and Anna C. Bramwell, eds., *Refugees in the Age of Total War* (London: Unwin Hyman, 1988), pp. 112–132.

14. Quoted in Ian Kershaw, *Hitler, 1936–1945: Nemesis* (New York: W. W. Norton, 2000), p. 246.

15. Michael R. Marrus, *The Unwanted: European Refugees in the Twentieth Century* (Oxford: Oxford University Press, 1985), pp. 225–226.

16. Richard C. Lukas, *The Forgotten Holocaust: Poles under German Occupation* (Lexington: University Press of Kentucky, 1986), p. 38. Roughly half of these victims were Jews who were killed not because they occupied German living space but as part of the Final Solution. For more on the fate of Poland during the war, see Norman Davies, *God's Playground: A History of Poland,* vol. 2, *1795 to the Present* (New York: Columbia University Press, 1982), pp. 435–491.

17. On the decreasing value of territory for national security, see Stephen Van Evera, "Primed for Peace: Europe after the Cold War," *International Security* 15, no. 3 (winter 1990/91): 7–57; Richard Rosecrance, *The Rise of the Virtual State: Wealth and Power in the Coming Century* (New York: Basic Books, 1999); and Carl Kaysen, "Is War Obsolete? A Review Essay," *International Security* 14, no. 4. (spring 1990): 42–64.

18. On the distinction between coercion and the "brute force" use of violence, see Thomas Schelling, *Arms and Influence* (New Haven: Yale University Press, 1966), pp. 2–18.

19. Mao Tse-Tung, *On Guerrilla Warfare,* trans. Samuel B. Griffith (New York: Praeger, 1961), pp. 44, 92–93.

20. For a discussion of the definition of terrorism see Bruce Hoffman, *Inside Terrorism* (New York: Columbia University Press, 1998), pp. 13–44.

21. This definition is similar to the one suggested by Caleb Carr: "terrorism is simply the contemporary name given to . . . warfare deliberately waged against civilians with the purpose of destroying their will to support either leaders or policies that the agents of such violence find objectionable." Caleb Carr, *The Lessons of Terror: A History of Warfare against Civilians* (New York: Random House, 2002), p. 6.

22. See Robert A. Pape, *Bombing to Win: Air Power and Coercion in War* (Ithaca, N.Y.: Cornell University Press, 1996), p. 269.

23. Quoted in ibid., p. 261.

24. Quoted in Ronald Schaffer, *Wings of Judgment: American Bombing in World War II* (Oxford: Oxford University Press, 1985), p. 36.

25. Ibid., p. 270.

26. See David Irving, *The Destruction of Dresden* (New York: Ballantine, 1965), p. 76, Anthony Verrier, *The Bomber Offensive* (London: B. T. Batsford, 1968), p. 301; and Michael Sherry, *The Rise of American Air Power* (New Haven: Yale University Press, 1987), p. 154.

27. Quoted in Sherry, *Rise of American Air Power,* p. 154.

28. Ibid., p. 260.

29. For more on the political and military use of famine, see Kurt Jonassohn, "Famine, Genocide and Refugees," *Society* 30, no. 6 (September/October 1993) pp. 73–74; John Mueller and Karl Mueller, "The Methodology of Mass Destruction: Assessing Threats in the New World Order," *Journal of Strategic Studies* 23, no. 1 (March 2000): 163–187; David Keen, *The Benefits of Famine: A Political Economy of Famine and Relief in Southwestern Sudan, 1983–1989* (Princeton: Princeton University Press, 1994); Jean Mayer, "Time to Ban the Use of Starvation as a Weapon of War," *Christian Science Monitor,* December 24, 1984, p. 12; and Karl Zinsmeister, "All the Hungry People," *Reason* 20, no. 2 (June 1988): 22–30.

30. Martin Gilbert, *The First World War* (New York: Henry Holt, 1994), p. 391. William Eckhardt estimates that eight hundred thousand civilians died as a result of blockade from 1914 to 1918. See "Civilian Deaths in Wartime," *Bulletin of Peace Proposals* 20 no. 1 (1989): 95.

31. John de St. Jorre, *The Brothers' War: Biafra and Nigeria* (Boston: Houghton Mifflin, 1972), p. 412; and Dan Jacobs, The Brutality of Nations (New York: Paragon House, 1988).

32. Alistair Horne, *A Savage War of Peace: Algeria 1954–1962* (New York: Viking, 1977), p. 538. On the strategic use of terror by Islamist guerrillas in Algeria in the 1990s, see Stathis N. Kalyvas, "Wanton and Senseless? The Logic of Massacres in Algeria," *Rationality and Society* 11, no. 3 (1999): 243–285.

33. See Guenter Lewy, *America in Vietnam* (New York: Oxford University Press, 1978), pp. 272–279; and Douglas Pike, *The Viet-Cong Strategy of Terror* (Saigon: United States Mission to Viet-Nam, 1970).

34. See Pape, *Bombing to Win*, 24–27.

35. On the other hand, some terrorist groups seem to have actively sought to provoke violent repression by the state in the hopes that this response will encourage the population to join the resistance. See Richard E. Rubenstein, *Alchemists of Revolution: Terrorism in the Modern World* (New York: Basic Books, 1987), pp. 90, 96–100.

36. For a similar argument, see Kurt Jonassohn and Frank Chalk, "A Typology of Genocide and Some Implications for the Human Rights Agenda," in Isidor Wallimann and Michael Dobkowski, eds., *Genocide and the Modern Age* (New York: Greenwood, 1987), pp. 13–14.

37. Paul Ratchnevsky, *Genghis Khan: His Life and Legacy* (Oxford: Basil Blackwell, 1991), pp. 160, 173.

38. Iris Chang, *The Rape of Nanking: The Forgotten Holocaust of World War II* (New York: Basic Books, 1997).

39. John Dower, *War without Mercy: Race and Power in the Pacific War* (New York: Pantheon Books, 1986).

40. Callum MacDonald, " 'Kill All, Burn All, Loot All': The Nanking Massacres of December 1937 and Japanese Policy in China," in Mark Levene and Penny Roberts eds., *The Massacre in History* (New York: Berghahn Books, 1999), pp. 223–245.

4. Communist Mass Killings

1. Rudolph J. Rummel, *Death by Government* (New Brunswick, N.J.: Transaction Publishers, 1994), p. 15. A team of six French historians coordinated by Stéphane Courtois estimates that communist regimes are responsible for between 85 and 100 million deaths. See Martin Malia, "Foreword: The Uses of Atrocity," in Stéphane Courtois et al., *The Black Book of Communism: Crimes, Terror, Repression* (Cambridge: Harvard University Press, 1999), p. x. Zbigniew Brzezinski estimates that "the failed effort to build communism" cost the lives of almost sixty million people. See Zbigniew Brzezinski, *Out of Control: Global Turmoil on the Eve of the Twenty-First Century* (New York: Charles Scribner's Sons, 1993), p. 16. Matthew White estimates eighty-one million deaths from communist "genocide and tyranny" and "man-made famine." See Matthew White, "Historical Atlas of the Twentieth Century," http://users.erols.com/mwhite28/warstat8.htm [June 2002]. Todd Culbertson estimates that communist regimes killed "perhaps 100 million" people. See Todd Culbertson, "The Human Cost of World Communism," *Human Events,* August 19, 1978, pp. 10–11. These estimates should be considered at the highest end of the plausible range of deaths attributable to communist regimes.

2. Author's estimate based on numerous sources. Estimates vary widely regarding both how many people died and how many deaths were intentional. See table 2.

3. Relatively high estimates of mass killings by these smaller communist states can be found in Rudolph Rummel, *Statistics of Democide: Genocide and Mass Murder since 1900* (Charlottesville: Center for National Security Law, 1997). See also Courtois et al., *Black Book of Communism*.

4. See James C. Scott, *Seeing like a State: How Certain Schemes to Improve the Human Condition Have Failed* (New Haven: Yale University Press, 1998); Robert Conquest, *Reflections on a Ravaged*

Century (New York: W. W. Norton, 2000); and Richard Pipes, *Communism: A History* (New York: Modern Library, 2001).

5. Isaiah Berlin, "On the Pursuit of the Ideal," *New York Review of Books,* March 17, 1988, pp. 11–18.

6. The main exceptions to this pattern have been regimes fighting significant internal guerrilla insurgencies. I discuss mass killing by these regimes in chapter 5.

7. See Mikhail Heller, *Cogs in the Wheel: The Formation of Soviet Man* (New York: Alfred A. Knopf, 1988); Orlando Figes, *A People's Tragedy: A History of the Russian Revolution* (New York: Viking Penguin, 1997), pp. 732–751; Karl D. Jackson, "The Ideology of Total Revolution," in Karl D. Jackson, ed., *Cambodia 1975–1978: Rendezvous with Death* (Princeton: Princeton University Press, 1989), pp. 66–78; and Kenneth M. Quinn, "The Pattern and Scope of Violence," in Jackson, *Cambodia 1975–1978,* pp. 189–194.

8. Alec Nove, "Victims of Stalinism: How Many?" in J. Arch Getty and Roberta T. Manning, eds., *Stalinist Terror: New Perspectives* (Cambridge: Cambridge University Press, 1993), p. 266; Jasper Becker, *Hungry Ghosts* (New York: Free Press, 1996), pp. 270–274; and Jean-Louis Margolin, "Cambodia: The Country of Disconcerting Crimes," in Courtois et al., *Black Book of Communism,* p. 591.

9. Niccolò Machiavelli, *The Prince* (London: Penguin Books, 1961), pp. 51–52.

10. Quoted in Stéphane Courtois, "Conclusion: Why?" in Courtois et al., *Black Book of Communism,* p. 749.

11. Alexander Dallin and George W. Breslauer, *Political Terror in Communist Systems* (Stanford: Stanford University Press, 1970), p. 6. For similar arguments, see Richard Pipes, *Communism,* p. 149; and Jonathan R. Adelman, "The Development of the Secret Police in Communist States," in Timothy Bushnell et al., eds., *State Organized Terror: The Case of Violent Internal Repression* (Boulder: Westview, 1991), pp. 106–107.

12. Leon Trotsky, *Terrorism and Communism: A Reply to Karl Kautsky* (Ann Arbor: University of Michigan Press, 1961), p. 58.

13. See David Zweig, *Agrarian Radicalism in China, 1968–1981* (Cambridge: Harvard University Press, 1989), pp. 44–45.

14. Quoted in Eugene Kamenka, ed., *The Portable Karl Marx* (New York: Penguin Books, 1983), p. 182.

15. See Conquest, *Harvest of Sorrow,* p. 120; and Courtois, "Conclusion: Why?" pp. 747–753.

16. Joseph V. Stalin, *Selected Works* (Davis, Calif.: Cardinal Publishers, 1971), pp. 257–258.

17. Quoted in George Leggett, *The Cheka: Lenin's Political Police* (Oxford: Clarendon, 1981), p. 114. See also Heller, *Cogs in the Wheel,* pp. 20–21, 95–97.

18. See Stephen Heder, "Class, Nationality and Race in Communist Crimes against Humanity: Theoretical and Historical Reflections on Marxist Racism and Violence," in Alexandre Kimenyi and Otis L. Scott, eds., *Anatomy of Genocide: State Sponsored Mass-Killing in the Twentieth Century* (Lewiston: Edwin Mellen, 2001), pp. 129–185.

19. For more on the political origins of modern famines, see Amartya Sen, *Poverty and Famines: An Essay on Entitlement and Deprivation* (Oxford: Oxford University Press, 1981); Karl Zinsmeister, "All the Hungry People," *Reason* 20, no. 2 (June 1988): 22–30; Kurt Jonassohn, "Famine, Genocide and Refugees," *Society* 30, no. 6 (September/October 1993): 72–76; Sylvia Nasar, "It's Never Fair to Just Blame the Weather," *New York Times,* January 17, 1993, p. E9; and Rone Tempest, "The Coexistence of Feast, Famine," *Los Angeles Times,* December 22, 1997, p. A1.

20. See Dimitri Volkogonov, *Stalin: Triumph and Tragedy* (New York: Grove Wiedenfeld, 1988), pp. 317–318; Felix Chuev and Albert Resis, eds., *Molotov Remembers: Inside Kremlin Politics* (Chicago: Ivan R. Dee, 1993), pp. 324–327; Robert C. Tucker, *Stalin in Power: The Revolution from Above, 1928–1941* (New York: W. W. Norton, 1992); pp. 475–480; Andrew G. Walder, "Cultural

Revolution Radicalism: Variations on a Stalinist Theme," in William A. Joseph, Christine P. W. Wong, and David Zweig, eds., *New Perspectives on the Cultural Revolution* (Cambridge: Council on East Asian Studies, Harvard University: 1991), pp. 41–61; Zhisui Li, *The Private Life of Chairman Mao* (New York: Random House, 1994), pp. 200–202, 232–234, 369; and David Chandler, *Brother Number One: A Political Biography of Pot* (Boulder: Westview Press, 1992), pp. 139, 156–157.

21. Figes, *A People's Tragedy*, p. 729.

22. See Conquest, *Harvest of Sorrow*, pp. 19–21.

23. See Silvana Malle, *The Economic Organization of War Communism, 1918–1921* (Cambridge: Cambridge University Press, 1985).

24. Figes, *A People's Tragedy*, pp. 617–622; and Conquest, *Harvest of Sorrow*, p. 45.

25. See Conquest, *Harvest of Sorrow*, p. 53.

26. Figes, *A People's Tragedy*, pp. 618–619; Conquest, *Harvest of Sorrow*, pp. 46–49; and Richard Pipes, *The Russian Revolution* (New York: Random House, 1990), pp. 721–738.

27. Pipes, *Russian Revolution*, pp. 736–737.

28. Orlando Figes, *Peasant Russia, Civil War: The Volga Countryside in Revolution, 1917–1921* (London: Phoenix, 2001), pp. 321–356; Oliver H. Radkey, *The Unknown Civil War in Soviet Russia: A Study of the Green Movement in the Tambov Region, 1920–1921* (Stanford: Hoover Institution, 1976); and Andrea Graziosi, *The Great Soviet Peasant War: Bolsheviks and Peasants, 1917–1933* (Cambridge: Ukrainian Research Institute, Harvard University, 1996), pp. 16–37.

29. Figes, *Peasant Russia*, p. 321. See also Chuev and Resis, *Molotov Remembers*, p. 246.

30. Radkey, *Unknown Civil War*, pp. 387–407; and Geoffrey Hosking, *The First Socialist Society: A History of the Soviet Union from Within* (Cambridge: Harvard University Press, 1992), p. 79.

31. Figes, *Peasant Russia*, p. 321.

32. Robert W. Davies, *The Socialist Offensive: The Collectivization of Soviet Agriculture, 1929–1930* (Cambridge: Harvard University Press, 1980), p. 39.

33. Conquest, *Harvest of Sorrow*, pp. 64–68.

34. Robert Himmer, "The Transition from War Communism to the New Economic Policy: An Analysis of Stalin's Views," *Russian Review* 53, no. 4 (October 1994): 515–529.

35. Quoted in Davies, *Socialist Offensive*, p. 37.

36. See Adam Ulam, *Expansion and Coexistence: The History of Soviet Foreign Policy, 1917–67* (New York: Praeger, 1968), pp. 164–167; and Tucker, *Stalin in Power*, pp. 74–76.

37. Quoted in Chuev and Resis, *Molotov Remembers*, p. 245.

38. John P. Sontag, "The Soviet War Scare of 1926–1927," *Russian Review* 34, no. 1 (January 1975): 76. Quoted in Chuev and Resis, *Molotov Remembers*, p. 245.

39. Davies, *Socialist Offensive*, pp. 39–41.

40. Ibid., p. 39.

41. James Hughes, *Stalin, Siberia and the Crisis of the New Economic Policy* (Cambridge: Cambridge University Press, 1991), pp. 138–148; and Moshe Lewin, *Russian Peasants and Soviet Power: A Study of Collectivization* (New York: W. W. Norton, 1968), p. 250–254.

42. Lewin, *Russian Peasants and Soviet Power*, p. 192.

43. Davies, *Socialist Offensive*, pp. 6–11.

44. Quoted in Lewin, *Russian Peasants and Soviet Power*, pp. 305–306.

45. For a brief review of some of these debates, see James R. Millar and Alec Nove, "Was Stalin Really Necessary? A Debate on Collectivization," *Problems of Communism* 25, no. 4 (July–August 1976): 49–62; and Chris Ward, *Stalin's Russia* (London: Edward Arnold, 1993), pp. 53–59.

46. Lewin, *Russian Peasants and Soviet Power*, pp. 241–242; and Hughes, *Stalin, Siberia*, pp. 174–179.

47. Stalin, *Selected Works*, p. 288.

48. Lewin, *Russian Peasants and Soviet Power*, pp. 251–252.

49. Ibid., p. 250.

50. Walter Laqueur, *Stalin: The Glasnost Revelations* (New York: Charles Scribner's Sons, 1990), p. 37. Laqueur concludes that both Stalin's "political and economic assumptions were wrong" but that these assumptions were also shared by the majority of the party leadership and thus formed the basis for the decision to collectivize in 1929. See also Leszek Kolakowski, *Main Currents of Marxism: Its Origin, Growth, and Dissolution,* vol. 3, *The Breakdown* (Oxford: Clarendon, 1978), pp. 40–41.

51. Hughes, *Stalin, Siberia,* pp. 137–148.

52. Martin Malia, *The Soviet Tragedy: A History of Socialism in Russia, 1917–1991* (New York: Free Press, 1994), p. 199.

53. Quoted in Davies, *Socialist Offensive,* p. 256.

54. Martha Brill Olcott, "The Collectivization Drive in Kazakhstan," *Russian Review* 40, no. 2 (April 1981): 139.

55. Lynne Viola, *Peasant Rebels under Stalin: Collectivization and the Culture of Peasant Resistance* (Oxford: Oxford University Press, 1996), p. 14.

56. Ibid., pp. 132–145.

57. Malia, *Soviet Tragedy,* pp. 192–193.

58. Lynne Viola, "The Case of Krasnyi Meliorator: Or 'How the Kulak Grows into Socialism,'" *Soviet Studies* 38, no. 4 (October 1986): 508–529.

59. Quoted in Conquest, *Harvest of Sorrow,* p. 114.

60. Ibid., p. 120.

61. See ibid., pp. 117–143; and Nicolas Werth, "A State against Its People: Violence, Repression, and Terror in the Soviet Union," in Courtois et al., *Black Book of Communism,* pp. 147–158.

62. Lynne Viola, "The Campaign to Eliminate the Kulak as a Class, Winter 1929–1930: A Reevaluation of the Legislation," *Slavic Review* 45, no. 3 (fall 1986): 503–524.

63. The low estimate is from Stephen G. Wheatcroft and R. W. Davies, "Population," in R. W. Davies, Mark Harrison, and Stephen G. Wheatcroft, eds., *The Economic Transformation of the Soviet Union 1913–1945* (Cambridge: Cambridge University Press, 1994), p. 77. The high estimate is from Conquest, *Harvest of Sorrow,* p. 306.

64. Dimitri Volkogonov, *Autopsy for an Empire: The Seven Leaders Who Built the Soviet Regime* (New York: Free Press, 1998), p. 104; and Conquest, *Harvest of Sorrow,* pp. 299–307.

65. Kolakowski, *Main Currents of Marxism,* p. 38.

66. Conquest, *Harvest of Sorrow,* pp. 322–326.

67. Nikita Khrushchev, *Khrushchev Remembers: The Last Testament* (Boston: Little, Brown, 1974), p. 109.

68. Conquest, *Harvest of Sorrow,* p. 232.

69. See ibid., pp. 217–224, 260–273; and James E. Mace, "Famine and Nationalism in Soviet Ukraine," *Problems of Communism* 33, no. 3 (May–June, 1984): 37–50. For a critical review of Mace's arguments along with Mace's reply, see Stephen G. Wheatcroft, "Ukrainian Famine," *Problems of Communism* 34, no. 1 (January–February, 1985), pp. 132–138.

70. Conquest, *Harvest of Sorrow,* p. 306; and Olcott, "Collectivization Drive," p. 136. Not all of these deaths were due to famine.

71. See Barbara B. Green, "Stalinist Terror and the Question of Genocide: The Great Famine," in Alan S. Rosenbaum, ed., *Is the Holocaust Unique? Perspectives on Comparative Genocide* (Boulder: Westview, 1996), pp. 137–161; and Heder, "Class, Nationality and Race," pp. 159–163.

72. Werth, "State against Its People," p. 167.

73. Ibid., pp. 167–168.

74. Quoted in Mark Mazower, *Dark Continent: Europe's Twentieth Century* (New York: Vintage, 1998), p. 119.

75. Robert Conquest, *The Great Terror: A Reassessment* (New York: Oxford University Press, 1990), p. 31.

76. Nikita Khrushchev, *The Anatomy of Terror: Khrushchev's Revelations about Stalin's Regime* (Washington, D.C.: Public Affairs, 1956), p. 70.

77. Malia, *Soviet Tragedy*, p. 244.

78. Leonard Schapiro, *The Communist Party of the Soviet Union* (London: University Paperbacks, 1966), p. 430.

79. Tucker, *Stalin in Power*, pp. 238–239.

80. J. Arch Getty and Oleg V. Naumov, *The Road to Terror: Stalin and the Self-Destruction of the Bolsheviks, 1932–1939* (New Haven: Yale University Press, 1999), p. 52. See also Jonathan Haslam, "Political Opposition to Stalin and the Origins of the Terror in Russia, 1932–1936," *Historical Journal* 29, no. 2 (June 1986): 395–417; and Malia, *Soviet Tragedy*, pp. 243–245.

81. For extended excerpts from the text of the Riutin platform, see Getty and Naumov, *Road to Terror*, pp. 54–58.

82. Quoted in Conquest, *Great Terror*, p. 24.

83. Getty and Naumov, *Road to Terror*, p. 59.

84. Roger R. Reese, "Red Army Opposition to Forced Collectivization, 1929–1930: The Army Wavers," *Slavic Review* 55, no. 1 (spring 1996): 24–45.

85. Haslam, "Political Opposition to Stalin," p. 409.

86. Quoted in Volkogonov, *Stalin*, p. 186.

87. Getty and Naumov, *Road to Terror*, pp. 71–72.

88. Conquest, *Great Terror*, p. 25.

89. Riutin was finally executed secretly on Stalin's orders in 1937.

90. Getty and Naumov, *Road to Terror*, p. 577.

91. Ibid., p. 139.

92. Volkogonov, *Stalin*, p. 200.

93. Tucker, *Stalin in Power*, pp. 264–265.

94. See Conquest, *Great Terror*, pp. 37–52; and Volkogonov, *Stalin*, pp. 201–213.

95. See Tucker, *Stalin in Power*, pp. 303–313. Getty and Naumov reject the notion that Stalin was planning the terror this far in advance. They argue that Stalin probably had not concluded that full-scale terror was necessary until as late as mid-1937. They acknowledge, however, that "there were hints as early as 1934 that the interests of Stalin and the other senior elites had begun to diverge." See Getty and Naumov, *Road to Terror*, p. 577.

96. J. Arch Getty and William Chase, "Patterns of Repression among the Soviet Elite in the Late 1930s: A Biographical Approach," in Getty and Manning, *Stalinist Terror*, p. 242.

97. Volkogonov, *Stalin*, p. 212.

98. Quoted in Chuev and Resis, *Molotov Remembers*, pp. 276–277, 278.

99. Werth, "State against Its People," pp. 186.

100. Quoted in Robert C. Tucker, *The Soviet Political Mind: Stalinism and Post-Stalin Change* (New York: W. W. Norton, 1971), p. 55.

101. See ibid., pp. 55–71.

102. Quoted in Volkogonov, *Stalin*, p. 188.

103. Killing family members may also have been intended to act as an additional deterrent to other potential oppositionists. See Getty and Naumov, *Road to Terror*, p. 487. On the persecution of "socially dangerous" wives and children in the Soviet Union, see Alexander N. Yakolev, *A Century of Violence in Soviet Russia* (New Haven: Yale University Press, 2002), pp. 29–47.

104. Werth, "State against Its People," pp. 186–187, 201.

105. Volkogonov, *Autopsy for an Empire*, p. 105. Much higher figures are possible, particularly if the period is expanded to include all the years between 1934 and 1945. For a detailed discussion

of the debate over the Gulag population and deaths due to the terror, see Edwin Bacon, *The Gulag at War: Stalin's Forced Labour System in the Light of the Archives* (New York: New York University Press, 1994), pp. 23–41.

106. Estimates of victims of Chinese communism are particularly hindered by a lack of evidence on the massive Chinese prison system, a scholarly history of which has yet to be written. See Jean Pasqualini, "Glimpses inside China's Gulag," *China Quarterly,* no. 134 (June 1993): 352–357.

107. For some examples of recent revelations about the brutality of Mao and his policies, see Jean-Louis Margolin, "China: A Long March into Night," in Courtois et al., *Black Book of Communism,* pp. 463–546; Becker, *Hungry Ghosts*; Andrew G. Walder and Yang Su, "The Cultural Revolution in the Countryside: Scope, Timing and Human Impact," *China Quarterly* 173 (March 2003): 74–99; Li, *Private Life of Chairman Mao*; Philip Short, *Mao: A Life* (London: Hodder and Stoughton, 1999); Jonathan Mirsky, "The Mark of Cain," *New York Review of Books,* February 5, 1998, pp. 31–33; Daniel Southerland, "Repression's Higher Toll," *Washington Post,* July 17, 1994, p. A1; and Daniel Southerland, "A Nightmare Leaves Scars, Questions," *Washington Post,* July 18, 1994, p. A1.

108. See Parris H. Chang, *Power and Policy in China* (University Park: Pennsylvania State University Press, 1975).

109. Frederick C. Teiwes and Warren Sun, *China's Road to Disaster: Mao, Central Politicians, and Provincial Leaders in the Unfolding of the Great Leap Forward, 1955–1959* (Armonk, N.Y.: M. E. Sharpe, 1999).

110. Mark Selden, "Cooperation and Conflict: Cooperative and Collective Formation in China's Countryside," in Mark Selden and Victor Lippit, eds., *The Transition to Socialism in China* (Armonk, N.Y.: M. E. Sharpe, 1982), p. 45.

111. Maurice Meisner, *Mao's China and After: A History of the People's Republic* (New York: Free Press, 1986), pp. 113–117.

112. Quoted in *The Selected Works of Mao Tse-Tung* (Beijing: Foreign Languages, 1977), 5:30.

113. Carl Riskin, *China's Political Economy: The Quest for Development since 1949* (Oxford: Oxford University Press, 1987), p. 40.

114. Quoted in *Selected Works of Mao Tse-Tung,* 4:416–417.

115. Vivienne Shue, *Peasant China in Transition: The Dynamics of Development Toward Socialism, 1949–1956* (Berkeley: University of California Press, 1980), pp. 41–43. See also Margolin, "China," p. 480.

116. See *Selected Works of Mao Tse-Tung,* 4:419.

117. Meisner, *Mao's China and After,* p. 80.

118. Frederick C. Teiwes, "The Establishment and Consolidation of the New Regime, 1949–57," in Roderick MacFarquhar, ed., *The Politics of China* (New York: Cambridge University Press, 1993), p. 34.

119. Meisner, *Mao's China and After,* p. 80. See also Julia C. Strauss, "Paternalist Terror: The Campaign to Suppress Counterrevolutionaries and Regime Consolidation in the People's Republic of China, 1950–1953," *Comparative Studies in Society and History* 44, no. 1 (2002): 99.

120. Teiwes, "Establishment and Consolidation," p. 35.

121. Shue, *Peasant China in Transition,* pp. 77–79.

122. Elizabeth J. Perry, "Rural Violence in Socialist China," *China Quarterly,* no 103 (September 1985): 418–420. Perry notes that many of these rebellions drew on members of religious sects opposed to the communist regime. Perry suggests that these rebellions were relatively rare, although her research is based primarily on contemporary Chinese press reports. In any case, the CCP clearly viewed this resistance as highly significant, and more recent research suggests that dissatisfaction with land reform was considerably greater than Perry and other scholars surmised. See Edward Friedman, Paul G. Pickowicz, and Mark Selden, *Chinese Village, Socialist State* (New Haven: Yale University Press, 1991).

123. Quoted in Strauss, "Paternalist Terror," p. 82.

124. Margolin, "China," p. 479. Maurice Meisner suggests that an estimate of two million executions and more than two million imprisoned in the first three years of the regime "is probably as accurate a guess as one can make." See Meisner, *Mao's China and After,* p. 81. A much lower, but nevertheless staggering, estimate of 400,000 to 800,000 executions is offered in Benedict Stavis, *The Politics of Agricultural Mechanization in China* (Ithaca, N.Y.: Cornell University Press, 1978), p. 29.

125. On the CCP's experience with violence in land reform prior to 1949, see John Byron and Robert Pack, *The Claws of the Dragon: Kang Sheng* (New York: Simon and Schuster, 1992), pp. 192–196; Short, *Mao,* pp. 307–308; and Friedman et al., *Chinese Village, Socialist State,* pp. 96–98, 104–107.

126. Shue, *Peasant China in Transition,* pp. 82–83.

127. Quoted in Strauss, "Paternalist Terror," p. 82; see also Short, *Mao,* pp. 436–438.

128. Quoted in Roderick MacFarquhar, Timothy Cheek, and Eugene Wu, eds., *The Secret Speeches of Chairman Mao: From the Hundred Flowers to the Great Leap Forward* (Cambridge: Council on East Asian Studies, Harvard University, 1989), p. 142.

129. Shue, *Peasant China in Transition,* pp. 278–279.

130. Friedman et al., *Chinese Village, Socialist State,* pp. 172–177.

131. Meisner, *Mao's China and After,* p. 123.

132. Selden, "Cooperation and Conflict," pp. 59–60.

133. Frederick C. Teiwes and Warren Sun, eds., *The Politics of Agricultural Cooperativization in China: Mao, Deng Zihui, and the "High Tide" of 1955* (Armonk, N.Y.: M. E. Sharpe, 1993), pp. 11–12.

134. *Selected Works of Mao Tse-Tung,* 5:184.

135. Ibid., p. 198.

136. Selden, "Cooperation and Conflict," pp. 72–78.

137. See Shue, *Peasant China in Transition,* p. 334; and Meisner, *Mao's China and After,* pp. 153–158.

138. Friedman et al., *Chinese Village, Socialist State,* pp. 185–213; and Dali L. Yang, *Calamity and Reform in China: State, Rural Society, and Institutional Change since the Great Leap Famine* (Stanford: Stanford University Press, 1996), p. 31.

139. James Kaising Kung, "Transaction Costs and Peasants' Choice of Institutions: Did the Right to Exit Really Solve the Free Rider Problem in Chinese Collective Agriculture?" *Journal of Comparative Economics* 17, no. 2 (June 1993): 495–497; and Teiwes, "Establishment and Consolidation," p. 64.

140. Strauss, "Paternalist Terror," p. 95.

141. Thomas P. Bernstein, "Leadership and Mass Mobilization in the Soviet and Chinese Collectivization Campaigns of 1929–30 and 1955–56: A Comparison," *China Quarterly* 31 (July–September 1967): 45.

142. Friedman et al., *Chinese Village, Socialist State,* pp. 198–203; Jean-Luc Domenach, *The Origins of the Great Leap Forward: The Case of One Chinese Province* (Boulder: Westview, 1995), pp. 42–45; and Becker, *Hungry Ghosts,* pp. 52–53.

143. Scholars disagree as to whether other party members forced Mao to accept a more moderate program or whether he was genuinely convinced of the necessity of such a retreat, at least temporarily. For the former position, probably the dominant interpretation, see Chang, *Power and Policy.* For the latter, see Teiwes and Sun, *China's Road to Disaster.*

144. Chang, *Power and Policy,* pp. 29–36.

145. Roderick MacFarquhar, "The Secret Speeches of Chairman Mao," in MacFarquhar et al., *Secret Speeches of Chairman Mao,* p. 14.

146. On the connection between Mao's long-term security concerns and his decision to launch

the Great Leap Forward, see Thomas J. Christensen, *Useful Adversaries: Grand Strategy, Domestic Mobilization, and Sino-American Conflict, 1947–1958* (Princeton: Princeton University Press, 1996), pp. 204–217.

147. See Teiwes and Sun, *China's Road to Disaster,* pp. 78–79. The name of the campaign comes from the phrase "let a hundred flowers bloom and a hundred schools of thought contend."

148. John King Fairbank and Merle Goldman, *China: A New History,* enlarged ed. (Cambridge: Harvard University Press, 1998), p. 364.

149. Frederick C. Teiwes, *Politics and Purges in China: Rectification and the Decline of Party Norms, 1950–1965* (Armonk, N.Y.: M. E. Sharpe, 1993), pp. 250–253; and Domenach, *Origins,* pp. 109–110.

150. Domenach, *Origins,* p. 110.

151. Jean-Louis Margolin estimates that between 400,000 and 700,000 people were arrested during the campaign. See Margolin, "China," p. 485. Frederick Teiwes suggests that 550,000 Chinese were "labeled rightists" but notes that although "reform through labor was apparently meted out on a large scale," not all of these people were actually arrested; see "Establishment and Consolidation," p. 82.

152. Friedman et al., *Chinese Village, Socialist State,* pp. 209–213.

153. In subsequent statements, Mao implied that China would overtake Britain in a matter of only one or two years. Teiwes and Sun, *China's Road to Disaster,* pp. 96–97.

154. MacFarquhar, "Secret Speeches of Chairman Mao," p. 15. For a similar view, see Michael Schoenhals, *Saltationist Socialism: Mao Zedong and the Great Leap Forward* (Stockholm: JINAB, 1987).

155. On the significance of this change in causing the famine, see Justin Yifu Lin, "Collectivization and China's Agricultural Crisis in 1959–1961," *Journal of Political Economy* 98, no. 6 (December 1990): 1228–1252.

156. For a description of these policies, see Friedman et al., *Chinese Village, Socialist State,* pp. 214–245.

157. Margolin, "China," p. 489.

158. Becker, *Hungry Ghosts,* pp. 70–82.

159. Thirty million excess deaths appears to be the most commonly cited figure, although other estimates vary from as low as fifteen million to as high as forty million. For reviews of estimates of the deaths resulting from the Great Leap Forward, see Becker, *Hungry Ghosts,* pp. 270–274; Yang, *Calamity and Reform in China,* pp. 37–39; and Southerland, "Repression's Higher Toll."

160. Thomas P. Bernstein, "Stalinism, Famine, and Chinese Peasants: Grain Procurements during the Great Leap Forward," *Theory and Society* 13, no. 3 (May 1984): 339–377.

161. See Friedman et al., *Chinese Village, Socialist State,* p. 230; and Teiwes and Sun, *China's Road to Disaster,* p. 119–176.

162. Becker, *Hungry Ghosts,* p. 81.

163. Ibid., pp. 86–88.

164. Quoted in ibid., p. 86. For a similar comment, see Alan P. L. Liu, *Mass Politics in the People's Republic: State and Society in Contemporary China* (Boulder: Westview, 1996), p. 38.

165. Quoted in Margolin, "China," p. 492.

166. Teiwes, *Politics and Purges in China,* pp. 312–329.

167. Although Peng retained his Politburo membership, this was merely a formality. He never attended another official meeting. During the Cultural Revolution he was sent to prison, where he died in 1974.

168. Becker, *Hungry Ghosts,* pp. 92–93.

169. Roderick MacFarquhar, *The Origins of the Cultural Revolution,* vol. 3, *The Coming of the Cataclysm, 1961–1966* (New York: Columbia University Press, 1997), p. 61.

170. Teiwes, *Politics and Purges in China,* p. 341.

171. See Becker, *Hungry Ghosts,* p. 93; and Yang, *Calamity and Reform in China,* p. 36.

172. Becker, *Hungry Ghosts,* p. 111.

173. Quoted in Rone Tempest, "Starving a Nation with the Politics of Illusion," *Los Angeles Times,* December 23, 1997, p. A1.

174. Becker, *Hungry Ghosts,* p. 103.

175. Margolin, "China," p. 498.

176. See ibid., p. 492; Becker, *Hungry Ghosts,* pp. 49–57; Teiwes, "Establishment and Consolidation," p. 63; and Yang, *Calamity and Reform in China,* pp. 27–28, 35–36.

177. John Wilson Lewis, "China's Secret Military Papers: 'Continuities' and 'Revelations,'" *China Quarterly,* no. 18 (April–June 1964): 76–77.

178. MacFarquhar, *Origins of the Cultural Revolution,* p. 70; and Zweig, *Agrarian Radicalism in China,* pp. 4–8.

179. MacFarquhar, *Origins of the Cultural Revolution,* p. 6; and Short, *Mao,* pp. 501–502.

180. Walder, "Cultural Revolution Radicalism," p. 51. See also Edward Friedman, "Maoism, Titoism, Stalinism: Some Origins and Consequences of the Maoist Theory of the Socialist Transition," in Selden and Lippit, *Transition to Socialism in China,* pp. 175–176.

181. Quoted in Walder, "Cultural Revolution Radicalism," p. 51.

182. Quoted in MacFarquhar, *Origins of the Cultural Revolution,* p. 364.

183. Ibid., p. 364.

184. Harry Harding, "The Chinese State in Crisis, 1966–9," in MacFarquhar, *Politics of China,* p. 153.

185. Fairbank and Goldman, *China,* p. 387. Three million cadres, approximately 20 percent of the party, were eventually rehabilitated in the late 1970s. See Harding, "Chinese State in Crisis," p. 243.

186. Quoted in Short, *Mao,* p. 551.

187. It is often said that Mao turned to the "masses" to carry out the Cultural Revolution against the party. In fact, the Red Guards represented a relatively small and highly unrepresentative slice of China's vast population.

188. Walder and Yang, "Cultural Revolution in the Countryside"; Zweig, *Agrarian Radicalism in China.*

189. See Margolin, "China," pp. 486–487, 529–530; Jonathan Unger, "Cultural Revolution Conflict in the Villages," *China Quarterly,* no. 153 (March 1988): 95–100; and Anne Thurston, *Enemies of the People* (New York: Alfred A. Knopf, 1987), p. 287.

190. MacFarquhar, *Origins of the Cultural Revolution,* p. 473. Alternatively, MacFarquhar speculates that Mao may have decided against more extensive executions out of concern that "even the most supine of his old comrades might have recoiled and perhaps rebelled at bare-faced brutality."

191. Margolin, "China," p. 524.

192. For a graphic description of the circumstances surrounding the death of Lui, see Thurston, *Enemies of the People,* pp. 151–153.

193. Harding, "Chinese State in Crisis," p. 149.

194. Quoted in Margolin, "China," p. 521.

195. Ibid., p. 513. Newly gathered evidence on the violence in the countryside during the Cultural Revolution suggests that these estimates, based mainly on deaths in urban areas, may need to be revised upward. Andrew Walder and Yang Su estimate that between 750,000 and 1,500,000 people died in the countryside alone from 1968 to 1971. See Walder and Yang, "Cultural Revolution in the Countryside."

196. Even then, many Khmer Rouge leaders were known outside the upper reaches of the party only by their pseudonyms.

197. See Kenneth M. Quinn, "Explaining the Terror," in Jackson, *Cambodia 1975–1978*," pp. 215–240.

198. Jackson, "Ideology of Total Revolution," p. 63.

199. Ibid., pp. 37–78.

200. Ibid., p. 77.

201. Ben Kiernan, *How Pol Pot Came to Power: A History of Communism in Kampuchea, 1930–1975* (London: Verso, 1985), p. 391.

202. Jackson, "Ideology of Total Revolution," pp. 39–49.

203. David P. Chandler, Ben Kiernan, and Chanthou Boua, eds., *Pol Pot Plans the Future: Confidential Leadership Documents from Democratic Kampuchea, 1976–1977* (New Haven: Yale University Southeast Asia Studies, 1988), p. xii.

204. Ben Kiernan, *The Pol Pot Regime: Race, Power and Genocide in Cambodia under the Khmer Rouge, 1975–1979* (New Haven: Yale University Press, 1996), p. 24.

205. Ben Kiernan, "New Light on the Origins of the Vietnam-Kampuchea Conflict," *Bulletin of Concerned Asian Scholars* 12, no. 4 (October–December 1980), pp. 61–65.

206. David P. Chandler, *Voices from S-21: Terror and History in Pol Pot's Secret Prison* (Berkeley: University of California Press, 1999), p. 42.

207. Charles H. Twining, "The Economy," in Jackson, *Cambodia 1975–1978*, p. 110; Elizabeth Becker, *When the War Was Over: Cambodia and the Khmer Rouge Revolution* (New York: Public Affairs, 1986), pp. 184–185.

208. Quoted in Chandler, Kiernan, and Chanthou, *Pol Pot Plans the Future*, p. 26.

209. David P. Chandler, "A Revolution in Full Spate: Communist Party Policy in Democratic Kampuchea, December 1976," in David A. Ablin and Marlowe Hood, eds., *The Cambodian Agony* (Armonk, N.Y.: M. E. Sharpe, 1987), p. 167.

210. Kiernan, *How Pol Pot Came to Power*, p. 368; and Quinn, "Pattern and Scope of Violence," p. 193.

211. Jackson, "Ideology of Total Revolution," p. 63.

212. Quoted in Chandler, Kiernan, and Chanthou, *Pol Pot Plans the Future*, p. 156.

213. Kiernan, *How Pol Pot Came to Power*, pp. 336–337.

214. Quinn, "Explaining the Terror," p. 227.

215. Kate G. Frieson, "Revolution and Rural Response in Cambodia: 1970–1975," in Ben Kiernan, ed., *Genocide and Democracy in Cambodia* (New Haven: Yale University Southeast Asia Studies, 1993), pp. 33–50.

216. Quinn, "Explaining the Terror," p. 218. See also Frieson, "Revolution and Rural Response," pp. 33–50; May Ebihara, "Revolution and Reformulation in Kampuchean Village Culture," in Ablin and Hood, *Cambodian Agony*, p. 35; and David Chandler, *The Tragedy of Cambodian History* (New Haven: Yale University Press, 1991), p. 239.

217. Kiernan, *How Pol Pot Came to Power*, p. 379.

218. Frieson, "Revolution and Rural Response," pp. 43–45; and Becker, *When the War Was Over*, pp. 153–155.

219. Chandler, "Revolution in Full Spate," p. 178; and Jackson, "Ideology of Total Revolution," p. 59.

220. Kiernan, *How Pol Pot Came to Power*, p. ix.

221. Quoted in Chandler, Kiernan, and Chanthou, *Pol Pot Plans the Future*, p. 127 (see also pp. 13–35).

222. For a description of the changes in village life under the Khmer Rouge, see Ebihara, "Revolution and Reformulation," pp. 16–61.

223. Margolin, "Cambodia," p. 604.

224. Chandler, *Voices from S-21*, p. 41.

225. Margolin, "Cambodia," p. 587.

226. See Stephen Heder and Brian Tittemore, *Seven Candidates for Prosecution: Accountability for the Crimes of the Khmer Rouge* (Washington, D.C.: War Crimes Research Office, American University, 2001), pp. 38–41.

227. Ibid., p. 41.

228. Becker, *When the War Was Over,* pp. 236–238.

229. See ibid., p. 234.

230. Margolin, "Cambodia," p. 634; emphasis in original. See also Chandler, Kiernan, and Chanthou, *Pol Pot Plans the Future,* p. 203; and Quinn, "Pattern and Scope of Violence," pp. 193–194, 201–204.

231. Kiernan, *Pol Pot Regime,* p. 62.

232. Jackson, "Ideology of Total Revolution," p. 47.

233. Kiernan, *Pol Pot Regime,* p. 48.

234. Margolin, "Cambodia," p. 591.

235. See Kiernan, *Pol Pot Regime,* pp. 251–309, 458.

236. Ibid., p. 26.

237. Stephen Heder, "Racism, Marxism, Labeling, and Genocide in Ben Kiernan's The *Pol Pot Regime,*" *South East Asia Research* 5, no. 2 (1996): 101–153.

238. Jackson, "Ideology of Total Revolution," p. 57.

239. Quoted in Francois Ponchard, *Cambodia: Year Zero* (New York: Holt, Rinehart and Winston, 1978), p. 50.

240. See Margolin, "Cambodia," pp. 588–591; Kiernan, *Pol Pot Regime,* pp. 456–460; Seth Mydans, "Cambodian Killers' Careful Records Used against Them," *New York Times,* June 7, 1996, p. A1; and Patrick Heuveline " 'Between One and Three Million': Towards the Demographic Reconstruction of a Decade of Cambodian History (1970–79)," *Population Studies* 52, no. 1 (March 1998): 58–61.

241. Margolin, "Cambodia," p. 591.

242. Heuveline " 'Between One and Three Million,' " pp. 58–61; and Margolin, "Cambodia," p. 591.

243. Margolin, "Cambodia," p. 601.

244. Ibid., p. 597.

245. For a general description of Khmer Rouge intra-party violence, see Becker, *When the War Was Over,* pp. 261–289.

246. Jackson, "Ideology of Total Revolution," pp. 56–57.

247. Kiernan, *How Pol Pot Came to Power,* pp. 328–329; and Becker, *When the War Was Over,* p. 202.

248. Chandler, Kiernan, and Chanthou, *Pol Pot Plans the Future,* p. 43.

249. See Kiernan, *Pol Pot Regime,* pp. 316–323; and Quinn, "Pattern and Scope of Violence," pp. 194–197. For some doubts regarding the existence of the coup, see Chandler, *Brother Number One,* p. 129.

250. Quinn, "Pattern and Scope of Violence," p. 195.

251. Quinn, "Explaining the Terror," p. 195.

252. Margolin, "Cambodia," p. 586.

253. Becker, *When the War Was Over,* p. 234; and Chandler, *Voices from S-21,* pp. 41–43.

254. Quoted in Kiernan, *Pol Pot Regime,* pp. 96–97; emphasis in original.

255. See Chandler, Kiernan, and Chanthou, *Pol Pot Plans the Future,* pp. 177–212; and Jackson, "Ideology of Total Revolution," pp. 56–57.

256. Chandler, *Voices from S-21,* pp. 41–49.

257. Quoted in Margolin, "Cambodia," p. 586.

258. Becker, *When the War Was Over,* p. 211.

259. Quinn, "Pattern and Scope of Violence," p. 201–202; and Chandler, *Voices from S-21,* pp. 37–38.

260. Quinn, "Pattern and Scope of Violence," p. 201.

261. Chandler, *Voices from S-21,* p. 44.

262. Ibid., p. 36.

263. Quinn, "Pattern and Scope of Violence," p. 207.

264. According to the 1937 census, the population of the Soviet Union was 162,003,225. See Bacon, *Gulag at War,* p. 33.

265. B. R. Mitchell, *International Historical Statistics: Africa, Asia and Oceania, 1750–1988* (New York: Stockton, 1995), p. 57.

266. In 1946 the population of Albania was 1,130,000; Bulgaria, 7,000,000; Czechoslovakia, 12,920,000; East Germany, 18,060,000; Hungary, 9,040,000; Poland, 23,770,000; Romania, 15,790,000; and Yugoslavia, 15,440,000. See B. R. Mitchell, *International Historical Statistics: Europe, 1750–1988* (New York: Stockton, 1992), pp. 84–86.

267. George W. Hoffman, "Rural Transformation in Eastern Europe Since World War II," in Ivan Volgyes, Richard E. Lonsdale, and William P. Avery, eds., *The Process of Rural Transformation: Eastern Europe, Latin America and Australia* (New York: Pergamon, 1980), p. 31. Joan Sokolovsky notes that collectivization in Czechoslovakia was not accomplished without some violence, coercion, and imprisonment, but she offers no estimates for the numbers affected. See Joan Sokolovsky, *Peasants and Power: State Autonomy and the Collectivization of Agriculture in Eastern Europe* (Boulder: Westview, 1990), pp. 161–163.

268. Figures from Lewin, *Russian Peasants and Soviet Power,* p. 21; Selden, "Cooperation and Conflict," pp. 52; and Twining, "Economy," p. 125.

269. Lewin, *Russian Peasants and Soviet Power,* pp. 420–421.

270. Frederic L. Pryor, *The Red and the Green: The Rise and Fall of Collectivized Agriculture* (Princeton: Princeton University Press, 1992), p. 99. On the Marxist classification of these regimes, see p. 363.

271. Ibid., pp. 12–13.

272. See Sokolovsky, *Peasants and Power,* pp. 31–85; and Melissa K. Bokovoy, *Peasants and Communists: Politics and Ideology in the Yugoslav Countryside, 1941–1953* (Pittsburgh: University of Pittsburgh Press, 1998).

273. Sokolovsky, *Peasants and Power,* p. 107.

274. Ibid., p. 147.

275. Ibid., pp. 145–147.

276. Tens of thousands of these refugees, however, drowned at sea trying to escape.

277. Pryor, *Red and the Green,* p. 100.

278. Robert Melson, *Revolution and Genocide: The Origins of the Armenian Genocide and the Holocaust* (Chicago: University of Chicago Press, 1992), p. 280. Rosemary H. T. O'Kane also claims that the ability of people to flee Cuba probably limited the scope of the killing. See *The Revolutionary Reign of Terror: The Role of Violence in Political Change* (Brookfield, Vt.: Edward Elgar, 1991), p. 166. Hugh Thomas estimates that five thousand people were executed in Cuba between 1959 and 1970. See *The Cuban Revolution* (New York: Harper and Row, 1971), p. 684.

279. After the fall of South Vietnam in 1975 more than 1.4 million Vietnamese fled the country. See George C. Herring, *America's Longest War: The United States and Vietnam, 1950–1975* (New York: McGraw-Hill, 1986), p. 270. Herring also notes that as many as fifty thousand Vietnamese "boat-people" perished in flight.

280. Bernard B. Fall, *The Two Vietnams: A Political and Military Analysis* (New York: Frederick A. Praeger, 1967), p. 154.

281. James Pinckney Harrison, *The Endless War: Fifty Years of Struggle in Vietnam* (New York: Free Press, 1982), p. 149.

282. Ronald A. Francisco, "Agricultural Collectivization in the German Democratic Republic," in Ronald A. Francisco, Betty A. Laird, and Roy D. Laird, eds., *The Political Economy of Collectivized Agriculture: A Comparative Study of Communist and Non-Communist Systems* (New York: Pergamon, 1979), p. 70.

283. William Stueck, *The Korean War: An International History* (Princeton: Princeton University Press, 1995), p. 22. Bruce Cumings contends, however, that not all of these refugees were actually fleeing communism. See *The Origins of the Korean War: Liberation and Emergence of Separate Regimes, 1945–1947* (Princeton: Princeton University Press, 1989), p. 425.

284. Documentation of the violence associated with the regime is not reliable enough to determine if a mass killing actually took place. For arguments that the North did not engage in mass killing (emphasizing the importance of the exodus as well as the moderate nature of collectivization in the North), see Cumings, *Origins of the Korean War*, pp. 416–417, 425–426; and Pryor, *Red and the Green*, pp. 84–85. For arguments that the North is guilty of mass killing, see Pierre Rigoulot, "Crimes, Terror, and Secrecy in North Korea," in Courtois et al., *Black Book of Communism*, pp. 547–564; and Rummel, *Death by Government*, pp. 365–379.

285. The second generation of leaders in these countries also implemented fewer radical plans for their societies. In fact, many of the radical policies and programs initiated by Stalin and Mao were discontinued or reversed by their successors.

286. Khrushchev, *Anatomy of Terror*, pp. 42, 34–35, 28.

287. Bokovoy, *Peasants and Communists*, pp. 84–89.

288. Ibid., p. 108.

289. Quoted in ibid., pp. 87–88, 108.

290. Richard West, *Tito and the Rise and Fall of Yugoslavia* (New York: Carroll and Graf, 1994), p. 231.

291. Ibid., p. 235.

292. Ibid., p. 236.

293. Conquest, *Reflections on a Ravaged Century*, pp. xi.

294. Pipes, *Communism*, p. 158.

295. See Francois Furet, *The Passing of an Illusion: The Idea of Communism in the Twentieth Century* (Chicago: University of Chicago Press, 1999); Forrest D. Colburn, *The Vogue of Revolution in Poor Countries* (Princeton: Princeton University Press, 1994), pp. 89–96; and Paul Hollander, *Political Will and Personal Belief: The Decline and Fall of Soviet Communism* (New Haven: Yale University Press).

296. Francis Fukuyama, *The End of History and the Last Man* (New York: Free Press, 1992).

5. Ethnic Mass Killings

1. During the Second World War, for example, the Nazis intentionally killed millions of non-Jewish Polish and Russian civilians. Although Nazi racial theories claimed that Poles and Russians were inferior to ethnic Germans, the primary rationale for the murder of these groups was the procurement of territory for German settlement. See Götz Aly, *Final Solution: Nazi Population Policy and the Murder of the European Jews* (London: Arnold, 1999).

2. See table 3 for estimates of the death tolls associated with these episodes.

3. For a discussion of the various bases of comparison between Hitler and Stalin, see Ian Kershaw and Moshe Lewin, eds., *Stalinism and Nazism: Dictatorships in Comparison* (Cambridge: Cambridge University Press, 1997); Steven Wheatcroft, "The Scale and Nature of German and Soviet Repression and Mass Killings, 1930–1945," *Europe-Asia Studies* 48, no. 8 (1996): 1319–1353; and

Peter Baldwin, ed., *Reworking the Past: Hitler, the Holocaust and the Historians' Debate* (Boston: Beacon, 1990).

4. Alan Bullock, *Hitler and Stalin: Parallel Lives* (New York: Random House, 1993), p. 343.

5. See Milica Zarkovic Bookman, *The Demographic Struggle for Power: The Political Economy of Demographic Engineering in the Modern World* (London: Frank Cass, 1997).

6. Aly, *Final Solution,* p. 89.

7. On these and other Nazi programs of social engineering, see Michael Burleigh and Wolfgang Wippermann, *The Racial State: Germany 1933–1945* (Cambridge: Cambridge University Press, 1991); Aly, *Final Solution*; Michael Burleigh, *Death and Deliverance: Euthanasia in Germany 1900–1945* (Cambridge: Cambridge University Press, 1994); and Robert Proctor, *Racial Hygiene: Medicine under the Nazis* (Cambridge: Harvard University Press, 1988).

8. See Milan L. Hauner, "A German Racial Revolution?" *Journal of Contemporary History* 19, no. 4 (October 1984): 669–687; and Sybil Milton, "The Context of the Holocaust," *German Studies Review* 13, no. 2 (May 1990): 269–283.

9. Aly, *Final Solution,* p. 89.

10. For similar arguments about the distinction between ethnic cleansing and genocide, see Norman M. Naimark, *Fires of Hatred: Ethnic Cleansing in Twentieth Century Europe* (Cambridge: Harvard University Press, 2001), pp. 3–4; Robert M. Hayden, "Schindler's Fate: Genocide, Ethnic Cleansing and Population Transfers," *Slavic Review* 55, no. 4 (winter 1996): 731–736; and Bookman, *Demographic Struggle for Power,* p. 135.

11. Hayden, "Schindler's Fate," p. 736.

12. Mark Danner, "America and the Bosnia Genocide," *New York Review of Books,* December 4, 1997, p. 59.

13. Christopher R. Browning, "Nazi Ghettoization Policy in Poland, 1939–1941," in *The Path to Genocide: Essays on Launching the Final Solution* (Cambridge: Cambridge University Press, 1992), p. 30. These deaths are nevertheless considered "intentional" by the definition utilized in this book because the Nazis "deliberately created conditions expected to cause widespread death" among the Jews and because the Jews were the direct object of the policies that created such conditions.

14. See Christopher J. Walker, *Armenia: The Survival of a Nation* (London: Croom Helm, 1980), pp. 86–89.

15. See Roderic H. Davison, "Nationalism as an Ottoman Problem and the Ottoman Response," in William W. Haddad and William Ochsenwal eds., *Nationalism in a Non-National State* (Columbus: Ohio State University Press, 1977), pp. 25–56; Roderic H. Davison, "Turkish Attitudes concerning Christian-Muslim Equality in the Nineteenth Century," *American Historical Review* 59, no. 4 (July 1954): 844–864; and Roderic H. Davison, *Reform in the Ottoman Empire: 1856–1876* (Princeton: Princeton University Press, 1963).

16. Davison, "Turkish Attitudes," p. 853.

17. For a description of the various Armenian political groups, see Walker, *Armenia,* pp. 125–131.

18. Richard Hovannisian, "The Armenian Question in the Ottoman Empire, 1876–1914," in Richard Hovannisian, ed., *The Armenian People from Ancient to Modern Times,* vol. 2, *Foreign Dominion to Statehood: The Fifteenth Century to the Twentieth Century* (New York: St. Martin's, 1997), pp. 212–215.

19. Walker, *Armenia,* p. 146.

20. Quoted in Ronald Grigor Suny, "Religion, Ethnicity and Nationalism: Armenians, Turks, and the End of the Ottoman Empire," in Omer Bartov and Phyllis Mack, eds., *In God's Name: Genocide and Religion in the Twentieth Century* (New York: Berghahn Books, 2001), p. 41. Scholars disagree as to how serious a threat these acts of "provocation" actually posed to Turkish rule. Almost all agree, however, that the regime perceived these acts to be highly threatening. For an ar-

gument stressing the Armenian provocation, see Stanford J. Shaw and Ezelkural Shaw, *History of the Ottoman Empire and Modern Turkey,* vol. 2, *Reform, Revolution, and Republic: The Rise of Modern Turkey, 1808–1975* (Cambridge: Cambridge University Press, 1977), pp. 200–205. For an argument stressing Turkish perceptions, see Robert Melson, "Provocation or Nationalism: A Critical Inquiry into the Armenian Genocide of 1915," in Richard Hovannisian, ed., *The Armenian Genocide in Perspective* (New Brunswick, N.J.: Transaction Books, 1986), pp. 61–84.

21. As such, these massacres seem closer to the imperialist mass killings described in chapter 3 than to ethnic mass killings. Indeed, Christopher J. Walker argues that the killings followed an "almost classic pattern" of imperial rule. See Walker, *Armenia,* p. 172. See also Suny, "Religion, Ethnicity and Nationalism," pp. 41–44; and Robert Melson, *Revolution and Genocide: The Origins of the Armenian Genocide and the Holocaust* (Chicago: University of Chicago Press, 1992), p. 69.

22. Vahakn N. Dadrian, *The History of the Armenian Genocide: Ethnic Conflict from the Balkans to Anatolia to the Caucasus* (Providence: Berghahn Books, 1997), pp. 160–161. A similar interpretation of the motives for the massacre is offered in Melson, *Revolution and Genocide,* pp. 44–53.

23. Roderic H. Davison, "The Armenian Crisis: 1912–1914," *American Historical Review* 53, no. 3 (April 1948): 482.

24. Naimark, *Fires of Hatred,* p. 24.

25. See A. L. Macfie, *The End of the Ottoman Empire: 1908–1923* (London: Longman, 1998), pp. 61–62; and Davison, "Armenian Crisis," p. 482.

26. Davison, "Armenian Crisis," pp. 483–484.

27. Melson, "Provocation or Nationalism," p. 72.

28. Macfie, *End of the Ottoman Empire,* p. 60.

29. G. S. Graber, *Caravans to Oblivion: The Armenian Genocide, 1915* (New York: John Wiley and Sons, 1996), pp. 47–48; and Walker, *Armenia,* pp. 182–189.

30. Dadrian, *History of the Armenian Genocide,* pp. 192–193; and Davison, "Armenian Crisis," pp. 484–485.

31. Richard Hovannisian, "Historical Dimensions of the Armenian Question, 1978–1923," in Hovannisian, *Armenian Genocide in Perspective,* p. 28. See also Dadrian, *History of the Armenian Genocide,* p. 198; Melson, *Revolution and Genocide,* pp. 159–169; and Macfie, *End of the Ottoman Empire,* p. 87.

32. These considerations also applied to Turkey's large Greek minority. Some have speculated that the Turks planned to deal with the Greeks as soon as the Armenian question was "solved." Indeed, Greeks also suffered horribly at the hands of the Turkish regime during the First World War. Many fled to Greece and some were deported to the interior alongside the Armenians. Tens of thousands of Greeks may have died. Greeks avoided the fate of the Armenians, however, because Greece itself remained neutral until July 1917 and was never a major combatant during the war. The Turks probably hoped to avoid a major confrontation with the Greek minority, which might have drawn Greece into the war. When conflict between Greece and Turkey did erupt between 1919–1923, however, the new Turkish regime under Mustafa Kemal quickly decided the time had come to cleanse Turkey of its remaining Greek population. Tens of thousands of Greeks died, but the death toll was probably lessened by the refugees' ability to flee to Greece and by the eventual international supervision of the population transfer. See Michael R. Marrus, *The Unwanted: European Refugees in the Twentieth Century* (Oxford: Oxford University Press, 1985), pp. 96–106; Ioannis K. Hassiotis, "The Armenian Genocide and the Greeks: Response and Records (1915–23)," in Richard G. Hovannisian, ed., *The Armenian Genocide: History, Politics, Ethics* (New York: St. Martin's, 1992), pp. 129–151; and Howard M. Sachar, *The Emergence of the Middle East: 1914–1924* (New York: Alfred A. Knopf, 1969), pp. 291–335.

33. Bernard Lewis, *The Emergence of Modern Turkey* (London: Oxford University Press, 1961), p. 350.

34. Vahakn N. Dadrian, "The Secret Young-Turk Ittihadist Conference and the Decision for the World War I Genocide of the Armenians," *Holocaust and Genocide Studies* 7, no. 2 (fall 1993): 190. As Dadrian notes, although the assassination plot was devised at a meeting of the Hunchak Party, there was no quorum at the meeting and the plot was approved only through illegitimate party procedures. One of the participants notified Turkish officials of the plot before the assassination attempt was made. Nevertheless, the incident was taken as evidence of the treacherous attitude of the entire Armenian population. Ironically, an Armenian nationalist seeking revenge for Talat's role in the genocide succeeded in assassinating him in Berlin in 1921.

35. Davison, "Armenian Crisis," pp. 484–505.

36. Dadrian, *History of the Armenian Genocide,* pp. 192.

37. Roderic Davison suggests that relatively few Armenian groups favored secession from Turkey, see "Armenian Crisis," pp. 483–485. For the view that Armenians favored independence, see Shaw and Shaw, *History of the Ottoman Empire and Modern Turkey,* pp. 314–317.

38. Dadrian, *History of the Armenian Genocide,* pp. 193–194.

39. See Macfie, *End of the Ottoman Empire,* pp. 132–133.

40. Ibid., p. 131. See also Edward J. Erikson, *Ordered to Die: A History of the Ottoman Army in the First World War* (Westport, Conn.: Greenwood, 2001), p. 103.

41. Gwynne Dyer, "Turkish 'Falsifiers' and Armenian 'Deceivers': Historiography and the Armenian Massacres," *Middle Eastern Studies* 12, no. 1 (January 1976): 106.

42. See Walker, *Armenia,* p. 200; and Naimark, *Fires of Hatred,* p. 29.

43. Quoted in Naimark, *Fires of Hatred,* p. 29.

44. Quoted in Ronald Grigor Suny, *Looking toward Ararat: Armenia in Modern History* (Bloomington: Indiana University Press, 1993), p. 113.

45. Quoted in Richard G. Hovannisian, *Armenia on the Road to Independence, 1918* (Berkeley: University of California Press, 1967), p. 52.

46. Quoted in Walker, *Armenia,* p. 210.

47. See Mim Kemal Öke, *The Armenian Question: 1914–1923* (Oxford: K. Rustem and Brother, 1988), pp. 133–136; and Shaw and Shaw, *History of the Ottoman Empire and Modern Turkey,* pp. 315–317.

48. See Christopher J. Walker, "World War I and the Armenian Genocide," in Hovannisian, *Armenian People from Ancient to Modern Times,* pp. 239–273; Dadrian, *History of the Armenian Genocide,* pp. 219–243; Suny, *Looking toward Ararat,* p. 111–115; Yves Ternon, *The Armenians: History of a Genocide,* 2d ed. (Delamar, N.Y.: Caravan Books, 1990), pp. 171–177; Melson, "Provocation or Nationalism," pp. 62–67; and Graber, *Caravans to Oblivion,* pp. 99–120.

49. Some scholars suggest that the Turks deliberately created harsh conditions during the deportation and at the camps in the attempt to exterminate the refugees. See Ternon, *Armenians,* pp. 187–220.

50. Quoted in Dadrian, "Secret Young-Turk Ittihadist Conference," p. 181.

51. Quoted in Graber, *Caravans to Oblivion,* p. 87. See also Ternon, *Armenians,* p. 171.

52. Erikson, *Ordered to Die,* pp. 101–102.

53. Dadrian, *History of the Armenian Genocide,* pp. 347–355. It has been estimated that 250,000 Armenians escaped to Russia during the genocide. See Walker, *Armenia,* p. 230.

54. Dadrian, *History of the Armenian Genocide,* pp. 356–374; and Suny, *Looking toward Ararat,* pp. 119–132.

55. Quoted in Dadrian, *History of the Armenian Genocide,* p. 208.

56. Erikson, *Ordered to Die,* p. 104.

57. On the political aspects of Nazi anti-Semitism, see Saul Friedländer, *Nazi Germany and the Jews,* vol. 1, *The Years of Persecution, 1933–1939* (New York: HarperCollins, 1997), pp. 90–112.

58. For a history of the protocols, see Norman Cohn, *Warrant for Genocide: The Myth of the Jew-*

ish World-Conspiracy and the Protocols of the Elders of Zion (New York: Harper and Row, 1967). On Hitler's belief in their authenticity, see Ian Kershaw, *Hitler, 1889–1936: Hubris* (New York: W. W. Norton, 1998), p. 153.

59. Philippe Burrin, *Hitler and the Jews: The Genesis of the Holocaust* (London: Edward Arnold, 1994), p. 30.

60. Arno J. Mayer, *Why Did the Heavens Not Darken? The "Final Solution" in History* (New York: Pantheon Books, 1988), esp. pp. 101–102.

61. Adolf Hitler, *Mein Kampf*, trans. Ralph Manheim (Boston: Houghton Mifflin, 1971), p. 326.

62. Quoted in Yehuda Bauer, *A History of the Holocaust* (New York: Franklin Watts, 1982), p. 91.

63. On the origins of Nazi biological racism, see Burleigh and Wippermann, *Racial State*, pp. 23–43; George L. Mosse, *Toward the Final Solution: A History of European Racism* (Madison: University of Wisconsin Press, 1985), pp. 77–112; and Paul Weindling, "Understanding Nazi Racism: Precursors and Perpetrators," in Michael Burleigh, ed., *Confronting the Nazi Past: New Debates on Modern German History* (New York: St. Martin's, 1996), pp. 66–83.

64. Hitler, *Mein Kampf*, p. 300.

65. Ibid., p. 65. For other statements by Hitler regarding his perception of the gravity of the Jewish threat for Germany and the world, see Yehuda Bauer, "Genocide: Was It the Nazis' Original Plan?" *Annals of the American Academy of Political and Social Science* 450 (July 1980): 38.

66. Bauer, "Genocide," p. 38–40; and Burrin, *Hitler and the Jews*, p. 37.

67. Bauer, "Genocide," p. 44.

68. This interpretation of the Nazi genocide incorporates elements from both schools of thought in the well-known intentionalist/functionalist debate on the Holocaust. Like the intentionalist interpretation, it suggests that Hitlerian-Nazi anti-Semitic ideology, not gradual bureaucratic radicalization, was the guiding force behind the Holocaust. Like functionalist explanations, on the other hand, it suggests that this ideology did not result in a genocidal intent until after the war had broken out. For reviews of this debate, see Browning, *Path to Genocide*, 87–121; Michael R. Marrus, *The Holocaust in History* (New York: Meridian, 1989), pp. 31–55; and Ian Kershaw, *The Nazi Dictatorship: Problems and Perspectives of Interpretation*, 2d, ed. (London: Edward Arnold, 1985), pp. 82–106.

69. Quoted in Friedländer, *Nazi Germany and the Jews*, p. 201.

70. Burrin, *Hitler and the Jews*, p. 52; Otto Dov Kulka, " 'Public Opinion' in Nazi Germany and 'The Jewish Question,' " in Michael R. Marrus, ed., *The Nazi Holocaust: Historical Articles on the Destruction of the European Jews in Nazi Europe*, vol. 5, *Public Opinion and Relations to the Jews in Nazi Europe*, vol. 1 (Westport, Conn.: Meckler, 1989), pp. 122–123; and Ian Kershaw, *Hitler, 1936–1945: Nemesis* (New York: W. W. Norton, 2000), p. 136.

71. Yehuda Bauer, *Jews for Sale?* (New Haven: Yale University Press, 1994), p. 35.

72. Christopher R. Browning, *The Final Solution and the German Foreign Office* (New York: Holmes and Meier, 1978), p. 14.

73. Bauer, *Jews for Sale?* pp. 30–43; and Burrin, *Hitler and the Jews*, pp. 59–61.

74. William D. Rubinstein, *The Myth of Rescue: Why the Democracies Could Not Have Saved More Jews from the Nazis* (New York: Routledge, 1997), pp. 16–17. As Rubinstein notes, these Jews must be distinguished from the millions of Jews outside the Reich who came under Nazi control after 1939. In addition, some Jews fled to countries such as France and Poland, where they were subsequently captured during the German occupation.

75. See Anna C. Bramwell, "The Re-Settlement of Ethnic Germans, 1939–41," in Michael R. Marrus and Anna C. Bramwell, eds., *Refugees in the Age of Total War* (London: Unwin Hyman, 1988), pp. 112–132; and Aly, *Final Solution*.

76. Aly, *Final Solution*, p. 97.

77. Quoted in ibid., p. 79.

292 NOTES TO PAGES 170–174

78. Hitler, *Mein Kampf,* p. 682.

79. Jewish emigration also continued during this period, although at a much reduced rate, as the doors of many Western nations closed to German refugees following the invasion of Poland.

80. For a detailed discussion of the various deportation plans, see Christopher R. Browning, "Nazi Resettlement Policy and the Search for a Solution to the Jewish Question, 1939–1941," in Browning, *Path to Genocide,* pp. 3–27; and Aly, *Final Solution.*

81. Browning, "Nazi Ghettoization Policy," p. 31.

82. Burrin, *Hitler and the Jews,* p. 71–72.

83. Quoted in Browning, "Nazi Resettlement Policy," pp. 15–16.

84. Browning, "Nazi Resettlement Policy," pp. 16–17. According to Himmler, Hitler explicitly approved of the memorandum.

85. Quoted in Aly, *Final Solution,* p. 3.

86. Browning, "Nazi Ghettoization Policy," p. 28–56.

87. See Browning, "Nazi Resettlement Policy," pp. 3–27; Aly, *Final Solution,* esp. pp. 88–104; and Kershaw, *Hitler, 1936–1945,* pp. 320–323.

88. Browning, *Final Solution,* pp. 35–43.

89. For the argument that the Nazis were never serious about resettlement, see Leni Yahil, "Madagascar—Phantom of a Solution for the Jewish Question," in Bela Vago and George L. Mosse, eds., *Jews and Non-Jews in Eastern Europe 1918–1945* (New York: John Wiley and Sons, 1974), pp. 315–334; and Philip Friedman, "The Lublin Reservation and the Madagascar Plan: Two Aspects of Nazi Jewish Policy during the Second World War," in *Yivo Annual of Jewish Social Science* 8 (1953): 151–177.

90. Marrus, *The Holocaust in History,* p. 63.

91. For a review of this debate, see Ian Kershaw, *The Nazi Dictatorship,* pp. 99–106.

92. See Raul Hilberg, *The Destruction of the European Jews, Student Edition* (New York: Holmes and Meier, 1985), p. 161; and Browning, "Nazi Resettlement Policy," p. 19.

93. Quoted in Kershaw, *Hitler, 1936–1945,* p. 520. See also Christian Gerlach, "The Wannsee Conference, the Fate of German Jews, and Hitler's Decision in Principle to Exterminate All European Jews," *Journal of Modern History* 70, no. 4 (December 1998): 786–787.

94. See Michael Burleigh, *The Third Reich: A New History* (New York: Hill and Wang, 2000), pp. 645–647; and Kershaw, *Hitler, 1936–1945,* p. 488.

95. Aly, *Final Solution,* p. 197.

96. Browning, "Nazi Resettlement Policy," p. 25.

97. Christian Gerlach, "German Economic Interests, Occupation Policy, and the Murder of the Jews in Belorussia, 1941/43," in Ulrich Herbert, *National Socialist Extermination Policies: Contemporary German Perspectives and Controversies* (New York: Berghahn Books, 2000), pp. 210–239; Kershaw, *Hitler, 1936–1945,* pp. 480–481; and Burrin, *Hitler and the Jews,* p. 119.

98. See Burrin, *Hitler and the Jews,* pp. 116–119; and Aly, *Final Solution,* pp. 173–177.

99. Burrin, *Hitler and the Jews,* pp. 119–120.

100. Quoted in Kershaw, *Hitler, 1936–1945,* p. 488.

101. Quoted in Martin Broszat, "Hitler and the Genesis of the 'Final Solution': An Assessment of David Irving's Theses," *Yad Vahem Studies* 13 (1970): 101. Even at this late date, however, Hitler still speaks of deporting the Jews to Russia.

102. See Broszat, "Hitler and the Genesis of the *'Final Solution,'* " p. 101; Kershaw, *Hitler, 1936–1945,* pp. 478–479; Gerlach, "Wannsee Conference," pp. 759–812; Mark Roseman, *The Wannsee Conference and the Final Solution: A Reconsideration* (New York: Metropolitan Books, 2002), pp. 48–78; and Mayer, *Why Did the Heavens Not Darken?,* pp. 234–275.

103. See Michael Geyer, "German Strategy in the Age of Machine Warfare, 1914–1945," in Pe-

S

ter Paret, ed., *Makers of Modern Strategy: From Machiavelli to the Nuclear Age* (Princeton: Princeton University Press, 1986), pp. 589–591; and Marrus, *The Holocaust in History,* p. 45.

104. Gerlach, "German Economic Interests," p. 227–228; Kershaw, *Hitler, 1936–1945,* pp. 480–481; and Roseman, *Wannsee Conference,* pp. 64–67.

105. Quoted in Hilberg, *Destruction of the European Jews,* p. 162.

106. Ibid., p. 339.

107. Bauer, *Jews for Sale?* pp. 252–253. Bauer argues that after the decision to kill the Jews was made sometime in 1941, subsequent Nazi proposals for emigration were merely tactical and the Nazis expected to recapture and murder all Jews who managed to escape.

108. Lucy S. Dawidowicz, *The War against the Jews 1933–1945* (New York: Bantam Books, 1986), p. 151. See also Gerald Fleming, *Hitler and the Final Solution* (Berkeley: University of California Press, 1984).

109. Quoted in Dawidowicz, *War against the Jews,* p. 106.

110. See Bauer, "Genocide," pp. 36–37; and Hans Mommsen, "The Realization of the Unthinkable: The 'Final Solution' to the 'Jewish Question' in the Third Reich," in Gerhard Hirschfeld, ed., *The Policies of Genocide* (London: German Historical Institute, 1986), pp. 108–109.

111. See Friedländer, *Nazi Germany and the Jews,* pp. 311–312; Kershaw, *Hitler, 1936–1945,* pp. 151, 478; and Mommsen, "Realization of the Unthinkable," pp. 107–110.

112. Browning, "Nazi Resettlement Policy," p. 17.

113. Quoted in Max Domarus, *Hitler: Speeches and Proclamations, 1932–1945,* vol. 3, *The Years 1939–1940* (Wurzburg: Domarus Verlag, 1997), pp. 1448–1449. On the ambiguous implications of this speech, see Marrus, *The Holocaust in History,* pp. 37–38.

114. Even Richard Brietman, who dates the decision for mass murder in early 1941, before Germany launched the war against the Soviet Union, cannot explain away these earlier actions. See "Plans for the Final Solution in Early 1941," *German Studies Review* 17, no. 4 (fall 1994): 483–493.

115. Christopher Browning, *Fateful Months: Essay on the Emergence of the Final Solution* (New York: Holmes and Meier, 1985), pp. 14–16.

116. For the argument that the Holocaust is unique, see Steven T. Katz, *The Holocaust in Historical Context,* vol. 1, *The Holocaust and Mass Death before the Modern Age* (New York: Oxford University Press, 1994). For a review of the debate on this question, see Alan S. Rosenbaum, ed., *Is the Holocaust Unique? Perspectives on Comparative Genocide* (Boulder: Westview, 1996); and Charles S. Maier, *The Unmasterable Past: History, Holocaust, and German National Identity* (Cambridge: Harvard University Press, 1988), esp. pp. 66–99.

117. The low figure for Jewish deaths in occupied Europe is calculated from Yehuda Bauer and Robert Rozett, "Estimated Jewish Losses in the Holocaust," in Israel Gutman, ed., *Encyclopedia of the Holocaust,* 4:1799. The high figure is from Dawidowicz, *War against the Jews,* p. 403. The world Jewish population in 1939 is estimated at 16.7 million.

118. Because scholars disagree on both the size of the pre-genocide Tutsi population and the number of people killed, estimates of the proportional death toll vary widely. Human Rights Watch estimates at least 500,000 killed from a population of approximately 650,000. Human Rights Watch, *Leave None to Tell the Story: Genocide in Rwanda* (New York: Human Rights Watch, 1999), pp. 15–16. Gérard Prunier estimates 800,000 to 850,000 killed out of a population of 930,000. Gérard Prunier, *The Rwanda Crisis: History of a Genocide* (New York: Columbia University Press, 1995), p. 264.

119. Estimates of the dead range from 200,000 to 1,500,000 (and even higher) from an initial population of between 1,750,000 to 2,000,000. For a discussion of the various estimates, see Christopher J. Walker, "Armenian Refugees: Accidents of Diplomacy or Victims of Ideology?" in Marrus and Bramwell, *Refugees in the Age of Total War,* p. 42.

S

120. For the history of this period, see Prunier, *Rwanda Crisis,* pp. 1–35.

121. Ibid., p. 39; and Philip Gourevitch, *We wish to inform you that tomorrow we will be killed with our families: Stories from Rwanda* (New York: Farrar, Straus and Giroux, 1998), p. 59.

122. Alan J. Kuperman, *The Limits of Humanitarian Intervention: Genocide in Rwanda* (Washington, D.C.: Brookings Institution, 2001), p. 7.

123. See Ogenga Otunnu, "Rwandan Refugees and Immigrants in Uganda," in Howard Adelman and Astri Suhrke, eds., *The Path of a Genocide: the Rwandan Crisis from Uganda to Zaire* (New Brunswick, N.J.: Transaction Publishers, 1999), pp. 3–29.

124. For an explanation of the timing of the invasions, see Ogenga Otunnu, "An Historical Analysis of the Invasion by the Rwandan Patriotic Army," in Adelman and Suhrke, *Path of a Genocide,* pp. 31–49.

125. Human Rights Watch, *Leave None to Tell the Story,* p. 48.

126. Ibid., p. 49.

127. Ibid., p. 135; and René Lemarchand, "Managing Transitional Anarchies: Rwanda, Burundi, and South Africa in Comparative Perspective," *Journal of Modern African Studies* 32, no. 4 (1994): 600–601.

128. Cyrus Reed, "Exile, Reform, and the Rise of the Rwandan Patriotic Front," *Journal of Modern African Studies* 34, no. 3 (1996): 491–492.

129. Human Rights Watch, *Leave None to Tell the Story,* pp. 31–32; and Prunier, *Rwanda Crisis,* p. 121.

130. Bruce D. Jones, *Peacemaking in Rwanda: The Dynamics of Failure* (Boulder: Lynn Rienner, 2001), pp. 61–64; and Alan J. Kuperman, "The Other Lesson of Rwanda: Mediators Sometimes Do More Damage than Good," *SAIS Review* 16, no. 1 (winter–spring 1996): 227.

131. Kuperman, *Limits of Humanitarian Intervention,* p. 9. Whether the French troops actually engaged the RPF in combat continues to be disputed. At a minimum, the troops helped secure the capital, Kigali, and other strategic sites, providing a deterrent and freeing up government forces. See Jones, *Peacemaking in Rwanda,* p. 30.

132. Joan Kakwenzire and Dixon Kamukama, "The Development and Consolidation of Extremist Forces in Rwanda, 1990–1994," in Adelman and Suhrke, *Path of a Genocide,* p. 66.

133. Bruce D. Jones, "The Arusha Peace Process," in Adelman and Suhrke, *Path of a Genocide,* p. 141.

134. See ibid., pp. 141–142.

135. Jones, "Arusha Peace Process," p. 141.

136. Both René Lemarchand and Gérard Prunier argue that the RPF's shift to guerrilla tactics and heavy recruitment among the internal Tutsi population following the initial failure of its conventional invasion led to increasing attacks by Hutu militias against Tutsi civilians as part of the extremists' counterinsurgency campaign. See Lemarchand, "Managing Transitional Anarchies," pp. 600–601; and Prunier, "The Rwandan Patriotic Front," in Christopher Clapham, ed., *African Guerrillas* (Oxford: James Curry, 1998), p. 132.

137. Quoted in Human Rights Watch, *Leave None to Tell the Story,* p. 52.

138. Prunier, *Rwanda Crisis,* p. 182.

139. Quoted in Eric Ransdell, "The Wounds of War: A Reconstruction of Rwanda's Genocide Suggests the Killing Could Return," *U.S. News and World Report,* November 28, 1994, pp. 67–75.

140. See Lemarchand, "Managing Transitional Anarchies," pp. 591–592, 596–602; and Human Rights Watch, *Leave None to Tell the Story,* pp. 125–126.

141. African Rights, *Rwanda: Death, Despair and Defiance,* rev. ed. (London: African Rights, 1995), p. 36.

142. See Human Rights Watch, *Leave None to Tell the Story,* pp. 76–78; and Hintjens, "Explaining the 1994 Genocide in Rwanda," *Journal of Modern African Studies* 37, no. 2 (1999): 264.

143. Quoted in Human Rights Watch, *Leave None to Tell the Story,* pp. 62–63; emphasis in original.

144. Prunier, *Rwanda Crisis,* p. 180; and Human Rights Watch, *Leave None to Tell the Story,* pp. 110, 126, 135.

145. Prunier, *Rwanda Crisis,* p. 175.

146. African Rights, *Rwanda: Death, Despair and Defiance,* p. 70; and Human Rights Watch, *Leave None to Tell the Story,* pp. 78–79.

147. On the enduring impact of the memory of the 1972 genocide, see René Lemarchand, "Genocide in the Great Lakes: Which Genocide? Whose Genocide?" *African Studies Review* 41, no. 1 (1998): 3–16.

148. Prunier, *Rwanda Crisis,* p. 226.

149. Others suggest that Habyarimana was killed by Hutu moderates or by the RPF in an attempt to replace him with someone more committed to the Arusha accords.

150. Quoted in African Rights, *Rwanda: Death, Despair and Defiance,* p. 98 (see also p. 46).

151. Ibid., p. 79.

152. Quoted in ibid., p. 89.

153. See Human Rights Watch, *Leave None to Tell the Story,* pp. 72–74; African Rights, *Rwanda: Death, Despair and Defiance,* p. 36; Hintjens, "Explaining the 1994 Genocide in Rwanda," p. 249; and Kakwenzire and Kamukama, "Development and Consolidation," pp. 61–91.

154. Quoted in Human Rights Watch, *Leave None to Tell the Story,* pp. 73–74.

155. Quoted in Philip Gourevitch, "After the Genocide," *New Yorker,* December 18, 1995, p. 85.

156. Quoted in African Rights, *Rwanda: Death, Despair and Defiance,* p. 65.

157. Prunier, "Rwandan Patriotic Front," p. 132; emphasis in original.

158. See Prunier, *Rwanda Crisis,* pp. 226–227; and Gourevitch, *We wish to inform you,* p. 98.

159. Quoted in African Rights, *Rwanda: Death, Despair and Defiance,* p. 39.

160. Human Rights Watch, *Leave None to Tell the Story,* pp. 295–297.

161. See African Rights, *Rwanda: Death, Despair and Defiance,* pp. 39, 77, 79; and Human Rights Watch, *Leave None to Tell the Story,* p. 204.

162. Prunier, *Rwanda Crisis,* pp. 226–227.

163. Human Rights Watch, *Leave None to Tell the Story,* pp. 204, 212–214.

164. Ibid., p. 172.

165. Prunier, *Rwanda Crisis,* pp. 169, 223–225.

166. See Jones, "Arusha Peace Process," pp. 151–152.

167. Prunier, *Rwanda Crisis,* p. 141.

168. Kuperman, *Limits of Humanitarian Intervention,* p. 16.

169. Prunier, *Rwanda Crisis,* p. 141.

170. Public opinion in Germany and Rwanda was discussed in chapters 1 and 2. Evidence regarding public opinion in Turkey is too limited to render a reliable judgment regarding overall Turkish support for anti-Armenian measures. There seems to have been substantial regional and local variation in attitudes. Christopher Walker does note, however, that at least some Turks "opposed the regime's violent policies . . . both at the official and the popular level" and that the "authorities had doubts about the popularity of their measures at the local level." See Walker, "World War I and the Armenian Genocide," pp. 261, 267–268.

171. For example, see Davison, "Nationalism as an Ottoman Problem," pp. 49–56; Lemarchand, "Managing Transitional Anarchies," pp. 603–604; Henry Ashby Turner Jr., *Hitler's Thirty Days to Power: January 1933* (Reading, Mass.: Addison-Wesley, 1996), esp. pp. 163–183; and Jones, "Arusha Peace Process," pp. 151–152.

172. John Battersby, "A Secret Network to Preserve White Power," *Christian Science Monitor,* August 24, 1992, p. 6.

173. See Bill Berkeley, *The Graves Are Not Yet Full: Race, Tribe and Power in the Heart of Africa* (New York: Basic Books, 2001), pp. 143–193.

174. On the value of within-case comparison for testing the validity of social science theories, see Stephen Van Evera, *Guide to Methods for Students of Political Science* (Ithaca, N.Y.: Cornell University Press, 1997), pp. 25–49; and Alexander L. George and Timothy J. McKeown, "Case Studies and Theories of Organizational Decision Making," *Advances in Information Processing in Organizations* 2 (1985): 21–58.

175. Friedländer, *Nazi Germany and the Jews,* pp. 34–36.

176. For a historical overview of ethnic cleansing, including several examples that were carried out without mass killing, see Alfred-Maurice De Zayas, "A Historical Survey of Twentieth Century Expulsions," in Marrus and Bramwell, *Refugees in the Age of Total War,* pp. 15–37; and Andrew Bell-Fialkoff, *Ethnic Cleansing* (New York: St. Martin's, 1996).

177. The size of the victim population *relative* to the perpetrators' may be particularly important since the resources that perpetrators can devote to easing the process of resettlement and the likelihood that victims will attempt to resist deportation are partially a function of relative rather than absolute population sizes.

178. See Charles Harrison, "Uganda: The Expulsion of the Asians," in Willem A. Veenhoven and Winifred Crum Ewing eds., *Case Studies on Human Rights and Fundamental Freedoms: A World Survey,* vol. 4 (The Hague: Martinus Nijhoff, 1976), pp. 289–315. Harrison notes that the actual number of Asians living in Uganda in 1972 may have been even lower (perhaps 40,000 to 50,000) since many had already fled during the two previous years.

179. Surplus People Project, *Forced Removals in South Africa,* vol. 1 (Cape Town: Surplus People Project, 1983), p. 5.

180. According to the Surplus People Project, although living conditions in the relocation areas were "generally very poor," they were, "on average, no worse than those found in other, established Bantustan communities [homelands] and in several instances may well be better." See ibid., pp. 18–20.

181. Although many thousands died during the expulsions, particularly in years before the deportations came under international supervision, the Turks did not seek to exterminate the Greeks, as the previous regime had done to the Armenians. See Marrus, *The Unwanted,* pp. 96–106.

182. For a similar argument, see Hayden, "Schindler's Fate," p. 740. A 1995 classified CIA report (issued prior to the Croatian ethnic cleansing of Serbs living in the Krajina region) found Serbs responsible for 90 percent of ethnic cleansing in the Bosnian war, with Bosnian Muslims by far the main victims. See Roger Cohen, "C.I.A. Report Finds Serbs Guilty in Majority of Bosnia War Crimes," *New York Times,* March 9, 1995, p. A1.

183. Steven L. Burg and Paul S. Shoup, *The War in Bosnia-Herzegovina: Ethnic Conflict and International Intervention* (Armonk: M. E. Sharpe, 1999), p. 172.

184. Tim Judah, *Kosovo: War and Revenge* (New Haven: Yale University Press, 2000), pp. 252–253 (death toll estimates on p. 310). Judah notes that while "the camps were hardly comfortable . . . compared to refugee camps in Africa and other parts of the Third World, these were certainly at the luxury end of the market." Over ninety thousand Kosovars were also airlifted to safety and temporarily resettled in Western countries.

6. Counterguerrilla Mass Killings

1. See table 5 for estimates of the death tolls associated with these episodes.

2. On the long history of guerrilla warfare, see Walter Laqueur, *Guerrilla: A Historical and Critical Study* (Boston: Little, Brown, 1976); Robert B. Asprey, *War in the Shadows: The Guerrilla in History* (New York: William Morrow, 1994); Robin Corbett, *Guerrilla Warfare: From 1939 to the Present Day* (London: Orbis, 1986); and Anthony James Joes, *Guerrilla Conflict before the Cold War* (Westport, Conn.: Praeger, 1996).

3. Of course, conventional armies, too, ultimately rely on civilians for many requirements, but in much less direct ways.

4. Mao Tse-tung, *On Guerrilla Warfare* (New York: Praeger, 1961), pp. 44, 92–93.

5. Roger Trinquier, *Modern Warfare: A French View of Counterinsurgency* (New York: Praeger, 1964), pp. 63–64. Despite the implications of this argument, it should be noted that Trinquier does not openly advocate violence against civilians.

6. Franklin A. Lindsay, "Unconventional Warfare," *Foreign Affairs* 40, no. 2 (January 1962): 265.

7. Corbett, *Guerrilla Warfare*, p. 112. For more on American atrocities during the war in Vietnam, see Edward M. Opton, "It Never Happened and Besides They Deserved It," in Nevitt Sanford and Craig Comstock, eds., *Sanctions for Evil* (San Francisco: Jossey Bass, 1971), pp. 49–70.

8. Lindsay, "Unconventional Warfare," p. 268.

9. See Edward E. Rice, *Wars of the Third Kind: Conflict in Underdeveloped Countries* (Berkeley: University of California Press, 1988), pp. 103–105.

10. See Bruce Hoffman, "A Nasty Business," *Atlantic Monthly,* January 2002, pp. 49–52.

11. Quoted in Joanna Bourke, *An Intimate History of Killing: Face to Face Killing in 20th Century Warfare* (New York: Basic Books, 1999), p. 177.

12. Quoted in Richard Overy, *Russia's War: A History of the Soviet War Effort: 1941–1945* (New York: Penguin, 1997), p. 144.

13. Quoted in Alexander Dallin, *German Rule in Russia 1941–1945* (Boulder: Westview, 1981), pp. 74–76.

14. See Martin Gilbert, *The Second World War: A Complete History* (New York: Henry Holt, 1989), pp. 309–310.

15. Alexander Werth, *Russia at War: 1941–1945* (New York: E. P. Dutton, 1964), pp. 710–726.

16. Quoted in Luzviminda Francisco, "The Philippine-American War," in Daniel B. Schirmer and Stephen Rosskamm Shalom, eds., *The Philippines Reader: A History of Colonialism, Neocolonialism, Dictatorship and Resistance* (Boston: South End, 1987), p. 11.

17. See Stanley Karnow, *In Our Image: America's Empire in the Philippines* (New York: Random House, 1989), p. 188.

18. Quoted in Asprey, *War in the Shadows,* p. 131.

19. Quoted in Francisco, "Philippine-American War," pp. 17–18.

20. Quoted in Karnow, *In Our Image,* p. 188.

21. Quoted in Asprey, *War in the Shadows,* p. 132.

22. See Rice, *Wars of the Third Kind,* pp. 95–98.

23. For nations willing and able to commit such resources to resettlement, however, the violence and mortality of relocation may be mitigated. Major population resettlement campaigns involving a vast commitment of resources, for example, were carried out by the French in Algeria and by the United States in Vietnam with relatively little violence. Nevertheless, the subsequent imposition of free-fire zones and the use of scorched-earth tactics in the depopulated regions resulted in widespread civilian deaths in both instances.

24. John J. McCuen, *The Art of Counter-revolutionary Warfare: The Strategy of Counter-Insurgency* (Harrisburg: Stackpole Books, 1966), p. 238.

25. Thomas Pakenham, *The Scramble for Africa: White Man's Conquest of the Dark Continent from 1876 to 1912* (New York: Avon Books, 1991), pp. 576–579.

26. Howard Bailes, "Military Aspects of the War," in Peter Warwick, ed., *The South African War: The Anglo-Boer War 1899–1902* (Essex: Longman, 1980), p. 98.

27. See Africa Watch, *Evil Days: 30 Years of War and Famine in Ethiopia* (New York: Human Rights Watch, 1991), p. 227; and Jason W. Clay, Sandra Steingraber, and Peter Niggli, *The Spoils of Famine: Ethiopian Famine Policy and Peasant Agriculture* (Cambridge: Cultural Survival, 1988), p. 17.

28. Robert D. Kaplan, *Surrender or Starve: The Wars behind the Famine* (Boulder: Westview, 1988), p. 120.

29. Africa Watch, *Evil Days*, pp. 211–230.

30. Quoted in Kaplan, *Surrender or Starve*, p. 101.

31. This counterguerrilla tactic should not be confused with more traditional scorched-earth policies used by retreating conventional armies in the effort to deny supplies to advancing armies.

32. Brian McAllister Linn, *The U.S. Army and Counterinsurgency in the Philippine War, 1899–1902* (Chapel Hill: University of North Carolina Press, 1989), pp. 25, 113; and Walden Bello, "Counterinsurgency's Proving Ground: Low-Intensity Warfare in the Philippines," in Michael T. Klare and Peter Kornbluh, eds., *Low-Intensity Warfare: Counterinsurgency, Proinsurgency, and Anti-Terrorism in the Eighties* (New York: Pantheon Books, 1988), p. 159.

33. See Francisco, "Philippine-American War," pp. 18–19.

34. African Rights, *Facing Genocide: The Nuba of Sudan* (London: African Rights, 1995), p. 93.

35. See Iris Chang, *The Rape of Nanking: The Forgotten Holocaust of World War II* (New York: Basic Books, 1997); and John Dower, *War without Mercy: Race and Power in the Pacific War* (New York: Pantheon Books, 1986), esp. pp. 284–290.

36. Chalmers A. Johnson, *Peasant Nationalism and Communist Power: The Emergence of Revolutionary China, 1937–1945* (Stanford: Stanford University Press, 1962), pp. 60–61.

37. Lincoln Li, *The Japanese Army in North China 1937–1941* (Oxford: Oxford University Press, 1975), p. 209. For more on the strategic motives for Japanese atrocities, see Callum MacDonald, "'Kill All, Burn All, Loot All': The Nanking Massacres of December 1937 and Japanese Policy in China," in Mark Levene and Penny Roberts, eds., *The Massacre in History* (New York: Berghahn Books, 1999), pp. 223–245; Ray C. Hillam, "Counterinsurgency: Lessons from the Early Chinese and Japanese Experience against the Communists," *Orbis* 12, no. 1 (spring 1968): 226–246; and Lloyd E. Eastman, "Facets of an Ambivalent Relationship: Smuggling, Puppets, and Atrocities during the War, 1937–1945," in Akira Iriye, ed., *The Chinese and the Japanese: Essays in Political and Cultural Interactions* (Princeton: Princeton University Press, 1980), pp. 275–303.

38. Johnson, *Peasant Nationalism and Communist Power*, p. 56.

39. Ibid., p. 58.

40. Dower, *War without Mercy*, pp. 295–296. Eight million deaths is a reasonable round estimate based on Dower's estimate of ten million total "war dead" and estimates cited by Dower of at least 1.3 million military fatalities. Not all of these deaths should be attributed to counterguerrilla operations. Japanese forces also engaged in terrorist and imperialist mass killing designed to coerce China into surrendering and cooperating with Japan's imperial ambitions.

41. Americas Watch, *El Salvador's Decade of Terror: Human Rights since the Assassination of Archbishop Romero* (New Haven: Yale University Press, 1991), p. 54.

42. Karnow, *In Our Image*, p. 153.

43. Hillam, "Counterinsurgency," pp. 230–231.

44. Jennifer Schirmer, *The Guatemalan Military Project: A Violence Called Democracy* (Philadelphia: University of Pennsylvania Press, 1998), p. 16. Vincente Collazo-Davila suggests that "hardcore rebel forces probably never exceeded more than two or three hundred men." See Vincente Collazo-Davila, "The Guatemalan Insurrection," in Bard E. O'Neill, William R. Heaton, and Donald J. Alberts, eds., *Insurgency in the Modern World* (Boulder: Westview, 1980), p. 116.

45. George Black, *Garrison Guatemala* (London: Zed Books, 1984), p. 82.

46. Michael A. Sheehan, "Comparative Counterinsurgency Strategies: Guatemala and El Salvador," *Conflict* 9, no. 2 (1989): 131; and Susanne Jonas, *The Battle for Guatemala: Rebels, Death Squads, and U.S. Power* (Boulder: Westview, 1991), p. 131.

47. Corbett, *Guerrilla Warfare*, p. 87.

48. Collazo-Davila, "Guatemalan Insurrection," pp. 112, 124–125.

49. Schirmer, *Guatemalan Military Project*, p. 16.

50. Michael McClintock, *The American Connection*, vol. 2, *State Terror and Popular Resistance in Guatemala* (London: Zed, 1985), pp. 83–94.

51. Schirmer, *Guatemalan Military Project*, p. 36.

52. Collazo-Davila, "Guatemalan Insurrection," p. 116.

53. Ibid.

54. Jonas, *Battle for Guatemala*, p. 69.

55. Collazo-Davila, "Guatemalan Insurrection," p. 117.

56. Cited in Stephen Schlesinger and Stephen Kinzer, *Bitter Fruit: The Untold Story of the American Coup in Guatemala* (New York: Anchor Books, 1982), p. 247. This figure probably includes those killed in the counterguerrilla campaign of 1966–1967.

57. See Arturo Arias, "Changing Indian Identity: Guatemala's Violent Transition to Modernity," in Carol A. Smith, ed., *Guatemalan Indians and the State: 1540 to 1988* (Austin: University of Texas Press, 1990), pp. 230–257.

58. Black, *Garrison Guatemala*, pp. 78–87.

59. Jonas, *Battle for Guatemala*, p. 139. See also McClintock, *American Connection*, pp. 152–156.

60. David Stoll, *Between Two Armies: In the Ixil Towns of Guatemala* (New York: Columbia University Press, 1993), esp. pp. 61–91.

61. Schirmer, *Guatemalan Military Project*, p. 41; and Beatriz Manz, *Refugees of a Hidden War: The Aftermath of Counterinsurgency in Guatemala* (Albany: State University of New York Press, 1988), p. 15.

62. Arias, "Changing Indian Identity," p. 255.

63. McClintock, *American Connection*, p. 161.

64. Schirmer, *Guatemalan Military Project*, p. 42; and Manz, *Refugees of a Hidden War*, p. 15.

65. Schirmer, *Guatemalan Military Project*, p. 41.

66. Manz, *Refugees of a Hidden War*, pp. 15–16.

67. Schirmer, *The Guatemalan Military Project*, p. 39.

68. Quoted in ibid., p. 42.

69. McClintock, *American Connection*, p. 221.

70. Schirmer, *Guatemalan Military Project*, p. 44.

71. Ibid., p. 44.

72. Michael Richards, "Cosmopolitan World View and Counterinsurgency in Guatemala," *Anthropological Quarterly* 58, no. 3 (1985): 95.

73. Quoted in Schirmer, *Guatemalan Military Project*, p. 49.

74. Ibid., p. 45; emphasis in original. For similar views on the motives behind the killings in Guatemala, see Richard E. Rubenstein, *Alchemists of Revolution: Terrorism in the Modern World* (New York: Basic Books, 1987), pp. 221–222; McClintock, *American Connection*, esp. pp. 240–259; Jonas, *Battle for Guatemala*, pp. 68–71, 148–152; and Saul Landau, *The Guerrilla Wars of Central America: Nicaragua, El Salvador and Guatemala* (New York: St. Martin's, 1993), pp. 184–186.

75. Schirmer, *Guatemalan Military Project*, p. 44.

76. Ibid., p. 56.

77. Allan Nairn, "Guatemala Can't Take Two Roads," *New York Times*, July 20, 1982, p. A23. See also Black, *Garrison Guatemala*, p. 129.

78. Even Ricardo Falla, whose account places a greater emphasis on the role of racism in the killing than many other scholars, concludes that "racism is a specific trait of counterinsurgency in Guatemala, but it is not the main motivation for it." See Ricardo Falla, *Massacres in the Jungle: Ixcán, Guatemala, 1975–1982* (Boulder: Westview, 1994), p. 186.

79. Schirmer, *The Guatemalan Military Project*, p. 4.

80. Patrick Ball, Paul Kobrak, and Herbert F. Spirer, *State Violence in Guatemala, 1960–1996: A*

Quantitative Reflection (New York: American Association for the Advancement of Science, 1999), p. 39.

81. Quoted in Nairn, "Guatemala Can't Take Two Roads," p. A23.

82. Quoted in ibid.

83. Quoted in Schirmer, *Guatemalan Military Project,* p. 47.

84. Quoted in ibid., p. 48.

85. Quoted in McClintock, *American Connection,* p. 230.

86. Schirmer, *Guatemalan Military Project,* pp. 52–55.

87. Americas Watch, *Human Rights in Guatemala: No Neutrals Allowed* (New York: Americas Watch Committee, 1982), p. 19.

88. Quoted in McClintock, *American Connection,* p. 247.

89. Quoted in Stoll, *Between Two Armies,* p. 84.

90. Christopher Dickey, "Guatemalan Village's Agony," *The Washington Post,* January 4, 1983, p. A11.

91. Falla, *Massacres in the Jungle,* p. 89.

92. Manz, *Refugees of a Hidden War,* p. 17; and McClintock, *American Connection,* p. 245.

93. Quoted in McClintock, *American Connection,* p. 243. See also Richards, "World View and Counterinsurgency," p. 97; and Manz, *Refugees of a Hidden War,* p. 105.

94. Manz, *Refugees of a Hidden War,* p. 148.

95. Carol A. Smith, "Conclusion: History and Revolution in Guatemala," in Smith, *Guatemalan Indians and the State,* p. 272.

96. Manz, *Refugees of a Hidden War,* p. 43.

97. Schirmer, *Guatemalan Military Project,* p. 58.

98. Tammy Arbuckle, "Counterinsurgency the Guatemalan Way," *International Defense Review* 21, no. 10 (1988): 1254.

99. Quoted in McClintock, *American Connection,* p. 258.

100. Americas Watch, *Creating a Desolation and Calling It Peace* (New York: Americas Watch, 1983).

101. Ibid., pp. 14–15.

102. Jonas, *Battle for Guatemala,* p. 149.

103. Americas Watch, *Creating a Desolation,* p. 9; and McClintock, *American Connection,* pp. 246–247.

104. Cultural Survival, "Counterinsurgency and the Development Pole Strategy in Guatemala," *Cultural Survival Quarterly* 12, no. 3 (1988): 15.

105. Americas Watch, *Human Rights in Guatemala: No Neutrals Allowed* (New York: Americas Watch Committee, 1982), p. 19. See also Cultural Survival, "Counterinsurgency and Development Pole Strategy," p. 15.

106. Schirmer, *Guatemalan Military Project,* p. 62.

107. Quoted in ibid., p. 64.

108. Quoted in ibid., p. 71.

109. Raymond Bonner, "Guatemala Enlists Religion in Battle," *New York Times,* July 18, 1982, p. A3.

110. Quoted in Schirmer, *Guatemalan Military Project,* p. 62.

111. McClintock, *American Connection,* p. 249.

112. Manz, *Refugees of a Hidden War,* pp. 42–43.

113. Schirmer, *Guatemalan Military Project,* pp. 64–124.

114. Sheehan, "Comparative Counterinsurgency Strategies," pp. 127–154.

115. Arbuckle, "Counterinsurgency the Guatemalan Way," p. 1254.

116. Rachael M. McCleary, *Dictating Democracy: Guatemala and the End of Violent Revolution* (Gainesville: University Press of Florida, 1999), p. 18.

117. Ibid., p. 190; and Susanne Jonas, *Of Centaurs and Doves: Guatemala's Peace Process* (Boulder: Westview, 2000), p. 31.

118. Marek Sliwinski, "Afghanistan: The Decimation of a People," *Orbis* 33, no. 1 (winter 1989): 39–56.

119. Mark Urban's otherwise excellent book, for example, acknowledges a policy of "deliberate depopulation" in certain areas but argues that "this does not amount to evidence of a centrally organised national policy." Instead, Urban speculates that as in "past guerrilla wars [such as Vietnam]" the violence may be explained "in terms of indiscipline, frustration and a sense of superiority on the part of the soldiers concerned." See Mark Urban, *War in Afghanistan* (New York: St. Martin's, 1988), pp. 110–111.

120. Quoted from a document translated in Lester W. Grau and Michael A. Gress, eds., *The Soviet-Afghan War: How a Superpower Fought and Lost* (Lawrence: University Press of Kansas, 2002), p. 24. The report goes on to say that this tactic "had the opposite effect" since the Afghan Pushtuns in the Mujahideen were "historically enemies" of some of these nationalities. This prompted greater resistance from the rebels. Nevertheless, this strategy is important because it shows that the Soviets were making efforts to reduce the impact of racism and nationalism during the conflict.

121. David C. Isby, "Soviet Tactics in the War in Afghanistan," *Jane's Defense Review* 4, no. 7 (1983): 692.

122. Anthony Arnold, "The Stony Path to Afghan Socialism: Problems of Sovietization in an Alpine Muslim Society," *Orbis* 29, no. 1 (spring 1985): 43; and Sylvain Boulouque, "Communism in Afghanistan," in Stéphane Courtois et al., *The Black Book of Communism: Crimes, Terror, Repression* (Cambridge: Harvard University Press, 1999), p. 709.

123. Boulouque, "Communism in Afghanistan," p. 711.

124. Robert L. Canfield, "Islamic Sources of Resistance," *Orbis* 29, no. 1 (spring 1985): 57–71; and Arnold, "Stony Path to Afghan Socialism," p. 44.

125. Urban, *War in Afghanistan*, pp. 27–28; and Arnold, "Stony Path to Afghan Socialism," pp. 51–52.

126. On the Soviet decision to intervene, see Raymond L. Garthoff, *Détente and Confrontation: American-Soviet Relations from Nixon to Reagan* (Washington, D.C.: Brookings Institution, 1985), pp. 915–938.

127. Diego Cordovez and Selig S. Harrison, *Out of Afghanistan: The Inside Story of the Soviet Withdrawal* (New York: Oxford University Press, 1995), pp. 35–37; and Michael Dobbs, "Secret Memos Trace Kremlin's March to War," *Washington Post*, November 15, 1992, p. A1.

128. Urban, *War in Afghanistan*, pp. 53–56.

129. Douglas M. Hart, "Low-Intensity Conflict in Afghanistan: The Soviet View," *Survival* 24, no. 2 (March/April 1982): 62.

130. See Barnett R. Rubin, *The Fragmentation of Afghanistan: State Formation and Collapse in the International System* (New Haven: Yale University Press, 1995), p. 123.

131. Edgar O'Ballance, *Afghan Wars: 1839–1992* (London: Brassey's, 1993), p. 97.

132. Urban, *War in Afghanistan*, pp. 64–65.

133. For an exception, see Grau and Gress, *Soviet-Afghan War*.

134. Anthony H. Cordesman and Abraham R. Wagner, *The Lessons of Modern War*, vol. 3, *The Afghan and Falklands Conflicts* (Boulder: Westview, 1990), pp. 38–46; and O'Ballance, *Afghan Wars*, p. 102.

135. Grau and Gress, *Soviet-Afghan War*, p. 24.

136. Hassan M. Kakar, *Afghanistan: The Soviet Invasion and the Afghan Response, 1979–1982*

(Berkeley: University of California Press, 1995), p. 215. See also Grau and Gress, *Soviet-Afghan War*, p. 29; Henry S. Bradsher, *Afghanistan and the Soviet Union* (Durham: Duke University Press, 1985), p. 211; and Edward Girardet, *Afghanistan: The Soviet War* (London: Croom Helm, 1985), p. 41.

137. David C. Isby, *War in a Distant Country: Afghanistan, Invasion and Resistance* (London: Arms and Armour, 1989), pp. 53–56.

138. Cordesman and Wagner, *Lessons of Modern War*, p. 7. Alex Alexiev estimates that this force represented 2.5 percent of overall Soviet force strength and between 1 and 2 percent of Soviet defense expenditures. See Alex Alexiev, "Soviet Strategy and the Mujahideen," *Orbis* 29, no. 1 (spring 1985): 32.

139. Alexiev, "Soviet Strategy and the Mujahideen," p. 32. For a similar argument, see Oliver Roy, *The Lessons of the Soviet/Afghan War*, Adelphi Papers, no. 259 (London: Brassey's, 1991), p. 20.

140. Roy, *Lessons of the Soviet/Afghan War*, p. 21.

141. Jeri Laber and Barnett R. Rubin, *A Nation Is Dying* (Evanston: Northwestern University Press, 1988), p. xiv. See also Alexiev, "Soviet Strategy and the Mujahideen," p. 32; and Boulouque, "Communism in Afghanistan," pp. 716, 718–719.

142. Jo Thomas, "Afghan War: Russians Tell of the Horror," *New York Times*, June 28, 1984, p. A10. For similar accounts from Russian veterans of attacks against civilians, see Svetlana Alexievich, *Zinky Boys: Soviet Voices from a Forgotten War* (London: Chatto and Windus, 1992); and Anna Heinamaa, Maija Leppanen, and Yuri Yurchenko, eds., *The Soldiers' Story: Soviet Veterans Remember the Afghan War* (Berkeley: University of California, 1994).

143. Marek Sliwinski, *Afghanistan, 1978–87: War, Demography and Society* (London: Central Asian Survey, 1988), p. 5.

144. For evidence that the Soviets used chemical weapons, see Cordesman and Wagner, *Lessons of Modern War*, pp. 214–218; and Isby, "Soviet Tactics," pp. 691–692. For a more skeptical view, see Urban, *War in Afghanistan*, pp. 56–57.

145. Edward B. Westermann, "The Limits of Soviet Airpower: The Failure of Military Coercion in Afghanistan, 1979–1989," *Journal of Conflict Studies* 19, no. 2 (fall 1999): 39–71; and Selig S. Harrison, "Afghanistan: Soviet Intervention, Afghan Resistance, and the American Role," in Klare and Kornbluh, eds., *Low-Intensity Warfare*, p. 193.

146. Rubin, *Fragmentation of Afghanistan*, p. 143; emphasis in original.

147. Quoted in Carlotta Gall and Thomas de Waal, *Chechnya: Calamity in the Caucasus* (New York: New York University Press, 1998), p. 97.

148. Laber and Rubin, *A Nation Is Dying*, pp. 77–104; Kakar, *Afghanistan*, pp. 153–168; and Boulouque, "Communism in Afghanistan," pp. 720–725.

149. Rubin, *Fragmentation of Afghanistan*, p. 137.

150. Ibid., p. 137.

151. Among the many analysts supporting this view, see Cordesman and Wagner, *Lessons of Modern War*, pp. 187–190; Isby, *War in a Distant Country*, pp. 30, 56; Joseph J. Collins, "The Soviet Military Experience in Afghanistan," *Military Review* 65, no. 4 (May 1985): 20; Sliwinski, "Afghanistan: Decimation of a People," pp. 49–51; Claude Malhuret, "Report from Afghanistan," *Foreign Affairs* 62, no. 2 (winter 1983–84): 431; and James Rupert, "Depopulation Campaign Brutally Changes Villages," *Washington Post*, January 15, 1986, p. A1. Oliver Roy argues that the Soviets did engage in collective reprisals against civilians but that there "was no systematic policy of displacing the population." See Roy, *Lessons of the Soviet/Afghan War*, p. 20.

152. O'Ballance, *Afghan Wars*, p. 104.

153. Boulouque, "Communism in Afghanistan," p. 717.

154. Kakar, *Afghanistan*, p. 239.

155. Malhuret, "Report From Afghanistan," p. 431.

156. O'Ballance, *Afghan Wars*, p. 154. See also Girardet, *Afghanistan*, p. 41.

157. Ali Ahmad Jalali and Lester W. Grau, *The Other Side of the Mountain: Mujahideen Tactics in the Soviet Afghan War* (Quantico: United States Marine Corps Studies and Analysis Division, 1999), pp. xix–xx.

158. Rupert, "Depopulation Campaign Brutally Changes Villages," p. A1. Other authors have referred to this policy as "migratory genocide." See Girardet, *Afghanistan,* p. 202.

159. Laber and Rubin, *A Nation Is Dying,* pp. xiv.

160. O'Ballance, *Afghan Wars,* p. 154.

161. For a description of these tactics, see Laber and Rubin, *A Nation Is Dying,* pp. 58–65; and Drew Middleton, "Soviet Target: Afghan Areas Aiding Rebels," *New York Times,* July 15, 1984, p. A7.

162. Alexiev, "Soviet Strategy and the Mujahideen," p. 33.

163. Boulouque, "Communism in Afghanistan," p. 719; Laber and Rubin, *A Nation Is Dying,* pp. 42–48; and Alexiev, "Soviet Strategy and the Mujahideen," p. 33.

164. Jalali and Grau, *Other Side of the Mountain,* pp. xix–xx; John M. Hutcheson, "Scorched-Earth Policy: Soviets in Afghanistan," *Military Review* 62 (April 1982): 29–37; Rubin, *Fragmentation of Afghanistan,* p. 143; Cordesman and Wagner, *Lessons of Modern War,* p. 189; and Isby, "Soviet Tactics," pp. 691.

165. Harrison, "Afghanistan," p. 189.

166. Arnold, "The Stony Path to Afghan Socialism," p. 51.

167. Rubin, *Fragmentation of Afghanistan,* p. 142. See also Fred Halliday and Zahir Tanin, "The Communist Regime in Afghanistan, 1978–1992: Institutions and Conflicts," *Europe-Asia Studies* 50, no. 8 (December 1998): 1366.

168. Halliday and Tanin, "Communist Regime in Afghanistan," p. 1369.

169. Cordesman and Wagner, *Lessons of Modern War,* p. 59.

170. Alan J. Kuperman, "The Stinger Missile and U.S. Intervention in Afghanistan," *Political Science Quarterly* 114, no. 2 (summer 1999): 219–263; Cordovez and Harrison, *Out of Afghanistan,* pp. 198–201; Sarah E. Mendelson, *Changing Course: Ideas Politics, and the Soviet Withdrawal from Afghanistan* (Princeton: Princeton University Press, 1998), pp. 97–100.

171. Cordesman and Wagner, *Lessons of Modern War,* p. 69.

172. Urban, *War in Afghanistan,* p. 221.

173. The low figure is from Cordesman and Wagner, *Lessons of Modern War,* p. 10. The higher estimate, based on newly released documents of the Russian General Staff, is from Grau and Gress, *Soviet-Afghan War,* pp. xix, 43–44.

174. Cordesman and Wagner, *Lessons of Modern War,* p. 95.

175. Mendelson, *Changing Course,* p. 74.

176. Quoted in Halliday and Tanin, "Communist Regime in Afghanistan," p. 1367.

177. Cordovez and Harrison, *Out of Afghanistan,* pp. 4–5. For a similar argument, see Mendelson, *Changing Course.*

178. I estimate that of seventy-five guerrilla conflicts since 1945, twenty-four, or roughly one-third, resulted in mass killing. See Benjamin Valentino, Paul Huth, and Dylan Balch-Lindsay, "Draining the Sea: Mass Killing International Organization and Guerrilla Warfare" 57, no. 1 (Winter 2004).

179. Timothy P. Wickham-Crowley, "Terror and Guerrilla Warfare in Latin America, 1956–1970," *Comparative Studies in Society and History* 32, no. 2 (April 1990): 226.

180. David Stoll suggests that while the guerrillas did receive broad public support, this support may have been primarily the result of the Guatemalan regime's overreaction to early political organization and low-level terrorism by the guerrillas. This vicious cycle resulted in broader government repression and, in turn, more guerrilla supporters. Stoll argues that the lack of strong, intrinsic support for the guerrillas' cause helps explain why the insurgency was so quickly suppressed. Without such a cause to motivate continuing sacrifices, many peasants decided that the best way

to avoid further violence was to accept army domination. See Stoll, *Between Two Armies,* esp. pp. 61–128.

181. Americas Watch, *El Salvador's Decade of Terror,* pp. 47–59.

182. Michael McClintock, *The American Connection,* vol. 1, *State Terror and Popular Resistance in El Salvador* (London: Zed Books, 1985), p. 428.

183. Americas Watch, *El Salvador's Decade of Terror,* p. 58.

184. Rubenstein, *Alchemists of Revolution,* p. 90.

185. Corbett, *Guerrilla Warfare,* pp. 90–93.

186. See Timothy J. Lomperis, *From People's War to People's Rule: Insurgency, Intervention, and the Lessons of Vietnam* (Chapel Hill: University of North Carolina Press, 1996), p. 205; and Corbett, *Guerrilla Warfare,* pp. 90–93. Corbett also suggests that the Malay Peninsula's geography helped the British by allowing them to more easily seal off the insurgency from outside sources of support.

187. Perhaps fifty thousand people actively supported the insurgency. See Lomperis, *People's War,* p. 216.

188. Ibid., p. 210.

189. Corbett, *Guerrilla Warfare,* p. 56. Over four hundred thousand people were resettled with relatively little resistance.

190. The Sandinistas did launch several cross border raids, but never used large numbers of troops or remained on Honduran territory for extended periods for fear of prompting direct U.S. intervention. See Robert Kagen, *Twilight Struggle: American Power and Nicaragua, 1977–1990* (New York: Free Press, 1996), p. 393.

191. William M. LeoGrande, *Our Own Backyard: The United States in Central America 1977–1992* (Chapel Hill: University of North Carolina Press, 1998), pp. 309, 490; Roy Gutman, *Banana Diplomacy: The Making of American Policy in Nicaragua, 1981–1987* (New York: Simon and Schuster, 1988), p. 301; and Robert J. McCartney, "U.S.-Backed Rebels Can't Win in Nicaragua, CIA Finds," *Washington Post,* November 25, 1983, p. A1.

192. Stephen Kinzer, *Blood of Brothers: Life and War in Nicaragua* (New York: G. P. Putnam's Sons, 1991), pp. 261–262.

193. See Russ Hoyle, "Moving the Miskitos," in *Time,* March 1, 1982, p. 22; and Kagen, *Twilight Struggle,* p. 359.

194. Norma J. Kriger, *Zimbabwe's Guerrilla War: Peasant Voices* (Cambridge: Cambridge University Press, 1992).

195. Laqueur, *Guerrilla,* p. 292.

196. Michael D. Shafer, *Deadly Paradigms: The Failure of U.S. Counterinsurgency Policy* (Princeton: Princeton University Press, 1988), pp. 232–234. See also Corbett, *Guerrilla Warfare,* p. 187.

197. Shafer, *Deadly Paradigms,* pp. 234.

198. See Lomperis, *People's War,* pp. 173–195.

199. Gay W. Seidman, "Blurred Lines: Nonviolence in South Africa," *PS: Political Science and Politics* 32, no. 3 (June 2000), 161–168. Other black resistance organizations, such as the Pan-Africanist Congress, did advocate escalating violent attacks on whites, including civilian targets. These groups, however, never received widespread support and carried out relatively few attacks.

200. Nelson Mandela, *Long Walk to Freedom* (Boston: Little, Brown, 1995), p. 365. See also Rubenstein, *Alchemists of Revolution,* p. 226.

201. See Heribert Adam, "The Manipulation of Ethnicity: South Africa in Comparative Perspective," in Donald Rothchild and Victor A. Olorunsola, eds., *State versus Ethnic Claims: African Policy Dilemmas* (Boulder: Westview, 1983), pp. 133–134, 138.

202. Although comprehensive figures for the entire apartheid era are not available, according to one estimate, South African security forces were responsible for roughly twelve hundred killings

from 1984 to 1988, a relatively violent phase of the conflict. See "South Africa Racial Toll Put at 4,000 in 4 Years," *New York Times*, March 5, 1989, p. A4.

203. "IRA Apologizes for Hundreds of Civilian Slayings," *Boston Globe*, July 17, 2002, p. A1.

204. Walter Laqueur, *The Age of Terrorism* (Boston: Little, Brown, 1987), p. 211.

205. Gall and de Waal, *Chechnya*, p. 97.

206. See Shafer, *Deadly Paradigms*, pp. 258–268. See also Frances FitzGerald, *Fire in the Lake: The Vietnamese and the Americans in Vietnam* (Boston: Little, Brown, 1972), pp. 123–125; and George C. Herring, *America's Longest War: The United States and Vietnam, 1950–1975* (New York: McGraw-Hill, 1996), pp. 98–99. For alternate (and sometimes contradictory) views on how the United States might have won the Vietnam War, none focusing on civic action, see Andrew Krepinevich Jr., *The Army and Vietnam* (Baltimore: Johns Hopkins University Press, 1986), pp. 258–275; Harry G. Summers, *On Strategy: A Critical Analysis of the Vietnam War* (Novato, Calif.: Presidio, 1982); and Michael Lind, *Vietnam: The Necessary War* (New York: Free Press, 1999), pp. 76–105.

Conclusion

1. Ervin Staub, *The Roots of Evil: The Origins of Genocide and Other Group Violence* (Cambridge: Cambridge University Press, 1989), pp. 274–283. See also Ervin Staub, "Preventing Genocide: Activating Bystanders, Helping Victims Heal, Helping Groups Overcome Hostility," in Levon Chorbajian and George Shirinian, eds., *Studies in Comparative Genocide* (New York: St. Martin's, 1999), pp. 251–260.

2. Helen Fein, "Accounting for Genocide after 1945: Theories and Some Findings," *International Journal on Group Rights* 1 (1993): 101.

3. Rudolph J. Rummel, *Death by Government* (New Brunswick, N.J.: Transaction Publishers, 1994), p. 27; emphasis in original.

4. William Jefferson Clinton, "A Commitment to Human Dignity, Democracy and Peace," *Issues of Democracy: USIA Electronic Journals* 1, no. 3 (May 1996).

5. Jack Snyder, *From Voting to Violence: Democratization and Nationalist Conflict* (New York: W. W. Norton, 2000). See also Edward D. Mansfield and Jack Snyder, "Democratization and the Dangers of War," *International Security* 20, no. 1 (summer 1995): 5–38; and Michael Mann, "The Dark Side of Democracy: The Modern Tradition of Ethnic and Political Cleansing," *New Left Review*, no. 235 (May/June 1999): 18–45.

6. Bruce D. Jones, *Peacemaking in Rwanda: The Dynamics of Failure* (Boulder: Lynn Rienner, 2001); and Alan J. Kuperman, "The Other Lesson of Rwanda: Mediators Sometimes Do More Damage than Good," *SAIS Review* 16, no. 1 (winter–spring 1996): 221–240.

7. See Leo Kuper, *The Prevention of Genocide* (New Haven: Yale University Press, 1985), pp. 209–228; Leo Kuper, "Reflections on the Prevention of Genocide," in Helen Fein, ed., *Genocide Watch* (New Haven: Yale University Press, 1992), pp. 135–161; Fein, "Accounting for Genocide," p. 101; and Ervin Staub, "The Origins and Prevention of Genocide, Mass Killing, and Other Collective Violence," *Peace and Conflict: Journal of Peace Psychology* 5, no. 4 (1999): 303–336.

8. Yahya Sadowski, *The Myth of Global Chaos* (Washington, D.C.: Brookings Institution, 1998), pp. 66–74.

9. See Noel Malcolm, "Bosnia and the West," *National Interest*, no. 39 (spring 1995): 3–14; and Jon Western, "Sources of Humanitarian Intervention: Beliefs, Information, and Advocacy in the U.S. Decisions on Somalia and Bosnia," *International Security* 26, no. 4 (spring 2002): 120, 128–133. Western notes that similar arguments may have delayed the American intervention in Somalia (p. 116).

10. Quoted in Samantha Power, *"A Problem from Hell": America and the Age of Genocide* (New York: Basic Books, 2002), p. 282. For a similar argument, see Conor Cruise O'Brien, "The Wrath

of Ages: Nationalism's Primordial Roots," *Foreign Affairs* 72, no. 5 (November/December 1993): 143–149.

11. "Press Briefing by National Security Advisor Tony Lake and Director for Strategic Plans and Policy General Wesley Clark," *US Newswire*, May 5, 1994. For more information on U.S. officials' views about the "tribal" roots of the conflict in Rwanda, see Human Rights Watch, *Leave None to Tell the Story: Genocide in Rwanda* (New York: Human Rights Watch, 1999), p. 624.

12. Henry Kissinger, "US Intervention in Kosovo Is a Mistake," *Boston Globe*, March 1, 1999, p. A15. Kissinger has stated, however, that he would have supported an intervention to prevent the genocide in Rwanda. See Alan J. Kuperman, *The Limits of Humanitarian Intervention: Genocide in Rwanda* (Washington, D.C.: Brookings Institution, 2001), p. 2.

13. I do not address here the other types of mass killing described in chapter 3 because I did not investigate these scenarios in detail in this book. In addition, these types of mass killing have been relatively rare in the twentieth century, and most of them seem likely to remain rare or become even less common in the future.

14. See Nancy MacLean, *Behind the Mask of Chivalry: The Making of the Second Ku Klux Klan* (New York: Oxford University Press, 1994), p. 197.

15. Philip Dray, *At the Hands of Persons Unknown: The Lynching of Black America* (New York: Random House, 2002), p. viii. As Dray notes, since this estimate was derived only from documented lynchings, the total number killed is almost certainly higher (p. x).

16. Kuperman, *Limits of Humanitarian Intervention*, p. 18.

17. Raul Hilberg, *The Destruction of the European Jews* (New York: Holmes and Meier, 1985), p. 339.

18. Power, *Problem from Hell*, pp. 345–348; and Michael Barnett, *Eyewitness to a Genocide: The United Nations and Rwanda* (Ithaca, N.Y.: Cornell University Press, 2002), pp. 329–389.

19. Quoted in Kuperman, *Limits of Humanitarian Intervention*, pp. 104–105.

20. An estimated two thousand Tutsi civilians were killed in Rwanda between the onset of the civil war in October 1990 and the genocide in April 1994. Kuperman, *Limits of Humanitarian Intervention*, p. 107.

21. Quoted in African Rights, *Rwanda: Death, Despair and Defiance*, rev. ed. (London: African Rights, 1995), p. 89.

22. For a description of the various forms of military intervention that might be utilized, see Barry R. Posen, "Military Responses to Refugee Disasters," *International Security* 21, no. 1 (summer 1996): 72–88; and Michael O'Hanlon, *Saving Lives with Force: Military Criteria for Humanitarian Intervention* (Washington, D.C.: Brookings Institution, 1997), esp. pp. 17–46.

23. On the requirements for international policing operations, see James T. Quinlivan, "Force Requirements in Stability Operations," *Parameters* 25, no. 4 (winter 1995–1996): 59–69.

24. John Mueller, "The Banality of Ethnic War," *International Security* 25, no. 1 (summer 2000): 42–70.

25. Others have suggested that even smaller numbers of foreign troops, if available early enough, might have been sufficient. See various estimates cited in Human Rights Watch, *Leave None to Tell the Story*, pp. 606–609.

26. Scott R. Feil, *Preventing Genocide: How the Early Use of Force Might Have Succeeded in Rwanda* (New York: Carnegie Corporation, 1998).

27. Kuperman, *Limits of Humanitarian Intervention*.

28. Ibid., p. 76.

29. Although ten Belgian peace-keepers were killed by extremist forces at the outset of the genocide, these troops were only lightly armed, isolated from the rest of the already small UN contingent in Rwanda, and not prepared for combat. See Linda Melvern, *A People Betrayed: The Role of the West in Rwanda's Genocide* (London: Zed Books, 2000), pp. 115–136.

30. Power, *Problem from Hell,* p. xxi.

31. Quoted in Michael Kelly, "A Perfectly Clintonian Doctrine," *Washington Post,* June 30, 1999, p. A31.

32. Steven Kull, "What the Public Knows That Washington Doesn't," *Foreign Policy,* no. 101 (winter 1995/96): 102–115.

33. Michael A. Fletcher and Steven Mufson, "Africa Conference's Huge Task: Turning Interest into Action," *Washington Post,* February 17, 2000, p. A2. The poll indicated that 60 percent believed the United States had an obligation to prevent genocide in Europe. For additional poll data suggesting strong support for the principle of intervention to prevent genocide, see the Program on International Policy Attitudes, *Americans on Globalization: A Study of U.S. Public Attitudes* (College Park, Md.: Program on International Policy Attitudes, 2000), pp. 36–37.

34. See Lawrence J. LeBlanc, *The United States and the Genocide Convention* (Durham, N.C.: Duke University Press, 1991); and Power, *Problem from Hell,* pp. 71–85, 155–169.

35. Eric V. Larson, *Casualties and Consensus: The Historical Role of Casualties in Domestic Support for U.S. Military Operations* (Santa Monica: RAND Corporation, 1996), p. 118.

36. For estimates of the number of lives saved by the intervention ranging from 10,000 to 500,000, see David D. Laitin, "Somalia: Civil War and International Intervention," in Barbara F. Walter and Jack Snyder, eds., *Civil War, Insecurity, and Intervention* (New York: Columbia University Press, 1999), p. 178.

37. Larson, *Casualties and Consensus,* p. 47.

38. Transcript of interview with James Woods, deputy assistant secretary for African affairs at the Department of Defense from 1986 to 1994, on the PBS Frontline documentary *The Triumph of Evil,* www.pbs.org/wgbh/pages/frontline/shows/evil/interviews/woods.html [October 2002]. On the importance of the "shadow of Somalia" on the reaction to the Rwandan genocide in the UN, see Barnett, *Eyewitness to a Genocide,* pp. 85–89.

39. For example, see Power, *Problem from Hell,* pp. 513–514.

40. Human Rights Watch, *Leave None to Tell the Story,* pp. 16–27, 635–660.

41. On the debate regarding the effectiveness of economic sanctions, see Robert A. Pape, "Why Economic Sanctions Do Not Work," *International Security* 22, no. 2 (fall 1997): 90–136; Kimberly Ann Elliott, "The Sanctions Glass: Half Full or Completely Empty?" *International Security* 23, no. 1 (summer 1998): 50–65; and Robert Pape, "Why Economic Sanctions *Still* Do Not Work," *International Security* 23, no. 1 (summer 1998): 66–77.

42. See Robert A. Pape, *Bombing to Win: Air Power and Coercion in War* (Ithaca, N.Y.: Cornell University Press, 1996).

43. It should be noted that in both Germany and Japan allied bombing aimed at forcing an unconditional surrender, not merely the cessation of mass killing. It is impossible to rule out the possibility, therefore, that bombing aimed at this more limited goal might have succeeded at an earlier date.

44. Pape, *Bombing to Win;* and Gar Alperovitz, *The Decision to Use the Atomic Bomb* (New York: Knopf, 1995).

45. Analysts of the campaign differ regarding the role of air power in compelling Slobodan Milosevic's decision to withdraw from Kosovo. Most analysts, however, suggest the decision was motivated at least in part by Milosevic's fear of an imminent NATO ground invasion, and some suggest this was his primary concern. For arguments pointing to the combined impact of air power, the fear of a ground invasion, and other pressures, see Daniel L. Byman and Matthew C. Waxman, "Kosovo and the Great Air Power Debate," *International Security* 24, no. 4 (spring 2000): 5–38; Ivo H. Daalder and Michael F. O'Hanlon, *Winning Ugly: NATO's War to Save Kosovo* (Washington, D.C.: Brookings Institution, 2000); Benjamin S. Lambeth, *NATO's Air War for Kosovo: A Strategic and Operational Assessment* (Santa Monica: RAND Corporation, 2001); and Stephen T.

Hosmer, *The Conflict over Kosovo: Why Milosevic Decided to Settle When He Did* (Santa Monica: RAND Corporation, 2001). For reports stressing Milosevic's fear of a ground invasion, see Michael Hirsh et al., "NATO's Game of Chicken," *Newsweek,* July 26, 1999, pp. 58–61; and Steven Erlanger, "NATO Was Closer to Ground War in Kosovo Than Is Widely Realized," *New York Times,* November 7, 1999, p. A4. For the argument that air power alone was sufficient to force Milosevic to back down, see Andrew L. Stigler, "A Clear Victory for Air Power: NATO's Empty Threat to Invade Kosovo," *International Security* 27, no. 3 (winter 2002/3): 124–157.

46. Tim Judah, *Kosovo: War and Revenge* (New Haven: Yale University Press, 2000), pp. 252–253. On the failure of air attacks to prevent Serb military forces from carrying out their missions, including ethnic cleansing, see Hosmer, *Conflict over Kosovo,* pp. 85–89.

47. I thank Alan Kuperman for alerting me to this important dynamic.

48. Vahakn N. Dadrian, *The History of the Armenian Genocide: Ethnic Conflict from the Balkans to Anatolia to the Caucasus* (Providence: Berghahn Books, 1997), pp. xxii–xxv.

49. Kuperman, "Other Lesson of Rwanda," pp. 221–240; and Jones, *Peacemaking in Rwanda,* pp. 61–64.

50. Hosmer, *Conflict over Kosovo,* pp. 50–52; Dusko Doder and Louise Branson, *Milosevic: Portrait of a Tyrant* (New York: Free Press, 1999), pp. 8–9, 260; Tim Judah, *Kosovo: War and Revenge* (New Haven: Yale University Press, 2000), p. 264; and Misha Glenny, *The Balkans: Nationalism, War and the Great Powers, 1804–1999* (New York: Viking, 2000), p. 658.

51. For arguments advocating partition as an effective solution to certain types of violent conflict, see Chaim D. Kaufmann, "Possible and Impossible Solutions to Ethnic Civil Wars," *International Security* 20, no. 4 (spring 1996): 136–175; Chaim D. Kaufmann, "When All Else Fails: Ethnic Population Transfers and Partitions in the Twentieth Century," *International Security* 23, no. 2 (fall 1998): 120–156; and Daniel L. Byman, "Divided They Stand: Lessons about Partition from Iraq and Lebanon," *Security Studies* 7, no. 1 (autumn 1997): 1–29. For arguments advocating partition in the former Yugoslavia, see John J. Mearsheimer and Robert A. Pape, "The Answer: A Three Way Partition Plan for Bosnia and How the U.S. Can Enforce It," *New Republic,* June 14, 1992, pp. 22–28; and John J. Mearsheimer and Stephen Van Evera, "Redraw the Map, Stop the Killing," *New York Times,* April 19, 1999, p. A23.

52. Robert Schaeffer, *Warpaths: The Politics of Partition* (New York: Hill and Wang, 1990); Radha Kumar, "The Troubled History of Partition," *Foreign Affairs* 76, no. 1 (January/February 1997), 22–34; Nicholas Sambanis, "Partition as a Solution to Ethnic War: An Empirical Critique of the Theoretical Literature," *World Politics* 52 (July 2000): 437–483; and Mark Kramer and Ana Siljak, " 'Separate' Doesn't Equal Ethnic Peace," *Washington Post,* February 21, 1999, p. B1.

53. For suggestions on ways to improve the provision of humanitarian assistance in conflict or post-conflict situations, see Daniel Byman et al., *Strengthening the Partnership: Improving Military Coordination with Relief Agencies and Allies in Humanitarian Operations* (Santa Monica: RAND Corporation, 2000).

54. On the difficulties facing Jewish emigrants and the possibility that greater international openness might have saved more from the Holocaust (both before and after the war began), see David S. Wyman, *The Abandonment of the Jews: America and the Holocaust, 1941–1945* (New York: Pantheon Books, 1984); Michael R. Marrus, *The Unwanted: European Refugees in the Twentieth Century* (Oxford: Oxford University Press, 1985), pp. 122–295; and Yehuda Bauer, *Jews for Sale?* (New Haven: Yale University Press, 1994).

55. William D. Rubinstein, *The Myth of Rescue: Why the Democracies Could Not Have Saved More Jews from the Nazis* (New York: Routledge, 1997), pp. 17–18. See also Frank W. Brecher, "The Western Allies and the Holocaust," *Holocaust and Genocide Studies* 5, no. 4, (1990): 423–446.

56. Kuperman, *Limits of Humanitarian Intervention,* pp. 74–77.

57. Power, *Problem from Hell,* pp. 378–379; and Melvern, *People Betrayed,* pp. 198–199.

58. The United Nations did authorize a new intervention force in Rwanda on May 17, but the United States and many other states refused to contribute troops. The United States held up for another month the shipment of the armored personnel carriers it had agreed to lease or sell to the UN for the mission. The new UN forces did not arrive until mid-August, by which time the genocide was already over. Nevertheless, the small UN contingent in Rwanda probably did save the lives of approximately twenty thousand Tutsi civilians who had taken refuge with UN forces in various locations around Kigali.

59. Beatriz Manz, *Refugees of a Hidden War: The Aftermath of Counterinsurgency in Guatemala* (Albany: State University of New York Press, 1988), pp. 148, 150–155.

60. For arguments stressing the lack of leadership, see Power, *Problem from Hell,* pp. 305, 509–510; Steven Kull and I. M. Destler, *Misreading the Public: The Myth of a New Isolationism* (Washington, D.C.: Brookings Institution, 1999); and Peter D. Feaver and Christopher Gelpi, "Casualty Aversion: How Many Deaths Are Acceptable?," *Washington Post,* November 7, 1999, p. B3. For arguments emphasizing public perceptions of the costs and benefits of military operations, see Larson, *Casualties and Consensus;* Eric Larson, review of *Misreading the Public,* by Steven Kull and I. M. Destler, *Public Opinion Quarterly* 63, no. 4 (winter 1999): 624–627; and John Mueller, "Public Support for Military Ventures Abroad," in John Norton Moore and Robert F. Turner, eds., *The Real Lessons of the Vietnam War* (Durham, N.C.: Carolina Academic Press, 2002), pp. 171–219.

INDEX